Read this book online today:

With SAP PRESS BooksOnline we offer you online access to knowledge from the leading SAP experts. Whether you use it as a beneficial supplement or as an alternative to the printed book, with SAP PRESS BooksOnline you can:

• Access your book anywhere, at any time. All you need is an Internet connection.
• Perform full text searches on your book and on the entire SAP PRESS library.
• Build your own personalized SAP library.

The SAP PRESS customer advantage:

Register this book today at *www.sap-press.com* and obtain exclusive free trial access to its online version. If you like it (and we think you will), you can choose to purchase permanent, unrestricted access to the online edition at a very special price!

Here's how to get started:

1. Visit *www.sap-press.com*.
2. Click on the link for SAP PRESS BooksOnline and login (or create an account).
3. Enter your free trial license key, shown below in the corner of the page.
4. Try out your online book with full, unrestricted access for a limited time!

Your personal free trial **license key**
for this online book is:

qxir-nm7c-96wy-bu8a

Using Crystal Reports® with SAP®

 PRESS

SAP PRESS is a joint initiative of SAP and Galileo Press. The know-how offered by SAP specialists combined with the expertise of the Galileo Press publishing house offers the reader expert books in the field. SAP PRESS features first-hand information and expert advice, and provides useful skills for professional decision-making.

SAP PRESS offers a variety of books on technical and business related topics for the SAP user. For further information, please visit our website: *www.sap-press.com*.

Jim Brogden, Heather Sinkwitz, Mac Holden
SAP BusinessObjects Web Intelligence
2010, 583 pp.
978-1-59229-322-3

Ingo Hilgefort
Reporting and Analytics with SAP BusinessObjects
2009, 655 pp.
978-1-59229-310-0

Larry Sackett
MDX Reporting and Analytics with SAP NetWeaver BW
2009, 380 pp.
978-1-59229-249-3

Daniel Knapp
SAP NetWeaver BI 7.0 Migration Guide
2008, 180 pp.
978-1-59229-228-8

Mike Garrett

Using Crystal Reports® with SAP®

Galileo Press

Bonn • Boston

Galileo Press is named after the Italian physicist, mathematician and philosopher Galileo Galilei (1564–1642). He is known as one of the founders of modern science and an advocate of our contemporary, heliocentric worldview. His words *Eppur se muove* (And yet it moves) have become legendary. The Galileo Press logo depicts Jupiter orbited by the four Galilean moons, which were discovered by Galileo in 1610.

Editor Erik Herman
Technical Reviewer Coy Yonce
Copyeditor Ruth Saavedra
Cover Design Jill Winitzer
Photo Credit Image Copyright Tischenko Irina. Used under license from Shutterstock.com.
Layout Design Vera Brauner
Production Editor Kelly O'Callaghan
Assistant Production Editor Graham Geary
Typesetting Publishers' Design and Production Services, Inc.
Printed and bound in Canada

ISBN 978-1-59229-327-8

© 2010 by Galileo Press Inc., Boston (MA)

1st Edition 2010

Library of Congress Cataloging-in-Publication Data
Garrett, Mike.
  Using Crystal Reports with SAP/ Mike Garrett.
      p. cm.
  Includes bibliographical references and index.
  ISBN-13: 978-1-59229-327-8 (alk. paper)
  ISBN-10: 1-59229-327-1 (alk. paper)
  1. Crystal reports (Electronic resource) 2. Business report writing—Computer programs. 3. SAP ERP. I. Title.

  HF5719.C793 2009
  651.7'8028553—dc22

                                                    2010007127

Contents at a Glance

Contents

Acknowledgments

I am grateful for the help of many who have encouraged me over the years and given me opportunities to grow and move on, even when I sometimes didn't want to. By nature I don't move unless something or someone outside me pushes. Here's to those who were willing to push.

First, I want to thank Blanchard and Lance at InfoTrain Solutions for getting me started with Crystal. You were willing to invest into getting me up and running and for that I am grateful.

Thanks to Bill and Geoff at EnQueue for taking a risk on someone who had never touched SAP before. Your confidence in me is greatly appreciated. If you had shown more sense I may have never gotten a start in the SAP world. I appreciate the lapse in judgment.

Many thanks also to Steve Lucas (formerly at Crystal Decisions). Your encouragement during the high tech drought in Denver kept me moving in the right direction. I wish you and your family all the best.

I also would like to thank all my former clients who have allowed me to continue to hone my craft while helping them. Anything of value in this business is learned through on the job training and I appreciate the chance to continue my education. The next client will appreciate it, too.

I'd also like to thank all my good friends who have supported me over the years through some pretty trying times. I especially want to thank John for his continuing support and friendship. It was always good to know we could talk whenever things got a little crazy.

I'd like to give my heartfelt thanks and appreciation to my father. You instilled in me many good things, just one of which is the understanding that any job worth doing is worth doing right. In many ways, that's what this book is all about.

Lastly, I want to express my deepest appreciation and love for Katy – my wife, life-long friend, and companion. You are proof that when an irresistible force meets an immovable object, things get moving. There is no way I would be where I am or who I am without you. Please never stop pushing.

Introduction

This book is not just about Crystal Reports. It's about you. As you turn the pages, you'll start seeing a lot about how to do this, that, or the other using Crystal Reports. But in the end, that's not really the point. This book is really more about recognizing who *really* runs your company. And one thing is for certain: it's *not* the person sitting in the big corner office.

This is not so say the person sitting in the big corner office is not important. Of course he or she's important. The point is that they are no more important than *you*, or the person sitting in the cube next to you, or down the hall, or anyone else in your company. And the ones who are the very best at "running" their companies will be the first to recognize that, at the end of the day; they really don't "run" anything at all.

More than ever before, decision making in any organization is a decentralized, democratized, and distributed process. Obviously decisions are made, and should be made, at the highest levels in any organization on a daily basis. And we all recognize that these are the types of decisions they typically have far-reaching implications and oftentimes affect every individual in the organization, sometimes in very profound ways. Many of us know firsthand the difference it can make to have the right person "at the wheel" of you company, especially during difficult and turbulent times.

That said; let's make what should be a painfully obvious point: *it is impossible to make every decision about what to do in your company from the top down*. Not going to happen. Not today, not tomorrow, not ever. In today's dynamic, rapidly changing economy it is more important than ever that *each* individual in any given organization be fully empowered to take quick, decisive action when faced with the question of what to do next.

You may be wondering why someone who is essentially a report writer would begin what is supposed to be a practical, hands-on book on creating reports with a diatribe on the best way to make decisions in an organization. And if you are, then you just might be the right person for the job and the type of person who should read this book. It could also be an indication that you possess a good balance of strategic, big picture thinking *and* in-the-trenches, hands on thinking, or, as you might call it, the Drucker-Adams combo.

Peter Drucker was, of course, one of the foremost experts of our time on the ins and outs of running any type of organization. Regardless of what you may think of his opinions and ideas about how best to operate a company, no one would deny that he was well informed, educated, and thought through his positions carefully. As the pioneer of modern management consulting, he could synthesize a wide variety of inputs and ideas to form a clear, concise, and sensible perspective. He was undeniably one of the world's foremost experts on organizational effectiveness.

Then you've got Scott Adams. Sometimes I think Scott was put on the earth for one purpose: to restore balance to the universe. Or perhaps to help us laugh before we cry. And again, regardless of what you might think of Scott's irreverent, no-holds-barred, sometimes painful look at the life of today's "knowledge worker," there's no denying he has struck a collective nerve in a big way. Just take a casual stroll through the cube farm of any IT department in the world and you'll see Dilbert literally everywhere.

In my opinion, it takes two kinds of people to run the world (or your company). It takes a Drucker and it takes an Adams. It takes a "here's the way it *should* work" person and it takes a "here's the way it *really* works" person. It takes the visionary and the realist. Without the visionary nothing ever gets started. Without the realist nothing ever gets finished.

I intentionally began this introduction by telling you the way things are *supposed* to be. Or at least the way *I think* things are supposed to be. You really *are* as important to the success of your organization as is the person at the top. It's the little decisions you make every day on the front lines that add up and determine the ultimate fate of your company – and whether you succeed or fail in the marketplace.

Well, that's the way things ought to be. Then you turn the page of your Dilbert desktop calendar, and wham, back to reality! This is of course what Scott Adams does so well. He takes the way things are *supposed* to be and shows us the way things *really* are. The unenlightened would label him a cynic. Those who "know" would say he's just saying it like it is, which is the first step toward any real change or growth. Until we fully recognize where we are, we are never able to truly move on.

So, in a perfect world, each individual in any given organization would be fully prepared and equipped to make the decisions they needed to get their job done effectively. We'll call this the Drucker ideal. It's right, it's reasonable, and it just makes sense.

Meanwhile, back over in the real world, things aren't so perfect. The world most knowledge workers find themselves in every day is one where many, if not most, of the pieces of the puzzle have come up missing. We'll call this the Adams reality.

Part of what drove me to write this book comes from my 20 plus years of experience working with end users of technology in a wide variety of capacities. I began my so-called career in technology after graduating college as a business major at Texas A&M University. This is back in the technology gold-rush days of the mid 80's when all you needed was a pulse and someone would be willing to teach you something that had to do with computers and put you on a job somewhere. Apparently I qualified because I was able to land a job at the university computer center where I quickly learned that whatever I thought I knew about computers yesterday no longer applied.

This, of course, was because new technologies, both hardware and software, were being rolled out at an amazing rate. Within a year or so of starting my new job my boss walked into my office and plopped down a funny looking beige box with a tiny screen and a handle on top. He told me it was a "Macintosh" computer.

"Some of the staff on campus has been talking about this new computer that just came out from a company called Apple Computer," he said. "I don't know what to make of it, but the computer center wants us to look into it and see how it works." I don't think I slept for the next week. I was immediately bitten by the Mac bug.

At the time I also had a Zenith PC on my desk and my job was to learn how both the PC and the Mac worked and then develop some training classes on how to use them for the university staff. It was like being a kid in a candy shop. Of course I didn't realize it at the time, but I was being given the unique opportunity of evaluating two differing world views, or at least two differing perspectives on how technology and people interact.

On one side of my desk I had the world view of the engineer, or technician. This was the world of the PC, especially at the time. Everything was in codes. Acronyms were everywhere. There were lots of colons and slashes. In short, a computer geek's dream come true. Everything exposed and readily available via a flashing command prompt, just the way it should be.

On the other side of my desk was a cute, little computer with a black and white screen that beeped and smiled at you when you started it up. And it had a new thing called a "mouse." And it was extremely addictive.

What was the difference? On the surface, you might be tempted to think it was the graphical interface, or the fact that word processing was WYSIWYG ("What You See Is What You Get"), or perhaps the mouse. Certainly all these factors contributed to the attraction of the original Mac, but underneath it all the real magic was "the human touch." You felt like someone understood that you were a human being and had made the effort to make a machine work the way you worked and not the other way around.

The reason the Mac was different was because it was conceived and created in an entirely new and different way. Whereas the design of the PC was driven primarily from a technician's perspective, the design of the Mac was driven primarily from a human perspective. It was technology that seemed more "real." It was the computer for "the rest of us."

I was so smitten by this new Mac that I ended up leaving my job at the university and going to work at Apple Computer. There I got an insider's look at the core philosophy that drove the design of Apple's products. And, at risk of bringing up the same old tired "Mac vs. Windows" debate, I did discover that there indeed *was* a true difference in perspective that pervaded the Apple culture. I call it the "so what" perspective.

As in, "That sounds really impressive and looks like it has cool new features and advanced, cutting edge functionality. But, *so what*? What can the average person *really* do with it?" You learned really quickly at Apple not to be overly impressed by impressive sounding technical jargon and cut right to the bottom line: what can someone do with it – *today*? If I can't pick it up and get at least *some* use out of it almost right away, I'm going to forget about it and move on to something else.

After about six years at Apple, the company hit a speed bump in the road called "Windows." Sales tanked, Bill Gates became a bizillionaire, and I along with thousands of other Mac zealots were asked to find something else to do with our lives. I then left and went to work for a small software company that sold and supported medical and dental software that ran on, you guessed it, the Mac. Looking back, this was an invaluable experience for me because it took me out of the "ivory tower" of the inside world of Apple and took me directly to the streets to see how this stuff actually worked in the real world.

Over the next few years I got what I would call a good dose of reality. True, the Mac was more user friendly than the PC. However, it was *still* a computer and still very much capable of creating frustration and anxiety in its own peculiar "user friendly" way. I began to develop a deeper appreciation for the resourcefulness of the everyday office worker. And how creative they can be when they have to be.

Around 1998 I was given the opportunity to join a new company that specialized in providing consulting and training services, primarily around a product called "Crystal Reports" (something I had never heard of before). 40 hours of training later, I was ready to *work* with clients to them create reports as a "certified" Crystal Reports consultant..

After several more years of learning and growing, I came across a small Crystal Reports consulting company that specialized in creating reports against SAP R/3. I had no idea what SAP was or how to create reports for it, but it seemed like the natural thing to do next. Thankfully, at that time hardly anyone else had any experience doing it either.

My first assignment was to work on a project for Multnomah County, Oregon where Crystal Decisions (the folks who produced Crystal Reports before Business Objects and now SAP) was installing a beta release of their Crystal Enterprise system (along with Crystal Reports) in an SAP BW environment. Crystal Reports had been previously integrated into SAP R/3, but this was the first integration of Crystal into SAP BW. This was cutting edge stuff and pretty difficult to make work.

A lot changed in the ensuing eight years. The integration steadily improved over until SAP announced they were cutting off their OEM agreement to bundle Crystal Reports with SAP BW and would be providing their own formatted reporting solution in the form of the Report Designer, due out with NetWeaver 2004s. While many professionals in my situation went on to do other things, I decided to stick it out and was able to find a few more "diehard" clients willing to stick it out with me, at least for awhile. But I knew the clock was ticking and I would eventually have to find something else to do.

In November of 2007, I received a phone call from a former director of professional services at Business Objects who I had done a project for in the past. "Check out the Business Objects website," he said. "You're not going to believe it." SAP had just bought Business Objects. Crystal Reports was back in town. And I looked like a genius.

I am excited both on a personal level as well as for the SAP end user community that Crystal Reports (and the entire the Business Objects BI toolset) is now front and center in the NetWeaver solution stack. I've had the opportunity to work with hundreds of SAP end users (both technical and business users) in implementing reporting solutions for SAP BW using Crystal Reports. I have seen over and over the difference the solution can really make. It just plain works. It's the workhorse of the new SAP BI toolset. I'm excited to have been given this opportunity to share the things I've learned over the past 8 years.

I hear a whole lot these days about some very impressive sounding business intelligence (BI) technologies. Take a casual stroll through any of the big BI websites and you'll come across all sorts of tools that provide such advanced functionality as online analytical processing (OLAP), ad-hoc query, data mining, business performance management, benchmarking, text mining, and predictive analytics, to name just a few. A lot is currently being said about these sort of highly advanced capabilities and the pros and cons of the various BI tools that provide them. Today, there are certainly some very nice advanced analytical tools available that can provide companies with ways to understand the meaning behind their data like never before. If you know how to use them, that is.

The most knowledge workers I rub shoulders with on a day-to-day basis are either not interested or are incapable of using any kind of advanced BI interface. And they shouldn't be made to feel like they should be.

In the right hands, the more advanced analytical tools in the market today, can provide invaluable insights into the inner workings of an organization and allow decision makers to see things they could never see without them. SAP and Business Objects take a balanced approach by presenting the end user base with a range of tools so that the right tool can be selected for the right job – *and* the right person.

One of Crystal Reports greatest strengths is its longevity. And in an industry that's prone to moving onto the "next thing" rather quickly, this is unique. It has quietly retained its place as the most popular BI tool in the world for over 15 years. And that's largely because Crystal's primary audience is the casual, non-technical business end user, and they're not going away any time soon.

Crystal Reports is one of the best tools on the market for meeting the majority of SAP knowledge workers business intelligence needs. However, as you'll find out in Chapter 2, while Crystal Reports is a great tool for creating BI content (reports) *for* the average end user, it's not necessarily meant to be used *by* the average end user.

Crystal Reports is a tool that is used by a small minority to create BI content for the majority of end users in an organization. However, once these reports have been created by the few, they can then be utilized by the many to meet their ongoing BI needs without the need for advanced knowledge or training.

This book was written with one goal in mind: to communicate clearly the processes and skills necessary to successfully *begin* creating Crystal Reports in an SAP BW environment. For that reason, you'll find certain things missing that you might find in a "generic" Crystal Reports how-to book. Rest assured, this was quite deliberate and stems from the philosophy that, when it comes to learning new technologies, less is more.

For instance, there are no chapters on formulas, charting, or cross-tabs in this book. It's not absolutely necessary that you master these topics in order to succeed in an SAP BW environment. I have learned from experience that the only real way to learn formulas in Crystal is to have a real-life need for them. Charts and cross-tabs are nice to know about, but not critical to getting started in this environment. You can learn these on your own as you make progress.

The material in this book has been time tested in a wide variety of scenarios. Much of it stems directly from the many custom on-site training sessions I have conducted over the past 8 years. Every effort has been made to make the lessons as practical and as universal as possible. And they are designed specifically to fully leverage the functionality and features of Crystal Reports in this environment

That's it for now. Time to get started. Thanks for taking the time out of your busy schedule to take a dive into the world of Crystal Reports and SAP BW. I certainly wish you the best and all the success in the world. Happy reporting!

Mike Garrett

It sure seems simple enough to store information. Why does it seem so hard to get it back? In this chapter, we attempt to shed some light on why your information seems to be playing "hard to get."

1 SAP BI for the Rest of Us

One thing is for certain: no one likes the feeling of being left out. Whether it's the high school prom, your (supposed) best friend's wedding, or that next rung on the ladder, it's never a good feeling to know you're *so* close to something really good, but you can't quite get there.

In the famous words of The Rhyme of the Ancient Mariner, when it comes to getting the information you need it can seem like there is "water, water everywhere ... and not a drop to drink." This first chapter is dedicated to all of those who have come to the water time and time again only to be turned away, thirsty as ever.

1.1 The Aging Information Age

Is that a little gray I see?

The Information Age is now *well* past middle age. The process of storing and retrieving information electronically has been going on now for over a half a century, dating back to the creation of the ENIAC computer in 1946. Since then, the hardware and software technologies used for capturing, storing, and retrieving data have been consistently improved and refined over and over, year after year. Newer, faster, more efficient and ever more "user-friendly" data systems are released that promise "information at your fingertips." We've seen the advent of relational database systems, SQL, data warehouses, data marts, and a seemingly endless supply of "natural" query languages and "user-friendly" reporting tools.

And yet, after over 50 years of steady progress, you would be hard pressed to find *any* decision maker in any business today who would say they are satisfied with the quality of information they receive daily to run their business. On the contrary, many would say they are quite unsatisfied.

What's wrong with this picture?

As you might suppose, understanding and agreeing upon all of the reasons for this apparent disconnect between a steady stream of advances in technology on the one hand and a persistent lack of satisfaction among end users on the other sounds like a nice idea but isn't likely to happen for a lot of reasons. But this doesn't mean we shouldn't make at least some effort at understanding the root causes of the current state of information gathering.

After all, there are *real* reasons why things are still as difficult as they are even after so much progress throughout the past decades. And if by identifying at least a few of these reasons we can gain some understanding as to why things are the way there are, then perhaps that will help us identify what we must do differently to move on.

One of the goals of this book is to help the reader understand some of the reasons it can often be so challenging to do what should be (at least on the surface) a seemingly straightforward, simple task: *accessing the information you need to run your business.* We'll do that briefly here at the beginning. The goal of the remainder of this book will be to provide some very practical advice and hands-on instruction for successfully retrieving data stored in the SAP NetWeaver® Business Warehouse (BW).

To begin, we need to look at the beginning: how information is *captured* in the first place (a phrase that isn't without a certain degree of irony).

1.2 The Good and Bad of the Relational Database

First, let's be clear about one point: the relational database was invented as a way to *store* information, *not* retrieve it. This is the one little secret that Ted Codd (the father of the relational database model) forgot to tell us. Without getting overly technical, the primary reason why this is true is simply because all of the information entered into the system (via a "frontend" application interface) isn't stored in one place but rather scattered about in various places (tables) in the database.

The relational database model was invented as a way to efficiently and accurately capture and store information entered using a frontend data entry screen, one screen at a time. You may have noticed that a typical application data entry screen is limited to a fairly narrow subject area (customer demographics, order entry, account management, etc.). Very few application screens give you the big picture, covering a wide range of data elements. When they do, the person creating the screen runs into the same issues you would if you were to try to create a report using those same elements — namely, finding and reassembling all of the various pieces you need.

As an example, let's look at a common scenario for entering and storing transactional data — recording the sale of goods and/or services. This is an activity that every commercial enterprise on the planet goes through many times every day (at least they would hope so).

In database terminology, all of the information that's entered into a data entry screen is stored in individual *tables.* Each table is custom designed to store a particular piece of information pertaining to a particular sales transaction. In the simplest scenario, this would require a minimum of two separate tables — a customer table and an orders table (Figure 1.1).

Figure 1.1 Simple Scenario with Two Separate Tables

When you think about it, this makes perfect sense. The alternative would be to store both the customer information and the sales-specific information in a single table. This would mean, among other things, that every time you enter a new sale you would have to reenter the customer information for that sale, which is a lot of extra work.

Thanks to the relational database, this isn't necessary. Instead, the customer information gets entered *once* in the customer table and is simply referenced whenever a new sale is made. This could be done one of two ways: either starting on a customer screen and initiating a new sale (perhaps by clicking an Enter Sale button) or by looking up the customer information from a sales screen. Either way, the point is you only have to enter the customer data once. From then on you simply use that existing data for each new sale.

When it comes time to create your sales report, the above scenario is quite simple: All you would need to do is connect (*join,* in database terminology) these two tables together and select the data you need from each table. Not too bad. However, it's rarely this simple in the real world.

Figure 1.2 shows a more typical example of the kinds of situations you run into when storing and retrieving data in a relational database.

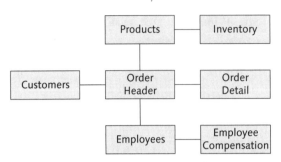

Figure 1.2 Typical Example of Storing and Retrieving Data in a Relational Database

Now things start to get a little more challenging when it comes time to create any sort of sales report. As long as your report covers only basic sales information (such as customer and order detail information), then things are the same as before, only in this case the sales information happens to be split between an order header and an order detail table. However, as soon as you begin expanding the scope of your sales reports, you begin to run into some challenges. Now you have to start bringing in (joining) additional tables, which increases the complexity of the report.

Besides the challenge of simply finding and assembling the correct data, there's the *dynamic nature* of transactional data. The data stored in transactional databases is real time, or up to the minute. In other words, it's constantly changing as your organization does business. This is great for getting a clear snapshot of current conditions, but not good at all for looking back in history.

For example, let's say you're a sales rep for the ACME Widget Company and you sell a carton of Widgets for Hikers to John McFerrin on January 1, 2009, for $100. If you entered this sale into a database. it might look something like Figure 1.3).

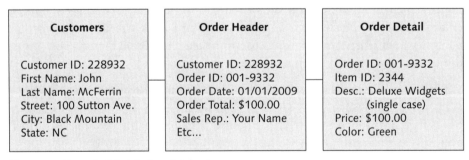

Figure 1.3 Example Sale Info in a Database

After entering this sale (along with other sales made that day), you might want to create a report for you boss that shows how busy you've been that day. No problem. At the end of the day you would simply join these three tables together and create a report something like the one in Figure 1.4).

ACME Daily Sale Report

Sales Rep: Your Name

Customer Last Name	Customer First Name	Order Date	Item Description	Total Amount
McFerrin	John	01/01/2009	Widgets for Hikers (single case)	$100.00
McKay	Ann	01/01/2009	Standard Widgets (carton)	$25.00
Barker	Robert	01/01/2009	Widgets for Hikers (carton)	$50.00
Heverly	Carolyn	01/01/2009	Widgets for Hikers (carton)	$50.00
Total Sales:				**$225.00**

Figure 1.4 Sample Report

Satisfied with your results, you print your report and hand it to the boss. However, your boss then tells you that recently the ACME Widget Company decided it would be a good idea to start keeping track of additional customer demographic information in its sales reports, namely *where* the sales are coming from. So your boss asks you to add the customers' zip codes to your daily sales report, which you do, and when you rerun the report it looks like Figure 1.5.

ACME Daily Sale Report

Sales Rep: Your Name

Customer Last Name	Customer First Name	Zip	Order Date	Item Description	Total Amount
McFerrin	John	28711	01/01/2009	Widgets for Hikers (single case)	$100.00
McKay	Ann	28308	01/01/2009	Standard Widgets (carton)	$25.00
Barker	Robert	28711	01/01/2009	Widgets for Hikers (carton)	$50.00
Heverly	Carolyn	28473	01/01/2009	Widgets for Hikers (carton)	$50.00
Total Sales:					**$225.00**

Figure 1.5 Customer Zip Codes on A Daily Sales Report

Now your boss has the additional information needed to determine where the biggest sales are coming from, which in your case is area code 28711. After seeing that well over half of your sales came from the same zip code, your boss asks you to do a little research and find out more about the area. As it turns out, area code 28711 is an area in western North Carolina that's part of the Appalachian mountain range. This would also help explain why the two sales made in this area code were for the Widgets for Hikers product.

The next day your boss asks you to run the report again for January 1 so he can take it to a meeting he has with the higher ups that morning. No problem. However, after running the report again, you discover a problem: One of the sales you made for area code 28711 has somehow been "moved" to a different zip code (Figure 1.6).

ACME Daily Sale Report

Sales Rep: Your Name

Customer Last Name	Customer First Name	Zip	Order Date	Item Description	Total Amount
McFerrin	John	28711	01/01/2009	Widgets for Hikers (single case)	$100.00
McKay	Ann	28308	01/01/2009	Standard Widgets (carton)	$25.00
Barker	Robert	28757	01/01/2009	Widgets for Hikers (carton)	$50.00
Heverly	Carolyn	28473	01/01/2009	Widgets for Hikers (carton)	$50.00
		Total Sales:			$225.00

Figure 1.6 Location of a Sale Has Moved

So what happened? Why has the location of one of your sales suddenly changed? What you've come up against is one of the biggest challenges when running reports against a transactional database system: ongoing changes to "master" data. In this case, the location of the sale didn't change, but the location of the *customer* changed. Without you knowing it, the customer moved this morning and called to update their address information in your system. Because your database only keeps the *current* demographic data for a particular customer, now that the address information has been updated, any sales report you run will reflect the new, updated address, even though the address may have been different at the time of the sale.

This is a simple example of a common issue with all transactional databases. The data that's directly associated with a particular sale (order date, items ordered, quantity, total amount, etc.) will never change, assuming it was entered correctly. This information is a record of an *event* that occurred at a particular point in time. So again, assuming the information was recorded correctly, that information will never change. It is what it is.

This isn't true, however, for information about any entity or entities *associated* with a given transaction. In the case of a sale, there's always at least one entity that's directly associated with a sales transaction: a customer. Usually there are two — a customer and a vendor (when you're reselling the product). In our case, something about the customer changed after the sale was recorded, namely, the customer's address. So even though your sale was actually made to a customer living in the 28711 zip code, it now appears to have been made in the 28757 zip code.

One way transactional systems deal with this issue is by maintaining a history of the information associated with a given entity. So instead of keeping just one current record, when the information is changed, an additional record is created with the new information while keeping the old record intact. What is then needed are "From Date" and "To Date" fields so you can determine the time period when that information was correct. In our example we would now have two entries in our customer table for Robert Barker (Table 1.1).

Customer ID	From	To	Last Name	First Name	Zip
228998	02/12/1978	01/01/2009	Barker	Robert	28711
228998	01/02/2009	12/31/9999	Barker	Robert	28757

Table 1.1 Two Entries in Customer Table for Robert Barker

As a side note, you may notice that the To date for Mr. Barker's current address is 12/31/9999. This is typically how you designate any record to be the current record in a database. Because you have to enter an actual date, you enter a To date that is well into the future. In this case, the year 9999 qualifies.

By maintaining a history of previous information, we can now create an accurate sales report that will reflect the actual customer demographic at the time of the sale. However, you just introduced a new level of complexity that quickly goes beyond the capabilities of the casual report developer. Even seasoned report developers can get tripped up by this need to synchronize the master data records across multiple entities. (For example, what was the current customer data, vendor data, organization structure, compensation plan, territory assignments, product mix, etc. at a *particular* moment in time?)

1.3 Set Your Data Free – the Data Warehouse

This historical data conundrum is the single biggest driver behind the need for and subsequent invention of the *data warehouse.* In its simplest form, you can consider a data warehouse a place where the master data values of all associated entities are *synchronized* over time. In other words, I can now go to a single place to see where all my customers lived at any particular time or what vendor I used to purchase a particular product or what my sales reps' compensation plan looked like. Or anything else that changes over time.

Once all of the master data is "time frozen," it becomes a relatively simple matter to look at all sorts of numbers (or *measures,* in data warehouse terminology, or *key figures,* in SAP NetWeaver BW terminology) and determine what my business world looked like at the time that number was generated. Typically the number or numbers would be associated with some sort of transaction, such as a sale, or an action, such as the hiring of a new employee. The two most common measures or key figures in any data warehouse are *quantity* and *amount.*

If you are familiar with data warehouses, you may also have heard of something called a *data mart* (often combined as *datamart*). Essentially a data mart is a scaled-down and more focused data warehouse. Whereas you might use a data warehouse to analyze data across the entire enterprise (across functional areas) a data mart is designed to provide a platform for analyzing a particular function within an organization (sales, accounting, human resources, etc.). For our purposes it's only important to recognize that, whether you're dealing with a data warehouse or a data mart, both are designed specifically to help facilitate historical reporting.

SAP NetWeaver Business Warehouse (BW) is the data warehouse solution provided by SAP, which will serve as the primary data source for us as we look at the various functions and features of Crystal Reports® throughout the remainder of this book. The primary focus of this book is to provide you with the knowledge and hands-on skills necessary to successfully create reports in an SAP NetWeaver BW environment using Crystal Reports.

SAP NetWeaver BW had its beginnings in the late 1990s as SAP R/3 customers began requesting an offline reporting solution that would allow them to more easily report off of and analyze R/3 data. We've already mentioned two of the most significant challenges facing report developers in a transaction environment — the fact that the data is scattered among various tables and the dynamic nature of transactional databases. With SAP NetWeaver BW, we get to add another challenge unique to the world of SAP R/3.

Things get even more interesting when you start looking at reporting directly off an ERP system such as SAP R/3 (now known as SAP ERP Central Component). Here's a little secret that most people who use SAP ERP Central Component every day don't realize: *SAP ERP Central Component isn't a database at all.* It's actually a very large collection of interrelated function modules that allow organizations to standardize, automate, track, and coordinate all sorts of otherwise disconnected business processes across an entire enterprise and eventually store the supporting data in your database of choice (typically Oracle or SQL Server).

This is a primary reason why reporting directly out of SAP ERP Central Component can be so challenging: not all of what you see in the application frontend is simply being pulled out of table somewhere and displayed on your screen. Much of what you end up seeing on the application frontend has been run through some sort of business logic first, depending on how the particular module you're working with was configured. This means that if you want to see the same number on a report that you currently see on your screen, you may not be able to simply go to a table somewhere in the database and pull it out.

So what SAP customers began to realize pretty quickly was that the very things that made SAP R/3 so powerful in helping them run their businesses were also making it more difficult to create and run reports. In terms of pure reporting, SAP R/3's greatest strengths became some of its greatest weaknesses.

Part of the fallout from this is that many SAP customers have ended up using SAP NetWeaver BW for what amounts to operational reporting, not for historical reporting as it was intended. If you bring over enough data at a high level of detail (document-level data) in SAP NetWeaver BW, it becomes a de facto operational reporting system. The only difference is that it's never *truly* real time. However, it isn't uncommon for SAP NetWeaver BW customers to set up a near real-time warehouse environment where updated data is loaded into the warehouse on an hourly basis or perhaps even more frequently.

This need to have operational reporting capabilities in SAP NetWeaver BW presents some significant technical challenges. Essentially these boil down to a very simple issue that can be quite difficult to figure out: how to transfer updates from the transactional environment (SAP R/3 or SAP ERP Central Component) into SAP

NetWeaver BW quickly enough to provide a near real-time experience without bringing your SAP R/3 or SAP ERP Central Component system to its knees. Fortunately, as the solution has progressed and with the addition of an advanced reporting solution like Crystal Reports there are other options now for providing detail-level operational reporting without having to move all of the data into the business warehouse.

SAP customers were also running up against another issue — the fact that not all of their operational data was in SAP R/3. Almost all SAP customers ran numerous other operational systems besides SAP R/3, and they often needed to be able to show data from these separate systems in a single report. This is another benefit of a data warehouse like SAP NetWeaver BW. It provides organizations with a way to gather data from multiple operational systems (in addition to SAP R/3 or SAP ERP Central Component) into a single reportable environment. Even the earliest versions of SAP NetWeaver BW provided a way to integrate non-SAP data into a common warehouse.

Here again is an area where Crystal Reports can provide an additional level of functionality to help facilitate the process of creating reports that combine SAP ERP Central Component data with non-SAP data sources. One of the strengths of Crystal Reports has always been its broad support for diverse data sources along with its ability to combine multiple data sources into a single report.

1.4 Finding Relief for Information Constipation

Important Disclaimer

In the next section we'll be dealing specifically with the process of specifying the requirements for developing *reports* using Crystal Reports, not the process of specifying the requirements for creating the *backend data objects* (InfoProviders) that are used as the ultimate data source for your reports. This process is referred to as "data modeling" and by its nature requires a significantly more rigorous specification process. This isn't to say, however, that you cannot or should not make improvements in the data modeling process as well.

Although the advent of data warehousing technologies like SAP NetWeaver BW provide for a more cohesive and integrated platform for accessing mission-critical information, there's more to accessing the right information than simply utilizing the best available technologies. Unfortunately for IT, it can't be done with better, faster, or cheaper hardware and software alone. At some point it takes people. And this is where things really start to break down, not because the *people* aren't working, but because the *process* isn't working.

What we're referring to is the classic "report specification process," or as it's sometimes referred to, the "go-away-and-leave-me-alone-can't-you-see-I'm-busy" process.

The most glaring indicator that things aren't working as they should is the sometimes hopelessly clogged information pipeline that exists in almost every organization. These organizations suffer from something we might call "information constipation."

The basic culprit is the traditional "waterfall" methodology that has been in common use in IT circles since the dawn of time. This process served us pretty well for many years until at some point the wheels started to fall off and the whole thing started falling apart. Not surprisingly, that was right about the time everyone started getting really busy.

And it's not just that people are busy, which they are. It's also that *they don't know what they don't know*. The classic top-down waterfall methodology assumes that end users know what they want before they get it, or in other words, that they're somehow able to recognize something they've never seen before.

So what exactly are we talking about? The traditional waterfall methodology for designing software systems is a multiphase linear process whereby each step in the process must be completed (accompanied by the mandatory sign off) before moving on to the next step. The typical steps in this process are shown in Figure 1.7.

```
Requirement Gathering Phase
      Design Phase
         Development Phase
            Testing Phase
               Rollout Phase
                  Support Phase
```

Figure 1.7   Steps in a Traditional Waterfall Methodology

This whole process is very methodical and, at least on the surface, seems quite reasonable as a logical system for helping ensure the success of an IT project. However, this approach has some significant shortcomings, particularly when you're dealing with the process of report design and development.

One of the biggest failings of this whole approach is that it makes the flawed assumption that the end user community is capable of correctly specifying a thorough, integrated set of requirements *before* they have seen the system (or report). In reality, end users rarely know exactly what they want at the beginning of the process. They simply don't know what they don't know.

This is especially true when developing Crystal Reports for the first time in an existing SAP NetWeaver BW environment. It's easier to develop reports for a new installation of SAP NetWeaver BW than an existing installation, because the end users at an existing site are familiar with the SAP BEx analyzer tool, and quite often it's all they know. Then one day you tell them you're going to start developing reports for them using Crystal Reports and you need their help designing the new reports. Guess what they're going to ask you to do? Re-create exactly their SAP BEx reports in Crystal Reports.

This happens because at this point in the game the world of SAP BEx (which is really Excel) is the only world they've ever known. So if you ask them what they want in their new "Crystal" report, they naturally are going to tend to ask for something they're familiar with. And even if they really don't especially like what they currently have, they don't have any real frame of reference from which to ask for something different.

There's another very practical problem with the idea of asking users to fully specify their reporting requirements *before* you begin development: it can take a *lot* of time. And one thing business end users don't have is a lot of time. We all know people are busy these days. Companies are doing more with less. Many of the people who are actually running the business are doing the work of two or sometimes three people. Asking them to take hours of their valuable time, especially in one big chunk, doesn't give them warm fuzzy feelings about your new "reporting initiative."

A word of caution: the final sticking point we would like to mention might dredge up some bad memories for certain people. It's a phenomenon that has derailed countless IT projects of all sizes and led to many a heated discussion between the business side and IT staff. It goes something like this: IT asks The Business what they want. The Business thinks about it. Talks about it. Has lots of discussions and questions and many meetings and debates. As time goes on, IT "encourages" The Business to hurry it up a bit, if possible. After all, we *are* on a deadline. Feeling pressure to come up with The Answer, The Business suddenly (and miraculously) finds its consensus and then presents its "final" requirements to IT. All is well. IT can now begin its work.

IT begins its development work in earnest. The Business goes on with, well, business. Some time later, after many long hours of development work, IT presents The Solution.

Long pause. Nervous glances around the table. The Business doesn't look happy. IT asks why. The Business says, "It's not what we need." IT says, "Yes, it is. We have the requirements right here." IT shows the requirements to The Business (with The Signature highlighted on the bottom).

The Business gives the requirements back to IT and says, "It may be what we asked for, but it's not what we *need.*" Then the fun really begins. Raised voices, hot collars – and no happy hour.

All this may sound a bit comical, but it's no laughing matter when it happens to a multimillion-dollar IT project, and it happens all the time. Chances are, if you're in the middle of a new reporting initiative in your organization, it's happening to you right now. And although everyone naturally wants to blame the other person, when it comes down to it, there's typically one primary culprit: *change.*

As we all know too well, the world isn't a static place. Things change. Business changes. People change. And *needs* change. Sometimes at a surprisingly fast rate.

What happened in our little scenario is something that happens naturally in any business environment and is perhaps the primary reason why the traditional, methodical, linear waterfall approach to designing software (or reports) is outdated and impractical. The business community learned something new. It could be about their business or about the capabilities of the technology or both. For whatever reason, the needs of the business end user community have changed since the initial requirement gathering took place, and the traditional waterfall approach is inherently resistant to change.

What's required is a flexible, iterative approach to report development that works the way people work.

1.5   Just-in-Time Report Design

We've all heard of "just-in-time" manufacturing. The basic idea is to create a manufacturing process that's able to respond quickly and efficiently to customers' changing needs. Yesterday your customers wanted blue, today they want red, tomorrow yellow. No problem. Deliver what they want, when they want it. And, if they don't want it tomorrow, still no problem, because we don't make any more than they want *right now.*

The reason just-in-time manufacturing has become so popular and widespread is simple: it makes sense — for everyone. Not just for the customer, but for the manufacturer as well. It's a classic win-win. And the reason why it works is because it's flexible, or nimble, or better yet, *agile.*

There's a somewhat underground movement in the IT world that has embraced a very similar concept and applied it to the process of designing and developing software systems. The movement's origin can be traced back to a meeting of 17 people at a ski resort in Utah in February 2001. What drew this small band together was a common desire for a new way of managing and driving new software implementations, especially large-scale implementations that require the coordinated efforts of many teams of people from both the business side of the house as well as IT.

What emerged from that meeting as a brief document entitled "The Agile Manifesto." It describes the 12 basic principles of the agile methodology and laid a foundation for a new way of looking at the process of designing and delivering software systems. The fallout from this little meeting created quite a firestorm among the IT community at large, for some very obvious reasons. First, it directly challenged the prevailing established industry standard waterfall methodology that virtually everyone adhered to at the time. Second, on the surface it looked uncomfortably too much like anarchy, a kind of "let's just wing it and see what happens" approach. Although agile proponents would rightly say nothing could be farther from the truth, nonetheless, you had to be a little bit "on the fringe" back then to openly support this new agile movement.

Today the whole agile approach has worked itself into many aspects of the IT world and is on the verge of becoming, and in many industry sectors has already become, mainstream. And there's perhaps no IT sector where it makes better sense to adopt a more agile approach than the realm of business report development.

▶ First, reporting is simply a process of looking at what already exists in a given database. Think about it: you're not *changing* anything.

▶ Second, reports are by their nature completely self-contained objects. In other words, they don't really interact with any other part of your IT software system in any significant way.

▶ Third, when you're developing reports in a reporting environment that's completely separate and distinct from your operational transaction systems (as with

SAP NetWeaver BW), there's absolutely *no chance* of adversely impacting the day-to-day operations of the business. After all, this is the primary benefit of an off-line data warehouse.

In other words, what are we all so worried about? It brings to mind the scene from the 1976 movie *The Marathon Man* where Lawrence Olivier's character leans over to Dustin Hoffman's character and whispers in a thick German accent, "Is it safe?"

Yes, it is, as a matter of fact.

Let's sit back for a moment and think about it. An organization makes the strategic decision that it needs to dramatically enhance and otherwise improve its business reporting capabilities. The first big practical result of that decision is the purchase and implementation of a data warehouse. As many now know firsthand, the process of getting from that decision to the completion of a fully functional data warehouse is neither simple nor quick. For reasons that we won't delve into here, a tremendous amount of effort is often required from both IT and the business community to pull something like this off effectively. It can easily take months, or even years, for any data warehouse to become fully operational. In many ways that's just the nature of the beast.

So now it's done. The warehouse has been designed, developed, and fully loaded with organized, sanitized, and de-normalized data, now ready and waiting for the business to dive in and explore to their heart's desire. The equivalent of the business analyst's promised land. A land flowing with milk and honey.

But wait a minute. Not so fast. You just can't go ahead and jump in. After all, you might hurt yourself. Or even worse, somebody else.

At least this is the message that many business end users get from the very folks that brought them their new data warehouse. It's a little like building a fancy playground for a bunch of school kids, complete with swings, merry-go-rounds, and see-saws and then telling them, "It's OK to take a look, but nobody touch anything. After all, we don't want you to get hurt." So, like a bunch of disheartened, wistful school kids at recess with nothing fun to do, many business end users continue on with business as usual, content to press on and just get by.

If all this sounds a bit melodramatic to you, you most likely come from the IT side of the house. If you're a business end user, you're most likely laughing or crying — or both.

Now, in defense of IT, it's no laughing matter to assemble a data warehouse from scratch. As we briefly discussed at the beginning of this chapter, the process of transforming and moving data from a transactional online system into a data warehouse can be extremely challenging and fraught with many a technical (and often political) challenge. Our hats go off to any IT professional who has worked on a data warehouse project and brought it successfully to fruition. As much as business users work to bring it all together, the hard reality is that IT works more. Usually a whole lot more. After all, they're the ones who have to *practically* bring it all together, and ultimately the success of the project is dependent on the talent, expertise, and determination of the IT staff.

And, humanly speaking, this significant investment of sweat and tears by IT can help explain why IT staff can sometimes come across as a bit overprotective when dealing with their new baby. We all know how it feels to take something that we've labored over and poured so much of our life into and hand it over to someone else. It can be a little hard to let go.

And, of course, there are some legitimate technical concerns IT might have about "cutting the business loose" on the new data warehouse. As we've said, the data warehouse is a totally separate environment, so your operational systems are perfectly safe from potential harm. But it can still break (at least figuratively speaking). To put it all in perspective, what exactly can go wrong in a data warehouse? It essentially comes down to two things: *data integrity* and *performance issues*.

First, one of the concerns IT might have about any type of "self-serve" reporting environment where the business basically takes care of itself is problems with data integrity. The way this plays out in practical terms is "my report doesn't match your report." So guess who's wrong? The other guy, of course.

From an IT perspective, most of the time and effort required to get a data warehouse up and running goes into the process of ensuring that the data that gets loaded from the operational system is accurate and clean. In other words, no garbage. It's all real, synchronized, and matched up across time. Again, this is no small task in even the smallest data warehouse implementations. If you're a business user who has been involved hands-on with setting up a data warehouse, you know firsthand how difficult it can be to simply define the things that get stored in a warehouse.

When is a sale really a sale? Well, that depends on who you ask. Ask a sales rep, and almost anything is a sale (especially at the end of the quarter). Ask an accountant, and it's not a sale until the money is in the bank. When is a shipment late? What's a direct versus an indirect cost? The list goes on and on.

When it comes to almost anything that's going to be captured and stored in a data warehouse, there are many times that at least some level of subjectivity comes into play. This is what can make the creation of a data warehouse so interesting. Perhaps unlike no other time, business users get to find out what other people are really thinking. And, as you might imagine, it can lead to some pretty lively discussions. But in the end it all somehow comes together, and you end up with a pool of data that has been discussed, debated, and eventually agreed upon as being "true." It really does represent the business.

So why can IT sometimes seem so uptight about allowing business users free access to the fruit of all this labor? After all, that's why they went through the whole process of ensuring the data was the real deal anyway, right? Well, yes, that's true, but there's one problem. Business users aren't always content to just look. They also want to get a chance to play.

As in "play" with the data. Although this sounds like a great idea to business users, it's the kind of thing that can keep IT folks up at night. And given what we've talked about up to now, you might see the reason why. Think about what's happening here: the entire organization just spent countless hours and a significant amount of money working through a process of ensuring that the business has available for its use a pristine reporting environment to support the decision-making processes of the business. And now the business wants to take that data and do whatever they want with it.

Let's get practical here. When we use the term *play* with the data, we're talking almost exclusively about the single most popular (and biggest) playground in business today: Microsoft Excel. With all of the end of the world disaster movies being such a craze these days, it's a wonder nobody has thought to come out with *The Day After Excel*. Probably too hard to imagine. All kidding aside, it truly is hard to imagine the business world without Excel. It has become part of the lifeblood of virtually every organization on the planet.

And for good reason. There's so much a savvy business end user can do with it. And virtually every organization has certain key people who have established themselves as the go-to people for handling all sorts of tricky and complicated data issues. As we all know, Excel allows you to do anything you want with any set of data. To a seasoned Excel user it's really just a starting point. The real power of Excel is that it let's you *make changes*.

But that also can be a potential problem, sometimes a big problem, especially from a control and governance perspective. As many corporations have found out (sometimes, unfortunately, in a very public way), it doesn't take a lot to get yourself in hot water when you start letting business users take the cleansed, tested, and verified data in your data warehouse and start "playing around" with it. Some have even found themselves on the front pages of the newspaper quicker than you can say "Sarbanes-Oxley."

A second common concern that IT often has when business users are given free reign in a data warehouse environment is performance. Often this is the most common real-world consideration. This is what IT is referring to when they say things like, "We can't let them do that. It'll bring the system down to its knees!"

Again, let's be practical: the number one concern that IT has here (and it can be a legitimate concern) is that, left unsupervised, unknowing end users might unleash a "run-away query" on the data warehouse that could slow the system down unacceptably for other users. In other words, one user could end up monopolizing the resources of the data warehouse at the expense of the other users of the system. The potential does exists for this to happen when you start putting more control into the hands of end users.

However, if managed properly, it's most certainly a risk worth taking because the potential for positive business outcomes is always going to be greater the closer you place the business users to the "inner circle" of the data warehouse. In plain language, the fewer hoops the business has to jump through, the greater their chances of success.

One of the very first practical lessons you'll learn in this book will be, as a report developer, how to prevent your queries from, as we said earlier, "bringing the system to its knees." There are just a few basic principles and "no-no's" you need to be aware of. Once you've got these figured out, there will be a much lower probability of anything going wrong. And after all, no business user is ever going to do any *real* damage to a data warehouse by running a report. It's simply not going to happen. Ever. As much as some IT people sometimes joke about smoke coming out of the server room, you can relax. You're not likely to set off any smoke alarms any time soon.

One thing that all sides can agree on is that ultimately the data warehouse exists to be used by business end users to help them in running the business. Although this may sound painfully obvious when you see it in print, the truth is that many IT departments don't really believe this in practice — or at least, not fully. At least to the point that they are willing for the warehouse to be used by end users right up to the point of *abuse*. In other words, to allow for some level of "unnecessary" stress on the system for the sake of providing a more open and usable reporting environment for the business.

As a side point, organizations often unknowingly become "penny wise and pound foolish" when making resource and budgeting decisions regarding a data warehouse environment. Although in terms of absolute dollars it can get pricey to upgrade the hardware for a particular data warehouse environment, compared to the potential cost savings and increased efficiencies that can be realized from a fully functioning, responsive data warehouse the true cost is often quite insignificant.

Additional memory costs money, but so does the wasted time business end users spend as they wait for a response to their queries. However, those costs aren't as obvious or as easily quantifiable as hardware expenditures are, which can often make it difficult to justify a hardware upgrade. The bottom line is that if the end users' wasted time could somehow be quantified and fed into an organization's accounting system, a lot of hardware upgrades would be done in short order.

1.6 So Why Not ... SAP BI for the Rest of Us?

This brings us back to the title of this chapter and the primary focus of this book: people. In particular, giving people (like yourself) power *over* the machine rather than making them feel subservient *to* the machine, in essence, closing the gap between knowledge of the business and knowledge of the tool.

One of the inherent inefficiencies of the report development process as it exists today is that you almost always are working with a divided effort that's difficult (at best) to bring together. The way most reports are currently developed is by pairing up someone from the business (an SME or business process expert) with a technical resource from IT.

Now the challenge becomes getting these two sides to work together effectively to produce the desired results. Anyone who has been involved with this process firsthand knows that it's fraught with difficulty, not least of which is simply trying to get these two people together to figure out exactly what needs to be done. That challenge alone has derailed many a reporting project. It just becomes too hard to get the two parties together and thinking along the same lines.

And even when you can get the two to communicate on a fairly regular basis, you then often have the problem of things getting lost in translation. Getting beyond just the standard differences in terminology and the sometimes excessive use of technical jargon, it can become very difficult for both sides to arrive at a common understanding of what exactly needs to be done. There's no real fault on either side. They just don't live in each other's world. Let's face it: many in-house IT resources are out of touch with the day-to-day operations of the business, and it gets much worse when outside contractors are brought in to help. As good as they may be with the technology, there's simply no way they're going to know the business as intimately as the business user, even if their resume' states that they possess years of "industry experience." Yes, they may know the industry, but they don't know *your* particular business the way you do.

This is what makes *you* so important to this whole process. Before we continue, let's take a minute to look at exactly who you are. We briefly mentioned in the introduction who the target audience is for this book. While there are definitely parts that will be of help to dedicated IT staff, the real purpose of this book is to empower business end users to develop their own reports using Crystal Reports, thereby eliminating the business-tool knowledge gap. Quite simply, the goal is to take someone who understands the business and teach him how to best use the tool to help run the business.

As we mentioned earlier, although the goal is to empower business end users to become as self-sufficient as possible, not every business end user is going to either want to, need to, or be able to create Crystal Reports themselves. Whereas it's extremely difficult to come up with an average, it would be safe to say that in the typical organization less than 10% of the end user population would qualify as good candidates for Crystal Reports development. In many organizations it would be in the low single digits.

So just what kind of person would make a good candidate for learning how to use Crystal Reports in an SAP environment? Perhaps the question on your mind right now is, "Do I have what it takes?" The first thing we should recognize is that in the end it's impossible to tell for certain whether or not any one individual will be able to successfully make the transition to producing reports using Crystal Reports. That said, there are, of course, certain key indicators and traits that can greatly improve your chances.

You can use the following checklist to help figure out where you stand (Table 1.2).

Question	Yes	No
Have you ever used a graphic design application?	2	0
Are you comfortable with creating and modifying Excel spreadsheets?	3	0
Have you ever written a report with any tool or modified a Bex worksheet?	4	0
Have you used Crystal Reports in the recent past (within the past two years)?	5	0
Are you personally motivated to create reports?	2	-2
Do you have sufficient time in your schedule to create reports for both yourself and for others in your work group?	0	-3
Do you have the support of your immediate supervisor?	0	-5

Table 1.2 Answer the above questions as best as you can and then total up your score

- ▶ 10 to 16 points – What are you waiting for?
- ▶ 5 to 9 points – You've got a good shot at it.
- ▶ 0 to 4 points – You may want to think about it.
- ▶ Under 0 points – Forget about it. Really.

> **Reality Check**
>
> You may score over 10 points and not ever get it, or you may score 5 points and do just fine. You'll never really know for sure until you get some actual hands-on experience.

It makes sense that the most heavily weighted factor is previous experience with Crystal Reports, especially if it's fairly recent (in the past two years or so). If you have had significant experience using Crystal Reports as a business end user, you're personally motivated, and the organization is behind you, then consider yourself a shoe-in.

Another factor that weighs heavily in your favor is experience using SAP BEx, especially in creating or modifying SAP BEx worksheets. Typically anyone who is adept at this is also going to be skilled at creating and modifying standard Excel spreadsheets. Possessing either skill is a good indicator that you may have what it takes to handle Crystal Reports.

You'll notice the biggest negative factor is a lack of support from your immediate supervisor. This doesn't require much in the way of explanation. You may have the background and the desire, but if your boss isn't behind you, your chances of success are greatly diminished.

So here's what you need to do. You need to stop and take the time to answer the above questions as honestly as possible. Be realistic about exactly where you are right now. If it turns out that you end up at the lower end of the scale (four or fewer points), you really need to give it further thought before moving on. It's tempting to say go ahead and give it a try, but we have to be realistic: it's going to require a significant commitment of time and effort on your part to learn not only the ins and outs of Crystal Reports, but basic reporting principles and skills as well.

Regardless of where you measure on the scale, keep in mind that the greatest single asset you bring to the table is your intimate knowledge of the business. Without that knowledge nothing of value gets done. It's that knowledge that makes a business end user the ultimate "double threat" when it comes to developing Crystal Reports.

1.7   I Can Do It Myself

If, for whatever reason, you've decided that you may not be quite ready for this at this particular time in your career, it's better to realize that now than to get further down the road only to end up frustrated. At least you've had a chance to learn a little about what goes on behind the scenes in the world of data warehousing and are perhaps a bit more educated on how the process works in the real world. A suggestion would be to pass this book on to a co-worker who you think may be a bit further along than yourself in terms of technical aptitude and skills. You never know – they may thank you for it later.

However, if after making your personal assessment, you've decided you do indeed have what it takes to succeed, then let us be the first to say "congratulations" on taking your first step. Our commitment to you is to walk with you every step of the way as you begin to build the knowledge and skills necessary to produce high-impact business content for your organization using Crystal Reports. You'll be learning in a detailed step-by-step fashion the critical steps to retrieving, formatting, and adding value to the data stored in SAP NetWeaver BW.

Yes, you *can* do it yourself. And we'll show you how.

1.8   Summary

- ▶ It is now over 50 years into the information age, and yet it's still difficult to find a decision maker in business who is satisfied with his or her access to critical business information.

- ▶ The relational database was designed as a way to quickly and efficiently capture information. However, it was *not* designed to provide easy access to that information once captured.

- ▶ Reporting off a relational database is a challenge for at least two reasons: the difficulty of reassembling the data and the inherent volatility of the data.

- ▶ The data warehouse was conceived as a way to overcome the shortcomings of reporting directly off of a relational database by providing an off-line repository where data can be cleansed, reassembled, summarized, and "time standardized" to allow for accurate historical reporting.

- ▶ The traditional waterfall methodology for running IT projects has some serious shortcomings when applied to the process of specifying, designing, developing, and testing reports. The report development process calls for a more agile approach to defining and refining the requirements and specifications for a given report. This "give-and-take" iterative approach to report development recognizes that the development of BI content is a process of discovery where each new step often reveals the next.

- ▶ For any BI initiative to succeed, there must be active, hands-on participation by the business end user community. One of the limitations of the current approach for developing BI content (such as reports) is that those who truly understand the business rarely get the opportunity to actively participate in the process in any substantive way.

- ▶ One of the primary goals of this book is to empower business end users to successfully develop their own high-quality BI content themselves using Crystal Reports. Although the percentage of business users who will be able to create their own reports will remain quite small, even a small number of business users equipped to create their own content using Crystal Reports can make a significant impact on a business's bottom line.

Before embarking on any kind of building project, the wise builder will take the time to identify and assess all the available tools and always use the right tool for the task at hand. If all you know is a hammer, then every problem becomes a nail.

2   Understanding the New SAP BI Toolset

Before we move on to the more practical, hands-on portions of this book, let's pause to consider why we're here in the first place. After all, you're about to embark on a journey that will require a significant degree of commitment of both time and energy, and chances are you don't have a tremendous reserve of either one.

So before you plunge headlong into the process of learning a particular tool, it might be a good idea to first determine exactly *what* it is you're trying to accomplish. Too often in the IT world we give someone a particular tool and then ask them what they want to do with it. We should be asking first what's to be done and then provide the correct tool for the job.

2.1   The Job of the Knowledge Worker

You've only heard it about a million times: we're currently living in the great Information Age. Let's just assume that's exactly the case. We *are* living in the information age. Just exactly what does that mean?

Among other things, it means that many of today's workers work primarily with information. If you're reading this book, chances are you don't produce or work with anything tangible in your job. Think about that for a minute. You, along with millions of other "knowledge workers," will go to work today and spend eight or more hours working what is probably a well-paying job, and at the end of the day you will shut down your computer, turn out the lights, and go home after having produced ... *what* exactly?

The cynical (and considerably less enlightened) response to that question would be, "Nothing" — at least, nothing you can actually touch or see.

Although it may be true that today's knowledge worker may not produce a visible, tangible product at the end of the day, is it also then true that nothing at *all* of value is being produced? The answer is a resounding "No."

But if it's true that today's knowledge workers are producing nothing tangible, exactly what then are they producing? At the end of the day, it boils down to one thing: *better decisions*. Because if what I do every day doesn't in the end directly produce a tangible product, then what I do must therefore be contributing in some tangible way to decisions about what to do and what not to do.

In case you think this is something unique and peculiar to the current Information Age, think again. For as long as time has been recorded, there have been productive, valued members of society that may not have produced anything at all tangible, but nevertheless proved themselves invaluable to those around them.

Take the scout, for instance. For as long as people have traveled into unknown (and many times dangerous) territories, there has been a need for the scout. But just what *exactly* did a scout produce? Many of them were well paid for their services and highly respected for their contributions. But at the end of the day they couldn't point to anything that they created that wasn't there before. In other words, they basically left everything the way it was.

But we all know the answer: it wasn't what the scouts *produced*, but *the service they provided* that made them valuable, namely, the *increased ability to make the right decision.* And these were the types of decisions that could mean the difference between life and death, not just the difference between a profitable and unprofitable quarter.

It was the scouts' ability to provide timely, relevant, and accurate information that made them invaluable for the successful outcome of a journey. And what made them so valuable was the fact that everyone else around them was headed into uncharted territory and needed experienced guides to help them get to their final destination. In other words, they provided the *information* necessary to get the job done.

So, if you want, think of yourself for a moment as a sort of scout for your organization. To keep with the analogy, let's assume there are others around you who lack the necessary information to safely arrive at their desired destination and who look to you, as their scout, to provide them with the information they lack to ensure a safe and successful journey.

If this is the case, it would be safe to assume that, at a minimum, your fellow travelers look to you for information that's timely, relevant, and perhaps above all, accurate. But what kinds of information? And in what form? And should it be delivered "as-is" or processed in some way?

2.2   The Information Processing Continuum

The job of the knowledge worker (more specifically, the report writer) can be broken down into one simple process: *the transformation of data into useful information*. This is "data processing" in the truest sense of the word. The idea behind this is that raw, unprocessed data that has been captured into computer systems can somehow be transformed into useful information by some process or series of processes. The question then becomes, "by what process (or processes) and by whom?" And, perhaps more importantly, "for what purpose?"

We'll start with the last question first: the *purpose* of the information being gathered. In other words, *why* are we seeking the information in the first place?

There can be many reasons why individuals or organizations may be seeking information. However, some of the most common reasons are:

▶ To see what's is happening *right now* (operational reporting)

▶ To see what has happened *in the past* (historical reporting)

▶ To see *why* things have happened (analytical reporting)

▶ To see what *will happen* in the future (predictive reporting)

Put another way, decision makers in any organization are constantly seeking information that will not only accurately represent to them the current status of their operations, but also give them an accurate picture of where they have come from, why things are progressing the way they are, and where things might go in the future based upon certain presumptions about the future.

If we were to place the corresponding reporting methodologies on a continuum it might look something like Figure 2.1.

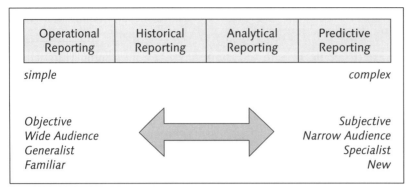

Figure 2.1 Corresponding Reporting Methodologies Continuum

At the left side of the continuum we have the granddaddy of them all, *operational reporting*. Operational reporting has been around since the dawn of time (at least in the computing world) and is by far the simplest and most familiar data processing method. Aside from the inherent challenges of simply finding and reassembling the data you need (as we discussed in the previous chapter), this method of reporting is the most widely recognized and utilized in the world.

Next we have *historical reporting.* This is the primary and most reliable function of the data warehouse. As we mentioned in Chapter 1, the data warehouse provides a way to "time freeze" all of the activities in your organization so that you can go back and see the exact business conditions that existed when that particular activity (e.g., a sale) occurred.

Third, we have analytical reporting (commonly referred to as *analytics*). We're now crossing over from what's primarily an objective exercise to a process that's considerably more subjective. The purpose of analytics is to look for cause and effect relationships. In other words, we're progressing from what's going on (operational) and what has happened (historical) into *why* things are happening the way they are and what's causing it. Because pure data analytics can only take you so far, at some point human judgment comes into play, which significantly increases the subjectivity of the analysis.

And speaking of being subjective, at the far right of our continuum lies the highly cerebral world of *predictive analytics*. This is where you start building models that are designed to help you predict what will happen (or is likely to happen) in the future of your business.

As you might imagine, the reliability of any sort of predictive analysis is question-able, at best. To be of any productive use at all it must be performed by highly trained, experienced specialists, and the results interpreted with a sizable grain of salt. This isn't meant to imply that predictive analytics can't be of any real value to an organization; it's only to say that it's important that everyone recognizes that, ultimately, you're trying to predict the future. So handle with care.

In case you're wondering where Crystal Reports sits along this continuum as a reporting tool, let's just say it has dominated the market for years as the opera-tional reporting tool of choice. Ever since it was introduced, it's been the industry "gold standard" for producing ongoing operational reports.

When Crystal Reports was first integrated with SAP NetWeaver BW in 2002, it suddenly became a player in the historical and (to a lesser degree) analytical areas of reporting simply because it was now able to access data stored in a data warehouse.

Another way to look at this is that with the addition of SAP NetWeaver BW as a backend data source Crystal Reports has been able to "cross over" into territory it couldn't cover before. This was more of a function of the integration of the two platforms than any real change in the tool itself. Crystal Reports is still, and most likely will always be, more of an operational tool than an analytical tool. That said, coupled with the robust data warehousing capabilities of SAP NetWeaver BW, you can now cover more ground with Crystal Reports than with just about any other tool on the market.

2.3 Information and the Conservation of Complexity

The process of transforming data into useful information is affected not only by the purpose of (or reason for) the information but also by the *initial condition* of the data. In other words, not all data is created equal.

Everyone has heard of the term "garbage in, garbage out." Ever since the very first typo, the problem of bad data in computer systems has plagued mankind and has made what should have been a fairly simple process many times more maddening. If you've ever had the privilege of being involved firsthand in a "data cleansing" project, you know exactly what we're talking about.

The problem begins at the beginning, when data is first entered into a relational database. First, you have simple typos, information entered incorrectly simply because it has been miss-typed. This is common in any frontend application because it's sometimes impossible to completely prevent this sort of data entry error. There's only so much that can be done to analyze each entry for spelling accuracy.

Then there's data that's spelled correctly but duplicated. This happens all the time and presents a huge problem when creating reports. This brings up the concept of "master data," where information about the various entities in your organization (such as customers, vendors, products, etc.) is kept in separate tables in your database and is referenced whenever someone inputs data into the transactional system. In other words, you don't enter a customer name into an order, but rather you look the name up in master data.

The idea of master data sounds great until you have to maintain it. The real difficulty is in keeping it "clean," which primarily means free of duplicate entries (e.g., two customers named Jane Smith when they are both the same person). Even more common is when the same master data item is entered more than once with a slightly different name (12" Big Screen TV vs. 12 inch Big Screen TV vs. 12" Big Screen Television, etc.).

There are other problems and challenges on the frontend involved with getting data input correctly from the beginning that we won't go into now. Suffice to say that it's virtually unheard of in any organization to have a situation where you can simply point a reporting tool at any operational database and pull back the data as-is. In almost every situation there will be at least some inconsistencies with the way the data was originally entered that will need to be corrected.

In addition to the data entry issues mentioned above, there's also the fundamental issue of the structure of the relational database when it comes to reporting. This was covered earlier in this chapter, so we won't elaborate much here but only remind the reader that even when dealing with pristine, accurate data, it's still quite challenging to create reports from a relational database owing to the inherent complexities of the relational database model (a series of tables joined together). Creating reports in this type of environment requires a high level of technical knowledge and an intimate knowledge of the underlying database structure (or schema).

This brings us to our topic at hand: *information and the conservation of complexity*. The conservation of complexity is based loosely upon the law of conservation of energy, which states that the total amount of energy in any closed system remains constant and can't be created or destroyed. It can only change form.

The Law of Conservation of Complexity

The total amount of complexity in any given computer system remains constant and can't be created or destroyed. You can only determine who has to deal with it.

At first glance you might conclude that it should be the goal of anyone who designs computer systems to eliminate as much complexity in the system as possible so that the end user has to deal with as little complexity as possible. This sounds like a good idea, at least until you realize that one of the drawbacks of this approach is that as you decrease the complexity of any system, you almost always must decrease the *functionality and/or flexibility* of the system at the same time. Often your greatest gains in eliminating complexity come specifically from eliminating functionality or flexibility, or both, from the system.

An argument can be made that there's no greater challenge for the designer of any end-user technology than arriving at the perfect balance of functionality, flexibility, and complexity. Or perhaps a simpler way to look at it would be to somehow strike the perfect balance between *power* and *ease of use*.

If a voice in your head just said "Apple," then you're getting the message. Apple Computer (now simply Apple) is arguably the very best hi-tech company in the world at achieving this elusive balance in the products they make. In essence, this is what sets Apple apart from the rest of the pack: the obsessive pursuit of the perfect balance of power and ease of use. As an old Apple commercial once said, *"What is the most powerful computer in the world? The one people actually use."*

So you can't just say that your goal in creating a computer system is to eliminate as much complexity as possible. It's not quite that simple. The real challenge is to reduce complexity while maintaining the appropriate level of functionality and flexibility to allow the user to accomplish the task at hand. As strange as it may seem, it's actually possible to make any system *too* easy to use. It becomes too easy at the point where you remove functionality or reduce flexibility to a degree where the end users are no longer able to do their jobs effectively.

Have you ever wondered why so many kinds of reporting tools are available on the market? Now you know why there isn't a one-size-fits-all reporting tool out there that will do the job for everyone. First, as we've seen, there are many reasons why someone may want to look at information regarding the state of their business. Second, not every end user requires or even desires the same mix of power versus ease of use in any reporting system. Some just want a one-click view of their world handed to them on a platter, and others want to be able to look at their world any way they want. And they'd appreciate it if you'd stay out of their way.

Again, the focus of this book isn't on all the things that can be done on the "backend" to decrease complexity while preserving functionality. Needless to say, many different types of technologies have been developed and advanced over the years to help reduce the level of complexity experienced by the report developer. One of these is the SAP BusinessObjects™ Universe, which is perhaps the most powerful "meta-layer" technology on the market for end-user reporting. Its purpose is to decrease the complexity inherent in reporting off a relational database while preserving as much functionality and flexibility as possible.

For now, as we move on to looking in detail at the various BI tools available from SAP, just keep in mind the law of conservation of complexity. If you want a fully utilize a tool that's both highly functional and flexible (like Crystal Reports), be prepared to invest the time and effort necessary to do so. And don't expect it to be easy. Likewise, if you want a tool that you can pick up and use almost immediately (and with little effort), don't expect to be rewarded with a lot of functionality or flexibility. While there may be additional functionality waiting beneath the hood (as there is with an end user tool like Web Intelligence), you must be willing to make the extra effort required to take advantage of it. Remember: you can only go so far before you have to deal with *some* level of complexity.

2.4   Introducing the New SAP BI Tools

When SAP announced it was buying BusinessObjects in October 2007, it introduced a significant change in direction regarding the frontend business intelligence (BI) tools for the SAP NetWeaver platform. Until then, the direction SAP had been taking was to continue developing and expanding the SAP BEx toolset internally to provide the additional functionality sought by its customer base, primarily formatted reporting capabilities not previously available in SAP BEx.

SAP had earlier introduced Report Writer as part of SAP NetWeaver 2004s, a formatted reporting tool that looked and operated somewhat like Crystal Reports, at least on the surface. As end users began to dig beneath the surface, however, it soon became apparent that Report Writer lacked the feature set and robustness of Crystal Reports, the product it had replaced. After considering its options, SAP decided to bring back Crystal Reports as the formatted report solution for SAP NetWeaver BI — along with three of its friends.

Now SAP customers not only have the option of using a world-class report design tool like Crystal Reports but also can use any of three other leading-edge BI tools: SAP BusinessObjects Web Intelligence® (sometimes referred to as Webi), SAP BusinessObjects Voyager, and SAP BusinessObjects Xcelsius® Enterprise (a dashboard and data visualization tool). This in many ways will prove to be a watershed moment for SAP customers as these tools begin to make their way into the SAP customer base.

This actually signals a homecoming of sorts for Crystal Reports, which was originally integrated with SAP NetWeaver BW 3.1 in the spring of 2002. The solution went through several major releases and upgrades in functionality until the announcement of Report Writer in NetWeaver 2004s. Now that SAP has bought the product and placed it front and center in its BI toolset lineup, the future of Crystal Reports (and for SAP's customer base) has never looked brighter.

So let's take a look at these new BI tools that SAP has obtained for their customer base. As we look at the toolset as a group, keep in mind the following:

► In a perfect world, the capabilities and feature sets of these four tools would be mutually exclusive.

► In reality, these four BI tools share some capabilities and parts of their feature sets. In other words, there are degrees of overlap of functionality.

► One of the keys for any business using an SAP system is to clearly define for its end user community the "sweet spot" of each tool in regard to functionality.

► Best practices dictate that the most appropriate tool be utilized in the correct way by the right person.

2.4.1 Xcelsius

Xcelsius was purchased by Business Objects in 2006. It's a data visualization tool that allows IT and power users to create interactive "what-if" dashboards that can be integrated directly into Crystal Reports 2008. Because Xcelsius dashboards are saved as Flash objects you can also embed them in any environment or container that supports Flash.

In terms of functionality, Xcelsius is designed to provide decision makers with a highly graphical, interactive interface for visualizing and interpreting information. To fully leverage its capabilities the dashboard designer would leverage the various interactive features of Xcelsius that allow decision makers to "play with the numbers" and instantly visualize the impact of those changes on various key metrics.

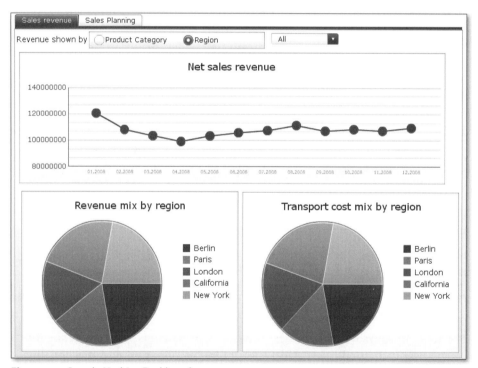

Figure 2.2 Sample Xcelsius Dashboard

As you can see from the sample dashboard (Figure 2.2), one of the primary appeals of SAP BusinessObjects Xcelsius Enterprise is its rich graphical interface. But there's much more to it than that. The product allows the skilled designer to create an intuitive and engaging interface that allows the end user to try various scenarios and receive instant feedback.

Xcelsius, much like Crystal Reports, is meant to be used by a highly skilled developer who can produce interactive dashboards for business end users. Anyone who is skilled with using Microsoft Excel would most likely feel quite at home using SAP BusinessObjects Xcelsius Enterprise to create content for end users. Keep in mind that it helps to have a good "eye" when creating dashboards and visualizations with this tool. To get the most out of it, you really need to be part developer and part graphic artist.

2.4.2 Voyager

Voyager is a true OLAP frontend tool, much like the current SAP BEx Excel analyzer and Web analyzer tools. A new version of Voyager (code named "Pioneer") is currently being developed. The stated direction from SAP is that "Pioneer" will eventually replace the current SAP BEx frontend toolset.

If you're unfamiliar with OLAP tools (such as the SAP BEx analyzer), the best way to describe this type of tool is as an Excel pivot table on steroids – that is, if you're familiar with Excel pivot tables. If not, then it's just important to know that OLAP interfaces like Voyager/Pioneer and the SAP BEx analyzers aren't really content creation tools (like Xcelsius and Crystal Reports) but are end-user interfaces that simply point to a backend OLAP data source (a data warehouse) such as SAP NetWeaver BW (see Figure 2.3).

It's also true that you can create and save "starting points" for users with these types of tools ("worksheets" in SAP BEx). But that's all it is: a starting point. The idea is that the end users would then be able to branch off from there and create all sorts of views of their data by "slicing and dicing" or by performing "drill downs" and/or "drill throughs."

The primary thing to remember about this type of tool is that it's highly interactive and isn't intended for the casual user. Typically the interface of an OLAP tool doesn't lend itself to producing highly (precisely) formatted output. It's really designed for on-screen interaction and for allowing the end user to look at the data in a variety of ways for performing data analysis.

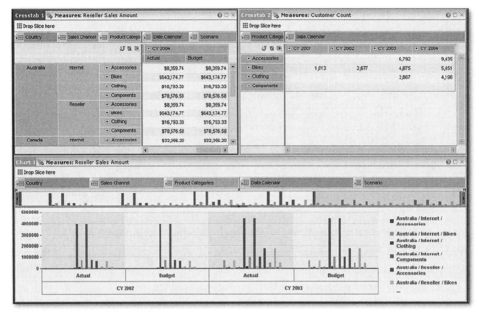

Figure 2.3 Sample "Pioneer" Report

2.4.3 Web Intelligence

SAP BusinessObjects Web Intelligence is a zero client end user ad-hoc reporting tool. It was initially introduced back in 1997 as a web-based alternative to the Desktop Intelligence reporting application, which for some time had been the premier ad hoc end user tool in the industry. Since that time Business Objects has steadily increased the functionality of Web Intelligence so that today it is now ready to replace Desktop Intelligence as the ad-hoc reporting tool of choice. SAP BusinessObjects Web Intelligence leverages a meta-layer technology called the Universe that provides developers and technically savvy end users with a way to create an abstract view of the underlying data and therefore reduce the amount of complexity presented to the ad-hoc report consumer.

SAP BusinessObjects Web Intelligence is an end-user tool that's designed to facilitate ad-hoc reporting and therefore provides the end user with the ability to both create and modify existing reports. Although it can be used for ongoing operational reporting needs, it's not designed specifically to handle large volume, highly formatted reports. It's meant to be used by end users to generate their own unique layout as needed (see Figure 2.4).

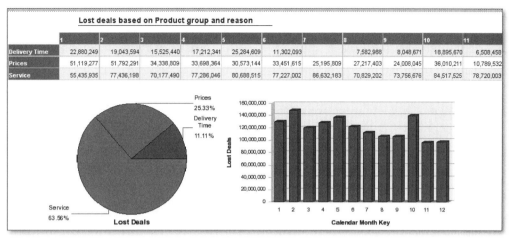

Lost deals based on Product group and reason										
1	**2**	**3**	**4**	**5**	**6**	**7**	**8**	**9**	**10**	**11**
Delivery Time 22,880,249	19,043,594	15,525,440	17,212,341	25,284,609	11,302,093		7,582,988	8,048,671	18,895,670	6,508,458
Prices 51,119,277	51,792,291	34,338,809	33,698,364	30,573,144	33,451,615	25,195,809	27,217,403	24,008,045	36,010,211	10,789,532
Service 55,435,935	77,436,198	70,177,490	77,286,046	80,688,515	77,227,002	86,632,183	70,829,202	73,756,676	84,517,525	78,720,003

Figure 2.4 Sample SAP BusinessObjects Web Intelligence Report

2.4.4 Crystal Reports

Crystal Reports has been around for a very long time, especially in terms of hi-tech years. Because the purpose of this book is to learn all we can about Crystal Reports, we'll take the time to dig a bit deeper into its history.

Crystal Reports began its life in the late 1980s as a product called Quik Reports, created by a company called Crystal Services. The original intent was to provide a way for users of their accounting software to create their own reports, but it soon got the attention of Seagate Technology, which bought the company in 1994 with the aim of developing the tool into a world-class report writer. This new software division was named Seagate Software.

The first major new product Seagate Software created was an exciting new report management and delivery system called Seagate Info. If Crystal Reports was the information package, Seagate Info was the shipping company. Seagate Info was the first system of its kind and provided a way for report developers to reliably and securely deliver their report content to end users. Seagate Info has since been revised several times into a completely web-based business content management system called Business Objects Enterprise.

Seagate Software was renamed Crystal Decisions in 2001 to take advantage of the brand equity it had built up around Crystal Reports. Altogether the two companies (really the same company with two different names) produced versions 4.0 through 9.0 of Crystal Reports.

Business Objects bought Crystal Decisions in December 2003. At the time, Business Objects was Crystal Decision's primary competitor, which often competed for the same business. Each company's flagship product (Crystal Reports on the one hand and Business Objects Classic, a.k.a. Desktop Intelligence on the other) had its own unique advantages that made the two platforms quite complementary.

Specifically, there were two primary differences in the two products that enabled them to sit side by side in the same product line:

▶ Crystal Reports was designed to be used by a report designer to produce a relatively static finished report to be consumed (viewed) by an end user. Desktop Intelligence (now SAP BusinessObjects Web Intelligence) was designed to be used by an end user who could either create his own ad hoc report and/or modify an existing report for his own use.

▶ Crystal Reports was designed to directly access a wide variety of data sources. One of its strengths has always been its ability to report off of just about anything. Desktop Intelligence was designed to leverage a meta-layer technology called the Universe, which was the real power behind the entire solution. The Universe was a way to assemble and simplify a wide variety of data sources to greatly simplify the process of creating and modifying ad hoc reports.

Crystal Reports was first integrated with SAP NetWeaver BW in 2002 when it was first bundled with SAP NetWeaver BW 3.1 as a solution for producing highly formatted reports. It remained the standard formatted reporting solution for SAP NetWeaver BW until it was briefly replaced by Report Writer in SAP NetWeaver 2004s.

By the time SAP purchased Business Objects in October 2007, Business Objects had captured close to 20% of the worldwide business intelligence market, with most of that attributable to the widespread success of Crystal Reports.

2.5 Comparing the New SAP BI Tools

Now that we've introduced the four new SAP BI frontend tools currently available (or in the case of "Pioneer," soon to be available) for SAP customers to use to access information stored in SAP NetWeaver BW, let's take a look at how they stack up against one another.

Doing any sort of comparison of these four BI tools is quite tricky and is *not* a completely objective exercise. The comparisons made here are intended to provide you, the reader, with a general idea of how these tools differ from each other in terms of specific end-user functionality. The numbers and rankings are presented here only as general guidelines, not as absolute truth.

Table 2.1 is provided as a guideline for comparing the four BI frontend tools available from SAP for use with SAP NetWeaver BW. Each comparison item will be further explained later.

	Crystal Reports	Web Intelligence	Voyager Pioneer	Crystal Xcelsius
End User Content *Creation* Tool	1	5	3	1
Operational "On-Going" Reports	5	3	2	1
Financial and External Reporting	5	3	2	1
Control over Formatting	5	3	1	1
Good for Ad-Hoc Reporting	1	5	3	1
Users Can "Play" with the Data	1	4	5	3
Good for Data Analysis	2	4	5	4
Good for Data Visualization	3	3	3	5
Good for "What If" Analysis	1	2	2	5
Total Score	**24**	**32**	**26**	**22**
Legend: 1= Poor, 2=Fair, 3=Good, 4=Very Good, 5=Excellent				

Table 2.1 A Guide for Comparing Four SAP BI Frontend Tools

2.5.1 End-User Content Creation Tool

This first point is perhaps one of the, if not *the most*, critical points to understand when evaluating these four BI tools. The emphasis here is on two points: who and what, as in *who can do what* with this particular tool, with the *who* being the end user and the *what* being the creation of usable business content.

The one thing to take away from this initial comparison is quite simple: Crystal Reports is definitely *not* a generalized end-user tool for the masses. It never has been and it never will be. For years the early producers of Crystal Reports (Seagate Software and Crystal Decisions) tried their best to "sprinkle" Crystal Reports among the business end-user community in hopes that some lasting fruit would somehow miraculously emerge. There was never a bumper crop.

Even though there are indeed many thousands of copies of Crystal Reports out in the end-user community today, even insiders within the Crystal Reports product team at SAP would admit that many of them simply aren't used on a day-to-day basis. Quite a few are just out there sitting on shelves.

This has nothing to do with the capabilities and functionality of the product but everything to do with who the target audience really is for this tool, and that's most definitely *not* the everyday, ordinary, nontechnical business end user.

> **Note**
>
> Remember our discussion of the conservation of complexity, where we said that when you increase the level of functionality and flexibility (power) of any given technology, you at the same time you typically increase the complexity? Welcome to Crystal Reports.

Although it's is true that Crystal Reports isn't the BI tool for the masses, when creating reports specifically using an SAP NetWeaver BW query as the data source, it does open the door to a greater number of ordinary business users to become actual report developers. This is because of the nature of a business warehouse: theoretically the data stored in a data warehouse is either report ready or near report ready.

What do we mean by "report ready?" In layman's terms, it means a lot of work (often a whole lot of work) has gone into transforming the original transactional (or *source*) data into a form that makes it much simpler to create reports. This is the same data that end users are already using whenever they view an SAP NetWeaver BW report using the SAP BEx Excel analyzer. The reason this works in the first place is because the data has been painstakingly nurtured to the point of making it report ready for the nontechnical end user.

Therefore, it makes sense that when working with a well-designed, cleanly implemented SAP NetWeaver BW implementation, you now have the opportunity to significantly expand the circle of Crystal Reports developers in your organization. And although the overall numbers may still be relatively small, it can end up being a good deal more than what you would normally have if working with a standard transactional data system.

At the other end of the scale, and leading the pack, we have SAP BusinessObjects Web Intelligence. Please keep in mind, however, that we're talking about the SAP BusinessObjects Web Intelligence user interface only, *not* the Universe Designer that's used to produce the data source for SAP BusinessObjects Web Intelligence. The Universe Designer, just like Crystal Reports, would rate a definite 1 on a 1–5 scale in this category as well.

This is what SAP BusinessObjects Web Intelligence has been designed to do from the ground up: provide the end-user community with an interface that will allow them to create and/or modify their own business content (reports) with little or no help from IT (except for the creation of the Universe as a data source). The idea is that once the Universe has been created, the end-user community can quickly and easily create new business content without having to know anything about complex database technology or arcane query language syntax.

Before we move on, keep in mind that once an experienced developer has created a report using Crystal Reports, that report becomes easily consumable business content for the rest of the end-user community. A fully developed and formatted Crystal Reports report is one of the easiest forms of business content for end users to get their hands on. So, although Crystal Reports may not be an end-user tool for content creation, it can be used to create easily consumable end-user content.

2.5.2 Operational Ongoing Reports

The second point of comparison is one of the greatest strengths of Crystal Reports. Think of Crystal Reports (when combined with SAP BusinessObjects Enterprise for report distribution) as an information pump, or perhaps an information engine. The whole premise of this solution is to provide a platform for facilitating the free flow of information throughout the organization. When you think of Crystal Reports and SAP BusinessObjects Enterprise, think about volume, as in increasing the volume of information flowing throughout the enterprise.

And when you think about it, day-to-day operational reporting (information used to run the daily operations of the business) is really more about volume than about almost anything else. At the operational level, most business end users are less concerned about the added value of the business content they receive than about just getting *enough* information to do their jobs correctly. We're not implying here that accuracy doesn't count. We all need accurate information. Just make sure there's enough of it.

How does this fit in with reporting off of SAP NetWeaver BW? After all, as we mentioned in the previous chapter, SAP NetWeaver BW isn't designed to be an operational reporting system, but rather a source for historical and analytical data. Does this mean Crystal Reports isn't well suited for nonoperational data sources like SAP NetWeaver BW?

This is a potentially big topic with a lot of implications for how reporting is to be carried out from both a strategic and an operational perspective. For now, just know that two real-world forces are at work here that help make this match work just fine.

On the one hand, although Crystal Reports is great at creating relatively static, operational reports, over the years it has also accumulated a fair amount of interactive capabilities that make it behave a bit more analytical. Crystal Reports provides simple drill-down and dynamic formatting capabilities along with some pretty sophisticated graphing functionality that combined provide the end user with some basic ways to analyze their data.

On the other side, as we mentioned earlier, SAP NetWeaver BW isn't strictly used for historical, analytical reporting. It's very common to see SAP NetWeaver BW being used in support of the day-to-day operation of a business. It all comes down to two things: how "fresh" does the data need to be and how often is the data "refreshed" in SAP NetWeaver BW?

It isn't uncommon for an SAP NetWeaver BW InfoProvider (InfoCube, DSO, etc.) to be refreshed with data from the transactional system once a day (normally overnight). It's also not uncommon for SAP NetWeaver BW InfoProviders to be refreshed with "delta" loads throughout the business day. The more frequent the data is refreshed, the more operational it becomes.

All this is to say that although Crystal Reports is not intended to be used as a truly analytical data warehouse interface (like "Pioneer"), it does provide enough flexibility in terms of user interaction to make it a good selection for many of your SAP NetWeaver BW reporting requirements.

2.5.3 Financial and External Reporting

When we talk about financial reporting here we're not talking about financial analytics, but about standard, regulatory financial reporting such as balance sheets, profit and loss statements, and so on — and especially any type of financial reporting that needs to go to someone outside of the organization.

It's a funny thing, but whenever information goes outside of a company it needs to be dressed up. That's just the nature of a world where perception is more important than reality, and anyone who's responsible for sending information to other organizations (regulatory agencies, shareholders, board of directors) knows the importance of putting on a good face. And that's one of the things Crystal Reports does best.

As it turns out, when combined with SAP NetWeaver BW as a data source, this becomes one of Crystal Report's better features. By fully leveraging hierarchies in SAP NetWeaver BW (you'll learn how to do this later in one of the hands-on sessions), you can easily create highly professional, beautifully formatted standard financial reports without having to re-create them every time (as is most often the case with SAP BEx).

2.5.4 Control Over Formatting

This is the primary reason why SAP originally began bundling Crystal Reports with SAP NetWeaver BW in 2002 — to make "pretty reports."

An Insider's Perspective

This is the part of Crystal Reports that drives some IT people crazy. "Oh, you want your report to look pretty, huh?" Let's just face it: left-brained IT people will never see the value of making something look pretty. Therefore, it's often not such a good idea to ask a left-brained IT person to make it look pretty. You might think about doing it yourself (so keep reading).

Crystal Reports is known for its ability to achieve "'pixel-perfect" formatting. There's no physical layout for a report that you can't create using Crystal Reports. And with the new view-time parameters in Crystal Reports 2008 you can now produce a wide variety of layouts, from high-level summary views to highly formatted detail reports using a single Crystal Report.

Having such a high degree of control over the final look and feel of your reports opens up a lot of possibilities. Some Crystal Reports have more the look of a form that a report, or perhaps a document. And control over formatting means control over pagination (determining where a page ends and the next one begins), which Crystal Reports handles quite nicely.

Ultimately this has always been the primary driver behind SAP's pursuit of Crystal Reports — the need for a high level of control over the final output of your report, something that has always been a challenge with the traditional SAP BEx tools.

You may notice that we gave "Pioneer" and Xcelsius very low marks for their ability to control formatting. Keep in mind that we're thinking primarily in terms of printed output in this case. Both of these products are capable of presenting to the user a very rich, full-featured interface to their world of information. However, these tools are highly interactive and rely on computer screens for presenting information.

2.5.5 Good for Ad Hoc Reporting

Now we begin to depart from the domain of Crystal Reports and turn the tables a bit. Crystal Reports definitely gets a low grade for its ability to satisfy the ad hoc reporting needs of end users. It's simply not a tool that's designed for allowing business end users to create their own business content on-the-fly.

The one tool in this bunch that's designed specifically for ad hoc reporting is SAP BusinessObjects Web Intelligence. This is exactly what it does, and it does it quite well. For more advanced end users who aren't afraid to "get their hands dirty," this is a nicely executed platform that provides a good mix of ease of use and flexibility. It has to be flexible, of course, simply because the whole idea is to provide users with a way to create a variety of "looks" of their data on their own. It has to be fairly easy to use or it would require too much time and training to learn how to use effectively.

SAP BusinessObjects Web Intelligence does a very good job of providing that ideal mix of functionality and simplicity so that the nonspecialist business user can create content without a heavy reliance on IT.

We give "Pioneer" a 3 (mid-level score) on this count simply because, technically speaking, it isn't intended to create any sort of report at all. It's more of an interactive real-time view of your data warehouse that the user can control not for the purposes of creating a final report, but for viewing and analyzing data on the screen. Although you can print a particular look that you might want to share with others in your organization, that's more of an afterthought than the central thought.

Xcelsius is rated at the bottom of the scale in this area for the same reason Crystal Reports is. No end user is going to create an ad hoc anything using Xcelsius — at least not anything that actually works and is recognizable. Dashboards created using Xcelsius are most definitely not ad hoc.

One last important thought before we leave this topic: our very low ranking of Crystal Reports in terms of satisfying the ad hoc needs of end users is made with the assumption that we're talking only about "true" ad hoc. So what do we mean by true ad hoc? One definition of ad hoc is "formed for or concerned with one specific purpose." Probably an even better definition in the case of reporting would be "improvised and often impromptu." For clarity, let's add a couple of adjectives: *unexpected* and *unusual*.

When viewed from a strict definition of the term, there are times in any organization when information needs to be retrieved and/or presented in some unique, never-before-realized fashion. Needs change. Situations change. Virtually every business operates in a dynamic, fluid environment that calls for an equally fluid and dynamic method for finding and delivering information as needed.

That said, much of what passes for ad hoc reporting in many organizations isn't ad hoc at all. It's what we'd call ongoing, predictable ad hoc, which of course is an oxymoron. We just said that something that's ad hoc is unexpected or unusual. It either has never happened before or has rarely occurred. If your business is generating a lot of ad hoc reports, you need to ask yourself a simple question: "Does our business really change that often?"

The confusion is understandable. The primary reason for the confusion is simple: we're confusing special and/or urgent requests with true ad hoc reporting. Just because someone urgently makes a special request for information doesn't necessarily make it ad hoc.

The most common occurrence of this (and it happens all the time) is when an end user needs to look at a particular *slice* (or piece) of information to meet a particular, sometimes unique need. "Well, you see, I don't need to see all divisions for the entire year. I only need the Network Data Storage division's sales numbers for August. Can you get that for me? Oh, and by the way, I need it in time for my one o'clock meeting with the board."

Most likely the company in our hypothetical example is already tracking and reporting sales by division and month. They most likely already have a report that shows each division's sales for the entire year. The problem is, today the Network Data Storage division chief is going before the board and needs just the numbers for her division and only for one particular month — and she needs more detail than the standard sales report provides. So off you go to fulfill yet another "ad hoc" request.

But let's think about this a minute. Chances are this same division chief is going to be back in your cube a few months from now just before the next board meeting looking for November's numbers this time instead of August's. Or perhaps she was here before looking for March's numbers. Or next month it could be another division chief looking for his particular numbers. These types of ongoing, somewhat predictable requests take on an ad hoc nature primarily for one reason: your front line of defense (your operational reporting) is too inflexible. It simply was not designed to adapt to a wide variety of needs.

This has always been the Achilles' heel of any operational reporting system: they tend to be fairly rigid and incapable of meeting the often changing needs of the end-user population. Therefore, the need for a more nimble, adaptable interface like a true ad hoc tool (such as SAP BusinessObjects Web Intelligence). And although Crystal Reports will never be the tool of choice for true ad hoc reporting, it can be a great tool to help you capture and fulfill the ongoing, predictable ad hoc requests that occur so regularly in any organization.

One of the goals of this book is to help you learn how to use Crystal Reports to create a much more flexible and comprehensive report for your end users that will allow them to quickly and easily find for themselves a particular slice of data to meet a specific need, without requiring the generation of yet another "one-off" report. This is perhaps the most important skill you'll learn in this book — so much so that if it were the only real Crystal Reports skill you learned, it would *easily* make your investment of time and energy more than worthwhile.

2.5.6 Users Can "Play" with the Data

If we were to include the SAP BEx Excel analyzer tool in this comparison, it would rate a 5 on this point, because ultimately SAP BEx is really Excel, and there's no better tool on the planet for playing with data than Excel. And because "Pioneer" is the most like Excel of all four of these tools, it makes sense that it would also rate a 5 in terms of providing end users with a way to play with (manipulate) data.

"Pioneer," being a true OLAP interface, is specifically designed to provide savvy end users with an initial view of their data and then give them a wide range of options for changing that view to fit their needs. In this case we're defining "play" as the ability not only to change the look (or presentation) of the data but also to add summaries, special calculations, charts, and so on to the initial view.

Once again, just as with ad hoc reporting, Crystal Reports rates a dead last in this area. It simply doesn't provide any way for the end user to truly play with the data. This always has been a deliberate feature of Crystal Reports: the end user can't change the content. In other words, it's "locked down."

It's true that users can export data from Crystal Reports into Excel and then manipulate it to their heart's content, but technically they are changing it not in Crystal Reports, but in Excel. The original data in Crystal Reports (which is still there after exporting) remains the same — untouched and unchanged.

> **Note**
>
> This is a significant point to remember about Crystal Reports in terms of corporate governance: it provides a way for an organization to produce and distribute enterprise-wide reports that become the gold standard for all other types of reporting that occur. This fact alone makes a case for making a tool like Crystal Reports a fixture in any organization's BI landscape.

Because Crystal Reports is specifically designed to prevent end users from manipulating the data (at least in its original Crystal Reports form), organizations can leverage this feature to create that elusive "one version of the truth" that can be used as a measuring stick to validate the sometimes wide variety of ad hoc reporting that occurs quite naturally (and at times almost spontaneously) in any organization.

Notice that we're giving Xcelsius a middle-of-the-road 3 when it comes to allowing users to manipulate the data. This is because we're making a distinction between the ability to play with (or modify) the data and the ability to perform "what if" analysis (which we'll look at shortly). These are similar in concept but are technically different needs that require different skills and approaches.

2.5.7 Good for Data Analysis

You might notice that the "other" three tools all get high marks in this department, with "Pioneer" edging out the competition with the highest mark possible. This is because, of the four tools, "Pioneer" is designed specifically to facilitate the process of data analysis. Without going into detail about exactly what constitutes data analysis, let's just say for now that the primary differentiator is the ability to go beyond the numbers to the reasons *behind* the numbers.

If you recall from our discussion of the primary drivers behind any organization's quest for information, the area of analytics gets beyond the "what's happening" and the "what happened" into the "why is it happening." This is when you begin trying to uncover causal relationships between the various entities and factors that affect your business. This is also where attempts are made at identifying and understanding those all-important yet elusive trends that can help identify where things are headed in the future.

SAP BusinessObjects Web Intelligence and SAP BusinessObjects Xcelsius Enterprise can also be useful in performing basic analytical functions, although not at as high a level as "Pioneer." However, Crystal Reports was never intended to be used to meet any type of true analytical need. The only reason we don't give it the lowest-level grade of 1 is because of its built-in crosstab and charting capabilities. Both of these features provide some very basic analytical functionality, albeit quite simplistic when compared to the rich feature set of a product like "Pioneer."

2.5.8 Good for Data Visualization

If you've been wondering when SAP BusinessObjects Xcelsius Enterprise was going to take off and fly, here it goes, off into the wild blue yonder. Data visualization is what Xcelsius is all about. This tool is meant to do one thing — and do it very well — and that is present numerical data in a highly graphical, intuitive interface.

By its nature, Xcelsius is meant to be viewed online. In a word, it's eye candy. Although you can certainly print an Xcelsius dashboard, you most likely won't want or need to (unless you're creating polished printouts for a presentation). Like any dashboard application, the whole goal of Xcelsius is to show as much information at a high level as possible, as quickly and as easily as possible.

More than any of these four tools, Xcelsius is as much art as science. This is because the real power of a tool like Xcelsius is its ability to create a *visual* representation of numerical data. This means much more than simply making the dashboard or visualization visually appealing. To be truly effective it must present a coherent, simple message that can be understood and absorbed readily by a wide audience. It's a great way to get everyone "on the same page" by providing a clear picture of key business metrics.

Is it possible to create a really bad dashboard? Absolutely. At this point the industry is going through a learning curve similar to that of desktop publishing in the early days of personal computing. Someone who can craft a truly elegant, focused, and relevant dashboard and who can do it in a creative, engaging manner is a valuable asset for any organization.

You may notice that Crystal Reports does a little better with data visualization than it did with data analysis — a 3 as opposed to a 2. This is because the same two features we mentioned concerning data analysis (crosstabs and charting) are even more effective here in terms of data visualization. After all, that's what they do. They take data and present it in either a summarized grid form or in the form of a chart, or graph. Although the charting capabilities in Crystal Reports don't compare with those of Xcelsius , they are nonetheless quite capable and adequate for many day-to-day visualization requirements. And as we mentioned earlier when we introduced Xcelsius, keep in mind that you can embed Xcelsius visualizations as Flash objects into Crystal Reports 2008 for the best of both worlds.

2.5.9 Good for "What If" Analysis

The final category in our beauty contest is the very specialized area of "what if" analysis. If you're good at Excel, you've most likely created at least one of these in a spreadsheet. The idea is that you have a set of baseline numbers (the current reality) and you "plug in" some variations of different numbers and then see the affect that variation has on the other numbers. "What if we decrease our order fulfillment time from an average of 3 hours to 2 hours?" You change the 3 to a 2 and, *voilà*, you see the effect on your bottom line.

Once again, Xcelsius stands above the pack concerning this type of functionality. It allows the developer to provide end users with a wide array of "widgets" that give the user the ability to dynamically alter various key metrics to see the potential effect of a change on the other metrics displayed in the dashboard.

Financial analysts love this sort of interface because it allows them to test various scenarios and see the combined effects of changes to key business metrics. Of course, the real trick behind this kind of analysis is making sure you've got all of the relationships right (remember the whole cause and effect thing?). As long as you ensure that these all line up and are correct, these "what if" dashboards can provide valuable insight into the inner workings of your business.

Crystal Reports ends up dead last here too, once again proving the point we made earlier about how no one tool can do it all — not even Crystal Reports.

> **Note**
>
> One final observation before we move on: recognizing again that our rankings are far from scientific, you may notice that SAP BusinessObjects Web Intelligence stands out from the other three tools in terms ranking across all categories (we must also note that no weighting is applied to the various categories). That said, it makes sense that SAP BusinessObjects Web Intelligence would produce the highest total of the three because it's designed to be the most general use tool of the four (i.e., it's the most well-rounded choice).

2.6 Making the Transition

To conclude this chapter (and before we move on to the more practical, hands-on aspects of this book), we'll go out on a limb and suggest a sort of framework for approaching the adoption and subsequent utilization of this new toolset available from SAP. In other words, what's a sensible approach to helping ensure the successful transition to the new BI toolset?

First, let's agree on one thing: like many things in life, there's no "one size fits all" strategy that we could suggest that will work in every situation. Not only is every organization unique in some way, but the situation and conditions that exist in any organization are often constantly changing, sometimes in subtle ways and sometimes in more dramatic fashion. Perhaps the most slippery factor is your individual corporate culture – and specifically your organization's perspective on and tolerance for change.

So, rather than try to devise some grandiose, overreaching strategy that can be shoehorned into every possible situation, we'll simply outline a series of basic principles — a set of simple guidelines to help you along the way as you move toward the adoption of one or more of these new BI tools.

2.6.1 The Question of Ownership

First, there must be a fundamental shift in perception regarding who within the organization owns the process of capturing and delivering mission-critical information to the business end-user community.

Before firing off some reflex answers, take a few seconds and think about this. Who *really* owns the process of collecting, organizing, preparing, retrieving, interpreting, analyzing, and in the end, acting upon the information that's stored in your organization's various databases? The answer to this question is critical and warrants some careful consideration.

Why is this so important? Because in business, as in life, ownership is everything, because ownership comes packaged with a lot of other things, namely responsibility. If I own something, ultimately I can do whatever I want with it because I'm responsible for it. In other words, I have the authority to do whatever I want with it. And this authority stems directly from my ownership. Ownership also determines accountability. If I own something, I'm accountable for it.

Much of the confusion and frustration that arises from the interaction of "the business" with "IT" over information processing in any organization stems from a lack of clarity over this very fundamental issue of ownership. And both sides are often guilty of part-time ownership, or perhaps a better way to say it would be good-times ownership. In other words, the process belongs to me until there's a problem. Then it belongs to you.

Perhaps you happen to be part of a progressive, open organization where this issue of ownership has been clearly thought through and articulated throughout all levels of the organization, so there's no confusion or question whatsoever regarding ultimate ownership of the information processes in the organization. If so, consider yourself lucky. In most organizations this is rarely spelled out explicitly.

In this book we'd like to make a case for saying that the ownership of the information in any organization belongs to the business, not to IT. Of course, someone could argue that, in the end, IT is part of the business, which of course is at least technically true. After all, all parties involved work for the same company (unless, of course, the entire IT department happens to be outsourced, which is close to the truth in some organizations). So, for sake of establishing ownership of the process we're making a distinction between the business and IT.

Why not say that IT actually owns the process? Or why not suggest some sort of joint ownership? The reason is simple: all of the information collected and stored in an organization is created by someone working in the day-to-day business operations of the organization. Every transaction recorded in a database had its origin with someone on the business side who initiated, carried out, and completed that transaction and subsequently entered it (or had someone else enter it) into a company databases system for "safekeeping."

The point here is that no business transaction can trace its origin to someone in IT. That's not the job of IT. It's the job of the business to carry out transactions.

If this is the case, the answer is sitting right there in front of us. If I create something, I own it. End of story. Now, as with anything else in life, anything owned can subsequently be sold. But unless there's the conscious conducting of a sales transaction, there's never a true change of ownership.

Once this concept of ownership is understood, communicated, and agreed upon by all interested parties, it can provide the proper framework, or foundation, for all subsequent decisions regarding the processing of information throughout the organization. Most of all, it provides clarity in times of conflict.

Anyone who has ever been involved firsthand in any sort of IT initiative knows that it's not at all uncommon for the business and IT to not see eye to eye over a particular decision regarding the direction of a given project. As in any relationship, disagreements are natural and unavoidable. These disagreements can be particularly difficult for those on the business side simply because they are, for the most part, navigating through uncharted waters. In other words, they find themselves in the rather uncomfortable position of having to make decisions about technical issues they know very little, if anything, about.

And depending on the individuals and the culture of the organization, there may be times when decision makers on the business side find themselves going along with a decision simply because they lack the know-how themselves and they feel they really shouldn't "rock the boat." So as IT makes its recommendations, the folks on the business side tend to sit and shake their heads and silently hope for the best.

But what happens (as it inevitably does) when "the best" fails to materialize? When things don't go according to plan, you tend to find out each party's perception of who owns the process, and as we alluded to earlier, it tends to suddenly become the other side. And because for all practical purposes IT tends to be the side that dominates the decision-making process, when things get a bit dicey, it becomes easy for the business to begin pointing fingers at the IT folks, and the blame game begins.

Let's propose a possible fix for all this: have both sides agree beforehand (perhaps formally) that the entire process belongs to the business side, from beginning to end. In other words, the business owns the process and runs the show. No questions asked.

This will immediately accomplish at least two things: first, it will place the entire responsibility for success or failure of the project on the business, and second, it will simultaneously give the business full authority to do whatever it sees as being in the best interest of the organization.

Perhaps a brief, real-world example will help make this a bit clearer. A few years ago one of the early adopters of this solution was about to implement a new project that involved the creation of a strategic plan data warehouse (consisting of a few targeted InfoCubes) that would be used in support of the company's yearly strategic planning meeting that occurred every late March. The end-user reports would be created primarily using Crystal Reports (the final product was to be a highly formatted PowerPoint presentation).

As is typical of these types of projects, the data modeling (backend) part of the project took longer than originally anticipated. By the time the InfoCubes were designed and loaded with data it was already well into the new year, with less than two months remaining until the yearly meeting. Now it was time to create the approximately 20 Crystal Reports required to complete the project.

A few weeks into the process it became clear to everyone involved that it was highly unlikely that the reports would be completed in time for the meeting at the pace they were being developed. Only a couple of reports had been completed, and time was running out. In an effort to increase production, an additional Crystal Reports specialist was brought in. After evaluating the situation, the specialist concluded that the project would most likely still not be completed in time, even with the addition of another resource. It was then suggested that the real solution to problem was not the addition of more resources, but a change to the process.

Up to that point the report development process had been proceeding according to the standard Dev-Q-P progression, where initial report development was taking place in a development environment, then moved to a quality (test) environment, and then finally sent on to the production environment. Of course, along the way the requisite approvals were being requested and subsequently granted using the appropriate forms. It was suggested that if the Crystal Reports development could be performed from start to finish in the production environment, this would greatly increase the chances of finishing the project in time for the yearly meeting.

To understand the IT's initial response to this proposal, you have to understand something first: this is simply not something that's done in an SAP production system. From a purely technical and control perspective, it's definitely not the right way to do things. But, in this particular case, it turned out to be the right thing to do for the business.

Once the business owners were apprised of the situation, and the proposed change of procedure was presented, the question was asked of IT: "Why not? Give us a good reason why we should *not* create Crystal Reports directly within the production environment?" A few technical and procedural reasons were presented, but in the end they all said essentially the same thing: it's just not done that way.

With a hard deadline looming and a world-wide strategic planning session on the line, you can imagine what the response was from the business owners: "We don't care where or how you get it done. Just get it done." From that point on, all Crystal Reports development was initiated and completed from within the production environment and, yes, the reports were completed in time. Mission accomplished.

This example (a true story) demonstrates clearly the importance and the power of clear ownership. There was never any question along the way about who owned the process of getting this project completed. Everyone involved understood that the final say in how things got done was in the hands of the business. And to the credit of the IT folks in this organization, they not only understood this clearly but were willing to step aside and allow the business to make a decision that they didn't feel comfortable with. Although they made it clear that it was not "standard" procedure, they also understood that there existed a greater need beyond the need to follow procedure.

We've spent quite a bit of time covering this issue of ownership for a good reason: whenever there's a question of ownership, there will inevitably be a questioning of authority, and whenever authority is questioned, it becomes very difficult to get anything done.

2.6.2 Close the "Knowledge of the Tool–Knowledge of the Business" Gap

We discussed this issue earlier in this chapter, but we include it here as a reminder and to emphasize how essential this is for a successful transition to the new SAP BI frontend toolset.

What we're talking about here is the traditional gap between those in the organization who know how to use the tools and those in the organization who understand the business of the organization. The real problem in the past has been that it's rare to find any one person who understands both the tools and the business.

This has always been the Achilles' heel of the existing SAP BEx frontend tools. In most cases the creation of a report for the business has required the direct involvement of a technical resource (typically an IT specialist) who would then work with someone from the business side to create a BW query to meet the particular business requirement. The logistical challenges alone can be enough to derail the entire process. But beyond this, there's the foundational issue of differences in perspective and language. It can be quite frustrating for the business side to simply communicate their needs clearly to the IT resource.

One of the foundational promises of these exciting new BI tools from SAP is the opportunity they bring to the business to become more directly involved in and in control of the creation of their business content. It simply makes sense that as more and more business end users develop the ability to create their own business content themselves, this will greatly increase the efficiency and effectiveness of the entire process.

Does this mean that with these new tools the level of direct participation by the business side in the process of content development will go from 3% to 20%? Possibly, but not likely. If your organization were to implement the full range of tools effectively and with close to full participation by the business, it isn't inconceivable that you could achieve those sorts of gains. However, a more realistic gain may be somewhere in the 5–10% range. Whatever the percentage gain, the point is that you'll have more business end users directly involved and controllingthe creation of their business content. And that can mean nothing but good things for any organization.

Perhaps the greatest benefit of this increased hands-on participation by the business is the sense of empowerment and control (ownership) that business users gain as a result of taking matters into their own hands. Almost universally the single greatest source of frustration for business end users is the fact that they're so often dependent on an often difficult to access outside resource that many times does not completely understand the real needs of the business.

If you're a business end user and are reading this book with the intention of ultimately being able to create you own business content using Crystal Reports, then you are to be congratulated. You're already playing a central role in this process of bringing the knowledge of the tool and the knowledge of the business together.

2.6.3   Develop a Dogmatic Pragmatism

Exactly what does it mean to be a "dogmatic pragmatist" concerning report development? It means a dogged commitment to doing whatever it takes to get the job done, regardless of how it gets done (within the appropriate ethical and legal boundaries, of course). When it comes to the process of report development, this means a commitment to results over a commitment to process.

Note

No one knows why, but in the world of IT there's no mistaking the fact that process is king. And there's no other environment where this is more true than in the SAP world. And although it can certainly be argued that there are some very legitimate reasons for this, there's no escaping the fact that when process is elevated over results everyone involved in the process ultimately loses.

We've already mentioned some examples of this in earlier discussions, most recently in our discussion of the importance of ownership, where we presented an example of a company that discarded standard procedure for the sake of getting the job done.

Of course, we're not advocating discarding all established procedure and protocol simply for the sake of getting things done. We recognize that, especially when dealing with financial and/or regulatory information, it's imperative that the process be orderly and the decisions made along the way be made deliberately and with the appropriate documentation. The point is not to shed all process and procedure, but to ensure that the process and procedure are absolutely necessary. Because if they're not necessary, then why do it?

In other words, what's necessary here is a sense of balance. Let's put it this way: if we told you that a particular report could be created that would ultimately save your company $1 million over the course of a single month, do you think someone in your company would be interested? Let's just say the answer to that question is a most definite "yes."

Now let's say we gave you two choices: you can follow all recognized and established procedures for getting this report done, and it will take one month to complete, or you can "fast track" the report by bypassing some of the less necessary parts of the process and get it done in two weeks. Realize that if you go for the first option, this report is going to end up costing your company over $500,000.

"Come again?" you say. How exactly is this report going to end up costing a half million dollars? Well, we just said that the information gathered in this report will result in at least $1 million in savings over the course of a month. If you go with plan A, your company will be foregoing two weeks of potential savings, or a half million dollars. However, if you streamline the process and produce the report in two weeks instead of one month, you begin realizing those savings two weeks earlier. In other words, the net gain for the company would be $500,000.

In business, they call this the cost of doing nothing. This is the most difficult cost to measure in the business world because you're trying to measure the effects of something that didn't happen.

Obviously, we're using a extreme example here to make a point. It would be unusual for any one report to result in a $1 million a month savings to the bottom line. But hopefully you get the point. The more valuable the information stuck in your organizational information pipeline is (i.e., information constipation) the more it's costing your company. That cost is very real and is going to the bottom line every single day, month, quarter, and year.

Of course, we're making a very basic assumption here: that you agree that there's inherent value in the data being stored in your organization and that there are real costs associated with the failure to make that information available to decision makers in a timely fashion. Then again, we assume that if you've made it this far, you probably have no issue with that assumption.

So remember, the important thing is that the information got there, not how it got there.

2.6.4   Build Your BI Baseline Using Crystal Reports

First, Crystal Reports is by far the most flexible and most far-reaching of all of the new BI frontend tools. (At least in terms of pure BI content creation. As we discussed earlier, SAP BusinessObjects Web Intelligence would be the overall leader in terms of content consumption and for ad hoc reporting.) You could say it's the "Swiss Army knife" of BI tools. Day in and day out, there's *very little* you can throw at Crystal Reports that it can't handle.

Are we saying that Crystal Reports can handle virtually any BI reporting requirement? Of course not. What we're saying, however, is that it can handle a lot more than any of the other three tools available from SAP, and more than almost any other tool out there on the market. Therefore, part of a winning strategy is to look to Crystal Reports to do your "heavy lifting" for the bulk of your BI requirements and then let the other specialist tools handle the rest.

Second, Crystal Reports provides a great way for your organization to deliver a consistent and reliable baseline of information that can be used as the one version of the truth whereby all other forms of information can be compared. In any organization there needs to be one set of these master reports that can function as a "true north" for the organization. Because these reports tend to go through a more rigorous design and testing cycle than other more ad hoc reporting, it makes sense that they would act as the standard by which all other reporting is to be measured.

Third, in terms of pure information consumption, Crystal Reports provides what is arguably the simplest and most intuitive interface of all of the available BI tools. Because Crystal Reports provides only the most basic types of navigation options, it can be easier for end users to navigate to and find the information they need than with some of the other tools. And once they do find what they need, it can typically be printed as a high-quality print-out if required.

Lastly, Crystal Reports provides a great way for technically savvy business users to "get their hands dirty" and immerse themselves in the inner workings of SAP NetWeaver BW without having to know a lot about the details of the backend. It's the kind of tool with which a business user can get some early wins by creating simple, high-level reports and gradually increase the level of complexity and detail.

Another way to look at this is that if all you could implement at your organization was one of the four new SAP BI frontend tools, you'd want to choose Crystal Reports. *None* of the other three tools provides you with the range of functionality and breadth of application that Crystal Reports does.

But of course, fortunately for you, you don't have to choose just one tool. Once you've established a solid baseline of consistent BI content using Crystal Reports, you can quickly move on to fill in the gaps with one or more of the remaining BI tools.

2.6.5   Power to the People

The last principle we'd like to pass on is, in some ways, the riskiest. What we mean by risky is this: it's a bit familiar, perhaps too familiar. What we're talking about is equipping your people to handle both the tools and the process themselves. We're talking about *training*.

If there ever was a Rodney Dangerfield of the IT world, it would be training. Training is always the last to get money and the last to get anyone's attention, if it ever does. Although we recognize that there are notable exceptions to this rule, in many organizations there simply isn't enough time, attention, or money left over for effective training.

Even when training is budgeted and planned for as part of an IT initiative, it's often inappropriate and/or ineffective. This is the primary reason why training doesn't get the respect it should — simply because much of it isn't worth the time people have to give up to participate.

For training to be effective it must be at least two things at once: *focused* and *relevant*. Focused training is training without the fluff. In other words, show me *exactly* what I need to know to do my job. Effective training is also relevant training — training that approximates as closely as possible the *real world* of the end user. We all know the most effective training tends to be on the job training. Even though it's frequently rushed, informal, and last minute, nevertheless it's often the most effective training simply because *you're learning your job while you're doing your job.*

Once again, the very fact that you're reading this book (and assuming you proceed on to the hands-on exercises) is proof that you, and most likely someone you report to in your organization, are committed to this very principle and are willing to put your money, time, and effort behind it.

However, as helpful and effective as we would hope this training will be for you, it still pales in comparison to learning to use your own data in your own environment. The best way to *learn how* to create reports in your unique environment and situation is to have someone *show you how* to create reports *in* your own unique environment and situation. "Canned" training can only take you so far. There's *no substitute* for having someone work alongside you and lead you through the process of creating business content using live data in your own SAP BI environment.

That said, any training is better than no training, assuming the material is appropriate and well written. Even though the hands-on exercises in this book by necessity won't utilize your unique organizational data, we'll be making every attempt to make the lessons as relevant as possible. And given the time pressures that exist in almost every organization today, you're to be commended for committing the time and making the extra effort to take on a new skill set.

So let's get on with learning how to successfully create Crystal Reports in an SAP BI environment.

2.7 Summary

▸ The knowledge workers today are in some ways like the scouts of former times: their primary value is in the transferring the knowledge they've gained into useful information to help guide the decision-making process.

▸ There can be many reasons why individuals or organizations seek information. Some of the most common reasons are:

▸ To see what's happening right now (operational reporting)

▸ To see what has happened in the past (historical reporting)

▸ To see why things have happened (analytical reporting)

▸ To see what will happen in the future (predictive reporting)

▸ The law of the conservation of complexity states that the total amount of complexity in any given computer system remains constant and can't be created or destroyed. You can only determine who has to deal with it.

▸ There's no perfect, one-size-fits-all BI tool. And in a perfect world there would be no overlap in the functionality and feature sets of the BI tools from a single vendor (such as SAP). In reality, although each tool will have its own particular design focus and strengths, there will inevitably be some overlap in functionality.

▸ SAP BusinessObjects Xcelsius Enterprise is a data visualization tool that allows IT and power users to create interactive, visually rich "what-if" dashboards.

▸ "Pioneer" (currently under development) will be a hybrid of the existing Voyager OLAP interface from Business Objects and the SAP BEx Excel analyzer tool. It's the only true OLAP tool among the SAP BI tools.

▸ SAP BusinessObjects Web Intelligence is a Web-based ad hoc end-user reporting tool that allows business end users to execute and modify existing reports.

▸ Crystal Reports is a "best of breed" report designer that's best known for its powerful and extensive formatting functionality that allows the skilled report designer to create virtually any report layout imaginable. It's also the most generalized tool among the SAP BI toolset in that it can be used to fulfill a wide range of reporting requirements.

- The primary business uses of Crystal Reports are:
- Ongoing operational reporting
- Financial or external reporting
- Highly formatted reports
- Some key steps to transitioning to the new SAP BI toolset are:
- Establish who owns the process of gathering and distributing information throughout the organization.
- Empower business end users to produce their own BI content.
- Be committed to doing whatever it takes to get the job done; a commitment to the people, not to the process.
- Build a solid BI foundation using Crystal Reports. Once this is established, you can fill the gaps as needed with the remaining BI tools from SAP.
- Provide relevant, contextual training for your end user community.

A wise person once said, "Watch your beginnings." This first practical, hands-on chapter sets the stage for everything else that is to follow, so pay careful attention. Much depends on getting this first part right.

3 SAP BW as a Crystal Reports Data Source

The purpose of this chapter is to help the reader understand how SAP BW functions as a data source for developing reports using Crystal Reports. This information is critical to the success of your Crystal Reports development effort because it forms the foundation of everything else we'll be covering in the remainder of this book.

> **Note**
>
> The information and techniques we'll be covering will benefit not only you as a Crystal Reports developer but also anyone who is responsible for the creation of BW queries in your organization. If someone else besides you creates or will be creating SAP NetWeaver BW queries for use with Crystal Reports, it's imperative that the information in this chapter be passed on that person *before* you begin your Crystal Reports development efforts.

First, we will cover some basic concepts and terminology concerning SAP BW. Next will be a brief discussion of a phenomenon peculiar to the world of data warehouses called "data explosion" and its potential impact on the Crystal Reports developer. Then we'll have a practical lesson covering the two SAP BW data sources available to the Crystal Reports developer: the BW query and the Data Store Object (DSO). Lastly, and most importantly, we'll get hands-on experience with creating a master BW query and a Crystal Reports template.

3.1 SAP NetWeaver Business Warehouse 101

Fortunately, as a Crystal Reports developer there's not a lot that you need to know about the inner workings of SAP NetWeaver Business Warehouse (or, as its better known, SAP NetWeaver BW). The goal here isn't to make you an expert on SAP NetWeaver BW, but to help you understand when to talk to someone who is.

Let's get one of the more difficult (and more delicate) items out of the way right up front: What is SAP BW and SAP BI, and are they one in the same? The confusion concerning SAP NetWeaver BW versus SAP BI stems from another case of a new marketing strategy coming head-to-head with a natural human trait commonly known as "resistance to change." It's a little like the ill-fated "New Coke" campaign that The Coca-Cola Company put on in 1985, only this time only the name changed and the product remained essentially the same.

To help understand where we have come from, you have to start with SAP NetWeaver BW. The *BW* stands for Business Warehouse. The *warehouse* part of the name comes from the fact that SAP NetWeaver BW is SAP's data warehouse product. SAP NetWeaver BW was originally developed and released in 1997 as SAP Business Information Warehouse (or BIW). Apparently this was about four too many syllables for the market to bear so the name was quickly abbreviated to SAP Business Warehouse, which was now only two words so naturally it was immediately acronym-ed into simple and short "SAP BW."

Once the market settled into SAP BW, things remained unchanged for many years until the release of NetWeaver 2004s, when SAP renamed SAP BW to SAP NetWeaver BI. Because thousands of SAP customers had been calling it SAP BW for so many years, it became immediately evident that almost all of them weren't going to be dropping the old familiar name for a new one any time soon. So SAP came up with a bit of a compromise: They retained the NetWeaver BI label for all the frontend tools and interfaces (the stuff the end user sees) and reverted back to the familiar SAP BW label for the backend data warehouse. So, technically speaking, when you're working with Crystal Reports, you're using a NetWeaver BI tool on top of SAP BW.

3.2 A Short Course on SAP NetWeaver BW Terminology

Like any other highly successful technology in the IT world, SAP NetWeaver BW has developed its own lingo and catch-phrases over the years, some of it official and some of it not so official. The following is a brief list of some of the more common terms and expressions, along with an attempt to convey their meanings.

By way of reminder, if you're a business-side end user who is interested in producing your own reports using Crystal Reports, it certainly is *not* a requirement that you understand all of the following terms along with the many others not listed that are associated with SAP NetWeaver BW. However, because the process of developing reports will almost certainly draw you closer to the IT side of the organization, it can be helpful to learn a little more about what the other side is talking about.

▶ **Cube**

In pure SAP BW–speak, the term is *Infocube*. From a business user's perspective, this is simply a place where business data is stored off-line (in a data warehouse) from the transactional system (where data is entered) for reporting purposes. A cube is also known as a *multi-dimensional* data structure. To get even more technical, a cube is the data structure used for OLAP (online analytical processing).

▶ **Query**

This can now take on two different functions. For the SAP BEx end user, a query is a report. The query is executed and data is returned into the SAP BEx analyzer. For Crystal Reports, a query is a data source for the Crystal Reports developer.

▶ **Key figure**

Known in other data warehouse circles as a *measure*, this is a simply a number that represents an aggregate (or summary). Two common key figures are the total number of an item sold (Quantity Sold) and the dollar amount (Revenue).

▶ **Aggregate**

This is a summary or total. The primary job of a data warehouse it to produce aggregates on-the-fly, or as you need them. An aggregate is a key figure that has been summarized across a set of characteristics (e.g., total sales by division and month).

▶ **Characteristic**

Similar to the data warehouse term *dimension*, this is something that can be used to identify or classify a business transaction (the name of a product, the zip code of the customer, the name of the division, etc.). The SAP NetWeaver BW Query Designer groups characteristics into dimensions.

▶ **Display attribute**

This is additional descriptive information associated with a particular characteristic. Color or size might be display attributes of the characteristic Product_ID. Crystal Reports treats display attributes as fields that can be added to the report. Adding a display attribute to a report has the same effect on aggregation as adding the characteristic itself.

▶ **Navigational attribute**
In SAP BEx, this is additional information associated with a particular characteristic that can be used to generate further aggregation. Adding the navigational attribute Color to a report that's currently aggregated on Product_ID will produce aggregates (or summaries) for each color.

▶ **InfoObject**
In SAP NetWeaver BW, key figures and characteristics are collectively known as InfoObjects.

▶ **Drill down**
This is the process of progressing to further details from a summary level. A common drill down would be to move from a summary of sales by year to sales by month. This is the most common analytic technique used in a data warehouse environment. Crystal Reports supports drill-down functionality.

▶ **Variable**
A variable appears to the SAP BEx end user as a prompt used for filtering the resulting data set from a BW query. When using a BW query as a data source, Crystal Reports automatically creates a parameter for each user variable in the query. These parameters are then presented to the end user when viewing Crystal Reports through a web browser.

▶ **Hierarchy**
This is a mechanism within SAP NetWeaver BW for organizing characteristic values in an ah hoc fashion. Because hierarchies are created manually and aren't driven by data values, they're by their nature a very flexible way to organize data, but at the same time they can be very maintenance intensive in a dynamic data environment. Crystal Reports fully supports the use of hierarchies in SAP NetWeaver BW.

▶ **Landscape**
This term is used primarily by IT personnel. It refers collectively to the three environments that normally exist in any SAP client site: development, test (or quality), and production, most commonly referred to as simply Dev, Q, and P.

▶ **Transport**
This is the process of moving code, or objects, from one SAP NetWeaver BW system to the next. An object is first created (or developed) in the development environment, then transported up to the quality environment, and then, after being tested and approved, finally transported into the production environment. Both BW queries and Crystal Reports are moved from development to production in this way.

3.3   Handle with Care: The Exploding Data Warehouse

Before we move on to the practical, hands-on lessons on creating SAP BI reports using Crystal Reports, it can be useful to explore a phenomenon unique to the world of data warehousing, something known as "data explosion." This is the tendency for data being stored and returned from a data warehouse to expand dramatically (sometimes exponentially) as the number of characteristics (or dimensions) increases.

This topic can get very technical and very confusing very quickly as you start to bring in such concepts as "sparse data" and "preaggregates" and a whole spectrum of very impressive-sounding words. Fortunately for us, we're only interested in how it directly effects our efforts to produce Crystal Reports against SAP NetWeaver BW (specifically, against an InfoCube in SAP NetWeaver BW).

Here's how it plays out for the Crystal Reports developer. As you add characteristics from your BW query to your Crystal Report, you're now requesting more summaries (aggregates) to be generated for you by SAP NetWeaver BW. This brings us to the one key difference between reporting off of a multidimensional data source (such as SAP NetWeaver BW) and reporting off of a relational data source (such as SAP R/3, Oracle, SQL Server, etc.).

> **Note**
>
> When you retrieve data from a relational database, you're asking for *N* rows (records) of data.
>
> When you retrieve data from SAP NetWeaver BW using a BW query, you're asking for *N* summary calculations to be generated. Each summary will return one row.

To look at it in a simplified way, when you retrieve data from a multidimensional data source like SAP NetWeaver BW, you're in reality asking it to create a set of summaries of whatever key figures (measures) you have included in your query. It makes sense that doing this will require a bit more work.

When you're dealing with relatively small amounts of data and fewer characteristics, this task can be quite easy and efficient for SAP NetWeaver BW (or any other multidimensional database) to handle. These smaller, focused queries can take just a second or two to process. However, things can change quite dramatically and quite suddenly as either one of two things happen: the size of the database increases and/or the number of characteristics (dimensions) increases.

To explain this, let's take a look at a simple scenario. Let's say we have an SAP NetWeaver BW InfoCube that contains sales transactions. Each sale, or transaction, in the InfoCube has three characteristics associated with it: Sales Division, Sales Representative, and Date of Sale.

This tells us the number of characteristics being stored in the cube but not the possible number of members in each characteristic. This is how things break out in this example:

► There are three sales divisions.

► There are 10 sales representatives.

► There are 30 days of data at any given time in the InfoCube (when a new day is added, the oldest day is dropped).

We know two critical pieces of information: the number of characteristics and the number of possible members in each characteristic. But we need one last, critical piece of information: How many sales transactions are there in the InfoCube?

The answer to that question of course depends on who this InfoCube belongs to. In other words, how big and how busy is the company (specifically the number of sales people in the company)? It would be one thing if we're talking about the local hardware store on the corner. It's a completely different thing if we're talking about Home Depot worldwide sales. For the sake of our discussion, we'll assume we're talking about a small, local business that makes around 100 sales per month.

We're now going to create a Crystal Reports report using a sales query against our SAP NetWeaver BW sales InfoCube. The first report we create is going to be very simple: Total Sales by Division. To do this, all we need to do is place the Sales Division characteristic on the report along with the Sales Revenue key figure. After the report is run, it may look something like Figure 3.1.

Division	Sales
Eastern	$10,000
Central	$20,000
Western	$15,000
Total	**$45,000**

Figure 3.1 Crystal Reports Report Using a Sales Query against Our SAP NetWeaver BW Sales InfoCube

Because the company has three divisions, the highest number of rows (and summaries) that would be returned is three. It's possible to have fewer than three, but it's not possible to have more because all we have is three divisions. And it doesn't matter if there were 10 sales or 10,000 sales that month. The number of aggregates (and therefore rows) returned is determined not by the number of sales, but by the total number of members in the current set of characteristics.

Let's take our report to the next level. We now want to see the sales not only for each division, but for each sales representative within that division. After adding the Sales Representative characteristic to our report, we'll see something like figure 3.2.

Division	Sales Rep	Sales
Eastern	John Roman	$5,000
Eastern	Louise Boardman	$2,000
Eastern	Jeff King	$3,000
Central	David Bennefield	$8,000
Central	Mike Brophy	$5,000
Central	Kent Welkener	$3,000
Central	Aan Coleman	$4,000
Western	Jim Johnson	$5,000
Western	Steve Kim	$5,000
Western	Edna Tokay	$5,000
Total		**$45,000**

Figure 3.2 Report with the Sales Representative Characteristic Added

Because there are a total of 10 sales representatives in the company, the highest number of summaries that would be returned would be 10.

So far, in our simple two-step progression, things have progressed in an almost linear fashion. We started with a Sales by Division report that produced three summaries, one for each of three divisions. We then moved on to a Sales Representative report that produced 10 summaries, one for each sales rep. In this case because each sales rep belongs to only one division, the number of divisions has no effect on the final number of summaries generated, but the number of sales reps is what now determines the number of summaries.

Now let's see what happens when we decide to go to the next level and create a report that breaks out the sales for each sales representative by date.

We've already stated that the sales InfoCube always holds exactly 30 days of sales. So what will happen when we add the Date characteristic to our report to show the sales for each day? Would we now get 30 summaries returned, one for each day? Yes, that would be the case if we placed the Date characteristic by itself in the report. However, in this example we're adding the Date characteristic to a report that already contains the Sales Division and Sales Representative characteristics. By doing this, we're asking SAP BW to summarize sales for *each* unique combination of sales division, sales representative, and date. Assuming each sales representative made at least one sale each day, we would then get as many as 300 summaries returned (10 sales reps × 30 days of sales).

This creates quite a big jump in the number of summaries (or aggregates) that SAP BW has to generate to run our report. So what would happen if we decided to add Product to the mix? The correct answer is, it depends, as in it depends on the total number of unique products that were sold. If the company sells 10 products (and each product was sold a least one time per day by each rep), you'd jump from 300 aggregates to 3,000. If there are 100 different products you'd go to 30,000 potential summaries.

At its most basic level this is a fairly simple and straightforward process: as you add characteristics from your BW query to your Crystal Reports report, you'll very likely increase the number of summaries or aggregates that SAP BW must generate. The reason why we say "very likely" is because not all characteristics will have the same effect on the total number of summaries generated.

Some characteristics will have a relatively low level of granularity (fewer unique members), and others will have a higher level of granularity (more unique members). An example of a common characteristic in SAP NetWeaver BW that would have a low level of granularity is Sales Channel. Most companies have relatively few sales channels. A characteristic that typically has a high level of granularity is Product. Most companies have a lot more products than they have sales channels.

This brings us to the most important thing you need to know about this concept of data explosion when creating reports against SAP NetWeaver BW. The characteristic with the highest level of granularity (the most unique members possible) is what we'll refer to as the "document level" characteristic. For sales information, this would be Sales Document. For accounting information it would be Accounting Document. In purchasing it would be a particular purchase order.

> **Note**
>
> Beware of the Document characteristic. It's by far the most explosive of all characteristics.

When you think about it, this makes perfect sense. You can't get any more granular in any business than an individual transaction (actually, one more level is possible — the *line item* level — but for all practical purposes you would never create a report in SAP NetWeaver BW at the line item level). In one sense, any business is ultimately the sum of all its transactions. And in even the smallest of businesses the number of transactions will (or should) dwarf the number of almost anything else you can think of within that business.

This brings us to our final topic regarding the inner workings of the data warehouse (or at least as much as you need to know as a Crystal Reports developer), and that is, "Does it make sense to include document-level transaction data in an InfoCube?"

First, many organizations use SAP NetWeaver BW to create detail-level reports at the transaction level, so it's very common to see document-level characteristics included in an InfoCube. This occurs because business end users are interested not only in high-level summary data. They also want to see the details. Because of this the people who build SAP InfoCubes often include transaction-level detail in their cubes.

Why would this be a problem? If this is what the business wants (and needs), why not give it to them? Well, this wouldn't be a problem if we lived in a world without limits, but unfortunately we do. And we sometimes hit those limits head on. This is what can happen when you try to do too much with too few resources. Things fall apart (or explode).

The practical fallout of all this is when you include a document-level characteristic from a BW query in your report, you run the risk of the report running out of resources on the SAP NetWeaver BW server. What this means ultimately is that the report will fail, with either a timeout or some sort of "out of memory" error. At a minimum the report may take a very long time to run. Either way, you always increase your chances of a significant performance issues when you include a document-level characteristic in your report, especially with very large data sets.

The obvious next question then becomes, "Is there a way to provide business users with transaction-level detail without potentially compromising performance?" Or perhaps another way to say this might be, "Is there a way to provide transaction-level detail in SAP NetWeaver BW without including it in the InfoCube?" The answer on both counts is "Yes."

We won't go into detail at this point, but when you introduce a powerful, highly versatile reporting tool like Crystal Reports into the mix, it introduces some interesting new possibilities for handling the "summary to detail" dilemma often encountered in data warehouses. Essentially it comes down to this: you leave the transaction-level detail out of the InfoCube entirely. This allows the InfoCube to do what it was designed to do: provide high-level summary data on-the-fly with a high level of performance (or at least it increases the chances of providing a high level of performance). The transaction-level detail can be left in a Data Store Object (DSO, which we'll describe later in this chapter when we look at the two different data sources in SAP BI), and Crystal Reports becomes the bridge between the two.

As you'll learn later in the hands-on exercises, Crystal Reports has a powerful feature known as a "subreport." If you're familiar with Crystal Reports at all, chances are you've at least heard of subreports. This is a very handy feature that, among other things, allows you as a report developer to "bridge" between two completely different data sources. You can use it to bridge between a BW query and a DSO or even a BW query and SAP ERP Central Component (or SAP R/3). This is very similar in concept to "jump" reports in the BEx analyzer.

It's now time to move away from the theoretical and on to some of the more practical aspects of developing Crystal Reports against SAP BW, which is why we're all here. The first step in the process is identifying and understanding the data sources in SAP BW that are available for use with Crystal Reports: the BW query and the Data Store Object (DSO). If you're a current SAP BEx end user, chances are you're at least somewhat familiar with the BW query. It's unlikely, however, that you'd have any idea what a Data Store Object is (unless you're an SAP BW developer). Let's take a look at both of these and see how they work with Crystal Reports.

3.4   The BW Query: Bedrock of SAP BEx

If you're an experienced SAP BEx end user, you've probably at least been introduced to the concept of the BW query. Whenever you run a report in the BEx analyzer you first open a BW query as your data source. You then typically respond to one or more prompts and run the query. The results are then displayed in the BEx analyzer (within Excel).

Some advanced end users have the ability to develop their own BW queries for their personal use and for other end users. However, in most organizations the development of BW queries is typically handled by someone in IT. If you don't have the ability to develop BW queries, you may want to find someone in your organization who does and show them the following section. What you (and they) are about to learn will probably save you both a lot of time and potential frustration. This is especially important if your organization has any history of developing BW queries for use with the SAP BEx analyzer.

3.4.1 Designing BW Queries for Use with Crystal Reports

The process of designing a BW query for use as a data source for Crystal Reports differs significantly from the standard process of designing queries for use with the BEx analyzer. Essentially the difference comes down to the fact that when used with SAP BEx, the query designer is in charge of creating the final look and feel of the report (the layout), whereas queries designed for Crystal Reports are simply a data source for the Crystal Reports designer. In this case the person developing the Crystal Reports report is responsible for the final layout of the report.

Therefore, creating queries for use with Crystal Reports is normally an easier process than creating queries for the BEx analyzer, simply because no consideration is given to the final layout of the report. Essentially all you're really doing is "staging" data into the query and making it available to the Crystal Reports developer. The organization of the query elements means absolutely nothing.

One of the greatest benefits of the MDX query driver used by Crystal Reports is that it allows the query designer to "load up" the query with as many characteristics and key figures as there are in the source InfoProvider. With the MDX query driver there's now (almost) no reason to create more than one query per Info-Provider, which makes the idea of a "master" query for reporting a reality. In the past, with the original BW query driver, it was necessary to custom tailor each BW query for a particular Crystal Reports report. Now that this is no longer necessary, the process of creating and maintaining BW queries for use with Crystal Reports is much more manageable.

> **Note**
>
> Although it's true that the MDX query driver allows the query designer to essentially "pass through" all of the characteristics and key figures defined in an InfoProvider, it's important to realize that this now places the burden of restricting the number of *active* characteristics and key figures on the Crystal Reports developer. As you'll recall from our earlier discussion of data explosion, it's especially important with larger data sets to be careful about how many characteristics you make active in a query.

So, although it's very convenient and advantageous from a query development and maintenance perspective to maintain a one-to-one ratio of queries to InfoProviders, it becomes very important that the Crystal Reports designer understand the implication of adding additional characteristics to a Crystal Reports report. We'll cover this in some detail in the next chapter when we begin our hands-on development with Crystal Reports.

Once you've created your master BW query for a particular InfoProvider, the next step is to create a Crystal Reports template that uses that BW query as its data source. This Crystal Reports template then becomes the starting point for anyone who wants to create a report against a particular InfoProvider.

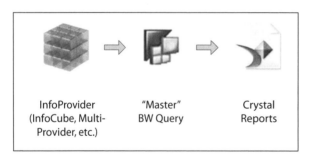

InfoProvider   "Master"   Crystal
(InfoCube, Multi-   BW Query   Reports
Provider, etc.)

Figure 3.3   Ideal Scenario

Although this is the ideal scenario, two characteristics of the BW query can (and will) stand in the way of achieving the goal of one template to one query to one InfoProvider: hierarchies and variables.

Our goal is to explain not what hierarchies and variables are and how they work, but their impact on the idea of creating a single master query for a given InfoProvider. Later, in the hands-on exercises, we'll look at both of these BW query elements and how they're handled in Crystal Reports.

If your organization utilizes hierarchies (and most do, especially in financial reporting), you'll find it necessary to create at least one additional query to handle your reports that require the use of a hierarchy. This is because once you assign a hierarchy to a characteristic in a query, there's no way in Crystal Reports to "unassign" the hierarchy. This means you'll always get not only the base line data (the "postable nodes") but all of the defined summary nodes as well. Although you don't have to actually re-create the structure of the hierarchy itself in Crystal Reports, you're still going to be stuck with additional summary nodes to deal with. So if your report does *not* require a hierarchy, you'll up with additional summary nodes you don't need.

There is a way within Crystal Reports to strip out the summary nodes of a hierarchy to get you back to the base nodes (postable nodes). This is primarily because in Crystal Reports if you know what you're doing, you can do just about anything. However, this is extremely time-consuming. It's best to just create another query without the hierarchy.

A second potential obstacle to achieving this ideal one-to-one-to-one scenario is *variables*. These are better known to end users as *prompts* and are used by SAP BEx users to filter the returned data set. Because not all reports against a particular InfoProvider require the same filters, this means it may become necessary to create a separate query for each set of end user variables (or prompts). This is because, much like hierarchies, once a variable is attached to a query characteristic, it's not possible to unattach it in Crystal Reports. As we'll see later in the hands-on exercises, Crystal Reports will always create a parameter for any variable it finds in the BW query, and that parameter will always get passed on to the end user when he runs the report.

We say "may become necessary" because it's possible to make a variable optional, allowing the end user to skip or ignore the variable when running the report. This now becomes an issue of usability and the end user's tolerance for seeing "extra" variables when running a report. We'll cover this in more detail later when we look in depth at end-user variables.

So although it may not always be possible to have a single BW query for each InfoProvider, with the MDX query driver it's possible to greatly reduce the number of queries necessary to provide your Crystal Reports designers with the data sources required to meet their BI reporting requirements.

3.4.2 Going "Flat" – the DSO

Before we move on with BW queries and, more specifically, how best to create queries for use with Crystal Reports, let's briefly explore the other, lesser known SAP BW data source: the Data Store Object (DSO).

First, here again there's been some name changing going on. The DSO was initially referred to as the ODS (Operational Data Store). In fact, the driver used in Crystal Reports 2008 is still called the SAP Operational Data Store driver.

In it's simplest form, a DSO is just transactional data (usually from SAP ERP Central Component or SAP R/3) that's been moved over to SAP BW. It may have been cleaned up a bit, but usually it's copied over from the transaction source system as-is. The primary difference between the DSO as a data source and a BW query is that the data isn't normally summarized and, if it is, it's stored as a summary only. In other words, unlike working with a BW query, you cannot ask for new summaries to be created for you on-the-fly. What you see is what you get.

In this way a DSO looks and feels just like any other relational (SQL) table (the standard way data is stored in virtually every transaction system on the planet — as a series of interconnected (related) tables). As you may recall from an earlier discussion, SAP R/3 (ECC) is run on a relational database. (As a side note, Crystal Reports includes a driver called the Open SQL driver that allows report developers to directly access the underlying transaction tables of SAP R/3 [SAP ERP Central Component]).

So what are DSOs used for in SAP BW? They're used almost exclusively to store transaction-level (detail) data to support the use of drill-down reporting in SAP BW. As you may recall from our discussion about the exploding data warehouse earlier in this chapter, it's inherently challenging (and contradictory) in a data warehouse environment to store transactional data in a multidimensional structure, or cube. Sometimes you can pull it off, but often it's is impractical owing to performance constraints.

3.4.3 Creating a Master Query

Let's look at an overview of creating a master BW query against an InfoProvider. Because the goal of this book is to teach you how to use Crystal Reports, not the SAP NetWeaver BW Query Designer, we're going to take a high-level look at developing basic queries. In the following section we'll assume that the reader has at least a basic understanding of developing queries using the SAP NetWeaver BW Query Designer and has previous hands-on experience.

Figure 3.4) shows the SAP NetWeaver BW 7.1 Query Designer with the Sales Overview InfoCube open in the InfoProvider pane at the left.

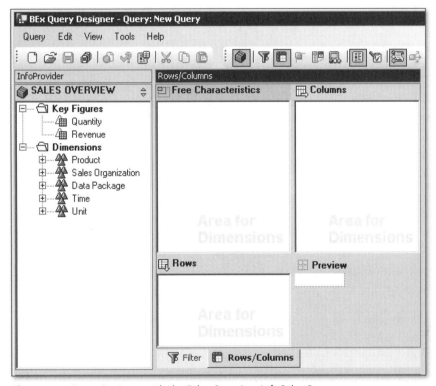

Figure 3.4   Query Designer with the Sales Overview InfoCube Open

Next we'll expand the Key Figures and Dimension nodes to see all of the available key figures and characteristics in this InfoProvider (Figure 3.5).

This InfoProvider is fairly limited in the number of available key figures and characteristics. Most real-world InfoProviders have significantly more than what is shown here. In this simple scenario all we need to do is drag all key figures and characteristics into the appropriate panes on the right.

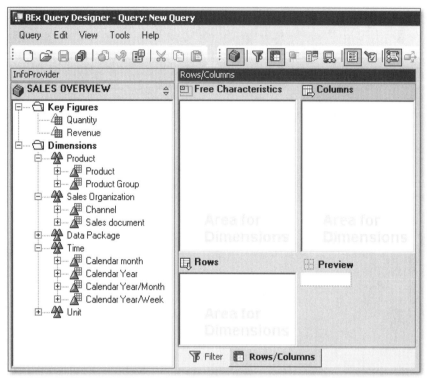

Figure 3.5 Expanded Key Figures and Dimension Nodes

Key figures always go in the Columns pane on the right. For queries designed for the BEx analyzer, where you place individual characteristics depends on how the SAP BEx end user is going to use them when the report is run. If you want to use the characteristic in the initial view of the report, you put the characteristic in the Rows pane. If you don't want it used for the initial view of the report but made available for the end user to create additional views (drill downs, slices), you place it in the Free Characteristics pane.

However, we're not developing this query with SAP BEx in mind, but for Crystal Reports. With Crystal Reports (using the MDX query driver) it makes no difference where you place your characteristics because Crystal Reports will treat them all as free characteristics until you use them in your Crystal Reports report. Then, and only then, do they become active characteristics.

So, where should you place your characteristics when developing a query for Crystal Reports? We recommend putting all characteristics in the Free Characteristics pane of the Query Designer in case an SAP BEx user attempts to run this query

98

using the BEx analyzer. It can be possible (given your particular security configuration) for an SAP BEx end user to accidentally run one of your master BW queries that you've designed for Crystal Reports. If this happens and you've made all your characteristics active row characteristics, the query may take a long time to run and will potentially return a lot of data. Plus, it will probably be a very busy report that makes little or no sense. However, if you placed all your characteristics in the Free Characteristics pane, the user running your query will get just the opposite: nothing. One other advantage of this approach is that the original SAP BW Query Driver (which has been deprecated by SAP but is still available for backward compatibility) is incapable of accessing free characteristics. So if you mistakenly use this driver instead of the current MDX query driver, you'll be unable to use any characteristics, rendering the query unusable.

Now we'll drag all of the available characteristics and key figures to their appropriate places on the right, as shown in Figure 3.6).

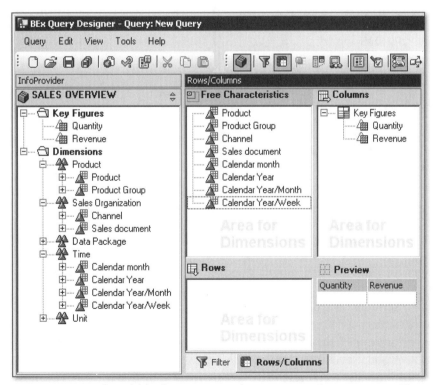

Figure 3.6 Drag All Available Characteristics and Key Figures to Their Appropriate Places on the Right

That's it! We've created a simple master query that a Crystal Reports developer can use to create any type of report that requires information from the Sales Overview InfoProvider. The only element we're missing that's in virtually every real-world query is at least one characteristic variable (for filtering the data).

We just need to make one more setting before saving our query. The name of the setting is Allow External Access to this Query. You get to this setting by going to the Properties pane on the right side of the Query Designer and selecting the Advanced tab (Figure 3.7).

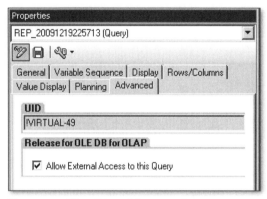

Figure 3.7 Allow External Access to Query

All you need to do is select this option to turn it on. Contrary to what you may hear elsewhere, you don't have to activate this to access a BW query in Crystal Reports as a data source. It *is* required, however, if you decide to change the data source of an existing Crystal Reports report to a different query. If the new query doesn't have this option selected, you won't be able to make the switch (this feature is called Set Location).

Let's now save what we have so we can proceed to the next step, which is the creation of a Crystal Reports template using this new query. When saving any BW query, you must supply both a description and a technical name. Depending on your organization, the description can be just about anything that adequately describes the query. Technical names, however, normally follow a predefined format. It's recommended that part of the technical name identify this query as one that was developed specifically for use with Crystal Reports. A common method is to insert "CR" into the technical name, as shown in Figure 3.8.

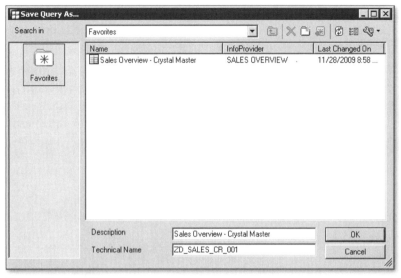

Figure 3.8 Save Query As

3.5   Summary

▶ A thorough understanding of how SAP NetWeaver BW functions as a data source for Crystal Reports is essential if you're to succeed in developing reports in an SAP NetWeaver BW environment.

▶ The world of SAP BW has its own lingo and practices. It's important that you become at least conversant so that you can understand others when discussing SAP BW.

▶ Data explosion can easily occur in any data warehouse environment. A data warehouse is designed to produce summaries (or aggregates) based upon a particular combination of characteristics. As you add characteristics into the mix, the number of summaries, or aggregates, tends to increase — sometimes exponentially. At some point you can "hit a wall," and the warehouse runs out of resources to complete your request.

▶ The most dangerous characteristic is the document-level (or transaction) characteristic. When this is added to a query (or in the case of Crystal Reports, to a report) it results in the maximum number of rows being returned.

▶ The primary advantage of using the new MDX query driver in Crystal Reports to create reports against an SAP NetWeaver BW query is that it treats all characteristics as free characteristics until used somewhere in the Crystal Reports report. This allows for the creation of master queries that can be used as the data source for a broad range of Crystal Reports reports.

▶ Although it may not always be possible to create a single query per InfoProvider, your goal should always be to minimize the number of queries and only create additional queries when absolutely necessary. The most common reason for having to create another query is the need for a different set of variables in a report.

Once you have created one or more master queries for a given InfoProvider, the next step is the creation of a Crystal Reports template for each master query. While it is tempting to skip this important step, the time taken is time well spent.

4   Creating the Crystal Reports Template

Sometimes a little can go a long way. Change your oil every 3000–4000 miles and your car might just last forever. Skip one or two changes and next thing you know, you're calling a tow truck. We all know the old saying, "An ounce of prevention is worth a pound of cure." If you really believe this is true, read on.

We highly recommend the next section for organizations that want to provide business end users with the ability to create and modify their own reports using Crystal Reports. The time savings that can (and will) be generated by following the guidelines outlined in this chapter will reap tremendous savings as you expand your report development efforts throughout your organization.

Some of the benefits of providing templates for your Crystal Reports developers when using BW queries as a data source are:

- They provide a consistent look and feel (common report headers, footers, and column headers).
- They shield the report developer from the technical names of query elements (especially key figures).
- Common calculations (formulas) can be included in the template, similar to shared calculated key figures in SAP BEx.

One point of clarification: For our purposes a Crystal Reports template is nothing more than a standard Crystal Reports report that you create as a starting point for further report development. Don't confuse this with the built-in template feature of Crystal Reports. When using SAP BW queries as a data source, the built-in template feature isn't of practical use.

Now here's where things are going to get a little tricky, because we're, in a sense, going to be getting ahead of ourselves. Because the creation of a BW query template is the first step toward the creation of an actual report, by necessity we're going to start by covering activities that are specific to the creation of a template. These won't be the same topics (or in the same order) that we'll cover when we proceed to the creation of the report itself.

So for now just follow along and catch what you can. The important thing is that you understand the importance of creating a template and the steps required to do so. After we're finished we'll move on to the basics of developing a simple report, and then you'll begin to see firsthand some of the reasons why we take the time to create a report template. So, without further delay, let's break out Crystal Reports, roll up our sleeves, and have some fun.

4.1 Creating a Template for Your Master Query

At this point it's critical that you've successfully completed the following three things:

▶ Install Crystal Reports 2008 your computer.

▶ Install the Integration Kit for SAP Solutions (client installation).

▶ Install the latest service pack from SAP (as of this writing, Service Pack 2).

In addition to this software installation, you must ensure that your SAP NetWeaver BW login has been added to a special SAP role that should have been created for Crystal Reports developers. This role allows you to access SAP BW queries as a data source from within Crystal Reports (among other things).

Note
If these steps haven't been completed you won't be able to proceed.

Once you've installed Crystal Reports on your computer (along with the Integration Kit for SAP Solutions and the latest Service Pack), you can launch Crystal Reports (START • PROGRAMS • CRYSTAL REPORTS 2008).

Once you've launched Crystal Reports, you should see the initial start page (Figure 4.1).

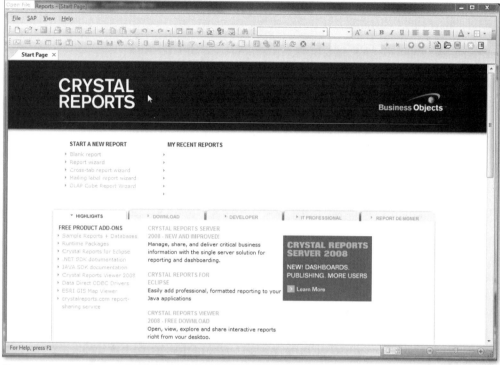

Figure 4.1 Crystal Reports Start Page

The next step is to change one important setting that pertains directly to accessing BW queries. This is done by clicking the Settings button on the SAP toolbar or by going to the SAP menu and selecting Settings (Figure 4.2).

Figure 4.2 The SAP Toolbar – Settings Button

You'll now see the Settings dialog box (Figure 4.3).

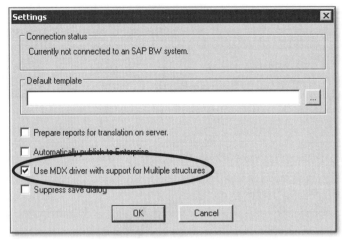

Figure 4.3   Settings Dialog Box

You select the Use MDX Driver with Support for Multiple Structures checkbox. It's critical that you complete this step before moving forward. This ensures that you're using the newer MDX query driver instead of the original BW query driver.

Click OK to exit the Settings dialog. Now we can access our master BW query to create our report template. To do this, click the Create New Report from a Query button on the SAP NetWeaver BW toolbar (Figure 4.4).

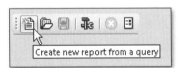

Figure 4.4   Create New Report from a Query

Next you'll be presented with the standard SAP logon dialog. You then select the appropriate SAP NetWeaver BW system (in our case the same system you created the master BW query on). After you've successfully logged on, you'll see the dialog shown in Figure 4.5.

You should then see your master query listed in your History. If you need help finding your master query, you can click the Find icon at the top right or simply enter the any part of the query technical name or description in the text box at the bottom right and press ⌈Enter⌋.

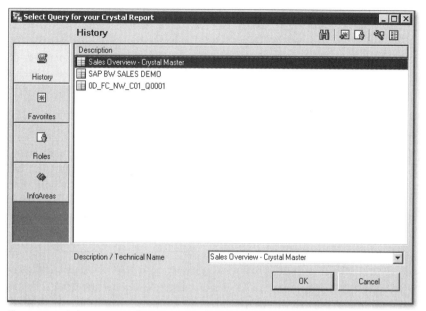

Figure 4.5 Select a Query for Your Crystal Report

In our case the master query we just created is the first item listed in our History. Double-click the query to open it in Crystal Reports, and you should see something like Figure 4.6.

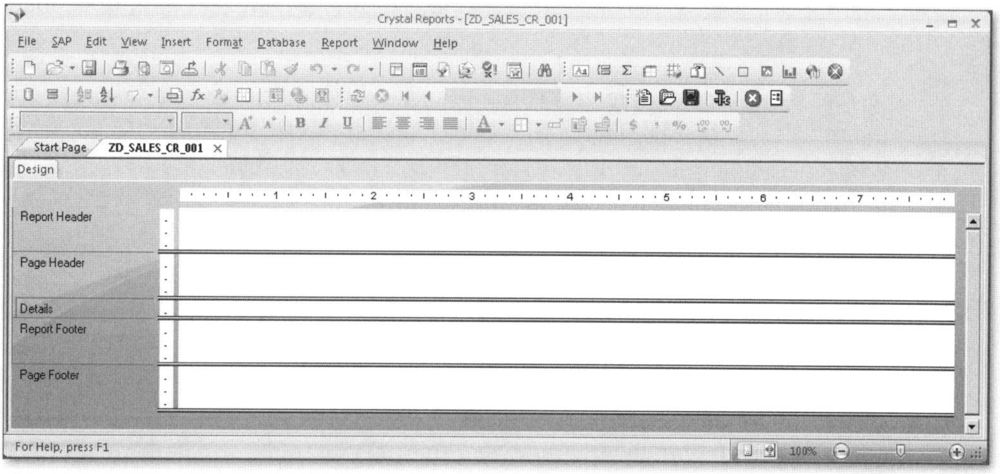

Figure 4.6 Design Tab in Crystal Reports

> **Note**
>
> As a reminder, the purpose of this section is to quickly cover the various aspects of creating a template for your master BW query. Therefore, we're going to skip some basic areas for now to focus on this specific task. We'll circle back around in the next chapter and start over from the beginning. For now, just follow along.

> **Note**
>
> In this example we're maintaining the default page orientation (portrait). Because most Crystal Reports end up being in landscape, it's a good idea to set the orientation of your template to landscape. That way you won't have to change it for the majority of your Crystal Reports. In this lesson we're going to keep it at portrait for a very practical reason: It's easier to fit the images on the relatively constrained pages of this book. To change the page orientation go to FILE • PAGE SETUP and select Landscape.

First, we need to cover some quick basics to get you oriented. You're looking at what is referred to as the Design tab of Crystal Reports. As the name implies, this is where almost all of the work of designing a Crystal Reports report is accomplished. Additional tabs come into play as you progress in developing your report (primarily a Preview tab that shows you what the report looks like with data).

The Design tab is initially divided into five sections. We'll cover these in detail in the next chapter. We'll be creating our standard header in the Page Header section, not the Report Header section. The reason for this will also be explained later. For now it's just important to know that it's not unusual for a report to not include a report header.

To create our header, we're first going to place a static text box for our fictitious company, the Hedijetijak Electronics Company (an international electronics manufacturing company based in Norway). To insert a text object, we first click the Insert Text Object button on the Insert toolbar (Figure 4.7).

Figure 4.7 Insert Toolbar

Now click and drag a text box in the page header section. Be sure to click and drag, not just click. And remember: You're determining the initial size of the text box as you click and drag, so give yourself enough room. You can always resize the text box later, if necessary.

You can now type the company name, "Hedijetijak Electronics Corporation" (Figure 4.8).

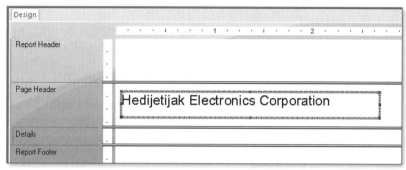

Figure 4.8   Page Header

You can now change the text size to 14 points and the style to bold by simply selecting these from the Formatting toolbar at the top (ensure that the text box is selected first by clicking on it) (Figure 4.9).

Figure 4.9   Formatting Toolbar – Bold

Depending on how big you made our text box, you may now need to resize it to accommodate the larger text size. To do this, simply grab one of the right "handles" of the text box and drag it to the right to increase the size of the box (Figure 4.10).

Figure 4.10   Resize Handles

The text box should now look something like Figure 4.11.

Figure 4.11   Page Header Resized

Next we'll add a special field that Crystal Reports uses to automatically generate a report title for your report. Before we do that, however, we'll enter the text for our report title using the Summary Info command under the File menu. Keep in mind that because this is a report template we're creating and not an actual report, it doesn't make sense to give the template a real report title. We recommend using a combination of the source BW query technical name and a description for your template report title.

Select FILE • SUMMARY INFO (Figure 4.12).

Figure 4.12 File – Summary Info

After selecting the Summary Info menu command, you should see the Document Properties dialog box. For now we're only going to enter the title of our report template, which will be "ZD_SALES_CR_001 (Sales Overview – Crystal Master)". Notice that Crystal Reports has already entered the technical name of your query as the report title, so you can simply append the query description as shown in Figure 4.13.

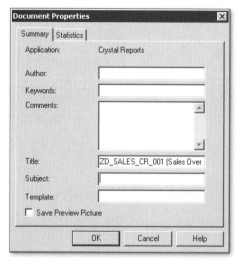

Figure 4.13 Document Properties – Report Title

You can now click OK. You may need to make your page header a little larger (taller) so we can place the report title beneath the company name. To do this, simply resize the section by grabbing the border below the section with your mouse. You'll know you've grabbed it when your cursor looks like the one shown in Figure 4.14.

Figure 4.14 Resizing a Section

You already know how to make the section bigger. Just click and drag the section border downward. You're getting your first taste of the power and control you have over formatting your reports using Crystal Reports. As you can tell as you drag the border, you have complete control over how little or big you want to make the section. For now, just resize it until it looks like you have enough space for another text box below the name.

Now that you've made room for the report title, we just need to add it to the page header. We do this by pulling it from the Special Fields section of the Field Explorer on the right side of your screen. If for some reason the Field Explorer isn't visible, simply click on the Field Explorer icon in the toolbar at the top of your screen (Figure 4.15).

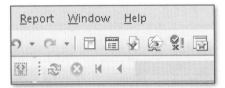

Figure 4.15   Field Explorer Button

The Field Explorer initially opens on the right side of your screen (Figure 4.16).

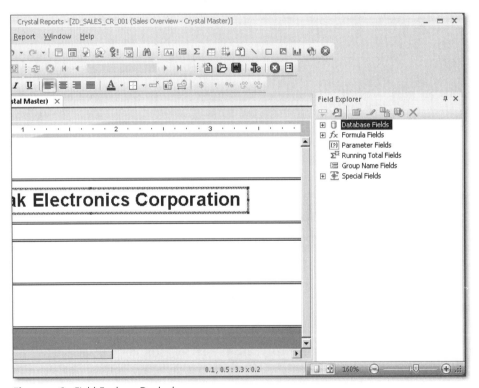

Figure 4.16   Field Explorer Docked

> **Note**
>
> In the next chapter we'll begin exploring the various parts of the Field Explorer in detail. For now, you just need to know that this is a very important dialog box that you'll use quite regularly when designing your reports. Think of it as the "building blocks" of your report.

To access the Report Title special field, click the plus sign (+) next to the Special Fields section of the Field Explorer. You should then see something like Figure 4.17.

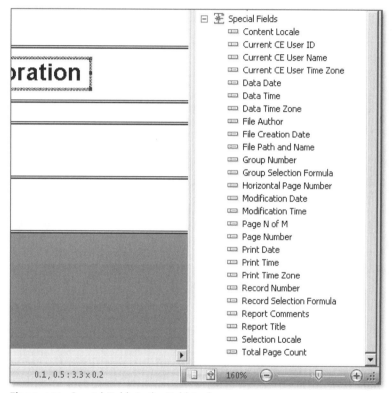

Figure 4.17 Special Fields in the Field Explorer

The Report Title special field will be near the bottom of the list. Now just click and drag it below the company name in the Page Header section. Change the font size to 12 points and make the font style bold. Resize the box to make it larger, as shown in Figure 4.18.

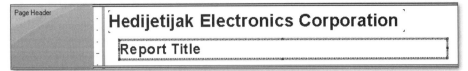

Figure 4.18   Report Title in the Page Header

In this example we've intentionally misaligned the two text boxes to show you how to use the Align Objects feature of Crystal Reports. If you haven't already, move the Report Title to the right so that the two text boxes are clearly not aligned with each other.

Now click on the company name at the top, hold down the Shift key, and click the Report Title beneath it. You can now release the Shift key. Next, right-click the company name at the top of the page header, select Align from the menu and then select Lefts (Figure 4.19).

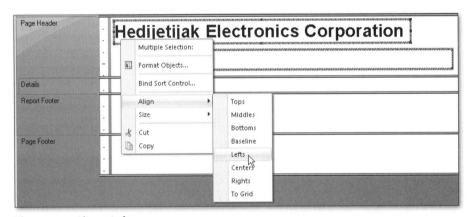

Figure 4.19   Align – Lefts

Now reselect both text objects by using your Shift key again. Press the left arrow key on your keyboard until both text objects bump up against the left border of the Design tab area and stop. Your page header should now look something like Figure 4.20.

Figure 4.20   Aligned Page Header

The last thing we're going to add to our page header is a horizontal line that spans the width of the page, but before we can do that we have a little housecleaning to do. Depending on the resolution of your screen, the Field Explorer on the right might be getting in the way of you seeing the entire width of your page, as it is in Figure 4.21.

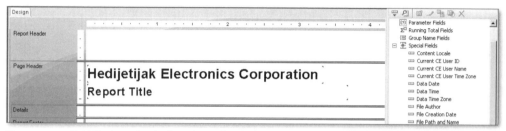

Figure 4.21   Field Explorer Docked on the Right

Except for very high-resolution screens, the default location of the Field Explorer (docked on the right side of the screen) is often inconvenient, as it is in this case. If the Field Explorer is covering part of the right side of your report design area, you can "un-dock" it by simply grabbing the top of the window and dragging it to the left (Figure 4.22).

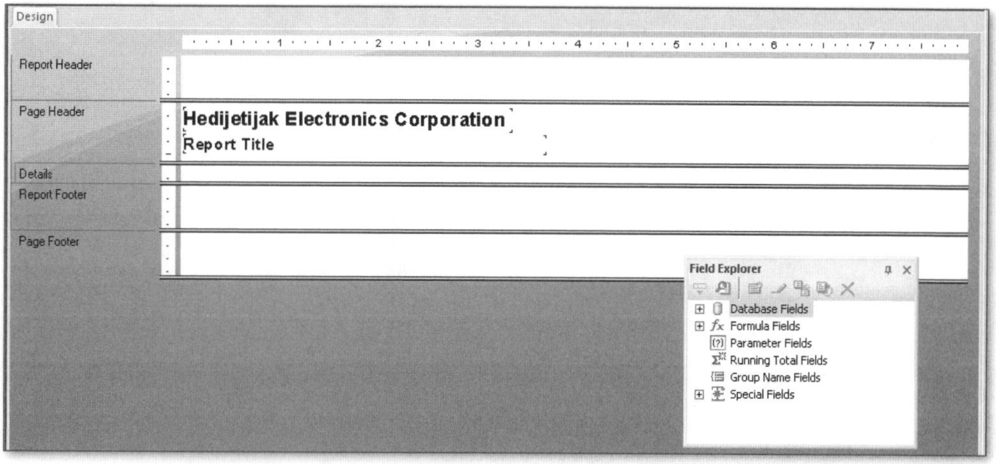

Figure 4.22   Field Explorer Undocked

Now the Field Explorer is floating on the screen, and we can see the full width of the report design area. You can now select the Insert Line tool from the Insert toolbar (Figure 4.23).

Figure 4.23   Insert Toolbar – Insert Line

Once you've selected this tool, simply click the far-left side of the report below the report title and drag all the way to the right margin; then let go. Now right-click the line and select Format Line (Figure 4.24).

Figure 4.24   Format Line

In the following dialog click the far-left Width selection (Hairline). This is the thinnest line possible in Crystal Reports (Figure 4.25).

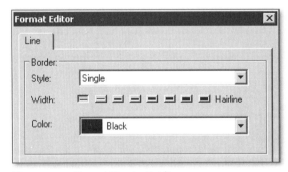

Figure 4.25   Format Line to Hairline

This takes care of our page header. Now let's create a standard page footer. We're going to add several common page footer elements: the date and time the report was run, a Page N of M field, and a confidentiality statement.

First, let's add the Page N of M special field at the center of the page footer, but before we do that, let's adjust the size of the page footer just a bit. Grab the bottom border of the page footer and move it up until it's even with the second notch on the left margin ruler. Next, expand the Special Fields node of the Field Explorer and drag the Page N of M special field to the center of the Page Footer section (Figure 4.26).

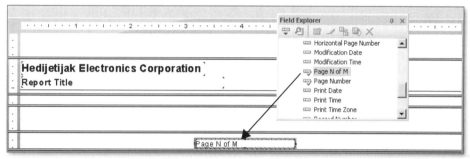

Figure 4.26   Adding Page N of M

Now the trick is to center the Page N of M field in the page footer. The best way to handle this is to select the Page N of M field and then click the Align Center button on the Formatting toolbar (Figure 4.27).

Figure 4.27   Formatting Toolbar – Align Center

You've now centered the text in the box. Now we need to center the box on the page. Some Crystal Reports developers like to stretch the text box from margin to margin, which does center the text on the page. The problem with this is that this isn't the only object we're going to add to the page footer, so we don't want to have overlapping objects (this is something we'll address again later). A better way to center anything on a report is to create a vertical guideline at the center point of the report and then align the object on the guideline.

Because we're introducing a new concept (guidelines), we'll take a moment to explain. Guidelines in Crystal Reports provide a way to align objects on your report. You create a guideline and then "attach" objects to the guideline. Once objects are attached, when you adjust the placement of the guideline, the objects move with it.

To see the guidelines in the Design tab, you must first go to FILE • OPTIONS and ensure that the Guidelines checkbox is selected, as shown in Figure 4.28.

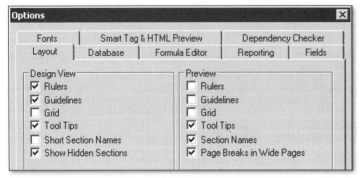

Figure 4.28 File – Options – Layout

Click OK when you're done.

Creating a guideline is quite simple. To create a vertical guideline you simply click the ruler at the top of the Design tab where you want to place the guideline. Because our current page layout is letter size (8½ by 11), our page orientation is portrait, and our margins are one-quarter inch, we have exactly eight inches of printable area. If we want a guideline at the exact center, we need to click the ruler at the four-inch mark (if you're using a landscape orientation, your midpoint will be at 5¼ inches) (Figure 4.29).

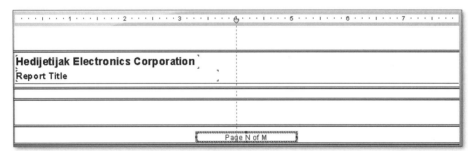

Figure 4.29 Guideline at the Center of the Page

Now we can attach the Page N of M special field to the guideline we just inserted at the center point of the text box. Just click the Page N of M special field and use you're the arrow keys on your keyboard to move it toward the guideline. Keep going until the center handle on the field locks on to the guideline. If you watch closely, you'll see it jump onto the guideline (much a like a magnet). You should also see two small red hash marks on the field once it attaches itself to the guideline (Figure 4.30).

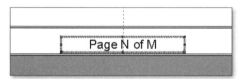

Figure 4.30 Page N of M Field Centered on Guideline

Now that the field is attached to the guideline, you can move it to the bottom edge of the page by pressing the down arrow until the field bumps up against the bottom. Once it reaches the bottom it won't move any further. The Page N of M field is now centered at the very bottom of the page.

The next step is to add a Run Date/Time field at the bottom left of the page footer. To do this, we'll combine two separate special fields: Data Date and Data Time. The Data Date and Data Time fields display the date and time that the report was executed (when the data was retrieved from the database).

First, we need to insert a text object so we can combine these two special fields with some static text in a single object. This is a handy feature of Crystal Reports that we'll explore in more detail in a later lesson. First, click the Insert Text Object button on the Insert toolbar (Figure 4.31).

Figure 4.31 Insert Toolbar – Insert Text Object

Now click and drag a text box at the far left of the page footer. Ensure that it's big enough. It should stretch almost to the Page N of M special field. Now type "Run Date/Time:" and be sure to include at least one space at the end of the text (Figure 4.32).

Figure 4.32 Insert Run Date and Time in the Page Footer

Next, we'll drag the Data Date special field onto the report. We're not going to place it directly in the text box we just created because we need to format the date first. Let's drag it temporarily into the report footer (Figure 4.33).

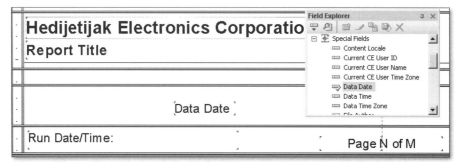

Figure 4.33 Insert Data Date into Report Footer

Right-click the Data Date special field and select Format Field. Select the 03/01/1999 date format (Figure 4.34).

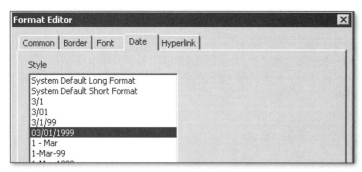

Figure 4.34 Format Date

Now we're ready to drag the Data Date special field into the text field we just created. Just click and drag the Data Date field on top of the Run Date/Time text field that you placed in the page footer (Figure 4.35).

> **Note**
>
> Here's the trick to making this work: Wait until the outline of the box you're dragging goes away and you see a vertical insertion line appear at the end of the text inside the text box. Then (and only then) let go.

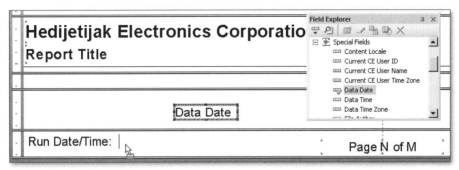

Figure 4.35 Insert Data Date into Text Box

If you've done this correctly, your text box should look something like Figure 4.36.

Figure 4.36 Data Date Inserted into Text Box

Now let's do the same thing with the Data Time field. Drag it to the report footer, right-click on the field, and select Format Field. Select the 1:23 pm formatting option.

Before you drag the Data Time special field next to the Data Date field in the text box, we first need to insert a space after the Data Date field. You can also do this afterward, but it's a bit easier to do this before you add the other field. Just double-click anywhere on the Run Date/Time text box. Now click *after* the Data Date special field inside the text box. Press the space bar once. Now you can drag the Data Time field and place it next to the Data Date field (remember to wait for the insertion line to appear before you let go) (Figure 4.37).

Figure 4.37 Data Time Inserted into Text Box

We're almost finished with the Page Footer section. All we need now is to put "H.E.C. Confidential" at the bottom right of the report footer. You should be able to handle this yourself by now. All you need is another text box (Insert Text Object button) at the bottom right of the page footer. Then just enter the text. Change the alignment to Right Aligned. Your page footer should now look like Figure 4.38.

Figure 4.38   Page Footer with Text Box Added

Now we just need some fine-tuning. First, we're going to reduce the font size for all three text objects from the default (10 points) down to 8 points.

To do this, we first need to select all three text objects at once. There are two ways to do this. One way is to use the "$\boxed{\texttt{Shift}}$ + click" method. You simply hold down the $\boxed{\texttt{Shift}}$ key and start clicking on the text objects you want to select. The second way is the "lasso" method. To lasso the objects, you click and drag your mouse pointer to select each text object. When you click and drag on any open space in the Design tab, you get an orange selection box. Anything the orange box touches is selected.

Whichever way you select the text boxes when they're all selected, they'll each have a blue box, as shown in Figure 4.39.

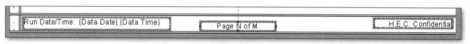

Figure 4.39   Page Footer with Objects Selected

Now go to the Formatting toolbar and change the font size to eight points. Then make the style Italic (Figure 4.40).

Figure 4.40   Arial Eight-Point Italic

The final step is to resize all of the text objects and align them with the bottom of the page. Because we've already done this with the Page N of M special field, we'll use this as our size and position "anchor" for the other two fields.

While all three fields are still selected, right-click the Page N of M special field. When you size and align objects it's important that you right-click the field that's currently the size and position that you want for all of the objects. It acts as your model. Now select Size and then Same Height. In this case we're not interested in making them the same width. You should now have something that looks like Figure 4.41.

Figure 4.41   Page Footer Objects Same Height

Now, finally, right-click Page N of M and select Align and then Bottoms. Figure 4.42 shows the final result.

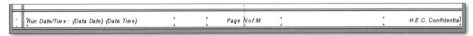

Figure 4.42   Page Footer Sized and Aligned

We're getting close to finishing the layout part of our report template. The only things remaining are a couple of column headings. We're putting these in the report template so the report developers will have samples for creating their own column headings.

First, let's back up and take a look at what we've done so far (Figure 4.43).

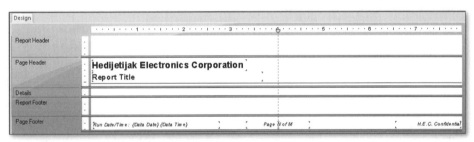

Figure 4.43   Page Header and Footer Complete

We've got a pretty good-looking page header and an equally impressive page footer. We now want to add some sample column headings.

The question is, Where do we put them? In the next chapter we'll discuss in detail each of the different sections in Crystal Reports and how they're used, along with what types of objects go in each section and why. For now, just go along for the ride. It'll all make more sense soon.

The sensible place to put column headings is in the page header. However, as you'll find out in a later lesson, there are times when you don't put column headings in the page header. You'll find out why later.

We have one small issue to deal with before we add our column headings. Our current page header doesn't have room for any column headings. You already know one simple way to handle this situation: Resize the section by dragging the bottom border. This would work just fine, but let's look at a better way.

Another (and more flexible) way to handle this is to *split* the page header into two sections instead of one. (Yes, you can have more than one Page Header section.) In fact, all of the sections in a Crystal Reports report can be divided up as many times as you require.

To split the page header, right-click its left margin (where it says Page Header) and select Insert Section Below (Figure 4.44).

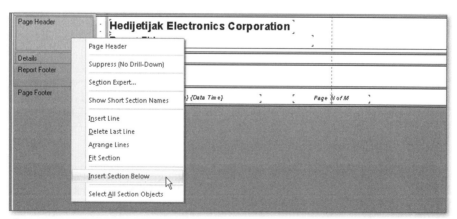

Figure 4.44 Splitting the Page Header

Figure 4.45 shows the results.

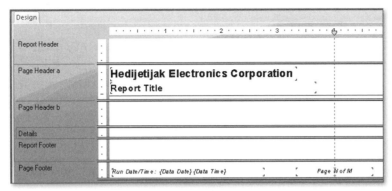

Figure 4.45   Page Header a and Page Header b

You now have Page Header a and Page Header b. At this point it's perfectly reasonable to ask, "Why is this better than simply expanding the existing page header?" Hold that thought for now. You'll find out soon. For now just think *flexibility*.

Now that we have room for our column headings, let's create them. Column headings are just text objects, so click the Insert Text Object button and drag a text box toward the left side of Page Header b. Type the words "Column Heading." You should see something like Figure 4.46.

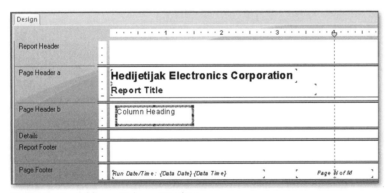

Figure 4.46   Adding a Column Heading

Now you need some formatting to make it look like a column heading. Select the text box and make the style bold and the alignment centered (you should know where these buttons are by now — on the Formatting toolbar).

Hot Tip

Don't use underline for column headings. It looks cheap. Instead, use a *bottom border*. These look better and are more flexible.

Crystal Reports has a nice border feature for text objects that works great for column headings. While the column heading is selected, click the Outside Borders button on the Formatting toolbar and then select Bottom Border (Figure 4.47).

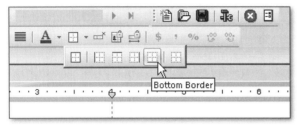

Figure 4.47   Bottom Border

You should now see something like Figure 4.48.

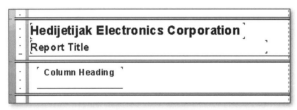

Figure 4.48   Column Heading Bold and Centered with a Bottom Border

Now we're going to "clone" the column heading to create a second "stacked" heading (two lines).

Hot Tip

Any object in Crystal Reports (text fields, data fields, formulas, charts, graphics, etc.) can be cloned (except for subreports). Cloning is faster and easier than doing a copy and paste. It's also more fun.

To clone any object in Crystal Reports, you simply hold down the `Ctrl` (Control) key on your keyboard and drag the object. So hold down the `Ctrl` key and drag the column heading text box to the right (Figure 4.49).

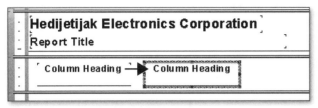

Figure 4.49 Cloned Column Heading

You've now created a copy of the original column heading. Double-click the new column heading on the right and then click in front of the word "Heading." Press `Enter` on your keyboard to create a stacked column heading (Figure 4.50).

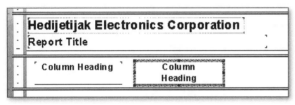

Figure 4.50 Stacked Column Heading

The next formatting step is to move the text in the left column heading down to the bottom of the text box. Double-click the original column heading on the left and then click in front of the word "Column." Now press `Enter` to move the text down within the text box (Figure 4.51).

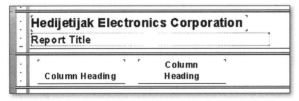

Figure 4.51 First Column Heading Moved Down

You may be wondering why the text box for the column heading on the left is as big (tall) as the one on the right when it's only a single line and the one on the right is two lines. At this point, it's just best to accept it as a good idea.

Also, it's not critical that the column headings in your template be aligned in any particular way. These only serve as templates for the report developers to create their own column headings.

Your report template should now look something like Figure 4.52.

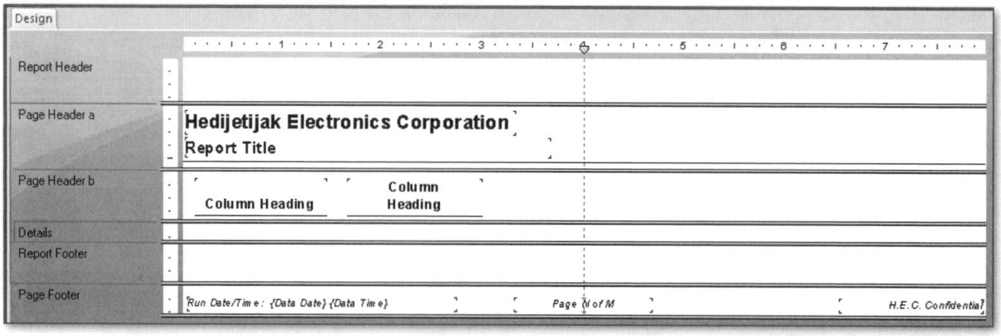

Figure 4.52   Formatted Report Template

There's one last formatting step to perform before we move on. Because it's optional to include a report header in a Crystal Reports report, we'll suppress the report header in our template. You'll learn a lot about the concept of suppressing sections and/or objects in your reports later. For now, it's just important to know that if we suppress any section in Crystal Reports, it doesn't show when you view and/or print the report. It simply goes away.

Hot Tip

What you're about to learn is something known as "absolute suppression." This means that, in our case, the report header will always be suppressed. Something much more powerful and flexible is "conditional suppression." In an upcoming chapter you'll learn how to fully leverage this powerful and very handy feature of Crystal Reports.

To suppress any section in Crystal Reports, you can simply right-click in the left margin (where the section names are) in the section you want to suppress and select Suppress (No-Drill-Down) (Figure 4.53).

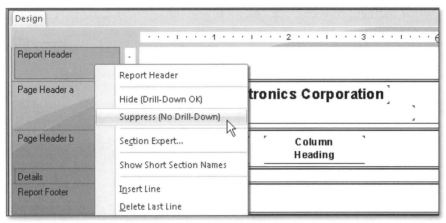

Figure 4.53   Suppressing the Report Header

The top of your design tab should now look like Figure 4.54.

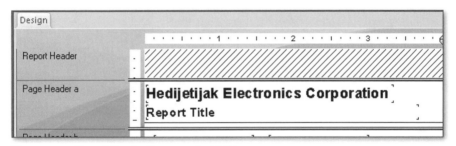

Figure 4.54   Report Header Suppressed – Visible

If your report looks like Figure 4.55, then we need to make a change to one of the layout options in Crystal Reports.

Figure 4.55   Report Header Suppressed – Invisible

Let's take a moment to look at this and a few other layout options that you can set in Crystal Reports. We looked briefly at the Options setting earlier when we turned on the guidelines. Go to FILE • OPTIONS and you'll see the Options dialog box (Figure 4.56).

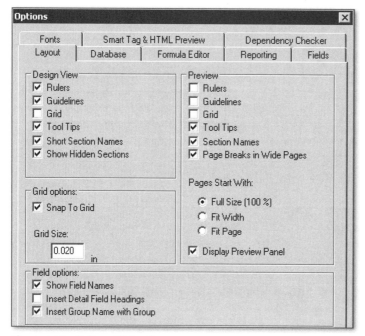

Figure 4.56 Options Dialog Box

If you could no longer see the report header at all after we suppressed it, you'll to select the Show Hidden Sections checkbox. Although this (like all of the layout options) is a matter of personal preference, we recommend that you show your hidden sections in your reports. The reason for this will become more apparent as we begin working with hiding and suppressing sections in a later chapter.

Another option we'll set now is the Grid Size. The Grid Size setting determines the size of the "steps" when you're moving objects in Crystal Reports. By default, the Snap to Grid option is selected. We recommend that you keep this setting so that as you move items in the Design tab (such as fields) they'll "snap" to an invisible grid. The default size of this grid is 0.083 inches (i.e., 1/12 of an inch). This grid size is too coarse (big) to allow for finer adjustments when placing and aligning objects. For this reason we suggest you change this setting to 0.02 inches which will allow you to move objects in much smaller increments.

One last option is Short Section Names. This option abbreviates the section names in the left margin of the Design tab (Report Header becomes RF and so on). If you're working with a smaller display (such as a 12–15-inch laptop display), you'll want to select this option. If you have a larger display (over 15 inches), you might want to leave this setting the way it is. As you might imagine, selecting Short Section Names simply gives you more horizontal space to work with on your display.

We'll make one last adjustment to our layout before we move on to the next section. Because we're not using our report header, let's adjust the size of the section down a bit to give us as much room as possible for our other sections. You learned how to resize sections earlier. In case you've forgotten, you simply grab the bottom border of the section and move it up or down. In this case grab the bottom border of the report header and move it up. The final layout should now look like Figure 4.57.

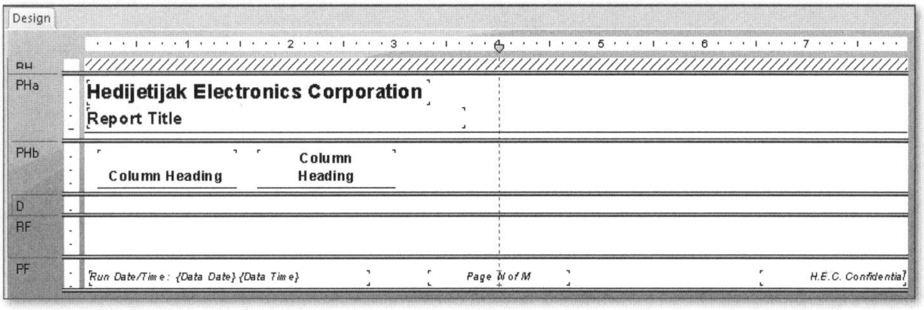

Figure 4.57 Formatted Report Template

We're now finished with the formatting part of creating a Crystal Reports template. We're going to move on next to one of the biggest time-saving (and frustration-avoiding) tips for creating reports against an SAP BW query: the deceptively simple "alias" formula.

4.2 The Alias Formula

A Crystal Reports template created using a BW query serves at least two main purposes, the first of which we just covered: providing a standard for producing a consistent look and feel for all reports. The second primary purpose, which we're about to cover, is definitely unique to working with BW queries: dealing with the complexity (and confusion) of SAP NetWeaver BW technical names in Crystal Reports.

Rather than trying to explain why this is important (actually essential) for ensuring the success of your Crystal Reports development efforts when using BW queries as your data source, it will be much simpler to show you why.

To begin, let's take another look at the contents of the Field Explorer. If you have closed the Field Explorer, you can always bring it back by clicking the Field Explorer button in the Standard toolbar (Figure 4.58).

Figure 4.58 Field Explorer Button

So far we've only looked at the Special Fields node of the Field Explorer when creating a standard layout for our template. The topmost node of the Field Explorer is the most important of all: Database Fields. This is where you access the fields from your selected data source, in our case a BW query (Figure 4.59).

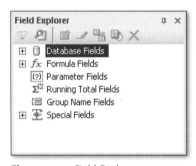

Figure 4.59 Field Explorer

Expand the Database Fields node of the Field Explorer. You should first see the technical name of your BW query. Expand that node and you'll see a series of additional nodes. The first node should be [Measures] (the key figures in the query), followed by additional nodes (one for each characteristic in the query). Expand the [Measures] node and you should see something like Figure 4.60.

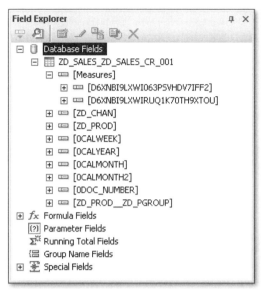

Figure 4.60 Field Explorer with Technical Names

What you're looking at are the technical names for the key figures and characteristics in your source query. You may recall from an earlier discussion that everything in SAP NetWeaver BW has a technical name and a description, the former not being fit for human consumption and the later being the user-friendly name that's actually recognizable. It actually is possible to figure out which characteristic is which from their technical names. However, there's absolutely no way to figure out the key figures. This is because key figures don't have technical names that are assigned by a developer, but have a unique, very long and very confusing alphanumeric code that's automatically generated when the key figure is created.

This issue with technical names also comes into play when you're creating formulas in Crystal Reports. We'll cover the whole topic of formulas in Crystal Reports in detail in later lessons, so for now we'll just say that formulas are just like they sound: They're special calculations that produce some result. They're very much like formulas in Excel.

To demonstrate the issue of technical names in formulas, we'll create (or at least begin to create) a test formula just for the purpose of seeing the formula editor. To do this, go to the Formula Fields node of the Field Explorer, right-click, select New..., and name the formula "Test" (Figure 4.61).

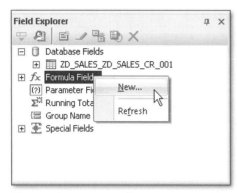

Figure 4.61 New Formula

Reminder

By necessity we're branching off into certain areas in Crystal Reports (in this case the Formula Editor) without much in the way of explanation. We'll have a chance to cover the Formula Editor again in future lessons.

Once you're in the Formula Editor, expand the BW query node (below Report Fields in the top-left pane) and then expand the [Measure] node. You should now see something like Figure 4.62.

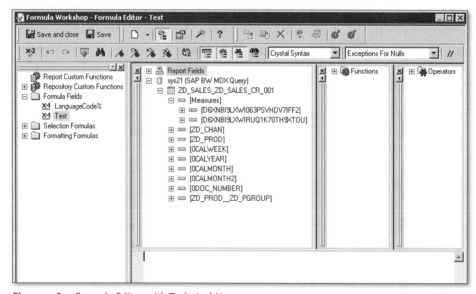

Figure 4.62 Formula Editor with Technical Names

As you can see, we have the exact same situation here in the Formula Editor that we had in the Field Explorer: unrecognizable SAP NetWeaver BW technical names.

Fortunately there's a quick fix in Crystal Reports that solves at least part of our problem. Click the Save and Close button at the top left of the Formula Editor. Now go to FILE • OPTIONS and select the Database tab. Change the Tables and Fields selection from the default (Show Name) to Show Description. Then click OK (Figure 4.63).

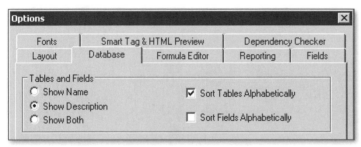

Figure 4.63 Database Options – Show Description

Now things should look a lot more familiar now in your Field Explorer (Figure 4.64).

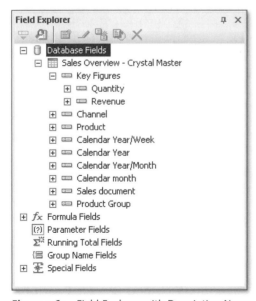

Figure 4.64 Field Explorer with Description Names

Now let's take a look at the test formula we created. Just expand the Formula Fields node and double-click Test (Figure 4.65).

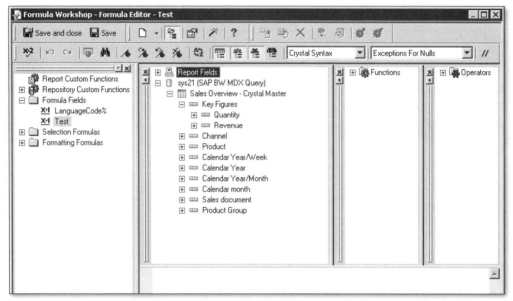

Figure 4.65 Formula Editor with Description Names

At first glance it appears that all is well again with just the click of a button. But not so fast. There's more than meets the eye. Let's say you want to use a key figure in a formula (a very common occurrence). To use any database field in a formula you simply double-click the field, and it will appear in your formula below. Let's double-click the Quantity key figure (Figure 4.66).

As you can see, even though the descriptive names appear in the database fields list in the upper-right pane of the Formula Editor, the technical name is what's actually entered into the formula. Once again, you can almost get by with using technical names in formulas for characteristics but it isn't not possible to use technical names for key figures. It just doesn't work.

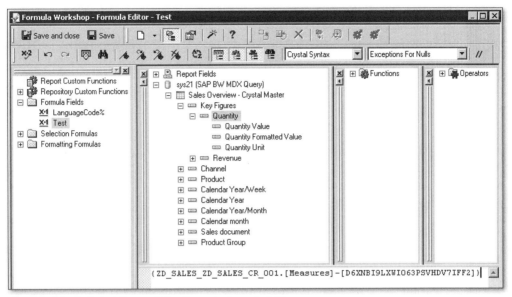

Figure 4.66 Technical Name of Key Figure in Formula Editor

Hot Tip

To eliminate the potential confusion of key figure and characteristic technical names in Crystal Reports, you should create an alias for each key figure and characteristic in the query.

This isn't just a hot tip, but the hottest tip. Once you understand this technique and apply it, you can pretty much skip the rest of the book and still come out way ahead. Of course, we hope you decide to stick around.

The fix for this unfortunate turn of events is exceedingly simple. It only requires a little time when creating your Crystal Reports templates and then you're done. Let's show you how.

You can stay right where you are in the Formula Editor because this is where we create our alias formulas. Essentially we're creating simple formula substitutes for the original key figure or characteristic. Click the New button at the top left of the Formula Editor window (Figure 4.67).

Great technique, but naming standards will be essential.

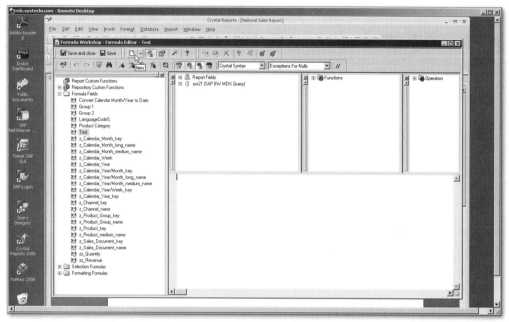

Figure 4.67 New Formula Button

Our first alias will be for the Quantity key figure. It's standard practice in SAP systems to preface any user-created object with the letter "z." In keeping with this practice we'll preface all our aliases with a "z." To help group the key figures together and keep them separate from the characteristics, we'll preface the key figures with "zz_" and the characteristics with "z_." With this in mind, we'll name this first alias "zz_Quantity" (Figure 4.68).

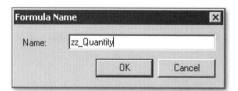

Figure 4.68 Naming the Quantity Formula

After you've entered the name, click OK. Don't bother saving the changes we made to the previous test formula. To create this first alias formula, all we need to do is double-click the Quantity key figure in the top left pane (Figure 4.69).

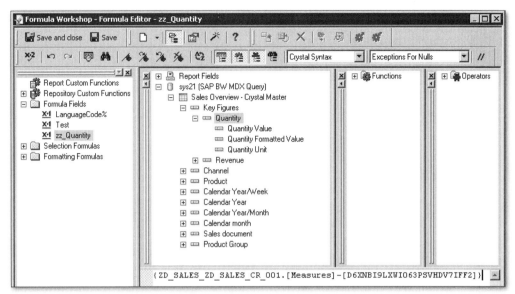

Figure 4.69 Quantity Alias Formula

That's it! This is the simplest type of formula you can possibly create. Just double-click whatever field (key figure or characteristic) you want to alias. To continue on to the next one, you simply click the New button again. Then enter the name of the next alias (in our case, we'd continue on to "zz_Revenue" and then on to the characteristics). Remember, the characteristics will begin with "z_," not "zz_" like the key figures.

Characteristics often require that you create not just one, but two or even three aliases. This is because characteristics often are referred to by a unique code (the key) and by a descriptive name (the name). For example, a product's unique identifier (key) might be something like SLL2290, and the descriptive name might be Super Light Laptop Computer. SAP NetWeaver BW provides the ability to attach up to three descriptive names to any characteristic.

Figure 4.70 shows the creation of an alias for the Channel characteristic key in the Formula Editor (notice that we've named this alias "z_Channel_key.")

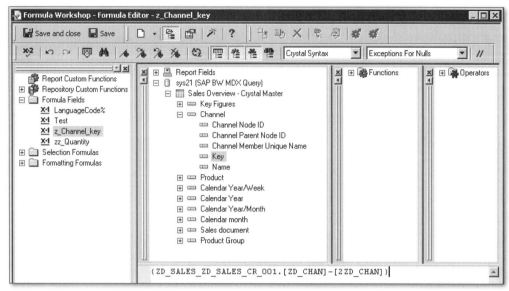

Figure 4.70   Channel Key Alias Formula

Now let's do the same for the Channel name (or description) (Figure 4.71).

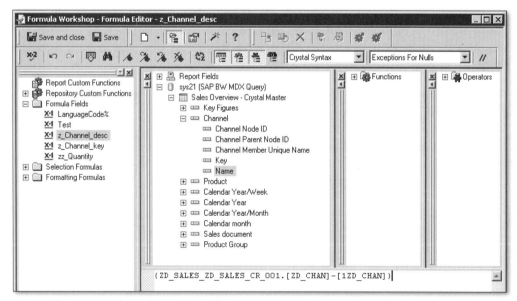

Figure 4.71   Channel Description Alias Formula

> **Important Note**
>
> In our example query here we only have one name for each characteristic. It's much more common to have more than one name for a characteristic. This is because in SAP NetWeaver BW you can assign any characteristic a short name, a medium name, and/or a long name (20, 40, and 60 characters maximum, respectively). However, it's uncommon to use every name for a characteristic. Normally only one or two will be populated with a value. And to make it even more confusing, sometimes two names (such as the medium and long names) will be populated with the exact same description. Unfortunately there's no standard approach to assigning descriptive names to characteristics.

So if you see more than one name associated with a characteristic, what should you do? Well, if you have the time you can track down whoever designed the original InfoCube and BW query to find out which of the name fields have actual descriptions, or you could simply alias all of them. Our recommendation is to do the latter. It doesn't take that much time, and if it turns out that a particular name has not been populated with a description, you can always delete it. After a while you'll start to figure out which names are populated in a given InfoCube.

In our example the Product characteristic has both a medium name and a long name associated with it. So we'd create an alias for both of these names (Figure 4.72).

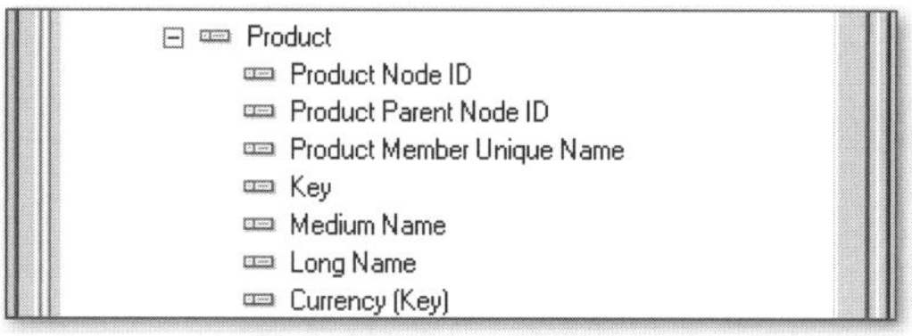

Figure 4.72   Product Medium and Long Names

Figure 4.73 shows what the Field Explorer looks like once we've finished creating all of our aliases for each key figure and characteristic in the query. This is what you would call a "fully aliased" Crystal Reports template, which is your objective. Each key figure and characteristic (including keys and names) has been aliased.

> **Hot Tip**
>
> From now on you can ignore the Database Fields. They don't exist anymore. Whenever you need to reference any key figure or characteristic in your report, always use its formula alias. If for some reason you missed one, create it (remember to create it in the original template).

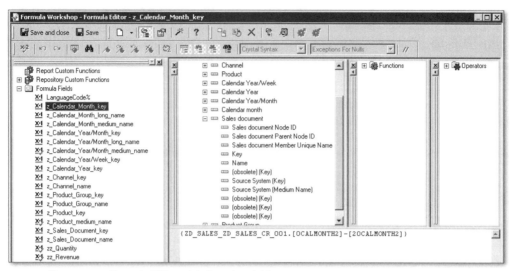

Figure 4.73 Formula Editor with Completed Aliases

To demonstrate one of the key benefits of this approach, we'll start another formula that references the Quantity key figure, but this time we'll double-click not the original database field, but the formula alias (found within the Report Fields node) (Figure 4.74).

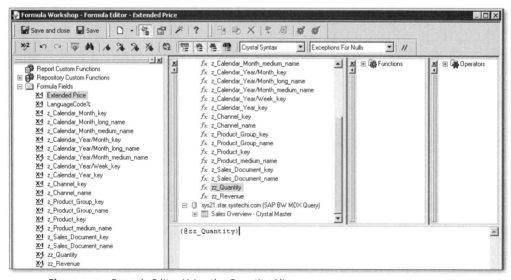

Figure 4.74 Formula Editor Using the Quantity Alias

Now there's no room for confusion. This technique benefits you not only here in the Formula Editor (the primary benefit) but in other places within Crystal Reports as well (groupings, summaries, etc.).

Once you've completed all your aliases, you're finished with your template (for now). The only thing you may need to add to any template beyond the standard header and footer formatting and the aliasing of characteristics and key figures would be formulas. When we get to the lesson on formulas you'll see some of the types of formulas that you might want to include in a report template.

The last thing we need to do is save the template. We'll give it the same name that we used earlier for the report title (the technical name of the query followed by the descriptive name in parentheses). In this case we'll save the template as "ZD_SALES_CR_001 (Sales Overview – Crystal Master)." This clearly identifies the source query that's being used for this template.

You'll want to establish a central location accessible by all Crystal Reports developers where you can safely store your report templates. This can be a file share on the network, a role in your SAP NetWeaver BW development system, or a common file repository such as SharePoint.

Congratulations! You've just completed a significant foundational step in your journey to becoming proficient at producing SAP NetWeaver BW reports using Crystal Reports. We can't emphasize enough how important this step is in ensuring that you reach your final goal. If you take the time to create a single BW query for each InfoProvider and a single Crystal Reports template for each query, this will have a tremendous multiplier effect on your time and effort spent creating reports going forward.

Lastly, if for some reason you decide against creating a report template for each query, ensure that you still make full use of aliases in all your Crystal Reports that use a BW query as the data source. You'll be glad you did.

We apologize again for the need to dive into various areas of Crystal early on, but we'll have plenty of opportunities ahead to circle back around and start from the beginning. So hang on, there's a lot more coming your way.

4.3 Summary

Some of the benefits of providing templates for your Crystal Reports developers when using BW queries as a data source are:

- ▶ They provide a consistent look and feel (common report headers, footers, and column headers).

- ▶ They shield the report developer from the technical names of query elements (especially key figures).

- ▶ Common calculations (formulas) can be included in the template, similar to shared calculated key figures in SAP BEx.

Even more important than the look and feel of the report is the creation of alias formulas when working with a BW query as a data source. These special formulas are unique to the integration of Crystal Reports and SAP NetWeaver BW and provide a way to shield Crystal Reports developers (especially those on the business side) from the technical names of various query objects, especially key figures.

In this chapter we began to cover some of the more basic aspects of developing reports using Crystal Reports — the placement and formatting of objects. In terms of overall efficiency it's very important that you become proficient at this particular skill because it will be something you repeat over and over in the course of developing reports.

Now we begin the process of creating a Crystal Reports against an SAP BW query in earnest. In this chapter, you learn the basics of adding fields to your Crystal report and how to perform some basic formatting tasks.

5 Getting Started with Crystal Reports and SAP NetWeaver BW

Now it's time to launch full speed ahead into creating reports in an SAP BW environment. But before we get into the hands-on exercises, we first need to cover a few more items.

5.1 Getting Set Up

In case you missed this in the previous chapter, you'll need to ensure that you've completed the following steps before you can start using Crystal Reports in an SAP BW environment:

▶ Install Crystal Reports 2008 on your computer.

▶ Install the Integration Kit for SAP Solutions (client installation).

▶ Install the latest Service Pack from SAP (as of this writing, Service Pack 2).

▶ Lastly, you'll have to be added to a special SAP role set up by someone on your BASIS team (usually called something like the Crystal Developer role).

Next, you'll need an SAP BW data source that you can use to follow along with the exercises. Here's where things might get a little tricky because there's no practical way to ensure that you'll have access to the same InfoProviders (InfoCubes, DSOs) that we'll be using in the hands-on exercises.

Most of the exercises in this book use queries built off of a Sales Overview Info-Cube that's part of the sample business content that comes with SAP BW 7.1. Unfortunately there's no way to ensure that your organization will have the exact same cube with the exact same data. So how are you to follow along with each exercise if your data is different?

The best way to handle this is to create a data source (in this case a BW query) in your organization's development environment that roughly approximates the data in the queries used in the exercises. We've tried to keep the exercises general enough that you can apply the same techniques regardless of the actual data in the query. The actual numbers and descriptions may differ, but the key is that you learn the technique or principle being taught. To be successful you'll need to be flexible and be able to apply the lesson to your own data environment.

> **Reminder**
>
> It's not critical that your data be exactly the same as the data used in the exercises. What's important is that you can learn the particular skill or technique being taught.

In one way, this acts as a sort of screening exercise that's built into each lesson. One of the keys to being successful at report development is the ability to adapt and think on your feet. You'll certainly need to be able to do so to follow along with each of the exercises. If you find yourself unable to incorporate your own environment into the exercises, it could be an indication that report development may not be for you.

5.2   A Simplified Approach to Reporting

Before we get started, it would be a good idea to think about what kind of approach we want to take when developing reports in Crystal Reports. Although it's true that we always want to prevent the *process* of developing reports to get in the way of the actual development, it's also true that most of the time you'll need some sort of written plan before you begin. This is especially true when you're developing reports for someone else. If the report is for your own needs, the written plan (better known as "report specification") can be minimal or even completely optional.

At least four factors determine the degree of planning required to develop a report in Crystal Reports:

▶ The experience level of the report developer

▶ The subject matter expertise of the report developer

▶ The robustness of the data the warehouse (SAP NetWeaver BW)

▶ The complexity of the report

The first three factors have an inverse relationship with the level of planning required. In other words, as they increase, the level of planning required tends to decrease. The final factor has direct impact on the level of planning required: as the complexity of the report increases, the planning requirements tend to increase.

Assuming your report requires at least a minimal level of planning, what kind of things do you need to put into a report specification document? Following is a checklist of items you typically include in any Crystal Reports specification using SAP BW as a data source:

- ▶ Basic information
  - ▶ Report ID (unique identifier for the report)
  - ▶ Report name
  - ▶ Priority (low, medium, high)
  - ▶ Complexity (low, medium, high)
  - ▶ Business sponsor name
  - ▶ Report developer name
  - ▶ Primary audience
  - ▶ Business purpose
  - ▶ Questions answered (up to five)
  - ▶ On demand or scheduled
  - ▶ Run frequency (if scheduled)
- ▶ Data source information
  - ▶ Name of query or DSO (if SAP BW)
- ▶ Data elements
  - ▶ Key figures
  - ▶ Characteristics
- ▶ Report logic/structure
  - ▶ Groupings
  - ▶ Summaries
  - ▶ Calculations
  - ▶ Filters

▶ Sample layout of the report

▶ Existing layout if a report already exists

Here are a few real-world observations about report specifications. First, no one likes to do these. Second, when forced to do a report specification, business end users tend to do as little as possible. This is only natural because they tend to be very busy people. Third, even if they take the time to complete these as thoroughly as possible, not all of the information is going to be right. If you recall from our discussion of this process in Chapter 2, it's not unusual for end users to have only a very vague idea of what they're looking for, especially when creating a completely new report in a new data environment.

Also, a few of these items can be so subjective as to be almost meaningless. The two biggest of these are priority and complexity. The problem with priority, of course, is that everything tends to end up being high priority, especially at the beginning of a reporting project. For complexity, the level of complexity for a report can be very difficult to determine early on, especially if the end user is the one figuring it out. It's usually best to leave it up to the report designer to determine how complex the report really is after development has gotten underway. Some reports that start off looking simple can evolve into more complex reports, whereas others that initially looked very hard end up being relatively easy. It's just too hard to tell sometimes until you dive into it.

As a reminder, one of the benefits of having the subject matter expert and the report developer being the same person is that it reduces the need for a rigorous report specification process. You can then afford to keep it pretty high level and simply cover the basics (business purpose, questions answered, primary audience, etc.).

And always keep in mind, whether the report has been specified by a coworker or by yourself, a report specification is only a starting point. Some of the best reports developed are the ones that evolved from an original idea into something at least partly different, if not sometimes radically different. That's perfectly natural and fully expected. Remember, the goal isn't to specify exactly what you want at the beginning and stick to it to the end. The goal is to create a report that meets a specific business need, regardless of whether or not it looks at all like the original report spec. If it bothers someone that the report ended up different than the original spec, and if the report is actually useful, rewrite the spec. Or write a new spec. Or better yet, everyone just agree that things turned out just fine and move on.

5.3 Starting with the Big Picture

One last word about the process of designing reports in a data warehouse environment like SAP NetWeaver BW. Because of the nature of a data warehouse, most (if not all) of your reports will be summary-level reports. In other words, you normally don't create detail-level, operation reports from a data warehouse. As we discussed in Chapter 3, this isn't a hard and fast rule because it's not unusual for SAP customers to include detailed (document-level) data in the warehouse, especially in a Data Store Object (SDO). However, because a data warehouse is designed specifically to create and deliver summarized data, you need to keep this in mind when designing your reports for Crystal Reports.

This is important for two reasons. first, it makes perfect sense to focus on "big picture" reports initially and then work your way to the more specific. One of the strengths of a data warehouse is its ability to provide business end users with a top-level view of the business, allowing users to recognize two key business indicators: relationships and trends. In other words, how does one entity in my business affect another entity, and which general direction are the various aspects of the business headed? The first question is answered by comparing different characteristics and their effects on the business, and the other is accomplished by observing a particular characteristic over time.

This is all to say that the whole structure and makeup of the data warehouse lends itself to starting with the big picture and then moving to the specific. Because of this, it makes perfect sense to initially design and create Crystal Reports reports that display top-level summary data with an eye toward revealing relationships and trends in your business.

The practical fallout of this is that one of the most important elements of your Crystal Reports reports is always going to be your *groupings*. Groups in Crystal Reports allow you to summarize data by some characteristic. The most common characteristic used for grouping data (by far) is time. Every transaction in every business in the world shares this common characteristic. Everything occurs at a specific time, and every transactional database ever made always records this information as part of the transaction record.

Of course, there isn't just a single time characteristic, but many. Year, month, week, fiscal period, day, and time of day are all examples of time characteristics, or dimensions. Virtually every InfoCube and therefore every BW query you'll work with in an SAP NetWeaver BW system is going to include at least one time dimension, and normally several.

Beyond the time characteristic falls a wide array of other common characteristics that are used to group and summarize the data in a data warehouse, such as Sales Division, Plant, Region, Personnel Group, and a host of others. The good news for the report developer is that the process of identifying and including the appropriate group characteristics has already been done by whoever designed and modeled the InfoCubes in your SAP BW environment. In fact, there's a good chance you may have been involved at some level in this process when your system was initially developed.

Because the total number of characteristics available for grouping your report has already been predetermined and loaded into the InfoCube, how do you decide which ones to include in a particular Crystal Reports report? This, of course, depends completely on what you're trying to convey in your report. One very important skill you'll learn in this book is how to use Crystal Reports to create reports that allow the end user to change the grouping or groupings on-the-fly, without having to run the report again. This new feature in Crystal Reports 2008 allows the developer to create a single report that can meet many individual reporting requirements. Before the addition of this feature, different grouping requirements required the creation of completely separate report objects. Essentially this allows a single report to function as many.

Once you've created your top-level summary reports and made them available to end users, it's quite common for the end user community to begin to request additional information, often information at a lower level of detail. You can handle this in Crystal Reports in one of two ways. The first (and best) choice is to include the lower-level detail in the original summary report, if at all possible. This creates what's called a "drill-down" report in Crystal Reports. A drill-down report provides a way for the user to easily move from the big picture to successively lower levels of detail. In previous versions of Crystal Reports this was always accomplished by double-clicking a particular summary characteristic, thereby revealing the next level of detail. We'll be showing you a second option in Crystal Reports 2008 that allows the user to select the level of detail via a parameter or user input.

The second option for moving from the summary report to more detail is to create a separate report and link the two together. These linked reports are called *subreports* in Crystal Reports. These are very similar in concept to SAP BEx jump reports. Subreports almost always use a completely different data source than the original (main) report. The data source could be another BW query, a DSO, or even data from SAP R/3 (SAP ERP Central Component) or any other data source on your network.

The main point to remember as we move forward to the particulars of using Crystal Reports in an SAP BW environment is to start small and think big. In other words, keep the report high level and focused at the beginning and keep the big picture in mind. You can always expand your focus as you and your end users gain further understanding.

5.4   Your First SAP BW Crystal Report

It's time to roll up our sleeves and begin the practical, hands-on process of creating reports in SAP BW using Crystal Reports. Right from the beginning we need to look at the two different ways to begin: from scratch or from an existing template. In the previous chapter we looked at the reasons why creating a template for a given BW query is a good idea. The primary reason why this is a good idea is that it keeps you as a report designer from having to create aliases of all your key figures and characteristics every time you create a report using a particular BW query (we'll cover aliases again in a minute).

The other two benefits of using a template, as you may recall, are that it provides a way to maintain a consistent look and feel across your reports by providing standardized headers and footers and it allows you to insert standard calculations (formulas) that can be used in each new report.

Because of these benefits, it makes perfect sense to create and utilize templates to support your Crystal Reports development efforts. However, we must also recognize that, for whatever reason, there may be times when you want to develop a report from scratch, or brand new. With this in mind, we'll show you how to start a report using both methods.

5.4.1   Creating a Crystal Report from Scratch

The first step to creating a report is to, of course, launch Crystal Reports (Figure 5.1).

If you can't find Crystal Reports 2008 under your Start menu, you may need to check that you've installed in correctly.

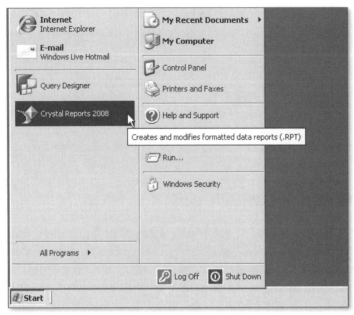

Figure 5.1 Starting Crystal Reports

Once Crystal Reports has launched successfully, you'll see something like the screen shown in Figure 5.2.

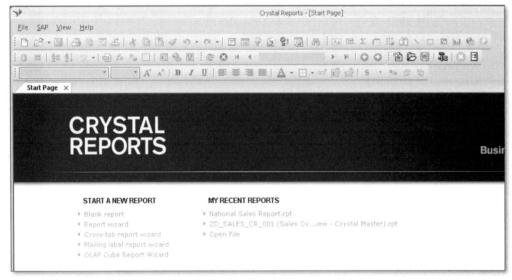

Figure 5.2 Crystal Reports Start Page

Important Note

If you don't see an SAP menu next to the File menu or the SAP toolbar, this means you haven't installed the Integration Kit for SAP Solutions client software on your computer. You'll need to do this before moving on. Also, once you've done this, you need to install the latest service pack from SAP (as of this writing, Service Pack 2).

Before we create a new report from a BW query, we need to ensure that we're using the MDX query driver. To check this, click the Settings button on the SAP toolbar (Figure 5.3).

Figure 5.3 SAP Toolbar – Settings Button

You'll now see the Settings dialog box (Figure 5.4).

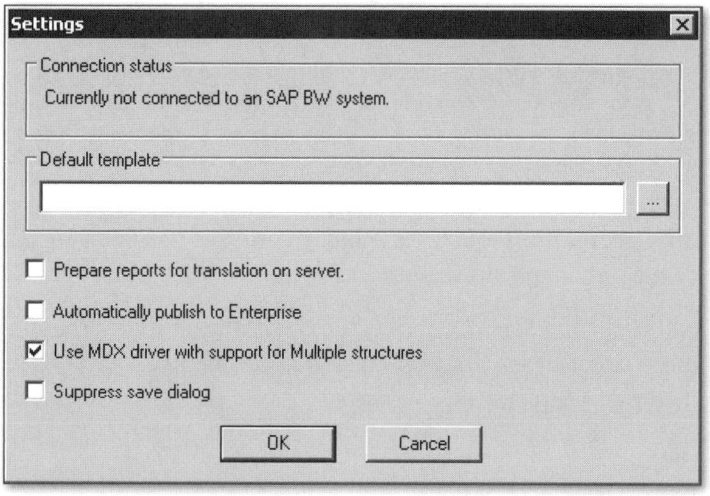

Settings

Connection status

Currently not connected to an SAP BW system.

Default template

☐ Prepare reports for translation on server.

☐ Automatically publish to Enterprise

☑ Use MDX driver with support for Multiple structures

☐ Suppress save dialog

OK   Cancel

Figure 5.4 Settings Dialog Box

You should then ensure that the Use MDX Driver with Support for Multiple Structures checkbox is selected. This should already be selected if you completed the lesson in the previous chapter. It's critical that you complete this step before moving forward. This ensures that you'll be using the newer MDX query driver instead of the original BW query driver.

Click OK to exit the Settings dialog. We can now create a new report from a BW query by clicking the Create New Report from a Query button on the SAP toolbar (Figure 5.5).

Figure 5.5 Create New Report from a Query

The next thing you'll see is the standard SAP logon screen where you can pick the SAP system you want to log on to. Normally you'll be using Crystal Reports in your SAP NetWeaver BW development environment (or perhaps your quality, or test, environment). If you're unsure which system is your SAP NetWeaver BW development environment, ask someone in your IT group.

Important Note
If you get any sort of error message when attempting to log on to your SAP system from within Crystal Reports, the most likely cause is that you haven't been added to the Crystal Developer role that should have been created for supporting Crystal Reports development in SAP NetWeaver BW. If this happens, you need to contact the appropriate person in your IT group (normally someone on your BASIS security team). If you get added to this role and you're still getting an error, there may be a problem with the Crystal Developer role. This would be up to your BASIS team to fix.

The first indication that everything — software and security — has been set up correctly is when you see the screen shown in Figure 5.6.

In our case we're looking for the Sales Overview – Crystal Master query that we created in the previous chapter (if you haven't created it, or one like it, you need to do so before proceeding). There are several ways to locate the query you need for your report. One way is to locate it in your History, as in this example. You can also save it to your Favorites area.

Another way to access queries is to navigate through the roles that you've been assigned to or through the various InfoAreas in your SAP NetWeaver BW system, as shown in Figure 5.7.

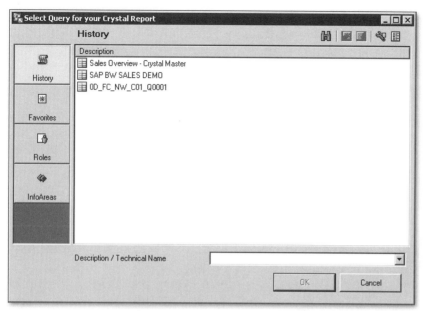

Figure 5.6 Select a Query for Your Crystal Report

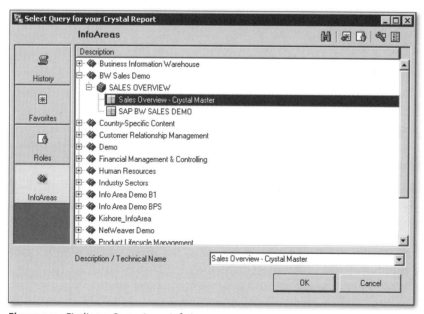

Figure 5.7 Finding a Query in an InfoArea

You can also search for your query in one of two ways. The first is to click the Find button at the top right of the window (see Figure 5.7 above). When you click it you'll see the screen shown in Figure 5.8.

Figure 5.8 Search for Queries Dialog Box

Next you type in your query's descriptive name or technical name (or usually part of the name) in the box at the top and click the Find button (no one ever uses the other options on this screen; they're a bit excessive for most people).

One last way to find your query is the one most people use. You simply type the query name (or part of the name) in the box at bottom of the Select Query screen and press Enter (Figure 5.9).

You'll then see a filtered list of all of the queries that contain that search string (Figure 5.10).

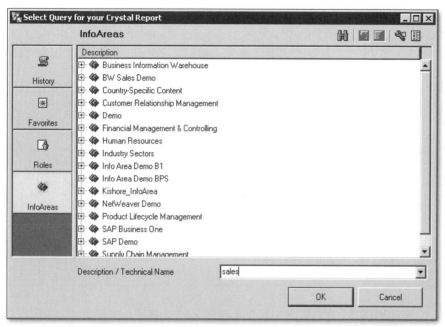

Figure 5.9 Find a Query by Entering Part of Name

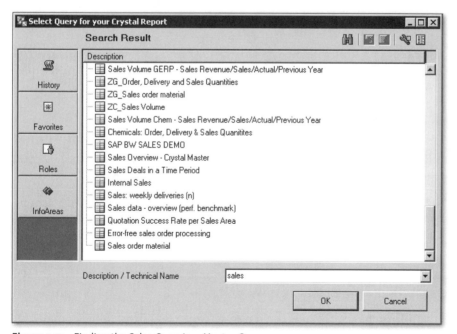

Figure 5.10 Finding the Sales Overview Master Query

You can select your query from the list. Whichever way you find and access your query, once you've selected it and clicked OK, you should be back in Crystal Reports and see something like Figure 5.11.

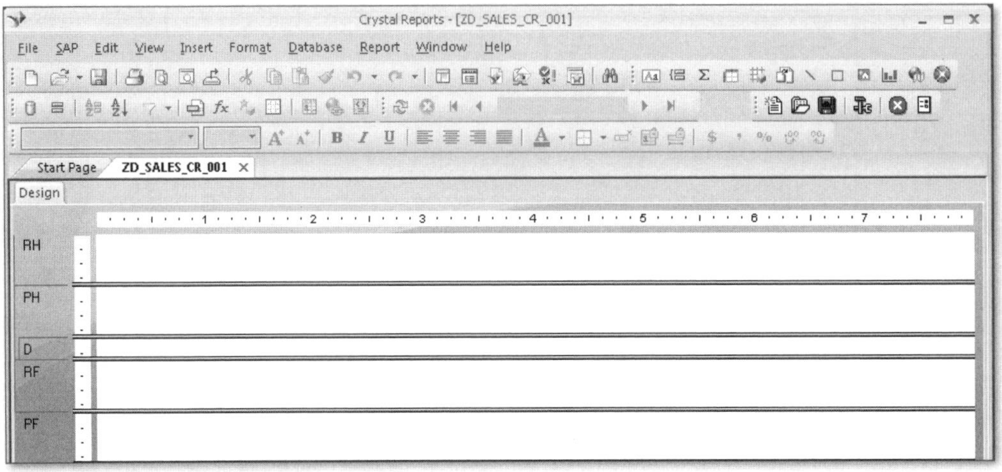

Figure 5.11 Starting a New Report Using a Query

Next to the Start tab is a new tab that displays the technical name of the query you just selected.

Before we move on to adding query elements to your report, let's look at how you start a report using a preexisting report template. As a reminder, this is the preferred method for beginning a new Crystal Reports report against a BW query.

5.4.2   Creating a Crystal Report from a Report Template

Creating a report beginning with a report template is very straightforward. All you do is open the Crystal Reports template, select Save As, and rename the report.

The only real issue is where to keep the templates so that your Crystal Reports developers can access them. You can save them in a file share on the network or even save them to SAP NetWeaver BW in a special role for Crystal Reports developers. Or you can store them in common file repository such as SharePoint. It doesn't really matter where you keep them. It only matters that each Crystal Reports developer has access to use them.

One last note on templates: You could create several templates for each query for each of three different printing options: letter, landscape, and legal. Landscape, of course, would be wider than letter (11 inches vs. 8½ inches), and legal would be 14 inches wide. This sounds like a good idea at first, but the problem is that it means you now have three separate templates to maintain. That's not too bad as long as they don't need to be changed. But if they ever do require modifications, you have to make the changes three times

Because of this we recommend creating and maintaining just one template per BW query. The changes required to move from landscape to portrait or even to legal-sized paper aren't very difficult for even the beginning developer. It's only a matter of moving a couple of items in the page footer.

5.4.3 Aliases: A Brief Review

Because we covered the reasons for creating aliases in a Crystal Reports report that uses a BW query in the previous chapter, we won't go into any further detail. It's is such an important first step, however, that it deserves repeating here. If for whatever reason you opt not to create a template for your Crystal Reports report, you'll need to create your aliases for the first time in your new report.

As a reminder, this is the most compelling reason to create a template as a starting point for your Crystal Report reports, because it's potentially the most labor-intensive part of the report creation process. You want to avoid having to go through this process more than once per query.

5.4.4 Arranging Toolbar Buttons

One last step of preparation before we begin building our first report. It will be helpful to arrange your toolbars to match the setup we'll be using in the exercises. This simply makes it easier to locate the various toolbar buttons we'll will be using. Figure 5.12 shows how our toolbars are arranged.

Figure 5.12 All Toolbars

The Standard toolbar is at the top left (this is the default location). Next to that we've placed the Insert toolbar. (To move a toolbar, simply drag the handle on the left of the toolbar.) Below the Standard toolbar on the left is the Experts toolbar.

Next to that is the Navigation toolbar, followed by the SAP Toolbar. Finally, at the bottom is the Formatting toolbar. Take a few minutes to arrange your toolbars accordingly. Once you become familiar with the various toolbars and buttons, you can to arrange them however you want.

5.4.5 Adding Objects to Your First Report

Now we're really ready to start building an actual report. At the beginning we aren't going to concern ourselves too much with making the report look perfect, or even "good." We simply want to understand the process of adding characteristics and key figures to a report and the impact this process has on the data set returned from SAP BW. We'll look at making it look "pretty" in a while.

In this exercise we'll use a report template as the starting point. All we need to do is open the template to get started. In our case we called the template ZD_SALES_CR_001 (Sales Overview – Crystal Master. To use it, simply go to FILE • OPEN and select the template (Figure 5.13).

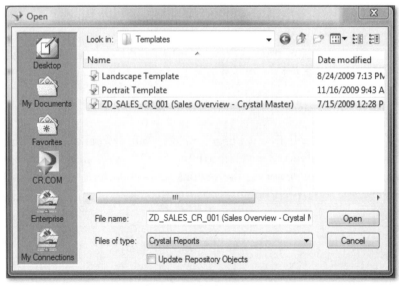

Figure 5.13 Opening a Crystal Reports Template

Before we begin placing objects on the Design tab of our report, we need to change just one more setting in Crystal Reports. By default, Crystal Reports inserts a column heading for any fields you place in the Detail section of your report. This isn't a very useful feature because it uses the name of the field (or formula) object for the column heading text. If you recall, we prefaced all our aliases with either "z_" or "zz_" (for example, zz_Revenue). This means Crystal Reports will create a column header that says zz_Revenue. You then have to edit the column header. It's quicker and easier to simply create column headers yourself.

To change this setting, go to FILE • OPTIONS. This takes you to the Layout tab. Unselect the Insert Detail Field Headings option then click OK (Figure 5.14).

Field options:
- ☑ Show Field Names
- ☐ Insert Detail Field Headings
- ☑ Insert Group Name with Group

Figure 5.14 Field Options

Our initial report is going to be a simple listing of sales by channel. All we need to do is place the sales channel description and the revenue key figure in the Detail section of our report. The Detail section of the Design tab is where you place the characteristics and key figures from the query when creating a simple list report. As you'll find out later as we explore sections in more detail, you're not required to use the Detail section at all. However, it's quite common to display data in the Detail section of a report.

Pop Quiz

Question: Where do you get the channel characteristic and revenue key figure to place onto your report?

Answer: You use the z_Channel_desc alias formula from the Formula Fields node of the Field Explorer. You do *not* use the Channel characteristic from the Database Fields node of the Field Explorer.

To add the Channel description to your report, simply expand the Formula Fields node and drag the z_Channel_desc alias formula to the Detail section on the left side of the Design tab (Figure 5.15).

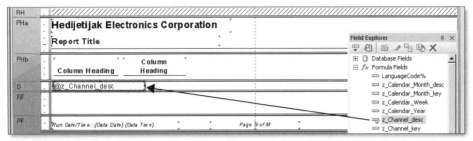

Figure 5.15 Adding the Channel Description Alias Formula

Now let's add the Revenue key figure. Just drag the zz_Revenue alias next to the channel description (Figure 5.16).

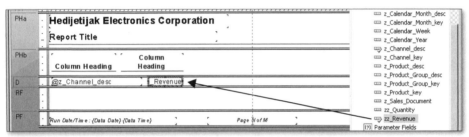

Figure 5.16 Adding the Revenue Alias Formula

That's all there is to it. You now have the basic elements of a simple sales report. To run the report, simply click the Refresh button on the Navigation toolbar (Figure 5.17).

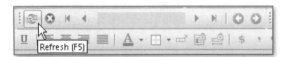

Figure 5.17 Refresh Button

You'll now be presented with the SAP logon dialog. You must enter the correct system identifier (SID) for your SAP NetWeaver BW system, the client number, a user name, and a password. Once the report has executed, you'll see something like Figure 5.18.

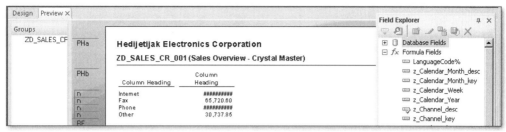

Figure 5.18 Initial Preview Tab

Notice that there's now a second tab next to the Design tab, called Preview. The Preview tab shows you what your report design looks like when you add data to it.

Crystal Reports will always let you know how many records (or rows) of data were returned from the data source (in our case, a BW query). You'll find this at the bottom middle of the window (Figure 5.19).

Figure 5.19 Record Counter

In this example we've retrieved four records. It's very important that you're always aware of how many records are being returned when running a report that uses a BW query as a data source. Recall from an earlier discussion about running reports in a data warehouse (such as SAP NetWeaver BW) that when you run a report, you're really asking SAP BW to generate *N* summaries for you and return them to the report. In this example SAP BW generated four summary values and returned them (along with the corresponding Channel description).

Before moving on, let's clean things up a bit. Notice that two of the summary values have been replaced by X's (as in Excel). This is because the numbers are too big (wide) for the current size of the field in our report.

One way to change the size of a field is to drag the handle on the right side of the field to the right. You can do this in either the Design tab or the Preview tab. The advantage of doing it in the Preview tab is that you can see right away if you've make the fields big enough (Figure 5.20).

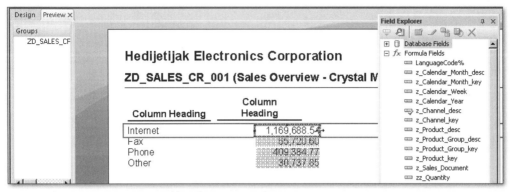

Figure 5.20 Resizing a Field in the Preview Tab

Simply place your mouse pointer over the handle on the right side of the Revenue field and drag it to the right until you can see all of the revenue numbers. We'll look in much more detail at basic formatting techniques and tricks a little later, but for now we need to focus on something that's critical to understanding how Crystal Reports reports "behave" when you use a BW query for a data source.

5.4.6 Data Explosion in Action

In the previous chapter we discussed a trait unique to data warehouses known as data explosion We'll now get a chance to see a little of this in action. Although we're not going to push things even close to what would be considered a genuine explosion of data, we'll at least get a chance to see how the process works and, most importantly, how to monitor and manage the process. And just in case this makes you a bit nervous, you can relax. Once you see how it works, you'll find it's quite simple to understand.

First, let's answer this simple question: Why did we get four rows back from SAP NetWeaver BW when we ran this report? Are there only four rows of data in SAP NetWeaver BW? After all, we didn't filter the data in any way. (Filtering data is a way of selecting only certain rows based upon some criteria.) If you've ever done any kind of reporting in a standard SQL environment (such as Oracle, SQL Server, etc.), you know that if you don't filter your query (or request), you'll get all of the rows from your data source.

So, because we haven't applied any sort of filter to our query, does that mean there are four rows of data for us to select from in SAP NetWeaver BW? The quick answer is, "No." There are potentially many more rows of data that can be returned from this (or any other) BW query. This is because of something we mentioned earlier in the previous chapter that bears repeating.

> **Note**
>
> When you retrieve data from a relational database, you're asking for *N* rows (records) of data.
>
> When you retrieve data from a multidimensional database, you're asking for *N* summary calculations to be generated.

So, in our case, exactly how did SAP BW know to only create and send back four summaries? SAP BW always looks at the characteristic (or characteristics) being used in the Crystal Reports report when determining how many summaries to create. This is why it's critical that you always know which characteristics are active (being used) in your Crystal Reports report at all times.

In our example SAP BW generated four summaries because the only characteristic being used in our report is Channel. In the source data (which is actually not the BW query, but the InfoProvider that the query points to), there are exactly four different Channels: Internet, Fax, Phone, and Other. Because this is the only characteristic in our report (thus far), SAP BW generated a summary of the Revenue key figure for each of these four channels. If there had been 10 channels, we would have received 10 summaries (and 10 records). If there had been 100, we would have received 100.

So how does data explosion work? Let's take a look. It's easy to expand the number of summaries being generated by SAP BW. All you have to do is add another characteristic to your report.

Before we go on, we need to explain this a bit further. Adding a characteristic doesn't always expand the number of summaries generated. It completely depends on the relative "granularity" of the characteristics and the order they are added to the report.

What we mean by granularity is that some characteristics have more unique members than others. The higher the number of unique members, the higher the granularity. In our example, Channel is a characteristic with a very low level of granularity because it has only four unique members. Other examples of characteristics with a low level of granularity are Division, Sales Organization, and Company. A highly granular characteristic would be something like Material Number or Personnel Number.

The type of characteristic with the highest level of granularity in any data warehouse is the document-level characteristic (Sales Document, Order Number, etc.). As we mentioned in the previous chapter, you need to be very careful when using any document-level characteristic in a Crystal Reports report, especially in a large data warehouse environment.

The best way to understand this is by seeing it in action. We're going to add the Product Group characteristic to our report. Before we do this, however, let's move the Revenue key figure to the right to give us some room. One way to do this is to go back to the Design tab (click the tab at the top left), select the Revenue field, and then use the Right Arrow on the keyboard to move the field to the right (Figure 5.21).

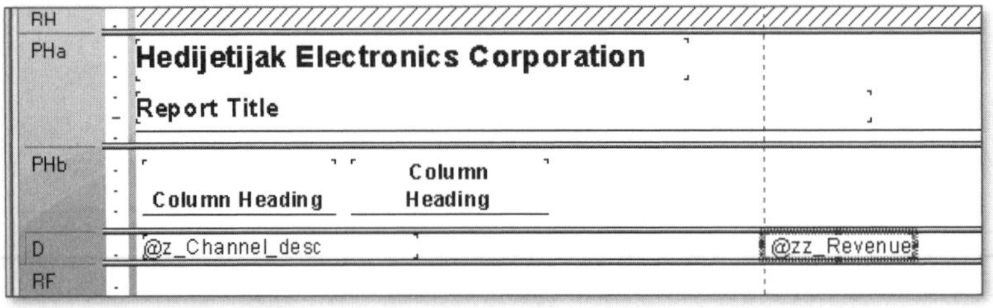

Figure 5.21 Moving the Revenue Field to the Right in the Design Tab

Now that we have room, let's drag the Product Group field (remember, use the z_Product_Group_desc alias formula we created in our template) next to the Channel field. When you switch back to the Preview tab, you should see something like Figure 5.22.

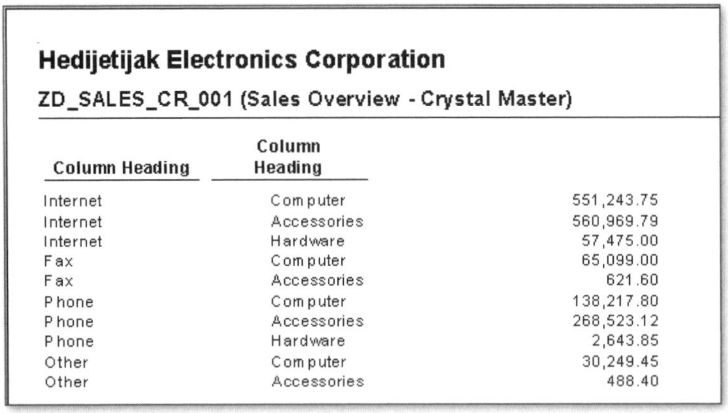

Hedijetijak Electronics Corporation

ZD_SALES_CR_001 (Sales Overview - Crystal Master)

Column Heading	Column Heading	
Internet	Computer	551,243.75
Internet	Accessories	560,969.79
Internet	Hardware	57,475.00
Fax	Computer	65,099.00
Fax	Accessories	621.60
Phone	Computer	138,217.80
Phone	Accessories	268,523.12
Phone	Hardware	2,643.85
Other	Computer	30,249.45
Other	Accessories	488.40

Figure 5.22 Adding Product Group Description

We now get 10 records back from SAP NetWeaver BW, simply because we added Product Group to our report because we're now asking SAP NetWeaver BW to no longer return total revenue figures for each channel, but for each possible combination of channel and product group. There are 10 combinations in this particular dataset.

If you look closely, you'll notice that three product groups are defined in this company. As we saw earlier, there are four channels. Then why aren't 12 totals (3 × 4) returned when we combine the two into one report? The reason is because, in this particular set of data, there are two "holes" in the data. No hardware was sold through either the Fax or Other channels. This could be because hardware isn't sold through either of these channels or because none was sold during this period, or for any other reason. This is why 10 totals were returned and not 12.

This brings up a good point. When you have holes like this in your data, they're returned not as zeros but rather as nothing at all. In other words, rather than a total equaling zero, no total is returned at all. In this case that would be just fine if hardware is never sold through either the Fax or Other channel. Why would we want to be shown a zero value when we already know it will always be zero?

However, if hardware can be and is sold through both of these channels, you may need to show zero values for hardware revenues for these two channels. The easiest way to handle this is by utilizing a feature in Crystal Reports called a *crosstab*. You'll learn how to use crosstabs in an upcoming chapter.

Let's add one more characteristic just to help drive the point home. We're going to add the Product medium description alias to the report. The result is something like Figure 5.23.

This time we end up with 19 rows (or summaries) in our report. In this example we intentionally began with a characteristic with few possible members (Channel), added a characteristic with slightly more possible members (Product Group), and ended by adding a characteristic with even more possible members (Product). The effect (driven completely by the data in this particular dataset) was to go from 4 to 10 to 19 rows. So in this case the addition of each characteristic approximately doubled our row set.

Hedijetijak Electronics Corporation

ZD_SALES_CR_001 (Sales Overview - Crystal Master)

Column Heading	Column Heading		
Internet	Computer	Ventra LX 2.33 1GB 300 GB	122,097.78
Internet	Computer	Ventra Ultra 3.00 2GB 750 GB	86,581.67
Internet	Computer	Ventra LXP 2.67 2GB 500 GB	342,564.30
Internet	Accessories	DigiPad Mousepad	9,395.04
Internet	Accessories	17" LCD Monitor	448,830.90
Internet	Accessories	UltraTouch USB Keyboard	64,767.60
Internet	Accessories	LightTouch Optical Mouse	37,976.25
Internet	Hardware	Computer Speakers	57,475.00
Fax	Computer	Ventra Ultra 3.00 2GB 750 GB	65,099.00
Fax	Accessories	DigiPad Mousepad	621.60
Phone	Computer	Ventra Ultra 3.00 2GB 750 GB	78,118.80
Phone	Computer	Ventra LXP 2.67 2GB 500 GB	60,099.00
Phone	Accessories	DigiPad Mousepad	9,226.32
Phone	Accessories	17" LCD Monitor	234,990.00
Phone	Accessories	UltraTouch USB Keyboard	15,992.00
Phone	Accessories	LightTouch Optical Mouse	8,314.80
Phone	Hardware	Computer Speakers	2,643.85
Other	Computer	Ventra LX 2.33 1GB 300 GB	30,249.45
Other	Accessories	DigiPad Mousepad	488.40

Figure 5.23 Adding Product Description

> **Note**
>
> Keep in mind that this is a very limited example in terms of the number of possible rows that could be generated. In the real world, the number of rows returned from SAP NetWeaver BW can start off much higher and expand much more quickly. It depends completely on the InfoCube you're working with.

We simply can't emphasize how important this concept is to grasp as we move forward in the process of developing reports against SAP BW. A firm understanding of how SAP BW responds to changes in report design can mean the difference between success and failure.

Remember, our real goal here is to put more power into the hands of the business end user (most likely someone just like you). One of the ways we're accomplishing this is by including in the BW query virtually anything you may want to use in a report that currently exists in the source InfoCube (the master query). By doing this we greatly reduce the amount of work required to create and maintain your source queries, and we provide the greatest amount of flexibility for the report designer.

However, with this increased flexibility comes the increased potential for something to go wrong. In this case it means allowing the report designer the freedom to add into one report essentially all of the characteristics that exist in a given Info-Cube at one time. And as we've discussed before (and are driving home now), in a real-world environment with a large backend dataset, you can end up creating a database query that either runs very long or never finishes running at all (times out).

But ultimately, when you think about it, isn't is worth the extra risk? Every day people are given new responsibilities, capabilities, or access to tools that provide them with an increased capacity to do both good and harm. Every time someone jumps in their car and starts it up, they increase the risk of getting either themselves or someone else, or both, seriously hurt or even killed. But you don't see many people lining up to turn in their keys.

It's the same sort of situation here (although, admittedly, the potential adverse consequences aren't quite so severe). Many technically savvy SAP system business end users have had to sit and wait for someone in IT to get the bandwidth to deal with their particular business need. This isn't a knock on IT. It's simply an acknowledgment that virtually every IT department on the planet is grossly outnumbered. No organization can afford the level of support it would take to fully service the needs of every business end user using only IT resources.

5.5 Making It All Look Pretty – Formatting 101

This is what Crystal Reports is known for: the ability to make reports look really nice. Ever since it was first integrated with SAP NetWeaver BW in 2002, it's always been positioned (and rightly so) as the best choice for creating "pixel perfect" reports.

But be warned: the formatting capabilities of Crystal Reports are both the best and (potentially) its worst features. In the hands of a skilled report developer they provide the ability to create an almost limitless array of reporting layouts. However, to the newbie (someone like you, for instance) they can turn into one of the biggest time wasters you can imagine.

It's easy with Crystal Reports (if you're not careful) to spend a lot of extra time "tweaking" a report ad infinitum. And we mean a *lot* of extra time. This is why we're are going to be working on this skill throughout the rest of the book. Each exercise will include some sort of tip or trick on how to make the formatting of your reports as effective and efficient as possible.

But before we go on, here's one quick observation: As your mother told you when you were a kid, neatness counts. Not everyone, of course, places the same value on making reports look pretty, but, in the end, the prettiest report wins. Just ask anyone in your marketing or sales department. Blame it on human nature, but you can present the exact same information in a plain, simple report and in a polished, elegant report, and guess which one will make the most impact?

This is something technical people will *never* understand. And this is why it's risky to have technical people create any type of report that will be seen in public, especially by anyone outside of your organization. Although there's the occasional technical person who has creative flair, don't count on it. It's sometimes better to take matters into your own hands.

> **Formatting Tip**
>
> *Know your limitations*. Not everyone is born an artist. And although it's true, as we just mentioned, that neatness counts, you don't have to go overboard either. Effective formatting in Crystal Reports requires skill, some artistic ability, and knowing when to say "enough."

For practice, we're going to start from the beginning again. We're going to assume that you've created at least the beginnings of a template against a BW query. We'll reopen our original template to begin a brand new report.

Go to FILE • OPEN and open your template.

> **Note**
>
> As a reminder, chances are your template won't be exactly like the template in these exercises, because it's unlikely that your SAP BW data source (InfoProvider) is identical to the one we used to create our template. The key to being successful from here on out is to remain as flexible and as creative as possible, which is also important because it just happens that those are two key traits of any successful report developer.

Once again, as we did in our previous example, we'll start by creating a simple list report (no groupings). To do this, all we need to do is place any information we need in our report in the Detail section of the Design tab. The simplest way to do this is by dragging the items from the Field Explorer into the Detail section.

In an effort to make these exercises as real-world as possible, we'll attempt to provide at least some sort of realistic scenario as a basis for our report development efforts. Although there's an almost limitless number of possible report requirement scenarios, we'll focus on some of the more common ones that you might run into in any organization. And, as you might imagine, we'll also start with some of the easiest.

In our case the requirement is a simple list of products sold by month. We'd like to see both the quantity sold for that month and the revenue. To accomplish this, all we need to do is drag the Calendar Year/Month and Product Description along with the Quantity and Revenue key figures into the Detail section.

In case you don't remember, to find these items go to the Formula section of the Field Explorer and use your alias formulas that you created when you first created your template. If you haven't created an alias for a particular characteristic or key figure, create the alias and then place it on the Design tab. And just to drill it home further, this is *not* an option when dealing with key figures.

The alias formulas we'll be using are:

▶ z_Calendar_Year/Month_medium_name

▶ z_Product_medium_name

▶ zz_Quantity

▶ zz_Revenue

After dragging these four items into the Details section of our report, it might look something like Figure 5.24.

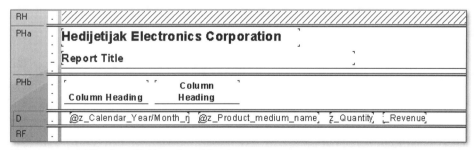

Figure 5.24 Adding Four Fields to Detail Section

At least that's what it might look like if you're already pretty good at placing fields next to each other and keeping them perfectly aligned. However, if you're new at this, you're probably not quite that good yet. We're going to shift our fields around a bit to show you how they might look when placed by a beginning report developer (Figure 5.25).

RH		//
PHa		**Hedijetijak Electronics Corporation**
		Report Title
PHb		Column Heading **Column Heading**
D		@z_Calendar_Year/Month_r @z_Product_medium_name z_Quantity Revenue
RF		

Figure 5.25   Four Fields Misaligned

As you can see, our four fields are now not so neatly lined up. This is a common occurrence when starting off using Crystal Reports. If you want to follow along and try this yourself, you'll first need to expand your Detail section to allow room for the misaligned field objects. This is something we covered briefly in our previous lesson on creating a Crystal Reports template, but in case you missed it, here's how. You simply move your mouse over the lower border of any section until it looks like Figure 5.26.

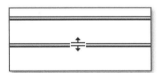

Figure 5.26   Resizing a Section

Once the cursor changes, you simply drag the bottom border either down to make the section bigger or up to make it smaller. In this example you want to make the Detail section a little bigger, so you drag the bottom border down.

It's easy to place fields on the report canvas in a way that leaves them misaligned, as above. Because you have complete control over everything that goes on in Crystal Reports in terms of report layout, it's easy to mess up a lot of things. And that brings us to our next big tip: Become good friends with Undo.

> **Note**
>
> The Undo command in Crystal Reports needs to become your best friend. In other words, you'll want to spend a lot of time with it and get well acquainted.

Once you realize how handy the Undo command is when creating report layouts, you'll begin to wear it out. It's not only the best way to handle a mistake, but it's also a great way to try out new ideas (I wonder how *this* would look?) without having to fully commit to them.

Perhaps the most basic (and common) use of Undo is when you make a formatting mistake. So when you do something really dumb, you can simply click Undo, and it all goes away.

If you're not comfortable using Undo, try it out now. We're not going to lead you through anything. Just start moving things around in the Design tab and then start clicking Undo until you get back to where you started. You can even click Redo (Undo's lesser-known cousin) if you want to go back and forth. Go ahead. We'll wait.

Now, keep in mind that Undo works great until you click Save. Once you do that, you've lost all opportunities to Undo anything you've done up to that point, which brings up another very important point: saving your work.

Crystal Reports does have an Autosave feature that you can set for a particular length of time so that every *N* minutes Crystal Reports will automatically save you work for you. (If you decide you want to use this feature, just go to FILE • OPTIONS and then select the Reporting tab). This is a tough call to make, because saving your work regularly is so important, but we'd like you to consider *not* using this feature, for the following reason.

The problem with the Autosave feature is that *you* no longer have any say about when your report gets saved. It just happens every *N* minutes. So what could be the problem with that? Well, let's say you're in the middle of trying out some new idea in a report you've been working on for some time. All you're trying to do is see how it would look. Then let's say that just then the Autosave kicks in and, wham, the new idea you were "just testing out" just became reality. Unless you have a backup of your original idea, you've lost it for good.

This is why we recommend that you don't rely on the Autosave feature of Crystal Reports and instead get used to saving reports yourself only when *you* want them saved. Of course, this means you probably need to do this more than every eight hours or so, or you'll risk losing a lot of work. So as long as you're consistent about saving your work yourself, it will work in your favor to not depend on Autosave.

> **Note**
>
> It's a good idea to get in the habit of "versioning" your reports. This means that it's time to make any kind of significant change to the design of report, you should open the report and immediately do a Save As. Then you attach a version number on the end of the report name (v2, v3, etc.). For simple reports you may only have two or three versions before finalizing the report. For more complex reports, it's not unusual to have 10 or more. You can always delete any versions you don't want to keep when you're finished. But it's always a good idea to keep your last few versions, just in case. End users have been known to change their minds.

5.5.1 Keeping Things Lined Up

Back to our misaligned field objects. Aside from using Undo and starting over again, to rectify this situation you have three choices:

▶ "Eyeball" it. In other words, just move the fields around with your mouse or the keyboard (arrow keys) to line them up visually.

▶ Use Guidelines to line things up.

▶ Use the Align command to line things up.

The first option isn't really an option if you don't like wasting time. The second option has been a favorite of Crystal Reports developers for many years, mainly because for a long time it was the only way to automatically line up anything in Crystal Reports. You may notice in our example that no guidelines were created for us automatically when we placed the four fields in the Detail section. This is because we've turned this option off by going to FILE • OPTIONS and unselecting the Insert Detail Field Headings checkbox (Figure 5.27).

Figure 5.27 Field Options with Insert Detail Field Headings Turned Off

As it turns out, when you turn off this option, it also prevents Crystal Reports from automatically inserting a guideline every time you place something in the Detail section. The reason you don't want Crystal Reports to insert a field heading (column heading) for you automatically is simply because most of the time (nearly all of the time) you end up re-creating the field heading anyway. This is because Crystal Reports simply takes whatever the name of the field happens to be and creates a column header with the same name. This works out great if your field happens to be named exactly what you want your column header to say, but this almost never happens. Normally you're placing a field that's called something like zz_Personnel_Group_medium_text.

Although guidelines can be quite useful (and many Crystal Reports developers use them every day), we recommend against using them primarily two reasons: They tend to "grab" fields and objects unintentionally, and they make it impossible to perform a "mass move" of fields.

The first reason has to do with the "magnetic" property of guidelines, which is an intentional feature that can go a bit awry. As you move guidelines back and forth on the ruler bar (much like a tab in Microsoft Word) they have a tendency to grab onto a field by accident. You then end up collecting additional fields and adding them to your guideline without meaning to.

The second reason for not using guidelines is the real killer, however. If you use guidelines to align a series of columns in Crystal Reports and then later find that you need to move all of the columns over a bit (a common occurrence), you have to move each column individually using its guideline. This can quickly turn into a time waster.

Fortunately an alternative called the Align command has been available for several versions of Crystal Reports. We're going to teach you how to use and encourage you to continue using the Align command to keep all your fields lined up in Crystal Reports. It's simple, effective, and leaves you with the most flexibility when it comes time to make any future changes to your layout.

To use the Align command, you first need to select at least two fields (or objects). In our case we need to align the four fields (aliases) we placed in the Detail section. You can accomplish this using any of the following three methods:

- ⌨ `Shift` + click (or `Ctrl` + click) on each object.
- Lasso the objects with your cursor.
- Use the Select All Section Objects command.

Shift + click (or Ctrl + click) works well when your goal is to select either just a few objects or items that are sitting among other objects that you don't want to select. You do this by simply holding down either the Shift key or the Ctrl key and then begin clicking on any objects you want to select. Try it now. To unselect everything that you just selected, you simply click on any white space in the Design tab canvas.

The second method, "lassoing" objects using your cursor, works only when the objects you're selecting are in the same general area and your goal is to select everything (or almost everything) in that area. This is quite easy to accomplish. All you have to do is click somewhere on the canvas (on white space, not on an object) and drag your mouse. You'll see an orange rectangle being created by your mouse. Anything that orange rectangle either touches or encloses is selected. Try it out now. Simply start at one end of the objects you want to select and work your way to the opposite end.

It can sometimes be useful to combine lassoing with the Shift + click method. Sometimes when using the lasso method you end up selecting objects that you didn't intend to select. To unselect only certain objects you can Shift + click them. Again, try this out for yourself. Try lassoing a series of objects and then go back and Shift + click several to unselect them.

However you decide to select these four objects, when you have them selected they'll all have a blue border, as shown in Figure 5.28.

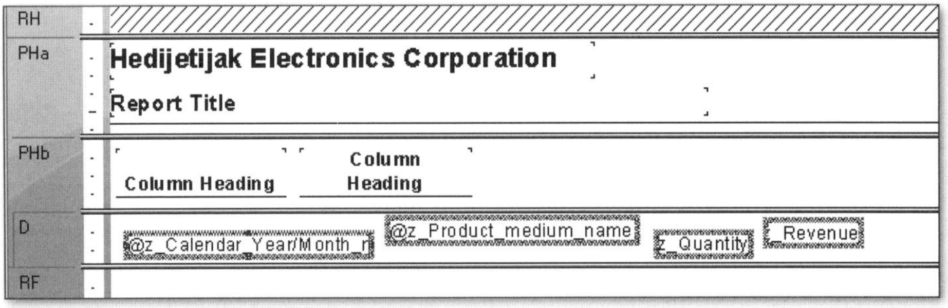

Figure 5.28 Four Objects Selected Showing Border

Now that we have the objects selected, let's use the Align command to line them up. The key to making this work correctly is to right-click the object that will be acting as the "anchor" for the rest of the objects. In other words, by right-clicking a particular object and selecting Align, you align all of the remaining objects to *that* object (it remains stationary and all the others move).

Now we'll right-click the Calendar_Year/Month_medium_name field on the left and then select Align (Figure 5.29).

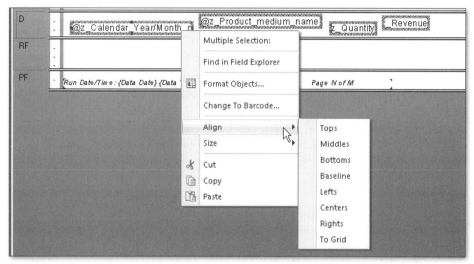

Figure 5.29   Align Menu

In our case, because we want to line these objects up horizontally across the page, we need to select one of the first four options (Tops, Middles, Bottoms, Baseline). Your choice depends on the relative size of the objects and how you want them to be aligned. In this example all four fields are the exact same height, so it really doesn't matter which one we pick. We'll look next at a situation where objects aren't the same size.

The Baseline option pertains to text objects, fields, and formulas only. This aligns the baseline portion of the text itself, not the edge of the border as the other three options do. We'll choose Baseline (Figure 5.30).

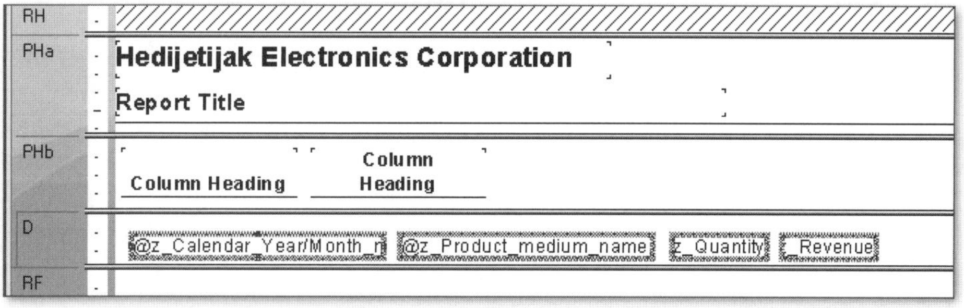

Figure 5.30   Four Objects Aligned Horizontally

Now that we've got the four field objects perfectly aligned, we need to remove any extra space from both above and below the fields. The way to do this is to first move all your field objects up until they are snug up against the top border of the Detail section. You do this by:

► Selecting all of the objects (we're assuming they're already sized the same and aligned horizontally).

► Using you're the Up Arrow on your keyboard and moving the field objects up until they jump *over* the top border into the section above.

► Pressing the Down Arrow on your keyboard once.

Now the fields are right up against the top border of the section. There are two ways to eliminate the white space below the field objects.

► Drag the bottom border using your mouse.

► Right-click in the left margin of the section and select Fit Section. The Fit Section command automatically moves the bottom border of the section up until it hits any object in the section.

Before we move on, it would be a good idea to take a few minutes and practice aligning objects. First, expand your Detail section. Then simply take a few fields (in our case alias formulas), set them in the Detail section, and deliberately misalign them. Now go through the steps we outlined above to align them, move them to the top of the section, and snug everything up.

5.5.2 Resizing Objects

Another fundamental formatting task that you'll find yourself doing all the time is resizing objects, whether they be field objects, formulas, text objects, lines, boxes, charts — you name it. Because you'll be doing this a lot, we're going to help you learn to do it as efficiently as possible. This is one of those little things that adds up quickly.

In this exercise we'll focus on resizing field, formula, and text objects because these are the most commonly resized objects. Let's take a look at the Preview tab of our example report and see what it looks like now that we've aligned all of the Detail fields.

> **Note**
>
> Before we look at the Preview tab of our example report, we need to share with you a very important tip that can potentially save you a lot of time as you continue in your report development efforts. In fact, this one tip alone is by *itself* worth the price of admission.

As you've seen, whenever you first run a report, it creates a Preview tab that shows you what the report currently looks like when you add data. You can then switch back and forth between the Preview and Design tabs as often as you need as you develop your report.

Let's say you go back to your Design tab and add another field to your layout. When you switch back to the Preview tab the report will automatically refresh itself. In other words, the report will be executed again and the data refreshed.

This makes sense because by adding a field that wasn't there before, you're forcing Crystal Reports to go back to the data source to retrieve the new field. This means that *every* time this happens you have to wait again until the refresh process has completed. This isn't much of an issue when the refresh time is a few seconds. But when it's a few minutes, that's another story.

This brings us to our time-saving tip. You want to avoid the situation where you're adding fields to the Design tab and switching over to the Preview tab, especially when the report takes more than a few seconds to refresh. It's best to place all of the fields you think you'll need for your report in the Design tab first, before you run the report the first time.

If you're careful to avoid the mistake of constantly adding new fields one at a time and switching over to the Preview tab, you'll save countless hours in your report development efforts.

Now, back to resizing field objects. You can resize any object in either the Design tab or the Preview tab. In fact, you can perform almost any design task in the Preview tab that you can perform in the Design tab. In general, it's best to avoid adding objects in the Preview tab, because this requires a lot more eye-hand coordination than it does in the Design tab. Also, as we just mentioned, you *never* want to add fields into the Preview tab because it causes a refresh every time you add one.

The Preview tab is a good place to resize fields because you can see how wide the field should be by looking at a sample of the data that's in that particular field. In other words, you see immediately the effects that resizing the field will have on your final output.

When we click on our Preview tab, we now see something like Figure 5.31.

Hedijetijak Electronics Corporation

ZD_SALES_CR_001 (Sales Overview - Crystal Master)

Column Heading	Column Heading		
JUL 2007	Ventra LX 2.33 1GB 300 GB	165.00	90,748.35
JUL 2007	Ventra Ultra 3.00 2GB 750 G	98.00	63,797.02
JUL 2007	Ventra LXP 2.67 2GB 500 GI	75.00	45,074.25
JUL 2007	DigiPad Mousepad	339.00	3,010.32
JUL 2007	UltraTouch USB Keyboard	120.00	4,797.60
JUL 2007	LightTouch Optical Mouse	95.00	1,519.05
JUL 2007	Computer Speakers	115.00	2,643.85
AUG 2007	Ventra LX 2.33 1GB 300 GB	12.00	6,599.88
AUG 2007	Ventra Ultra 3.00 2GB 750 G	30.00	19,529.70
AUG 2007	Ventra LXP 2.67 2GB 500 GI	390.00	########
AUG 2007	DigiPad Mousepad	758.00	6,731.04
AUG 2007	17" LCD Monitor	1,650.00	########
AUG 2007	UltraTouch USB Keyboard	530.00	21,189.40
AUG 2007	LightTouch Optical Mouse	1,475.00	23,585.25
AUG 2007	Computer Speakers	1,300.00	29,887.00

Figure 5.31 Four Columns in the Preview Tab

As you can see, things can use a little touching up:

- The Calendar Month/Year field is too wide.
- The Product field is just a little too narrow (some of the text is truncated).
- The Revenue field is too narrow, and some of the numbers are masked with # symbols.

The fields weren't sized correctly to begin with because Crystal Reports doesn't do anything for you in terms of automatically resizing fields to accommodate the text or numbers in that field. There's is no Autosize function like there is in Excel. The initial size of the field is determined by the type of the field and, for string fields, the defined length of the field. It's up to you to determine how wide to make any individual field.

Let's resize our fields in the Preview tab. To do this, you simply grab the center handle on the right side of the field (Figure 5.32).

JUL 2007	Ventra LXP 2.67 2GB 500 GE
JUL 2007	DigiPad Mousepad
JUL 2007	UltraTouch USB Keyboard

Figure 5.32   Grabbing a Resize Figure on a Field

Notice that when you grab the handle, your cursor changes to a double arrow. We're trying to make this field smaller, so we'll drag the mouse to the left. When finished, the Calendar Month/Year field should look something like Figure 5.33.

Column Heading	Column Heading		
JUL 2007	Ventra LX 2.33 1GB 300 GB	165.00	90,748.35
JUL 2007	Ventra Ultra 3.00 2GB 750 G	98.00	63,797.02
JUL 2007	Ventra LXP 2.67 2GB 500 GE	75.00	45,074.25
JUL 2007	DigiPad Mousepad	339.00	3,010.32
JUL 2007	UltraTouch USB Keyboard	120.00	4,797.60

Figure 5.33   Resized Calendar Month/Year Field

Now let's make the Product field just a bit wider so the text isn't truncated. Just as before, simply grab the handle on the right side of the field, but this time move it to the right (Figure 5.34).

Column Heading	Column Heading		
JUL 2007	Ventra LX 2.33 1GB 300 GB	165.00	90,748.35
JUL 2007	Ventra Ultra 3.00 2GB 750 GB	98.00	63,797.02
JUL 2007	Ventra LXP 2.67 2GB 500 GB	75.00	45,074.25
JUL 2007	DigiPad Mousepad	339.00	3,010.32
JUL 2007	UltraTouch USB Keyboard	120.00	4,797.60
JUL 2007	LightTouch Optical Mouse	95.00	1,519.05

Figure 5.34   Resized Product Field

Finally, we'll make the Revenue field a bit wider to accommodate the larger numbers. The final result should look something like Figure 5.35.

Hedijetijak Electronics Corporation

ZD_SALES_CR_001 (Sales Overview - Crystal Master)

Column Heading	Column Heading		
JUL 2007	Ventra LX 2.33 1GB 300 GB	165.00	90,748.35
JUL 2007	Ventra Ultra 3.00 2GB 750 GB	98.00	63,797.02
JUL 2007	Ventra LXP 2.67 2GB 500 GB	75.00	45,074.25
JUL 2007	DigiPad Mousepad	339.00	3,010.32
JUL 2007	UltraTouch USB Keyboard	120.00	4,797.60
JUL 2007	LightTouch Optical Mouse	95.00	1,519.05
JUL 2007	Computer Speakers	115.00	2,643.85
AUG 2007	Ventra LX 2.33 1GB 300 GB	12.00	6,599.88
AUG 2007	Ventra Ultra 3.00 2GB 750 GB	30.00	19,529.70
AUG 2007	Ventra LXP 2.67 2GB 500 GB	390.00	234,386.10
AUG 2007	DigiPad Mousepad	758.00	6,731.04
AUG 2007	17" LCD Monitor	1,650.00	387,733.50
AUG 2007	UltraTouch USB Keyboard	530.00	21,189.40
AUG 2007	LightTouch Optical Mouse	1,475.00	23,585.25
AUG 2007	Computer Speakers	1,300.00	29,887.00

Figure 5.35 All Fields Resized

Here's another time (and potential frustration) saver. If you're finding it a little hard to manipulate objects in the Design tab, it could be because of the small size of the objects at the default zoom setting of 100%. It can be particularly hard to grab the borders of sections or the resize handles of objects.

To help with this, you should get used to zooming your Design tab up by either clicking the + button on the zoom control or by moving the slider to the right. The zoom control is located at the bottom right of the window (Figure 5.36).

| Records: 23 | 4.7, 2.5 : 0.8 x 0.2 | | 100% |

Figure 5.36 Zoom Control

Even the best Crystal Reports developers can find it challenging to work at the 100% zoom level, especially when working on a high-resolution monitor. In the following example we've clicked once on the + sign to zoom up to 130% (Figure 5.37).

You may find it useful to do much of your design work at a higher zoom level than 100%. This is especially true when working with a "crowded" report when the text is small (under 8 points). The main point to remember is to get used to zooming in when necessary to make it easier to work with resizing and moving objects.

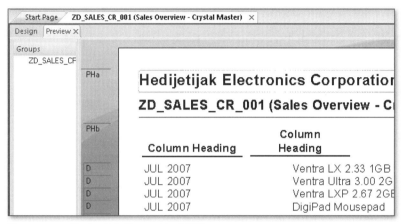

Figure 5.37   Design Tab Zoomed to 130%

Before we move on to moving objects, let's cover one more way to resize objects, this time in the Design tab. If you'd rather not use your mouse, you can use your keyboard to resize objects. Keep in mind, however, that this feature doesn't work in the Preview tab — only in the Design tab.

To resize an object in the Design tab using your keyboard, follow these steps:

▶ Select the object using your mouse.

▶ Hold down the ⟨Shift⟩ key on your keyboard.

▶ With the ⟨Shift⟩ key held down, use you're the Arrow keys on your keyboard to resize the object.

Try it now. Simply navigate to the Design tab and follow the above directions. If you'd like, you can try it with multiple objects at a time by simply selecting more than one before you use the Arrow keys.

5.5.3   Moving Objects

Now that we've gotten our first look at resizing objects in Crystal Reports, let's look at how to move them around.

First, just like resizing, it's very common to have to move objects around in Crystal Reports. As you're probably realizing by now, the Crystal Reports Design tab is very much a free-form environment. You can pretty much do whatever you want in terms of where you want to place objects.

We briefly cover the grid when creating our template. You use the grid in Crystal Reports to help align objects. With the grid on (the default setting), as you move objects they're forced to "step" through the grid. Depending on the size of the grid, you may or may not notice these steps as you move the object.

We recommend that you keep the grid turned on in Crystal Reports. We also recommend that you decrease the size of the grid from the default setting of 0.083 inches (1/12 of an inch) to either 0.04 or 0.02 inches. The reason for this is that this setting won't allow you to make finer adjustments when positioning objects on your report. We don't recommend setting it any lower than 0.02 inches.

You can also determine whether or not you want to see the grid in Crystal Reports. The default setting is for the grid to be invisible. This is a matter of personal preference. You'll find that if you set the grid to a smaller size, you won't want to see it. It turns your Design tab canvas grey because of all the dots. If you want to change any of the grid settings, just go to FILE • OPTIONS and go to the Layout tab.

Just as the Preview tab isn't a good place to add objects to your report, it's also not a good place to move them. In fact, you probably *never* want to move anything in the Preview tab unless you're very good with a mouse. This, of course, means you'll end up doing virtually all of your moving of objects in the Design tab.

Let's start moving. It's always best to resize all of your objects before you begin moving them, just as we've done in this exercise. If you don't, you'll find yourself moving objects more than once. Also, it's generally best to start at the left side of the Design canvas and work your way to the right. In almost every report the data will start on the left side of the page and progress to the right.

> **Note**
>
> When moving objects horizontally or vertically in the Design tab, always use the Arrow keys on your keyboard, not your mouse. There's no "constrain" key in Crystal Reports that you can hold down to restrict your movement to a perfectly vertical or perfectly horizontal direction when dragging objects with your mouse.

We'll now begin moving all of the fields in our Design tab over to the left. We could simply move one at a time, but we'll show you a technique that's a bit more efficient at getting the job done.

First, select all of the fields in the Detail section (remember, you can Shift + click them, use the mouse to lasso them, or use the Select All Section Objects command in the left margin of the Detail section).

Now press the Left Arrow key on your keyboard. Keep pressing it until the left-most field bumps up against the left margin. In many columnar reports you'll want to place your first field right up against the left margin. You cannot go past the left margin, but you *can* go past the right margin.

As soon as the leftmost field bumps up against the left margin, stop pressing the Left Arrow key on your keyboard. Now you can Shift + click on the leftmost field to unselect it. Press the Left Arrow again until the next field is close to the first field.

> **Note**
>
> How do you know when to stop? How close should you get to the adjacent field? This is part of the "art" of using Crystal Reports. There's no automatic way to set the gap between each field in the Detail section. You just need to learn how to position the fields visually.

Once the second field is in position, you can Shift + click it to unselect it and continue the process until all fields have been repositioned. When finished, the Detail section should look something like Figure 5.38.

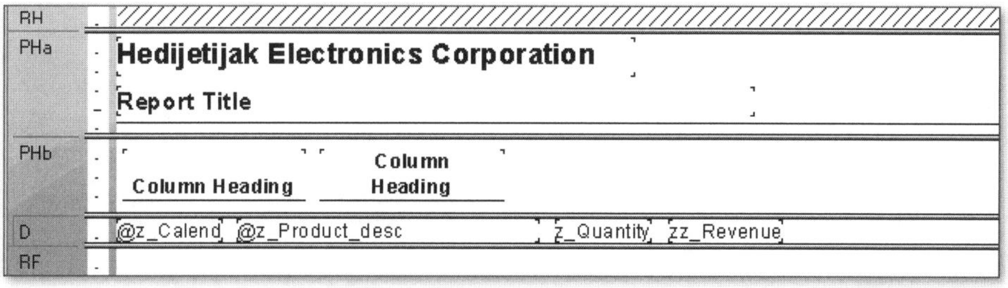

Figure 5.38 All Fields Moved in the Design Tab

When we look at our report in the Preview tab, we can see that the look has been much improved (Figure 5.39).

Hedijetijak Electronics Corporation

ZD_SALES_CR_001 (Sales Overview - Crystal Master)

Column Heading	Column Heading		
JUL 2007	Ventra LX 2.33 1GB 300 GB	165.00	90,748.35
JUL 2007	Ventra Ultra 3.00 2GB 750 GB	98.00	63,797.02
JUL 2007	Ventra LXP 2.67 2GB 500 GB	75.00	45,074.25
JUL 2007	DigiPad Mousepad	339.00	3,010.32
JUL 2007	UltraTouch USB Keyboard	120.00	4,797.60
JUL 2007	LightTouch Optical Mouse	95.00	1,519.05
JUL 2007	Computer Speakers	115.00	2,643.85
AUG 2007	Ventra LX 2.33 1GB 300 GB	12.00	6,599.88
AUG 2007	Ventra Ultra 3.00 2GB 750 GB	30.00	19,529.70
AUG 2007	Ventra LXP 2.67 2GB 500 GB	390.00	234,386.10
AUG 2007	DigiPad Mousepad	758.00	6,731.04
AUG 2007	17" LCD Monitor	1,650.00	387,733.50
AUG 2007	UltraTouch USB Keyboard	530.00	21,189.40
AUG 2007	LightTouch Optical Mouse	1,475.00	23,585.25
AUG 2007	Computer Speakers	1,300.00	29,887.00

Figure 5.39 All Fields Moved in the Preview Tab

Before we move on to some additional formatting tasks, we need to make one important observation concerning the formatting of reports using Crystal Reports.

> **Note**
>
> Because the resizing and moving (positioning) of objects in Crystal Reports requires a lot of eye-hand coordination and manual dexterity (along with a good eye for proportions), this is where some people find out they may not have what it takes to get the job done. If after practicing for a while, you still find it unnatural or difficult to perform these sorts of tasks, you may want to reconsider becoming a report developer. There's simply no getting around these very essential functions, and you end up doing them *all* the time.

5.5.4 The Finer Touches

You might consider what we've covered so far in terms of formatting as laying the foundation. The resizing and accurate positioning of objects is an essential first step in the process of creating a report in Crystal Reports. Now let's look at some other common formatting tasks that will further enhance the visual appeal of our report.

The first thing we'll do is reduce the decimal places of our Quantity field (Figure 5.40). The default display for any numeric field in Crystal Reports is to display two decimal places. The easiest way to change this to zero decimal places for the Quantity field is to simply select the field and then click the Decrease Decimals button in the Formatting toolbar two times.

Figure 5.40   Decrease Decimals Button

Now we'll format the Revenue field to display a dollar sign. The quickest way to do this is to select the Revenue field and then click the Currency button in the Formatting toolbar. However, when we do this we get a "floating" currency symbol, which looks like Figure 5.41.

JUL 2007	Ventra LX 2.33 1GB 300 GB	165	$90,748.35
JUL 2007	Ventra Ultra 3.00 2GB 750 GB	98	$63,797.02
JUL 2007	Ventra LXP 2.67 2GB 500 GB	75	$45,074.25
JUL 2007	DigiPad Mousepad	339	$3,010.32
JUL 2007	UltraTouch USB Keyboard	120	$4,797.60
JUL 2007	LightTouch Optical Mouse	95	$1,519.05
JUL 2007	Computer Speakers	115	$2,643.85
AUG 2007	Ventra LX 2.33 1GB 300 GB	12	$6,599.88
AUG 2007	Ventra Ultra 3.00 2GB 750 GB	30	$19,529.70
AUG 2007	Ventra LXP 2.67 2GB 500 GB	390	$234,386.10

Figure 5.41   Floating Currency Symbol

If this is fine for your reporting requirement, then you can do it this way. However, if your requirement calls for a fixed currency symbol (this is standard for most financial reporting), you cannot simply click the Currency button. You need to format the field by right-clicking the Revenue field and selecting Format Field (Figure 5.42).

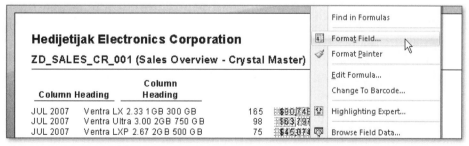

Figure 5.42   Format Field Menu Item

Selecting Format Field takes us to the Format Editor for numeric fields (Figure 5.43).

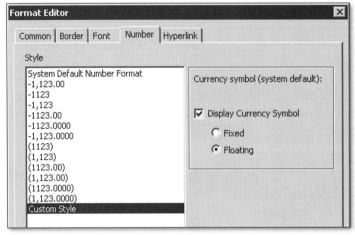

Figure 5.43 Format Editor for Numeric Field

As you can see from Figure 5.43, we now have the option to select Fixed for the currency symbol. Most business users prefer it this way. Once you add the currency symbol and select Fixed, you might have to resize your field if some of the values have been masked with a series of #s. If so, you should know by now how to resize the field without much difficulty.

There are many other ways you can format a field to suit your needs in Crystal Reports. Most of these are common formatting options that you're probably already familiar with: font, style, color, size, and so on. Some of the options are unique to Crystal Reports, and we will address several of these as we progress through our lessons (such as formatting dates). For now, we'll finish up our first report layout.

The final steps for our first simple list report will be to create some column headings and change the report title. To create the headings, we'll start with the sample column headings that we included with our report template. If for some reason you don't have a sample included with your template, you can simply create a new text object by clicking the Insert Text Object button.

As a side note, normally you'd use the same font and point size used for your data fields and set the style to bold. Also, as you might recall from our lesson on creating a report template, it's not a good idea to underline column headers. It's much more appealing to use a bottom border instead.

To create our first column header, all we need to do is change the first sample column header (the single-line header). To do this, first double-click the text box. This "activates" the box and puts you in Edit mode. Now just change the text. You can highlight the entire text string and retype the new text. We're going to change it to "Month/Year."

The next step is to select an alignment for the column that works with the corresponding field. Notice that we didn't say "matches" the corresponding field, because the alignment of the column heading doesn't have to be the exact same as the field alignment, although often it is. Here are some simple rules:

▶ For text field columns, you'll almost always match the alignment with the corresponding field, which will either be left aligned or centered. You typically use centered for any text that's of uniform length, in other words, when all of the values in the field are the same length (such as a product code).

▶ For numeric field columns, you'll almost always match the alignment with the corresponding field, which will always be right aligned. There are some times when you'll want to center the column heading rather than keep it right aligned, but that would be the exception to the rule.

▶ For date fields, you'll almost always center the column heading because date fields are typically centered (when formatted as MM/DD/YYYY). If the date is a period (normally a month or month/year) then you'd follow the rules for text fields.

Now our first column heading looks like Figure 5.44.

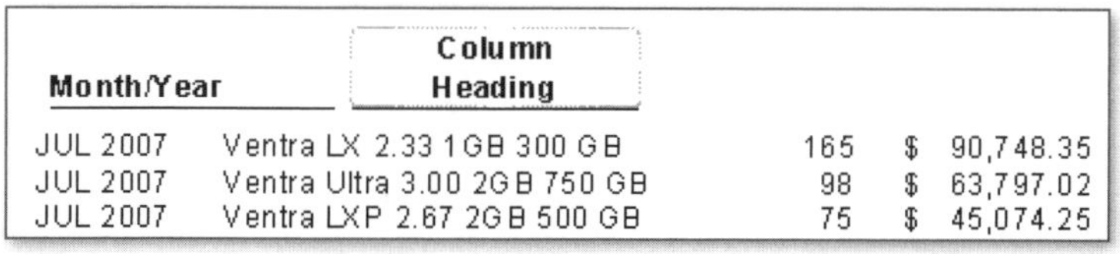

Month/Year	Column Heading		
JUL 2007	Ventra LX 2.33 1GB 300 GB	165	$ 90,748.35
JUL 2007	Ventra Ultra 3.00 2GB 750 GB	98	$ 63,797.02
JUL 2007	Ventra LXP 2.67 2GB 500 GB	75	$ 45,074.25

Figure 5.44 *Month/Year Column Heading*

All we need to do now is resize the column header, match the size of the header to the field below, and then line them up vertically. First we'll resize the header either by dragging the resize handle on the right side of the text box to the left or by using the Left Arrow key on the keyboard (remember to hold the ⌈Shift⌋ key down). If you want to use your Arrow key, please remember that this only works in the Design tab. Because in this case the column header text is just a bit wider than the month field below, we'll resize the header down until the "Month/Year" text just fits inside the box.

Now right-click the field (not the header) and select ALIGN • LEFTS. We right-click the field and not the header because we want the header to line up with the field below (because it's positioned correctly), not the other way around.

Your column heading should now look something like Figure 5.45.

Month/Year	Column Heading		
JUL 2007	Ventra LX 2.33 1GB 300 GB	165	$ 90,748.35
JUL 2007	Ventra Ultra 3.00 2GB 750 GB	98	$ 63,797.02
JUL 2007	Ventra LXP 2.67 2GB 500 GB	75	$ 45,074.25

Figure 5.45 *Month/Year Column Heading Resized and Aligned*

Before creating the other column headers, it would be a good idea to move the other three fields over a bit *because* the Month/Year column heading is crowding the next field.

Pop Quiz

Question: What's the fastest way to move the three fields to the right?

Answer: Move them in the Design tab using your Right Arrow key.

Once we've moved the other three fields to the right, we need to create the remaining three column headers. At this point the biggest decision we need to make is whether or not a particular column header is going to require one or two lines of text (sometimes you might need three, but you want to avoid this if at all possible).

Because the remaining three headers will be Product, Qty, and Revenue, we'll only require a single line for each column header. Because of this we'll delete the two-line column header sample that was part of the original template.

To create another one-line header for the Product field we can simply clone the first column heading.

> **Note**
>
> You can clone any object in Crystal Reports. Cloning is the fastest way to make a copy of anything. To clone something, all you do is hold down your Ctrl key and then drag the object.

After we make a clone of the first header we simply double-click the header and enter the new text. Now we have a new column heading for our Product field (Figure 5.46).

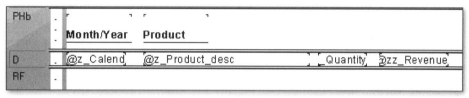

Figure 5.46   Product Column Header

Notice that the Product column header is currently significantly narrower than the Product_desc field. In this situation it's a good idea to make the column header the same size as the field. Just select both the header and the field, right-click the field, and select SIZE • SAME WIDTH. Follow this up immediately with a right-click and then select ALIGN • LEFTS (or Center or Right, because the two objects are now both the exact same width).

Now make another clone of the Month/Year column to make a header for the Quantity field. Why didn't we clone the Product header? We could have, but the Month/Year header is smaller and easier for us to handle. It's also closer to the size we need for the Quantity header.

We now need to rename the Quantity column header "Qty." Also, because Quantity is a numeric field, we need to make the text right-aligned. You can do this by just clicking the Align Right button in the Formatting Toolbar (Figure 5.47).

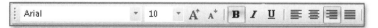

Figure 5.47   Align Right Button

Finally, clone the Qty column header to make the final column header for Revenue. Because the Qty header was already right-aligned, the cloned header will already be right-aligned as well. All you need to do is change the text to "Revenue." Be sure to resize both headers to match the width of the field below and align them vertically.

When you're finished, you'll need to ensure that all of the column headers are aligned with each other horizontally. Just select all four and then right-click one, select Align and then Bottoms. When finished, your headers should look something like Figure 5.48.

PHb				
	Month/Year	Product	Qty	Revenue
D	@z_Calend	@z_Product_desc	Quantity	@zz_Revenue

Figure 5.48 All Four Column Headers Completed

The final step for now is to change our report title. Currently the title is the name of the original report template that we used to begin this report. Go to the File menu and select Summary Info. Enter "National Sales Report" for the Title (Figure 5.49).

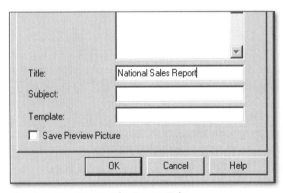

Figure 5.49 Entering the Report Title

When we go to the Preview tab, our initial list report looks complete (Figure 5.50).

Hedijetijak Electronics Corporation			
National Sales Report			
Month/Year	**Product**	**Qty**	**Revenue**
JUL 2007	Ventra LX 2.33 1GB 300 GB	165	$ 90,748.35
JUL 2007	Ventra Ultra 3.00 2GB 750 GB	98	$ 63,797.02
JUL 2007	Ventra LXP 2.67 2GB 500 GB	75	$ 45,074.25
JUL 2007	DigiPad Mousepad	339	$ 3,010.32
JUL 2007	UltraTouch USB Keyboard	120	$ 4,797.60
JUL 2007	LightTouch Optical Mouse	95	$ 1,519.05
JUL 2007	Computer Speakers	115	$ 2,643.85

Figure 5.50 Completed National Sales Report

The reason why the title now appears in the page header of our report is because the template we started from had the special field, "Report Title," in the page header. It's important that you always provide a report title this way by going to FILE • SUMMARY INFO.

That's it! Congratulations. You just completed your first Crystal Reports report using a BW query as a data source. This is just the beginning of many good things to come.

5.6   Sharing with Others

Before we continue on to the next chapter, we need to briefly discuss an important procedural issue — the process of making your new report available to others in your organization. Because this can become a bit technical and therefore tedious, we don't want to interrupt the momentum we've built up in this current lesson. However, we do need to at least mention it here so that you're aware of the issues involved and introduced to the basic process. We'll discuss this in detail at the end of the book in Chapter 11, Getting Published.

For now we'll just give you an idea of the steps involved in making your report available to others in your organization. Of course, we're making the assumption that this is something you want or need to do, which is usually the case. Most report developers don't create reports only for themselves.

First, some definitions are in order. What you've just begun learning is something known as *content creation*. Specifically, you've learned the basics of creating a report in Crystal Reports using SAP NetWeaver BW as a data source, and you'll soon be learning even more. As you begin developing real-world content on your own SAP NetWeaver BW system, you're (probably) going to need a way to distribute it to others. This is where a *content distribution* system (or platform) comes into play.

The content distribution platform that's used for Crystal Reports content is called SAP BusinessObjects Enterprise. As of this writing, the current version is Enterprise XI 3.1. Enterprise is a Web-based business intelligence content distribution and management system that provides a way for developers to make their content available to each end user in the organization. End users access the system to consume (view) BI content using a standard web browser.

SAP Business Objects also produces a mid-market version of the Enterprise system called SAP Business Objects Edge as well as an entry level version called Crystal Reports Server (for distributing Crystal Reports only). However, neither of these platforms integrates with SAP BW.

To get your report into SAP BusinessObjects Enterprise so others in your organization can access it, you publish it. The process of publishing reports into SAP BusinessObjects Enterprise in an SAP BW environment differs in some significant ways from publishing reports in other standard SQL environments (such as Microsoft SQL Server or Oracle). Fortunately for you as a report developer, you probably won't need to be involved first-hand in the details of putting your reports into your production environment. Typically all you'll be doing is getting the process started.

At this point we have to make one basic assumption: that someone either within your organization or from an outside consulting company has already installed and configured SAP BusinessObjects Enterprise and integrated it successfully into your SAP BW landscape. By "landscape" we're referring to the standard Development, Quality/Test, and Production environments that exist within every SAP customer site.

Assuming this is the case, the basic process from the report developer's perspective is this: The report is usually saved into an SAP BI role in your SAP BW development environment (much like a query would be saved) and then published into the corresponding SAP BusinessObjects Enterprise development server. This process can be (and typically is) configured to happen simultaneously. For the report developer it's as simple as saving a report. The only difference is where and how you're saving it.

For now, we're going to have you save your report locally on your computer's hard drive. To do this, you do *not* select FILE • SAVE. When saving a report that uses a BW query as its data source, if you select FILE • SAVE the report will be saved directly into SAP NetWeaver BW. Normally this is what you would do when you're ready to publish your report. But we won't be publishing any of the reports we create in this book, so you'll need to do a Save As command and save the report somewhere on your local hard drive. You should name it "Chapter 5 – National Sales List Report."

Again, we'll cover this process of publishing reports in detail in a later chapter. For now, let's continue on to the next topic: creating groups and summaries in Crystal Reports.

5.7   Summary

- When specifying the design of a Crystal Report it's usually a good idea to start with a broad, general idea of what the report should do and gradually work toward the specifics.

- It's important to keep in mind when specifying any report that most end users don't have the time (or motivation) to fully commit to the process. You must learn to make do with what you get. The key is to produce results as quickly as possible, which often will help motivate all interested parties to become more involved in the process. The longer the process drags out without any results, the more likely it is that everyone will lose interest entirely.

- Although we do explain how to create a Crystal Reports report directly from a BW query, it's always best to begin with a report template.

- It's very important that you understand the effect of adding additional characteristics to your Crystal Reports report when your data source is a BW query. When adding a characteristic, keep in mind that it might result in the generation of additional summaries (or aggregates) by SAP NetWeaver BW.

- This chapter, more than any other, is about mastering a set of manual skills. The process of adding, moving, resizing, aligning, and copying objects in Crystal Reports is repeated over and over with each new report. Early on you must take the time to become as efficient as possible in performing these tasks. A little progress in these areas can go a long way.

Now we dive into the next logical step beyond a simple list report – creating groups and summaries. This is where we begin organizing our data in ways that help us make sense of our data and begin to reveal trends and patterns. Think of it as a first step toward the world of analytics.

6   Summing It All Up

In this lesson we look at what is, beyond formatting skills, perhaps the most common task you perform when creating a report in Crystal Reports: creating groups and summaries. You group data primarily for creating summaries of any key figures (numbers) in your report, so the two go hand in hand.

The quickest way to recognize the need for a group when creating a report is whenever you see or hear the word *by* when discussing the report design. "I would like to see sales *by* division." "We need to list all products *by* type." "Can I get a list of employees *by* personnel area and seniority?"

Creating groups and summaries in a report that uses a BW query as its data source is a bit different than creating them in a report that gets its data from a transactional database. The difference is that the data coming back from a BW query is almost always already summarized. The only exception to this is when running a report at the document (or transaction) level from SAP BW. In every other case you're actually summarizing summarized data.

However, that's not important to understand. Our goal here is simply to help you understand why you need groups, how to create them, and how to leverage your groups to summarize the data in your report.

6.1   Creating Groups

Before we get into the specifics of creating a group in Crystal Reports, it would be a good idea to explore the various reasons why you would want to create a group in the first place.

Groups provide a way to, well, *group* your data. The primary benefit of grouping your data is that it gives you the ability to see the big picture and therefore compare and contrast the members of the group across various *metrics* — some sort of measure, or number, that indicates how a particular member is performing (or behaving).

The most common method for grouping data in any report is to group directly on a characteristic (or characteristics) from the data set. You may be wondering how else you would group your data. We'll get to that soon.

Creating a group directly from a characteristic is the simplest way to create a group. The most common type of characteristic to group by is a text (or string) characteristic. The second most common is a date characteristic. This is characteristic whose data type is a date field, not some other time characteristic (such as month or period) that would be defined as a text field. The least common type of field to group by is numeric, although it's certainly possible to do so.

The trickier type of group to create is when you find yourself having to group by something that's not in the data — at least not directly. Although it may not seem immediately evident, this is something that occurs quite regularly in any organization. Business end users are constantly creating new ways to look at their data. This could be driven by the need to track the impact some new initiative (marketing campaigns, promotions, etc.) or perhaps in reaction to some unforeseen industry development or to respond to the latest government regulation. A brief example will help explain.

Let's say you work for a hospital and are working on a new resource utilization report required by the board of directors. The goal of the report is to show the utilization of various resources (people, equipment, supplies) within the hospital by department and by floor. It's a six-story hospital. and the board wants to get a feel for how each floor is being utilized.

As you begin to group your report, you can quickly locate a Department characteristic that can obviously be used to group the data by department. Easy enough. But as you continue looking through the data, you find (to your dismay) that there's no *Floor* characteristic. Apparently whoever was putting the hospital database together didn't think to map each department to its floor in the hospital. And although the people in the hospital may know the floor of each department, unfortunately for you, the database doesn't have a clue.

There are essentially three ways to handle this sort of situation, each with its own pros and cons (and set of issues). The first way is to change the structure of the database. The second is to transform the data in the source database either on–the–fly or as you transfer it to a separate reporting environment (the data warehouse approach). The final approach is to handle it within the report itself.

Let's look at the first approach (change the source database). The benefit of this approach is that the change is both global and permanent (or at least until you change the structure again). The problem with this approach is that it typically takes an act of Congress to get it done, and even then it may take months or years to complete. Sometimes (especially with proprietary databases) it's not even possible to do this.

In the SAP world, this customization of the database is supposed to be done during the system configuration process that SAP customers go through when setting up SAP R/3 (or SAP ERP Central Component). During this initial configuration the "base" SAP system is customized to meet the unique needs of a particular customer. The process can require a significant amount of effort on the part of both IT and the business to identify and define the various data elements necessary to run that particular business. So, in our example, someone should have stepped up and mentioned that it would be a good idea to associate each department with the floor it's on.

However, it appears that, for whatever reason, this wasn't the case, because there's no such association in the source data. What happened? Usually one of two things: Either the need existed at the time of the initial configuration and it was simply missed, or (more likely) a particular business need has changed since the original configuration took place.

In our example that's exactly what happened. The requirement to track utilization of resources by floor is a recent development that arose out of a recent decision by the board of directors. Unfortunately all of this happened after the SAP ERP Central Component system was initially configured. The result is the business now needs to see something that, according to the system, doesn't exist.

So again, in this scenario one option is to reconfigure the system to incorporate a new data element (in this case, floor). However, as we mentioned earlier, this is typically not something that's done overnight. Sometimes not even close. And sometimes not ever. It completely depends on how complex the change is and whether or not IT considers it both feasible and worthwhile. And part of the reason why IT might not consider it worthwhile is that there are other options that (like surgery) may not be quite so invasive.

One likely option is to utilize something called a *hierarchy* in SAP ERP Central Component (as we'll see in a later lesson, SAP BW also uses hierarchies). A hierarchy is simply a way to structure, or organize, a particular characteristic. Perhaps the most common hierarchy across all SAP systems worldwide is a G/L Account hierarchy. This provides a way to take all of the base G/L accounts (the ones with numbers) and group them into your organization's own unique chart of accounts.

So, in our example, another option would be to have someone in IT help us create a new hierarchy for the Department characteristic. Given the relatively few departments and floors and the fact that the relationship between departments and floors is relatively stable (departments rarely, if ever, move across floors), this is an attractive and viable option.

However, when there are many different associations (hundreds or thousands) to maintain and/or a high degree of volatility in the relationship (associations change regularly), a hierarchy isn't a good option. In these cases the best option is to go back to the beginning and change the source system.

For simpler custom grouping scenarios you can also leverage a feature of BW queries called a structure. A structure is simply a way to organize members of a characteristic within a BW query. One difference between a hierarchy and a structure is that you're limited to a single level within a structure. Hierarchies can accommodate multiple levels.

Before the integration of Crystal Reports with SAP NetWeaver BW you were limited to the aforementioned choices when faced with this situation where no existing characteristic can be used to group your data to meet your business need. But fortunately, as you're about to see, Crystal Reports provides you with another level of options for creating custom groups.

One thing to keep in mind before moving on is that this idea of "regrouping" your data isn't uncommon and, depending on the volatility of your business environment, can even become quite commonplace. The question then becomes how best to handle it. In general, the closer you handle it toward the backend (the source system), the more time and effort it takes, and as you move to the frontend (in our case, Crystal Reports), less time and effort is required.

Although it's impossible to generalize on this across all industries and organizations, virtually every organization on the planet has to deal with at least some degree of change. Depending on the industry, the prevailing economic conditions, and the competitive environment, that degree of change can be a little or a lot — sometimes a *whole* lot.

> **Note**
>
> Our main point here is that the source data systems in your organization are designed to capture that portion of your business that's relatively stable and rarely changes over time. Those parts of your business that change regularly and are often temporary in nature are best handled either in some sort of meta-layer or with a frontend BI tool (such as Crystal Reports).

And although it's certainly true that the optimal approach is always to make the change in the source system data, the pressing nature of business needs often makes this impossible, at least in the short run. Given the transient nature of many of these changes, it may not even make sense to go to all the trouble of affecting a more permanent change. After all, what do you do when the business need changes again next month?

Before we venture into the world of custom groups in Crystal Reports, let's start with the more common situation of grouping on an existing characteristic.

6.1.1   Creating a Standard Group

You use the Group Expert in Crystal Reports to create any type of group. To create a "standard" group you simply select the characteristic you want to group by from within the Group Expert.

We'll begin our grouping exercises by opening the report we saved at the end of Chapter 5, which we named Chapter 5 – National Sales List Report. Before making any changes, let's save the report with a new name. Go to FILE • SAVE AS and change the name to "Chapter 6 Exercise 1 – Standard Group."

You should now see something like Figure 6.1.

Hedijetijak Electronics Corporation
National Sales Report

Month/Year	Product	Qty	Revenue
JUL 2007	Ventra LX 2.33 1GB 300 GB	165	$ 90,748.35
JUL 2007	Ventra Ultra 3.00 2GB 750 GB	98	$ 63,797.02
JUL 2007	Ventra LXP 2.67 2GB 500 GB	75	$ 45,074.25
JUL 2007	DigiPad Mousepad	339	$ 3,010.32
JUL 2007	UltraTouch USB Keyboard	120	$ 4,797.60
JUL 2007	LightTouch Optical Mouse	95	$ 1,519.05
JUL 2007	Computer Speakers	115	$ 2,643.85
AUG 2007	Ventra LX 2.33 1GB 300 GB	12	$ 6,599.88
AUG 2007	Ventra Ultra 3.00 2GB 750 GB	30	$ 19,529.70
AUG 2007	Ventra LXP 2.67 2GB 500 GB	390	$ 234,386.10
AUG 2007	DigiPad Mousepad	758	$ 6,731.04
AUG 2007	17" LCD Monitor	1,650	$ 387,733.50
AUG 2007	UltraTouch USB Keyboard	530	$ 21,189.40
AUG 2007	LightTouch Optical Mouse	1,475	$ 23,585.25
AUG 2007	Computer Speakers	1,300	$ 29,887.00
SEP 2007	Ventra LX 2.33 1GB 300 GB	100	$ 54,999.00
SEP 2007	Ventra Ultra 3.00 2GB 750 GB	225	$ 146,472.75
SEP 2007	Ventra LXP 2.67 2GB 500 GB	205	$ 123,202.95
SEP 2007	DigiPad Mousepad	1,125	$ 9,990.00
SEP 2007	17" LCD Monitor	1,260	$ 296,087.40
SEP 2007	UltraTouch USB Keyboard	1,370	$ 54,772.60
SEP 2007	LightTouch Optical Mouse	1,325	$ 21,186.75
SEP 2007	Computer Speakers	1,200	$ 27,588.00

Figure 6.1 Initial List Report

Although this may not have been evident when we created this report, the reason we call this type of report a "list" report is because the report doesn't contain any groups. Before we begin transforming this list report into a grouped report, we'll first add two grand total summaries to the report. Whenever you have a list report, the only type of summary you can create is a summary of all of the data in the report (or a "grand" summary").

To create our first grand summary, from the Design tab right-click the zz_Quantity field in the Detail section and select Insert and then Summary (Figure 6.2).

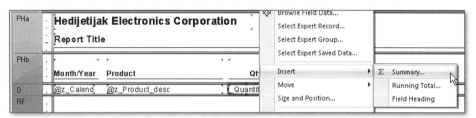

Figure 6.2 Insert Summary Menu Item

Next you should see the Insert Summary dialog box (Figure 6.3).

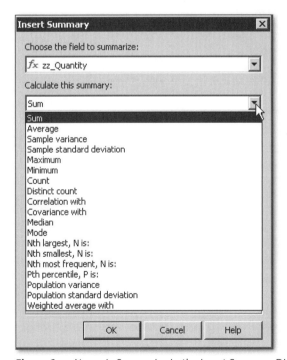

Figure 6.3   Insert Summary Dialog Box

One of the options in the Insert Summary dialog box is a drop-down dialog box where you can select the type of summary you want to insert. If you pull down the list, you should see the dialog box shown in Figure 6.4.

Insert Summary

Choose the field to summarize:

fx zz_Quantity

Calculate this summary:

Sum

| Sum |
| Average |
| Sample variance |
| Sample standard deviation |
| Maximum |
| Minimum |
| Count |
| Distinct count |
| Correlation with |
| Covariance with |
| Median |
| Mode |
| Nth largest, N is: |
| Nth smallest, N is: |
| Nth most frequent, N is: |
| Pth percentile, P is: |
| Population variance |
| Population standard deviation |
| Weighted average with |

OK   Cancel   Help

Figure 6.4   Numeric Summaries in the Insert Summary Dialog

The types of summaries you see in this list depend on the data type of the field you're summarizing. Usually you'll be summarizing a numeric field, which is the case here for our first summary. Some of these options will look familiar (such as Sum and Average) and others not so familiar (such as Covariance With and Pth Percentile, P Is:). We won't take the time to explain each summary type here but only say that there are many built-in summary functions for you to choose from in Crystal Reports.

The most common summary function by far (positioned at the top of the list) is the Sum function. We'll select this summary to create a grand total of the zz_Quantity field.

Before clicking OK, note that the second option in the Insert Summary dialog box is Summary Location. Because our current report is a list report (with no groups), the only option we have here is Grand Total (Report Footer).

In Crystal Reports the location of a summary determines the range of data that's summarized. If you want to summarize all of the data in a report, you place the summary in either the report footer or report header (the built-in summary functions work fine in header sections). When you start creating groups, you begin to get additional options to place the summary in either the group footer or group header.

After clicking OK, you should see Figure 6.5 when on the Design tab.

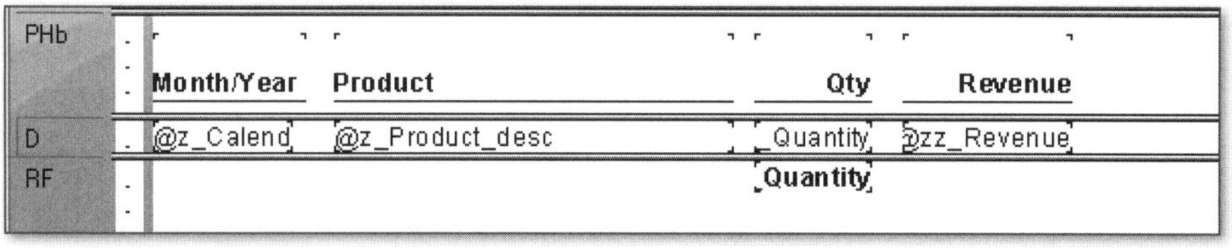

Figure 6.5 Quantity Grand Total

When you switch over to the Preview tab, you should see Figure 6.6.

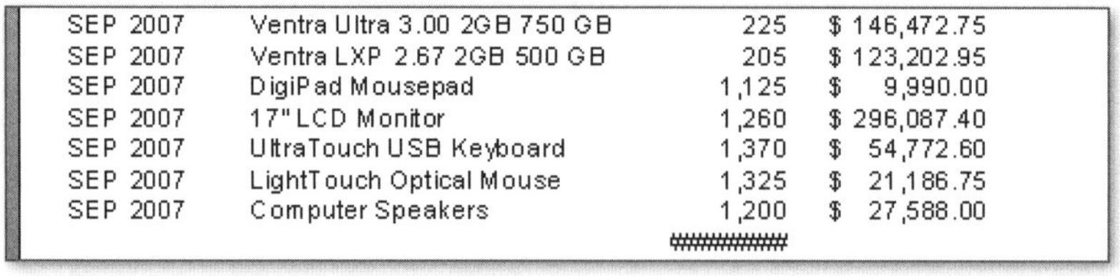

SEP 2007	Ventra Ultra 3.00 2GB 750 GB	225	$ 146,472.75
SEP 2007	Ventra LXP 2.67 2GB 500 GB	205	$ 123,202.95
SEP 2007	DigiPad Mousepad	1,125	$ 9,990.00
SEP 2007	17" LCD Monitor	1,260	$ 296,087.40
SEP 2007	UltraTouch USB Keyboard	1,370	$ 54,772.60
SEP 2007	LightTouch Optical Mouse	1,325	$ 21,186.75
SEP 2007	Computer Speakers	1,200	$ 27,588.00

Figure 6.6 Quantity Summary in the Preview Tab

Notice that the summary we inserted in the report footer is masked with #s. This is because the width of the summary object won't accommodate the size of the grand total figure. Recall from our previous lesson how to resize an object in Crystal Reports. As a reminder, the best place to resize a field so that you can immediately see the result is in the Preview tab.

> **Note**
>
> When resizing a numeric summary, it makes sense to "stretch" the summary object to the left rather than to the right. That way the right side of the summary remains aligned with the field above. To do this, simply grab the handle on the left side of the summary object and drag it to the left.

After you resize the summary field it should look like Figure 6.7.

SEP 2007	DigiPad Mousepad	1,125	$ 9,990.00
SEP 2007	17" LCD Monitor	1,260	$ 296,087.40
SEP 2007	UltraTouch USB Keyboard	1,370	$ 54,772.60
SEP 2007	LightTouch Optical Mouse	1,325	$ 21,186.75
SEP 2007	Computer Speakers	1,200	$ 27,588.00
		13,962.00	

Figure 6.7 Quantity Summary in the Preview Tab Resized

The last thing we need to do with this summary is format it. First, we'll change the decimal places to 0 decimal places to match the zz_Quantity field. To do this, while the summary is selected, click the Decrease Decimals button two times (Figure 6.8).

Figure 6.8 Decrease Decimal Button

The next thing we want to do is add a top border to the summary by clicking the Top Border button in the Formatting Toolbar (Figure 6.9).

JUL 2007	DigiPad Mousepad	355	$ 3,010.32
JUL 2007	UltraTouch USB Keyboard	120	$ 4,797.60
JUL 2007	LightTouch Optical Mouse	95	$ 1,519.05

Figure 6.9 Top Border Button

Now the zz_Quantity summary should look something like Figure 6.10.

SEP 2007	DigiPad Mousepad	1,125	$	9,990.00
SEP 2007	17" LCD Monitor	1,260	$	296,087.40
SEP 2007	UltraTouch USB Keyboard	1,370	$	54,772.60
SEP 2007	LightTouch Optical Mouse	1,325	$	21,186.75
SEP 2007	Computer Speakers	1,200	$	27,588.00
		13,962		

Figure 6.10 Quantity Summary with Border

No try the same thing with the zz_Revenue field. Once you've completed this, the two summaries should look like Figure 6.11.

SEP 2007	DigiPad Mousepad	1,125	$	9,990.00
SEP 2007	17" LCD Monitor	1,260	$	296,087.40
SEP 2007	UltraTouch USB Keyboard	1,370	$	54,772.60
SEP 2007	LightTouch Optical Mouse	1,325	$	21,186.75
SEP 2007	Computer Speakers	1,200	$	27,588.00
		13,962	**$**	**1,675,531.76**

Figure 6.11 Two Grand Totals in the Preview Tab

Now we have two grand total summaries in our report footer. Let's move on to the main reason we're here: creating groups and summaries.

As we stated earlier, the primary reason for creating a group in a report is so that group can summarize one or more numeric fields (key figures). When you create totals for a group, it's called a subtotal. Looking at our current report, we have two active characteristics in the Detail section: Calendar Year/Month and Product. Let's assume that our business requirement is to see the two key figures totaled by Calendar Year/Month. To do this, we first need to create a group on the Calendar Year/Month characteristic.

To create a group, click the Group Expert button in the Expert toolbar (Figure 6.12).

Figure 6.12 The Group Expert Button

You should next see the Group Expert dialog box (Figure 6.13).

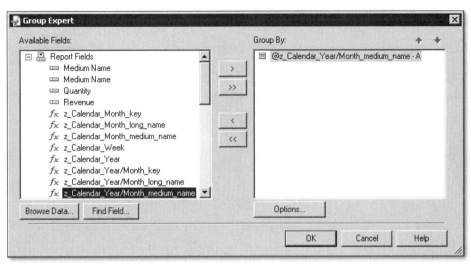

Figure 6.13 Group Expert Dialog

On the left side of the Group Expert dialog box are all of the fields that are currently being used in the report, followed by all of the defined formulas. Below that is the full list of all available fields from the data source being used in the report.

> **Important Reminder**
>
> As you'll recall, we spent a lot of time discussing the importance of creating aliases for all of the key figures and characteristics in your source BW query. The ideal way to do this is to create them in a report template before you get started on your actual report.
>
> In the preceding dialog box we get a chance to see another reason why we take the time to do this. At the top of our list of fields are two fields, each with the name Medium Name. One is the medium name for Calendar Year/Month, and the other is the medium name for Product.

We're going to group our report initially by Calendar Year/Month. Rather than group by the original characteristic, we'll use the alias we created as part of our original template: z_Calendar_Year/Month_medium_name. Simply click this and then click the right arrow, or double-click the alias to move it to the right side of the dialog box.

Before moving on we need to cover a few of the basic options you can set when creating a group in Crystal Reports. While z_Calendar_Year/Month_medium_name is highlighted on the right, click the Options button at the bottom right of the dialog box (or right-click the field and select Options). You'll then see the following (Figure 6.14).

Figure 6.14   Change Group Options

The first most basic option to set for any group is the sort order of the group. The options are ascending order, descending order, specified order, and original order. The first two options are self-explanatory. We'll look later in this chapter at specified order. Original order means the group will be ordered according to how it was retrieved from the database (no order). We'll see later that this option is used in one particular case: when grouping on a BW hierarchy. We'll leave this group sorted in ascending order.

Next select the Options tab at the top of the dialog box. You'll now see the tab page shown in Figure 6.15.

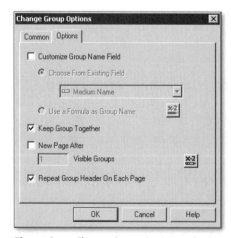

Figure 6.15   Change Group Options – Options Tab

We'll look at the Customize Group Name Field option soon. For now we'll discuss the Keep Group Together and Repeat Group Header On Each Page options.

Keep Group Together perhaps would be better named "Attempt to Keep the Group Together on One Page – If Possible." That's exactly what this option does. It tells Crystal Reports to try to keep the group on one page. The net effect is that if the next group won't fit on the current page, Crystal Reports starts the group at the top of the following page.

The last option on this screen is Repeat Group Header On Each Page. This does what it sounds like it does. It repeats the group header at the top of every page for a group that spans multiple pages.

You almost always want to turn both of these options on, so as a matter of habit you should turn them on when you create any group. After you click OK, the Preview tab should look something like Figure 6.16.

Month/Year	Product	Qty	Revenue
AUG 2007			
AUG 2007	Ventra LX 2.33 1GB 300 GB	12	$ 6,599.88
AUG 2007	Ventra Ultra 3.00 2GB 750 GB	30	$ 19,529.70
AUG 2007	Ventra LXP 2.67 2GB 500 GB	390	$ 234,386.10
AUG 2007	DigiPad Mousepad	758	$ 6,731.04
AUG 2007	17" LCD Monitor	1,650	$ 387,733.50
AUG 2007	UltraTouch USB Keyboard	530	$ 21,189.40
AUG 2007	LightTouch Optical Mouse	1,475	$ 23,585.25
AUG 2007	Computer Speakers	1,300	$ 29,887.00
JUL 2007			
JUL 2007	Ventra LX 2.33 1GB 300 GB	165	$ 90,748.35
JUL 2007	Ventra Ultra 3.00 2GB 750 GB	98	$ 63,797.02
JUL 2007	Ventra LXP 2.67 2GB 500 GB	75	$ 45,074.25
JUL 2007	DigiPad Mousepad	339	$ 3,010.32
JUL 2007	UltraTouch USB Keyboard	120	$ 4,797.60
JUL 2007	LightTouch Optical Mouse	95	$ 1,519.05
JUL 2007	Computer Speakers	115	$ 2,643.85
SEP 2007			
SEP 2007	Ventra LX 2.33 1GB 300 GB	100	$ 54,999.00
SEP 2007	Ventra Ultra 3.00 2GB 750 GB	225	$ 146,472.75
SEP 2007	Ventra LXP 2.67 2GB 500 GB	205	$ 123,202.95
SEP 2007	DigiPad Mousepad	1,125	$ 9,990.00
SEP 2007	17" LCD Monitor	1,260	$ 296,087.40
SEP 2007	UltraTouch USB Keyboard	1,370	$ 54,772.60
SEP 2007	LightTouch Optical Mouse	1,325	$ 21,186.75
SEP 2007	Computer Speakers	1,200	$ 27,588.00
		13,962	**$ 1,675,531.76**

Figure 6.16 Calendar Month Group in the Preview Tab

You've just created what might be considered a standard, or perhaps basic, group in Crystal Reports. This is when you simply select a field (or characteristic) and a sort order of ascending or descending to create your group. You'll find that most groups you create using Crystal Reports will be this type of group.

However, there are times when you need to do a little more work to create a group that will work for your particular requirement, as is the case with our current report.

6.1.2 Grouping by Date Using a Text Field

If you look closely, you'll see that we have an organizational problem with our Calendar Year/Month group. With an ascending sort order the group is now in alphabetical order (AUG – JUL – SEP) instead of the preferred chronological order (JUL – AUG – SEP).

We need to order our data in date order using a text field. Even though the Calendar Year/Month field (characteristic) represents a particular month and year, it does it using text, which when put in either ascending or descending order won't produce groups organized in date (or chronological) order.

When we first created our group using the Calendar Year/Month field, we had four sort options available to us: ascending, descending, specified, and original. The specified order sort option is a way to organize your group in a custom (or specified) order and at first glance appears to be a good option for us to remedy our current sort order problem. But although it would be a way to fix our immediate problem, it wouldn't work at all as a long-term solution.

The problem is that, although we can manually order the three calendar months currently in our report, what happens next time we run the report for completely different months? Our specified order would be completely wiped out, and we would have to rebuild it again based on the new set of calendar months. (We'll cover another situation soon where it makes sense to use a specified order grouping.)

If you cannot use an ascending, descending, or specified order grouping to create the correct sort order, what can you do? Situations like this call for the creation of a *custom* group, which is one of the best and most flexible features of Crystal Reports. You create a custom group in Crystal Reports by grouping on a formula instead of a characteristic (or field).

This is one of those places where we get things a little out of order — for a reason. We're about to dive right into creating formulas in Crystal Reports, which is a sizable topic all by itself. Notice that we haven't dedicated any one lesson to creating formulas, which is intentional for a couple of reasons:

► The best way to learn about formulas is to create them in context. All of the formulas in this book are created in the context of performing a specific task or function.

► There are as many types of formulas as there are different reasons for creating formulas — and there are many different reasons to use formulas when building a Crystal Reports report. We're intentionally focusing on types of formulas that are commonly used when creating reports specifically against SAP BW and therefore will "weave" them into each lesson as needed.

The current situation is a great example of a need specific to the world of SAP BW that requires a particular type of approach using a particular type of formula. It's very common with BW queries to only have string fields to represent various time periods (usually weeks, months, and years; sometimes quarters). Perhaps the most common time period found in any BW query is month or period (specifically, fiscal period).

One of the advantages of using the SAP BEx interface with a BW query is that the Bex analyzer puts these time periods in the correct chronological order automatically. However, in Crystal Reports they're treated just like any other string (or text) field and are therefore put in alphabetical order ascending or descending unless you do something different.

That "something different" is to convert the string time period into a date. Once you do that, you'll be able to use the standard grouping features of Crystal Reports, because Crystal Reports is good at grouping on dates.

We introduced you (briefly) to the Formula Editor in Crystal Reports in our first hands-on lesson when we created our initial report template. In that lesson you learned how to create a very simple alias formula (actually, the simplest formula you could possibly create). We're now going to go back to the Formula Editor, this time to create a formula that can be used to group our report in chronological order.

> **Note**
>
> The best thing to do for now is just hang on for the ride and follow along. For now we're not going to spend a lot of time explaining the particulars of this custom group formula. We'll explain why after we're finished.

To create a new formula, right-click the Formula Fields node in the Field Explorer and select New.... Then enter the following formula:

```
local numberVar nYear:= tonumber({@z_Calendar_Year_key});
If {@z_Calendar_Month_medium_name} = 'JAN'
  then Date(nYear,1,1)
else
if {@z_Calendar_Month_medium_name} = 'FEB'
  then Date(nYear,2,1)
else
if {@z_Calendar_Month_medium_name} = 'MAR'
  then Date(nYear,3,1)
else
if {@z_Calendar_Month_medium_name} = 'APR'
  then Date(nYear,4,1)
else
if {@z_Calendar_Month_medium_name} = 'MAY'
  then Date(nYear,5,1)
else
if {@z_Calendar_Month_medium_name} = 'JUN'
  then Date(nYear,6,1)
else
if {@z_Calendar_Month_medium_name} = 'JUL'
  then Date(nYear,7,1)
else
if {@z_Calendar_Month_medium_name} = 'AUG'
  then Date(nYear,8,1)
else
if {@z_Calendar_Month_medium_name} = 'SEP'
  then Date(nYear,9,1)
else
if {@z_Calendar_Month_medium_name} = 'OCT'
  then Date(nYear,10,1)
else
if {@z_Calendar_Month_medium_name} = 'NOV'
  then Date(nYear,11,1)
else
if {@z_Calendar_Month_medium_name} = 'DEC'
  then Date(nYear,12,1)
```

Before we go any further, we need to go through a mid-term reality check. It's important that you're as objective and honest as possible.

Rate your comfort level with what we've just completed. We aren't asking you how well you understood the particulars, just how *comfortable* you felt about the process of creating a formula.

Rate yourself on a scale of 1 to 5, with 1 being you felt very uncomfortable and 5 being you're doing just fine (perhaps just waiting for some additional explanation).

> **Note**
>
> If you have rated yourself a 1 or a 2, this could be an indication that Crystal Reports development may not be the best use of your time. The formula we just entered would be considered a mid-range formula in terms of overall complexity. Although it's hard to generalize, formulas with this level of complexity will most likely be a common occurrence if you decide to proceed as a Crystal Reports developer.

We have intentionally inserted a formula at this point to help you gauge your level of comfort about having what it takes to succeed as a Crystal Reports developer. As we discussed in an earlier chapter, although one of the primary goals of this book is help equip business end users with the necessary skills to develop their own reports, we must recognize that this doesn't mean most business end users will have what it takes to be successful.

However, if you've ranked your comfort level at 3 or above, you can take this as an encouraging sign (by the way, give yourself extra credit if you used copy and paste to complete the preceding formula).

Now let's rewind a bit and explain what we've just done. Keep in mind the objective of this formula: to produce a *date* from a time period text field because only date fields can be sorted in chronological order in Crystal Reports. Doing something like creating a date isn't something you want to code yourself. Fortunately for us, many of these really tricky jobs can be accomplished by leveraging one of the many built-in functions that come with Crystal Reports. The function we'll be using to create our date is appropriately named the Date function.

Here's is how all functions in Crystal Reports work: you supply the function with raw material (in technical terms an *argument* or *arguments*), and it returns a *result* to you. As you might imagine, each function is quite particular about what it "eats" so you have to be very careful what you "feed" it. Some functions require only one argument; others several. Often certain arguments are optional.

The Date function requires three arguments to do its job: a year, a month, and a day. As we mentioned, functions are very picky eaters. The Date function expects each of these to be in the form of a number. In other words, it expects to see three *numeric* arguments.

Now let's start dissecting the various parts of our date conversion formula:

```
local numberVar nYear:= tonumber({@z_Calendar_Year_key});
```

Our sample formula starts off by creating the first of these three arguments: a numeric year. We achieve this by utilizing a popular function in Crystal Reports called the ToTumber function, which takes a number that's stored as string (text) and converts it into a numeric data type.

The Calendar Year characteristic is a four-digit year stored as a string. This is standard for SAP NetWeaver BW. Our first line takes the Calendar Year and converts it to a number using the ToNumber function. It also takes that number and assigns it to a local variable that we've called nYear. We then use this numeric year value as the first argument for the Date function.

We'll revisit variables at least once more before the end of this book. For now it's just important to know that a local variable like the one we're using here is just a form of shorthand. It keeps us from having to use the ToNumber function over and over throughout the remainder of the formula. The keyword "local" here determines the *scope* of this particular formula. A *local* variable can only be referenced (used) within this one formula. The other two possible scopes for a variable are *global* and *shared*. Global variables can be referenced across formulas. A shared variable is used to pass values between a main report and a subreport. Later in Chapter 10 when we look at subreports you'll have a chance to use a shared variable.

After you have declared a scope for your variable you must declare a variable *type*. In our example we are declaring a numeric variable so the type is "numberVar." The two most commonly used variable types besides numberVar are stringVar (for text) and dateVar (for dates).

Lastly, we must give our variable a name. The name can be anything that makes sense but cannot be the name of a function, keyword, or operator. In our example we could not name our variable "Year" because this is the name of a Crystal function. Therefore we named the variable "nYear." The name also cannot contain any spaces.

After you provide a scope, type, and name for a variable you can then assign a value to the variable in the same statement. This is what the ":=" is for. It is the *assignment* operator.

```
If {@z_Calendar_Month_medium_name} = 'JAN'
 then Date(nYear,1,1)
else ...
```

The rest of the formula is a series of *If* statements. The *If* statement is used extensively in Crystal Reports development (along with its cousin the Select Case function). It's is a series of tests that checks the value of the Calendar Month medium name alias and creates a date via the data function using the numeric value for the month (JAN = 1, FEB = 2, etc.) and a 1 for the day (the day for us is irrelevant; we're only interested in the month. We couldn't use a real day value even if wanted to because we don't have access to one in this query. All we have is the year, month, and week.

Now that we've created our date formula, click Save and Close at the top left of the Formula Editor. Back in the Design tab we'll place our new formula in the Detail section to the right of Revenue and make it bold.

When you go the Preview tab, your report should look like Figure 6.17.

Hedijetijak Electronics Corporation

National Sales Report

Month/Year	Product	Qty	Revenue	
AUG 2007				
AUG 2007	Ventra LX 2.33 1GB 300 GB	12	$ 6,599.88	8/1/2007
AUG 2007	Ventra Ultra 3.00 2GB 750 GB	30	$ 19,529.70	8/1/2007
AUG 2007	Ventra LXP 2.67 2GB 500 GB	390	$ 234,386.10	8/1/2007
AUG 2007	DigiPad Mousepad	758	$ 6,731.04	8/1/2007
AUG 2007	17" LCD Monitor	1,650	$ 387,733.50	8/1/2007
AUG 2007	UltraTouch USB Keyboard	530	$ 21,189.40	8/1/2007
AUG 2007	LightTouch Optical Mouse	1,475	$ 23,585.25	8/1/2007
AUG 2007	Computer Speakers	1,300	$ 29,887.00	8/1/2007
JUL 2007				
JUL 2007	Ventra LX 2.33 1GB 300 GB	165	$ 90,748.35	7/1/2007
JUL 2007	Ventra Ultra 3.00 2GB 750 GB	98	$ 63,797.02	7/1/2007
JUL 2007	Ventra LXP 2.67 2GB 500 GB	75	$ 45,074.25	7/1/2007
JUL 2007	DigiPad Mousepad	339	$ 3,010.32	7/1/2007
JUL 2007	UltraTouch USB Keyboard	120	$ 4,797.60	7/1/2007
JUL 2007	LightTouch Optical Mouse	95	$ 1,519.05	7/1/2007
JUL 2007	Computer Speakers	115	$ 2,643.85	7/1/2007
SEP 2007				
SEP 2007	Ventra LX 2.33 1GB 300 GB	100	$ 54,999.00	9/1/2007
SEP 2007	Ventra Ultra 3.00 2GB 750 GB	225	$ 146,472.75	9/1/2007

Figure 6.17 Calendar Month Group in the Preview Tab

As you can see, we now have a date for each month in our report. Remember, the day isn't important — only the month and year.

The next step is to change our group so that it now uses our new date formula to group by. (It wasn't necessary to add our conversion formula to the Design tab to group by it. We only do it here temporarily to see the result of the formula in the Preview Tab.) To change any group, right-click in the left margin of the Design tab within the group header or group footer of that group (Figure 6.18).

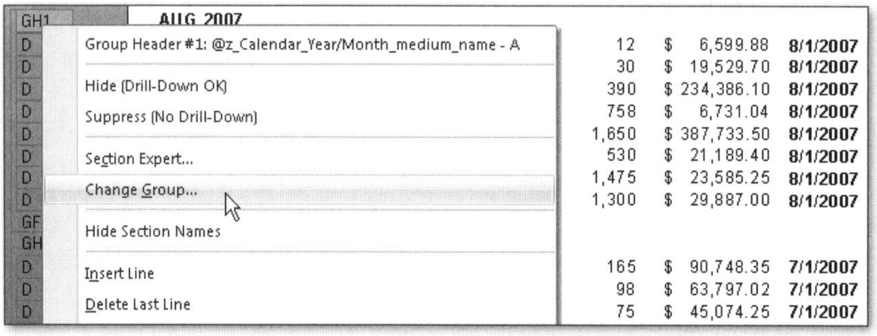

GH1	AUG 2007				
D	Group Header #1: @z_Calendar_Year/Month_medium_name - A	12	$	6,599.88	8/1/2007
D		30	$	19,529.70	8/1/2007
D	Hide (Drill-Down OK)	390	$	234,386.10	8/1/2007
D	Suppress (No Drill-Down)	758	$	6,731.04	8/1/2007
D		1,650	$	387,733.50	8/1/2007
D	Section Expert...	530	$	21,189.40	8/1/2007
D		1,475	$	23,585.25	8/1/2007
D	Change Group...	1,300	$	29,887.00	8/1/2007
GF					
GH	Hide Section Names				
D	Insert Line	165	$	90,748.35	7/1/2007
D		98	$	63,797.02	7/1/2007
D	Delete Last Line	75	$	45,074.25	7/1/2007

Figure 6.18   Change Group Menu Item

Next you'll see the Change Group dialog box. Now you can change the field that's being used for this report from z_Calendar_Year/Month_medium_name to the Convert Calendar Month to Date formula (Figure 6.19).

Notice that when we switch our group to a date field (or in this case, a formula), we get an additional option that says This Section Will Be Printed:, followed by a pull-down menu with various date groupings. The one we want for our report is For Each Month. We hope it makes sense to you that it would not make sense to group by anything less than a month (such as week or day) because our date formula only uses the month and year.

When you click OK and preview the report, you should now see the report in date order (JUL-AUG-SEPT) (Figure 6.20).

Figure 6.19   Grouping by a Date Formula

Month/Year	Product	Qty	Revenue
7/2007			
	Ventra LX 2.33 1GB 300 GB	165	$ 90,748.35
	Ventra Ultra 3.00 2GB 750 GB	98	$ 63,797.02
	Ventra LXP 2.67 2GB 500 GB	75	$ 45,074.25
	UltraTouch USB Keyboard	120	$ 4,797.60
	DigiPad Mousepad	339	$ 3,010.32
	Computer Speakers	115	$ 2,643.85
	LightTouch Optical Mouse	95	$ 1,519.05
8/2007			
	17" LCD Monitor	1,650	$ 387,733.50
	Ventra LXP 2.67 2GB 500 GB	390	$ 234,386.10
	Computer Speakers	1,300	$ 29,887.00
	LightTouch Optical Mouse	1,475	$ 23,585.25
	UltraTouch USB Keyboard	530	$ 21,189.40
	Ventra Ultra 3.00 2GB 750 GB	30	$ 19,529.70
	DigiPad Mousepad	758	$ 6,731.04
	Ventra LX 2.33 1GB 300 GB	12	$ 6,599.88
9/2007			
	17" LCD Monitor	1,260	$ 296,087.40
	Ventra Ultra 3.00 2GB 750 GB	225	$ 146,472.75
	Ventra LXP 2.67 2GB 500 GB	205	$ 123,202.95
	Ventra LX 2.33 1GB 300 GB	100	$ 54,999.00
	UltraTouch USB Keyboard	1,370	$ 54,772.60
	Computer Speakers	1,200	$ 27,588.00
	LightTouch Optical Mouse	1,325	$ 21,186.75
	DigiPad Mousepad	1,125	$ 9,990.00
		13,962	**$ 1,675,531.76**

Figure 6.20   Grouped by Date in the Preview Tab

Now that we have the report grouped by month and in the correct order, let's clean things up a bit. Notice that our new date group currently displays the first day of the month as the Group Name. Let's format the Group Name so that it displays the month and year as July 2007 and so on. To do this, we can leverage Crystal Reports' built-in formatting functionality.

Right-click the Group Header and select Format Field... You should then see the Format Editor showing the options for formatting date fields (Figure 6.21).

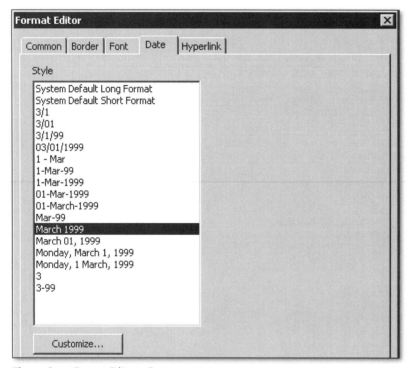

Figure 6.21 Format Editor – Date

We'll select the March 1999 option. If you want to get a feel for some of the custom options available to you for formatting a date field, you can click the Customize button. When finished (after expanding the Group Name field), your report will look like Figure 6.22.

Hedijetijak Electronics Corporation

National Sales Report

Month/Year	Product	Qty	Revenue	
July 2007				
JUL 2007	Ventra LX 2.33 1GB 300 GB	165	$ 90,748.35	**7/1/2007**
JUL 2007	Ventra Ultra 3.00 2GB 750 GB	98	$ 63,797.02	**7/1/2007**
JUL 2007	Ventra LXP 2.67 2GB 500 GB	75	$ 45,074.25	**7/1/2007**
JUL 2007	DigiPad Mousepad	339	$ 3,010.32	**7/1/2007**
JUL 2007	UltraTouch USB Keyboard	120	$ 4,797.60	**7/1/2007**
JUL 2007	LightTouch Optical Mouse	95	$ 1,519.05	**7/1/2007**
JUL 2007	Computer Speakers	115	$ 2,643.85	**7/1/2007**
August 2007				
AUG 2007	Ventra LX 2.33 1GB 300 GB	12	$ 6,599.88	**8/1/2007**
AUG 2007	Ventra Ultra 3.00 2GB 750 GB	30	$ 19,529.70	**8/1/2007**
AUG 2007	Ventra LXP 2.67 2GB 500 GB	390	$ 234,386.10	**8/1/2007**
AUG 2007	DigiPad Mousepad	758	$ 6,731.04	**8/1/2007**
AUG 2007	17" LCD Monitor	1,650	$ 387,733.50	**8/1/2007**
AUG 2007	UltraTouch USB Keyboard	530	$ 21,189.40	**8/1/2007**
AUG 2007	LightTouch Optical Mouse	1,475	$ 23,585.25	**8/1/2007**
AUG 2007	Computer Speakers	1,300	$ 29,887.00	**8/1/2007**
September 2007				
SEP 2007	Ventra LX 2.33 1GB 300 GB	100	$ 54,999.00	**9/1/2007**
SEP 2007	Ventra Ultra 3.00 2GB 750 GB	225	$ 146,472.75	**9/1/2007**
SEP 2007	Ventra LXP 2.67 2GB 500 GB	205	$ 123,202.95	**9/1/2007**
SEP 2007	DigiPad Mousepad	1,125	$ 9,990.00	**9/1/2007**
SEP 2007	17" LCD Monitor	1,260	$ 296,087.40	**9/1/2007**
SEP 2007	UltraTouch USB Keyboard	1,370	$ 54,772.60	**9/1/2007**
SEP 2007	LightTouch Optical Mouse	1,325	$ 21,186.75	**9/1/2007**
SEP 2007	Computer Speakers	1,200	$ 27,588.00	**9/1/2007**
		13,962	**$ 1,675,531.76**	

Figure 6.22   Group Name Formatted as Month and Year

Now we'll get rid of the redundant Month/Year field in the first column and the date formula we temporarily placed in the Detail section. It's standard procedure to remove a field (or characteristic) from the Detail section once you've grouped by that field.

Tip

It's not unusual to place things like formulas (such as our convert to date formula) in a report temporarily to test them to see what value is returned. If it isn't going to be used in the final report, you can either delete it or suppress it in some way (we'll look at suppressing objects later).

Once we have done this, we'll have our completed report grouped by date (Figure 6.23).

Hedijetijak Electronics Corporation

National Sales Report

Month/Year	Product	Qty	Revenue
July 2007			
	Ventra LX 2.33 1GB 300 GB	165	$ 90,748.35
	Ventra Ultra 3.00 2GB 750 GB	98	$ 63,797.02
	Ventra LXP 2.67 2GB 500 GB	75	$ 45,074.25
	DigiPad Mousepad	339	$ 3,010.32
	UltraTouch USB Keyboard	120	$ 4,797.60
	LightTouch Optical Mouse	95	$ 1,519.05
	Computer Speakers	115	$ 2,643.85
August 2007			
	Ventra LX 2.33 1GB 300 GB	12	$ 6,599.88
	Ventra Ultra 3.00 2GB 750 GB	30	$ 19,529.70
	Ventra LXP 2.67 2GB 500 GB	390	$ 234,386.10
	DigiPad Mousepad	758	$ 6,731.04
	17" LCD Monitor	1,650	$ 387,733.50
	UltraTouch USB Keyboard	530	$ 21,189.40
	LightTouch Optical Mouse	1,475	$ 23,585.25
	Computer Speakers	1,300	$ 29,887.00
September 2007			
	Ventra LX 2.33 1GB 300 GB	100	$ 54,999.00
	Ventra Ultra 3.00 2GB 750 GB	225	$ 146,472.75
	Ventra LXP 2.67 2GB 500 GB	205	$ 123,202.95
	DigiPad Mousepad	1,125	$ 9,990.00
	17" LCD Monitor	1,260	$ 296,087.40
	UltraTouch USB Keyboard	1,370	$ 54,772.60
	LightTouch Optical Mouse	1,325	$ 21,186.75
	Computer Speakers	1,200	$ 27,588.00
		13,962	**$ 1,675,531.76**

Figure 6.23 National Sales Report Grouped by Date

Let's add subtotals for each of our two key figures. The only choice we have is where to put them — in the header or the footer. Although summaries work perfectly well in either location, it's advantageous to put your group summaries in the group header rather than the footer.

First, it makes it easier to read the summaries and associate them with the group. Second, and more importantly, it's an important step to turning your report into a drill-down report that first displays the summary values only and then displays the details along with the summaries. You'll learn how to create this type of report in a later lesson.

There are two ways for us to create the subtotals we need. We could right-click each key figure and select INSERT • SUMMARY and then change the location of the summary to Group #1. This would place the subtotal in the group footer, and you could then move it to the group header. Although this works perfectly well, we'll show you another method you may find a bit easier.

Once you've created a summary for a particular key figure (or numeric field) you can easily clone it to create another summary to place in a different section. We already have a grand total summary for each key figure in the report footer. All you need to do is hold down your Ctrl key and drag each summary into the group header. Once you've done this, you'll want to remove the top border by selecting the summary and then clicking the No Border button (Figure 6.24).

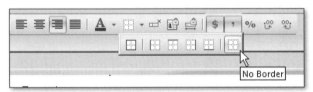

Figure 6.24   No Border Button

Now would be a good time to practice your alignment skills. Recall from our previous lesson how we can select multiple objects and align them by right-clicking on one of the objects and selecting Align.

Pop Quiz

Question: When aligning objects, does it make a difference which object you right-click when selecting the Align command?

Answer: Yes. You always right-click the "anchor" object — the one that every other selected object will align itself to. It will remain stationary while the other objects move.

After you've either used the INSERT • SUMMARY command or cloned the existing grand totals and placed them in the group header, your report should look something like Figure 6.25.

Hedijetijak Electronics Corporation

National Sales Report

Month/Year	Product	Qty	Revenue
July 2007		**1,007** $	**211,590.44**
	Ventra LX 2.33 1GB 300 GB	165	$ 90,748.35
	Ventra Ultra 3.00 2GB 750 GB	98	$ 63,797.02
	Ventra LXP 2.67 2GB 500 GB	75	$ 45,074.25
	DigiPad Mousepad	339	$ 3,010.32
	UltraTouch USB Keyboard	120	$ 4,797.60
	LightTouch Optical Mouse	95	$ 1,519.05
	Computer Speakers	115	$ 2,643.85
August 2007		**6,145** $	**729,641.87**
	Ventra LX 2.33 1GB 300 GB	12	$ 6,599.88
	Ventra Ultra 3.00 2GB 750 GB	30	$ 19,529.70
	Ventra LXP 2.67 2GB 500 GB	390	$ 234,386.10
	DigiPad Mousepad	758	$ 6,731.04
	17" LCD Monitor	1,650	$ 387,733.50
	UltraTouch USB Keyboard	530	$ 21,189.40
	LightTouch Optical Mouse	1,475	$ 23,585.25
	Computer Speakers	1,300	$ 29,887.00
September 2007		**6,810** $	**734,299.45**
	Ventra LX 2.33 1GB 300 GB	100	$ 54,999.00
	Ventra Ultra 3.00 2GB 750 GB	225	$ 146,472.75
	Ventra LXP 2.67 2GB 500 GB	205	$ 123,202.95
	DigiPad Mousepad	1,125	$ 9,990.00
	17" LCD Monitor	1,260	$ 296,087.40
	UltraTouch USB Keyboard	1,370	$ 54,772.60
	LightTouch Optical Mouse	1,325	$ 21,186.75
	Computer Speakers	1,200	$ 27,588.00
		13,962 $	**1,675,531.76**

Figure 6.25 Report Grouped by Month with Subtotals

The last thing we'll do with our first grouped report is add a detail-level sort. Sorting is always done at the detail (or record) level. In our example, we want to see the detail records (products) sorted by Revenue in descending order so that we see the biggest sellers at the top of the list.

To add a sort to our report, just click the Record Sort Expert button (Figure 6.26).

Figure 6.26 Record Sort Expert Button

After clicking this button, you'll then see the Record Sort Expert dialog box (Figure 6.27).

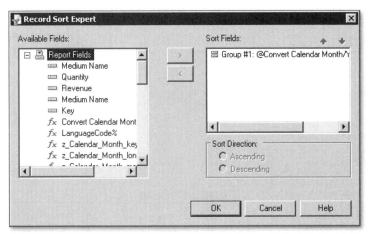

Figure 6.27 Record Sort Expert Box

Now we simply select the field we want to sort by on the left and move it to the right of the expert. In our case we'll want to select the Revenue key figure. We could select the original query field (toward the top of the list), but for sake of consistency we'll select the zz_Revenue alias we created earlier. After selecting this and moving it to the right, select Descending for the Sort Direction (Figure 6.28).

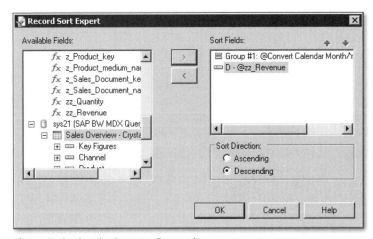

Figure 6.28 Sort by Revenue Descending

Now our report should look something like Figure 6.29.

Month/Year	Product	Qty		Revenue
July 2007		**1,007**	**$**	**211,590.44**
	Ventra LX 2.33 1GB 300 GB	165	$	90,748.35
	Ventra Ultra 3.00 2GB 750 GB	98	$	63,797.02
	Ventra LXP 2.67 2GB 500 GB	75	$	45,074.25
	UltraTouch USB Keyboard	120	$	4,797.60
	DigiPad Mousepad	339	$	3,010.32
	Computer Speakers	115	$	2,643.85
	LightTouch Optical Mouse	95	$	1,519.05
August 2007		**6,145**	**$**	**729,641.87**
	17" LCD Monitor	1,650	$	387,733.50
	Ventra LXP 2.67 2GB 500 GB	390	$	234,386.10
	Computer Speakers	1,300	$	29,887.00
	LightTouch Optical Mouse	1,475	$	23,585.25
	UltraTouch USB Keyboard	530	$	21,189.40
	Ventra Ultra 3.00 2GB 750 GB	30	$	19,529.70
	DigiPad Mousepad	758	$	6,731.04
	Ventra LX 2.33 1GB 300 GB	12	$	6,599.88
September 2007		**6,810**	**$**	**734,299.45**
	17" LCD Monitor	1,260	$	296,087.40
	Ventra Ultra 3.00 2GB 750 GB	225	$	146,472.75
	Ventra LXP 2.67 2GB 500 GB	205	$	123,202.95
	Ventra LX 2.33 1GB 300 GB	100	$	54,999.00
	UltraTouch USB Keyboard	1,370	$	54,772.60
	Computer Speakers	1,200	$	27,588.00
	LightTouch Optical Mouse	1,325	$	21,186.75
	DigiPad Mousepad	1,125	$	9,990.00
		13,962	**$**	**1,675,531.76**

Hedijetijak Electronics Corporation
National Sales Report

Figure 6.29 Report Group by Month with Subtotals and Sort

Congratulations! You've just completed your first grouped report. Before moving on, let's save a copy. Go to FILE • SAVE AS and name the report "Chapter 6 – Sales Report by Month."

If you got past our initial formula without too much stress, you deserve extra congratulations. Rest assured, we'll be returning to the Formula Editor a few more times before we finish. In fact, there's another need for a formula coming up.

6.1.3   Keeping Up with Business – Creating Custom Groups

We can't emphasize enough how powerful the ability to create custom groups is when creating reports in Crystal Reports. This one skill will get you out of more jams than almost any other skill you'll learn in this book.

We hope that by now you're getting the impression that the world of reporting isn't a static environment. Reporting requirements often change a lot because (especially these days) business changes a lot. The way you look at things today may not be the way you looked at them yesterday, and it may not be exactly the same tomorrow. And, as we mentioned earlier, it's very difficult to keep up with the pace of business changes on the backend of any data system (either at the source or *transactional* system or in a data warehouse system like SAP NetWeaver BW).

One of the benefits of any frontend tool like Crystal Reports is that it enables the report designer to move at the "speed of business" to react to changing business conditions. Business decision makers are constantly being challenged to look at their business activities and functions in some new way. Obviously the level of volatility varies widely from industry to industry and even among individual organizations within an industry, but it's safe to say that no organization is immune to having to deal with changing business conditions within their reporting systems.

To help illustrate how handy this feature is, let's look at some hypothetical examples. These are just a few examples of the almost countless ways you can leverage this highly flexible functionality in Crystal Reports.

Currently the products at Hedijetijak Electronics Corporation can be organized in a variety of ways. The InfoCube that we're accessing for our report (via a BW query) provides us with two options: Channel and Product Group.

Pop Quiz

Question: We just completed a report where products were grouped by calendar month. True or false?

Answer: This is a bit of trick question. It's not technically correct that we grouped products by calendar month. Think about it a second. How do products relate to time (other than when they are created)? In our previous report we were grouping product sales by calendar month. While products don't occur within a month, product sales do.

To begin, let's open the report we just created (Chapter 6 – Sales Report by Month) and do a Save As. Save it as "Chapter 6 – Sales Report by Specified Order Group."

The first thing we're going to do is change the group on our report from our date conversion formula to Channel (z_Channel_name). To do this, we need to right-click in the left margin of the Group 1 header (or footer) and select Change Group. In the Change Group Options dialog box change the field from the Convert Calendar Month to Date formula we created earlier to the z_Channel_Name alias formula. Keep the sort order as ascending. When finished, your report should now look like Figure 6.30.

Hedijetijak Electronics Corporation

National Sales Report

Month/Year	Product	Qty	Revenue
Fax		**170**	**$ 65,720.60**
	Ventra Ultra 3.00 2GB 750 GB	100	$ 65,099.00
	DigiPad Mousepad	70	$ 621.60
Internet		**10,388**	**$###########**
	17" LCD Monitor	1,910	$ 448,830.90
	Ventra LXP 2.67 2GB 500 GB	570	$ 342,564.30
	Ventra LX 2.33 1GB 300 GB	222	$ 122,097.78
	Ventra Ultra 3.00 2GB 750 GB	133	$ 86,581.67
	UltraTouch USB Keyboard	1,620	$ 64,767.60
	Computer Speakers	2,500	$ 57,475.00
	LightTouch Optical Mouse	2,375	$ 37,976.25
	DigiPad Mousepad	1,058	$ 9,395.04
Other		**110**	**$ 30,737.85**
	Ventra LX 2.33 1GB 300 GB	55	$ 30,249.45
	DigiPad Mousepad	55	$ 488.40
Phone		**3,294**	**$ 409,384.77**
	17" LCD Monitor	1,000	$ 234,990.00
	Ventra Ultra 3.00 2GB 750 GB	120	$ 78,118.80
	Ventra LXP 2.67 2GB 500 GB	100	$ 60,099.00
	UltraTouch USB Keyboard	400	$ 15,992.00
	DigiPad Mousepad	1,039	$ 9,226.32
	LightTouch Optical Mouse	520	$ 8,314.80
	Computer Speakers	115	$ 2,643.85
		13,962	**$ 1,675,531.76**

Figure 6.30 National Sales Report Grouped by Channel

Before we move on, we have a couple of housecleaning items to take care of. First, our group header needs to be updated. In the Design tab, double-click the Month/Year column header, *triple*-click to select all of the text (or drag across the text with your mouse), and then enter "Channel." Fortunately for us "Channel" fits nicely into our existing text box, so no re-sizing is required.

The next item is to expand our Revenue column a bit. You may notice that the subtotal for the Internet channel contains more digits than can displayed given the current width of the summary field (Crystal Reports masks the subtotal with #s). To fix this we have to resize the field.

We covered resizing objects in Crystal Reports when we created our first report, but this example is a bit trickier because it requires the simultaneous and synchronized resizing of multiple objects. Here's how best to handle this:

▸ We'll need to re-size four objects at once: the detail Revenue field (or key figure), the Channel subtotal, the grand total, and the column header. To do this we need to select all four at once. Although this can be done in the Preview tab, we strongly suggest doing this in the Design tab.

▸ In the Design tab select these four objects. As you'll recall, there are a couple of ways you can do this. You can use the ⎡Shift⎤ + click method or use the lasso method by dragging a rectangle across the objects with your mouse (Figures 6.31 and 6.32).

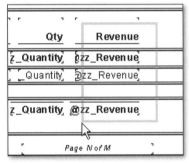

Figure 6.31 Selecting Multiple Objects

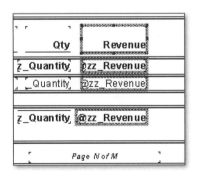

Figure 6.32 Multiple Objects Selected

▶ Now you can resize all four of these objects at one time. One way is to hold down the Shift key and press you're the Right Arrow key on your keyboard while in the Design tab. The other way is to switch to Preview and resize them by clicking and dragging the resize handle. Only one of the objects will have a resize handle (in our example the column header at the top).

Pop Quiz

Question: What's the advantage of resizing objects in the Preview tab?

Answer: You immediately see the result on your final output.

Feel free to try both methods to get a feel for the difference. If you decide to resize objects in the Design tab, you'll need to toggle over to the Preview tab to see the result.

Important Reminder

Whenever you're trying out different formatting options (such as resizing objects), remember that you can always click Undo to get back to where you started before your change was made. It's a good idea to get used to using Undo rather than trying to reverse the change yourself.

This would be a good place to put this into practice. Try resizing the objects and then clicking Undo (or Ctrl + Z). Then try clicking the Redo button. The more comfortable you get using Undo in Crystal Reports, the more confident and adventurous you'll become. You'll begin to find it very easy to try something new in your layout when you understand that you're just one click away from getting back to where you came from.

Once you've made these two cosmetic changes, your report should look something like Figure 6.33.

Now, on to some examples of why you might want to create a custom group in Crystal Reports.

Our first example will be simply a matter of sort order. In this case, we want the Other group member to be last. Currently it's the third member of the group because our sort order is Ascending. For obvious reasons Descending won't work either. Because these are the only two ways for Crystal Reports to automatically order a group for us, we need to come up with a way to take matters into our own hands.

Hedijetijak Electronics Corporation

National Sales Report

Channel	Product	Qty	Revenue
Fax		**170**	**$ 65,720.60**
	Ventra Ultra 3.00 2GB 750 GB	100	$ 65,099.00
	DigiPad Mousepad	70	$ 621.60
Internet		**10,388**	**$ 1,169,688.54**
	17" LCD Monitor	1,910	$ 448,830.90
	Ventra LXP 2.67 2GB 500 GB	570	$ 342,564.30
	Ventra LX 2.33 1GB 300 GB	222	$ 122,097.78
	Ventra Ultra 3.00 2GB 750 GB	133	$ 86,581.67
	UltraTouch USB Keyboard	1,620	$ 64,767.60
	Computer Speakers	2,500	$ 57,475.00
	LightTouch Optical Mouse	2,375	$ 37,976.25
	DigiPad Mousepad	1,058	$ 9,395.04
Other		**110**	**$ 30,737.85**
	Ventra LX 2.33 1GB 300 GB	55	$ 30,249.45
	DigiPad Mousepad	55	$ 488.40
Phone		**3,294**	**$ 409,384.77**
	17" LCD Monitor	1,000	$ 234,990.00
	Ventra Ultra 3.00 2GB 750 GB	120	$ 78,118.80
	Ventra LXP 2.67 2GB 500 GB	100	$ 60,099.00
	UltraTouch USB Keyboard	400	$ 15,992.00
	DigiPad Mousepad	1,039	$ 9,226.32
	LightTouch Optical Mouse	520	$ 8,314.80
	Computer Speakers	115	$ 2,643.85
		13,962	**$ 1,675,531.76**

Figure 6.33   Report Grouped by Channel with Formatting Changes

One option is a built-in feature of Crystal Reports called *specified order* grouping. As the name implies, this feature allows you, the designer, to specify your own custom order for any group. To make this change, right-click in the left margin of the group header and select Change Group (be forewarned: from now on we're just going to say, "Change the group").

Now change the sort order to In Specified Order. You'll see another tab appear called Specified Order. Select that tab. Here's where you enter the names for the group members in the order you want them to appear in your report. The names don't have to match the actual member name (for instance, you could name the Phone member "Telephone"). In most cases, however, you just enter the actual name of the group member.

We want our group to be in the following order:

- ▸ Internet
- ▸ Phone
- ▸ Fax
- ▸ Other

To accomplish this, simply enter the name of each member and press Enter. When you're finished, the Specified Order tab should look like Figure 6.34.

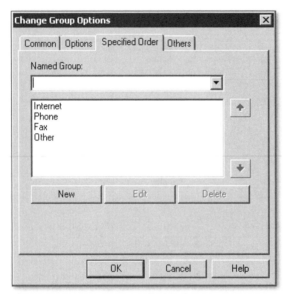

Figure 6.34 Creating a Specified Order Group

If you need to adjust the order of your entries, just select one and click the up or down arrow on the right. Now double-click the Internet entry at the top of the list, and you'll see the Define Named Group dialog box (Figure 6.35).

This is where you determine which value for Channel Name gets to be in the Internet group. Because we gave our groups the same name as the value we need, we don't need to make any changes here. However, if your group name doesn't exactly match the characteristic value, you'll need to change it. For example, if we had named our Phone group Telephone, we'd have to change the value from Telephone back to Phone, because that's the actual value in the data. If this sounds confusing at all, don't worry. We'll be covering an example of this next.

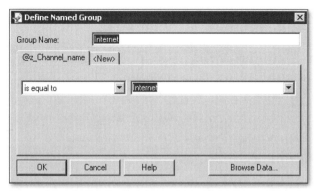

Figure 6.35 Define Named Group Dialog Box

Click OK here and OK again to go back to our report. It should now look like Figure 6.36.

Hedijetijak Electronics Corporation

National Sales Report

Channel	Product	Qty	Revenue
Internet		**10,388**	**$ 1,169,688.54**
	17" LCD Monitor	1,910	$ 448,830.90
	Ventra LXP 2.67 2GB 500 GB	570	$ 342,564.30
	Ventra LX 2.33 1GB 300 GB	222	$ 122,097.78
	Ventra Ultra 3.00 2GB 750 GB	133	$ 86,581.67
	UltraTouch USB Keyboard	1,620	$ 64,767.60
	Computer Speakers	2,500	$ 57,475.00
	LightTouch Optical Mouse	2,375	$ 37,976.25
	DigiPad Mousepad	1,058	$ 9,395.04
Phone		**3,294**	**$ 409,384.77**
	17" LCD Monitor	1,000	$ 234,990.00
	Ventra Ultra 3.00 2GB 750 GB	120	$ 78,118.80
	Ventra LXP 2.67 2GB 500 GB	100	$ 60,099.00
	UltraTouch USB Keyboard	400	$ 15,992.00
	DigiPad Mousepad	1,039	$ 9,226.32
	LightTouch Optical Mouse	520	$ 8,314.80
	Computer Speakers	115	$ 2,643.85
Fax		**170**	**$ 65,720.60**
	Ventra Ultra 3.00 2GB 750 GB	100	$ 65,099.00
	DigiPad Mousepad	70	$ 621.60
Other		**110**	**$ 30,737.85**
	Ventra LX 2.33 1GB 300 GB	55	$ 30,249.45
	DigiPad Mousepad	55	$ 488.40
		13,962	**$ 1,675,531.76**

Figure 6.36 Specified Order Group in Preview

That's it. As you can see, the our group is now ordered according to our specified order list.

Before we go on you'll want to save our current report. Go back and select Save As and save the report as "Chapter 6 – Sales Report by Specified Order Group 2" (just add a "2" to the end of the name).

For this example, let's change our group so that we're now grouping on Product Group rather than Channel (you'll need to select z_Product_Group_name when you select your field to group by).

> **Reminder**
>
> We warned you earlier that we were going to stop giving you the steps for changing a group. If you've forgotten how, go back a few pages to look it up. This is the way it's going to be for the remainder of this book. Once you've learned something, we stop telling you how.

After you change your group to Product Group, your report should look like Figure 6.37.

	Hedijetijak Electronics Corporation		
	National Sales Report		
Channel	**Product**	**Qty**	**Revenue**
Accessories		**10,047**	**$ 830,602.91**
	17" LCD Monitor	1,910	$ 448,830.90
	17" LCD Monitor	1,000	$ 234,990.00
	UltraTouch USB Keyboard	1,620	$ 64,767.60
	LightTouch Optical Mouse	2,375	$ 37,976.25
	UltraTouch USB Keyboard	400	$ 15,992.00
	DigiPad Mousepad	1,058	$ 9,395.04
	DigiPad Mousepad	1,039	$ 9,226.32
	LightTouch Optical Mouse	520	$ 8,314.80
	DigiPad Mousepad	70	$ 621.60
	DigiPad Mousepad	55	$ 488.40
Computer		**1,300**	**$ 784,810.00**
	Ventra LXP 2.67 2GB 500 GB	570	$ 342,564.30
	Ventra LX 2.33 1GB 300 GB	222	$ 122,097.78
	Ventra Ultra 3.00 2GB 750 GB	133	$ 86,581.67
	Ventra Ultra 3.00 2GB 750 GB	120	$ 78,118.80
	Ventra Ultra 3.00 2GB 750 GB	100	$ 65,099.00
	Ventra LXP 2.67 2GB 500 GB	100	$ 60,099.00
	Ventra LX 2.33 1GB 300 GB	55	$ 30,249.45
Hardware		**2,615**	**$ 60,118.85**
	Computer Speakers	2,500	$ 57,475.00
	Computer Speakers	115	$ 2,643.85
		13,962	**$ 1,675,531.76**

Figure 6.37 Grouped by Product Group

Take a look again at the results of our last group change. The group did indeed change from Channel to Product Group (we still need to change the column header). However, notice what happened to the detail data. Most of the products have been split into two entries. This behavior is unique to working with BW queries in Crystal Reports. Our key figures are temporarily aggregated by not only Product Group but by both Product Group and Channel.

To illustrate, let's temporarily add Channel back into the Detail section to the right of the Revenue key figure. Once we do this, it becomes apparent why we're getting the duplicate rows (Figure 6.38).

Hedijetijak Electronics Corporation

National Sales Report

Channel	Product	Qty		Revenue	
Accessories		**10,047**	**$**	**830,602.91**	
	17" LCD Monitor	1,910	$	448,830.90	Internet
	17" LCD Monitor	1,000	$	234,990.00	Phone
	UltraTouch USB Keyboard	1,620	$	64,767.60	Internet
	LightTouch Optical Mouse	2,375	$	37,976.25	Internet
	UltraTouch USB Keyboard	400	$	15,992.00	Phone
	DigiPad Mousepad	1,058	$	9,395.04	Internet
	DigiPad Mousepad	1,039	$	9,226.32	Phone
	LightTouch Optical Mouse	520	$	8,314.80	Phone
	DigiPad Mousepad	70	$	621.60	Fax
	DigiPad Mousepad	55	$	488.40	Other
Computer		**1,300**	**$**	**784,810.00**	
	Ventra LXP 2.67 2GB 500 GB	570	$	342,564.30	Internet
	Ventra LX 2.33 1GB 300 GB	222	$	122,097.78	Internet
	Ventra Ultra 3.00 2GB 750 GB	133	$	86,581.67	Internet
	Ventra Ultra 3.00 2GB 750 GB	120	$	78,118.80	Phone
	Ventra Ultra 3.00 2GB 750 GB	100	$	65,099.00	Fax
	Ventra LXP 2.67 2GB 500 GB	100	$	60,099.00	Phone
	Ventra LX 2.33 1GB 300 GB	55	$	30,249.45	Other
Hardware		**2,615**	**$**	**60,118.85**	
	Computer Speakers	2,500	$	57,475.00	Internet
	Computer Speakers	115	$	2,643.85	Phone
		13,962	**$**	**1,675,531.76**	

Figure 6.38 Duplicate Rows Caused by Channel

Because we had grouped by Channel before we changed the group to Product Group, our report is now aggregated by both characteristics. You just didn't know that before because Channel was being used to create a group and wasn't being displayed on the report. It isn't important that you understand why this happens, only that you know that it does happen from time to time and that you know how to readjust the summaries (aggregates) in your report when it does.

First, we'll remove the Channel characteristic from the detail section. Now we need to refresh the report so that we can get SAP NetWeaver BW to return the correct aggregates for Product Group only. After being refreshed, our report now displays the correct aggregates (Figure 6.39).

Hedijetijak Electronics Corporation

National Sales Report

Channel	Product	Qty	Revenue
Accessories		**10,047**	**$ 830,602.91**
	17" LCD Monitor	2,910	$ 683,820.90
	UltraTouch USB Keyboard	2,020	$ 80,759.60
	LightTouch Optical Mouse	2,895	$ 46,291.05
	DigiPad Mousepad	2,222	$ 19,731.36
Computer		**1,300**	**$ 784,810.00**
	Ventra LXP 2.67 2GB 500 GB	670	$ 402,663.30
	Ventra Ultra 3.00 2GB 750 GB	353	$ 229,799.47
	Ventra LX 2.33 1GB 300 GB	277	$ 152,347.23
Hardware		**2,615**	**$ 60,118.85**
	Computer Speakers	2,615	$ 60,118.85
		13,962	**$ 1,675,531.76**

Figure 6.39 Correct Aggregates After Refresh

> **Hot Tip**
>
> As you make changes to the structure of any Crystal Reports report that uses a BW query as its data source, you may need to refresh the report from time to time to get the correct number of aggregates.

The CEO of Hedijetijak Electronics is set to present the latest sales figures to the board of directors tomorrow morning. However, he has a big problem and he needs you to fix it. Today.

Somehow when the master data was set up for Product Group, someone got things a bit backward, and the CEO isn't happy about it. For some reason, Accessories and Hardware have gotten switched around. After a series of frantic emails are passed among the various accused parties, it appears that no one knows for certain how this happened. However, the CEO doesn't appear to be too concerned about how it happened. He just wants it fixed. Now.

So what do you do? The board of directors meeting is at 8:00 tomorrow morning, so changing the data on the backend (in SAP BW) isn't an option. Then you remember hearing about a feature in Crystal Reports called something like specified order grouping. Let's give it a try.

First, you need to change your group and change the order from In Ascending Order" to In Specified Order. Now select the Specified Order tab, enter "Accessories," and press `Enter`.

Double-click the Accessories entry, and you should see the Define Named Groups dialog box. You can now determine what value for the Product Group characteristic to use to create the Accessories member of the Product Group group. You can do this in one of two ways: You can enter the value into the box on the right or click the pull-down menu to pick the value from the list.

> **Warning**
>
> Be very careful about clicking the pull-down menu to pick the value from a list. Crystal generates the list by running your query. If your query takes a long time to run, you'll be waiting a long time to get your list. For larger data sets it's best to enter the value yourself — unless you have lots of extra time on your hands.

Because our query is a "quick runner," we'll select the correct value from the pull-down list (Figure 6.40).

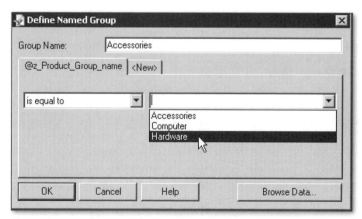

Figure 6.40 Define Named Group for Product Group

To correct our master data issue we'll select Hardware from the list. What we're now saying is that all records where Product Group is equal to Hardware will be placed in the group member called Accessories.

Now let's do the same thing (only opposite) to the Hardware group member. First, create the Hardware member by entering "Hardware" in the Named Group box on the Specified Order tab of the Change Group Options dialog box and pressing Enter. Double-click the Hardware entry and enter "Accessories" for the group member value and then click OK. Lastly, enter a "Computer" member. You don't need to change its value because the value for this group member is going to remain the same.

After we're done, let's change the order of the group to the following:

▶ Computer

▶ Hardware

▶ Accessories

You can do this by using the up and down arrows on the Specified Order tab of the Change Group Options dialog box. When everything is done (after changing the first column heading), your report will look like Figure 6.41.

Hedijetijak Electronics Corporation

National Sales Report

Product Group	Product	Qty	Revenue
Computer		**1,300**	**$ 784,810.00**
	Ventra LXP 2.67 2GB 500 GB	670	$ 402,663.30
	Ventra Ultra 3.00 2GB 750 GB	353	$ 229,799.47
	Ventra LX 2.33 1GB 300 GB	277	$ 152,347.23
Hardware		**10,047**	**$ 830,602.91**
	17" LCD Monitor	2,910	$ 683,820.90
	UltraTouch USB Keyboard	2,020	$ 80,759.60
	LightTouch Optical Mouse	2,895	$ 46,291.05
	DigiPad Mousepad	2,222	$ 19,731.36
Accessories		**2,615**	**$ 60,118.85**
	Computer Speakers	2,615	$ 60,118.85
		13,962	**$ 1,675,531.76**

Figure 6.41 Product Group Specified Order Group

Now all is well with the world again. You print your new report and hand it to the CEO. He smiles. Everyone breathes a sigh of relief, and you get to be the hero.

Admittedly, this is a pretty extreme example, but we do this for a reason. As far fetched as this may sound, these types of situations do come up all the time because it's not unusual for the data to get out of step with the business. In our fictitious example the problem was a mistake with master data. The more common scenario is when the need for a new way of looking at the data arises that isn't supported directly by the data. We'll look at an example of this type of situation next.

If someone from IT is reading this section, right about now they're probably on the verge of a heart attack. They might be saying something like, "This is crazy. You would never correct problems with master data in a *report.*" And they would be right. At least you don't fix the problem permanently. But this isn't meant to be a permanent fix. It's meant to provide a less than ideal solution to a difficult problem. The key is that it works and it works on time.

This is where best practices come face to face with hard, cold reality. Best practices often don't work best in less than ideal situations. Although no one would dispute that best practice dictates that this problem be fixed in the source system by fixing the master data, the fact of the matter is everyone was out of time. In these situations best practice takes a back seat to doing whatever it takes to meet the immediate need. There's always time later to do it the right way.

Again, we use a somewhat extreme example here to make a point. And the point is this: the *best* best practice is the practice that bends. It gives. It's pliable. This point recognizes that we don't live in an ideal world and that sometimes, in the words of Larry the Cable Guy, you've just got to "get 'er done."

Reminder
True best practice puts the needs of the business first.

Let's get even more practical. Let's say you agree (at least in principle) that there are indeed situations where you may need to make adjustments to your data inside a report. However, if we're going to handle these types of changes inside individual reports for any length of time, we need to pay attention to two very important considerations: *maintainability* and *portability*.

The degree of importance given to these two considerations is in direct proportion to the permanence of the fix. In other words, if the fix being handled by the report is temporary (as it would be in our previous example), then it doesn't matter much if the solution is either maintainable or portable. After all, it's only around for a very short while. This is the nature of an emergency fix.

However, as we all know too well, some temporary fixes have a way of becoming a bit more permanent, often quite unintentionally. Again, this isn't the ideal situation, but it does happen. If you think your temporary fix might stick around longer than you thought, there are ways to make it more manageable.

The one potential problem with using a specified order group is that it's difficult to maintain and not at all portable. This is because it's buried inside a single Crystal Reports report and must be maintained within that one report. In our previous example the need was to fix a single report. But what if 10 reports were affected? Or what about 100? At that point specified order grouping begins to lose its appeal.

This is why it's often best to use a formula to handle these kinds of situations in Crystal Reports. There are two primary reasons why this is true:

▶ First, you can do a lot more with a formula in terms of business logic than is possible with specified order groups. With a specified order group you're only able to evaluate the value of the characteristic being used for the group (in our examples it was first Channel and then Product Group). With a formula there's no limit to the number of conditions you can apply when forming your group.

▶ Second, and perhaps most importantly, formulas can be shared among multiple Crystal Reports, much like how objects (calculated key figures, structures, variables) can be shared among BW queries. You make formulas shared in Crystal Reports by saving them to the SAP BusinessObjects Enterprise *repository*. This is what makes formulas both maintainable and portable.

To give you an example of how this might work, let's take the exact same emergency requirement we just completed using specified order grouping and handle it using a formula.

First, be sure to save your previous report. Then do another Save As and call this report "Chapter 6 – Custom Group Using a Formula."

Now let's create our custom group, this time using a formula. Create a new formula (hint: open the field explorer) and call it "Product Group Custom Group." Then enter the following formula:

```
If {@z_Product_Group_name} = 'Computer'
  then 'Computer'
else
if {@z_Product_Group_name} = 'Accessories'
  then 'Hardware'
else
  'Accessories'
```

This is a multiple condition If statement, which is quite common in Crystal Reports. We created one earlier when we created a custom group at the beginning of this chapter. Now we get a chance at look at another example here.

Again, your ability to understand this formula would be a good leading indicator as to your long-term viability as a Crystal Reports developer. In simple terms, we first evaluate the Product Group name to see if it's equal to Computer. If so, we make the value of this formula 1Computer. If not, we check to see if it's equal to Accessories. If so, we make the value of this formula 2Hardware. If the Product Group name isn't equal to either of these two values, we set the value of this formula to 3Accessories (remember, in our example the requirement is to switch the Hardware and Accessories groups).

Click Save and Close at the top left of the Formula Editor. The next step is to change our first group so that we're now grouping on our newly created formula (Product Group Custom Group).

Pop Quiz

Question: What should we use for the sort order?

Answer: Specified order grouping.

In this case because part of the requirement is to order the groups in a particular order, we'll still be using specified order grouping just to determine the order of the group. The logic behind creating the group members is completely contained within our custom group formula.

Change the field we're grouping on for Group 1 to the Product Group Custom Group formula. Once you've done this, change the sort order to By Specified Order. Now you can enter the order for this group: Computer, Hardware, and then Accessories. Once you've created these, you can click OK to see your group.

We won't bother inserting another graphic of the report because it now looks identical to what it looked like before, when we were handling all of the logic in the specified order group definition. Or at least it should. Check yours and make sure that's the case.

There are many other examples of how this kind of flexibility to meet the often dynamic and sometimes unpredictable needs of the business end user community makes Crystal Reports a terrific tool for getting both you and your organization out of a tight space. Let's look at a just one more example of how you might use this flexibility to solve some tricky report requirements.

For this next exercise you'll need to open an existing report to use as a starting point. Save the current report and then open the "Chapter 6 – Sales Report by Month" report that we created earlier. Immediately do a Save As and name the new report "Chapter 6 – Custom Group Using a Formula 3."

The VP of sales has assigned the sales department at Hedijetijak Electronics to track certain types of sales for the months of July, August, and September to help gauge the success of a new mid-summer sales promotion. Specifically, the report should break out sales by three product categories:

▶ Strategic Products

▶ New Products

▶ Legacy Products

Because you're good at writing reports and are familiar with the sales process at Hedijetijak, you've been asked to help create this new report. The first step in the process (as with any report) is to determine the data source for your report. After checking with your IT department, you decide that the best data source for your report is an InfoCube that was created specifically for the sales department.

Fortunately for you, someone in the IT department has already created both a BW query and a Crystal Reports master template that uses this InfoCube as its data source. Upon opening the template in Crystal Reports, you open the Field Explorer to begin work. When you begin scanning through the available characteristics, however, it begins to look like the product categories aren't available, at least not in the template.

Upon further investigation you're told that this characteristic isn't available in either the BW query or the InfoCube. Furthermore, it's not even available in the source system (SAP R/3). The reason you're given is that the sales department just recently created these product categories and haven't added them to the source database structure and won't add them until after the system upgrade scheduled next month.

This isn't a good thing because the VP of sales wants this information now.

From a purely technical perspective, the IT department would be correct in stating that the sales department never did actually create these three new product categories because they don't exist in the database. Someone might even say that this is purely an "internal sales department initiative." And although that's certainly true technically, current business needs require that the sales department be able to track sales by these product categories, whether they officially exist or not.

Perhaps this sounds familiar. We're not faulting IT or anyone else for that matter. As the line goes in the movie *Babe,* "It's the way things are." But that doesn't mean nothing can be done about it.

Fortunately for you, you recently learned of a way to create custom groups in Crystal Reports by using a formula. All you need to know is which products belong in which category, which is easy enough to find out. So you set out to create your custom group by creating the following formula (which you name Product Category):

```
If {@z_Product_key} in ['PDS01', 'PDS06']
  then 'Strategic Products'
else
if {@z_Product_key} in ['PDS02', 'PDS04', 'PDS07']
  then 'New Products'
else
if {@z_Product_key} in ['PDS03', 'PDS05', 'PDS08']
  then 'Legacy Products'
```

We use the IN operator here along with an array (the text in square brackets) to determine which products belong in which category. You may notice that we're using not the product name (or description) in our arrays but the product key (or code). It's always best to use keys or codes in formulas when at all possible because this greatly reduces the chances of getting an error. If you were to use the product names, there's a good chance you would introduce a typo and the formula wouldn't work correctly.

When we close and save this report, we now need to use this new formula to create a Product Category group. Figure 6.42 shows what our report looks like before adding our new group.

Hedijetijak Electronics Corporation

National Sales Report

Month/Year	Product	Qty	Revenue
July 2007		**1,007** $	**211,590.44**
	Ventra LX 2.33 1GB 300 GB	165	$ 90,748.35
	Ventra Ultra 3.00 2GB 750 GB	98	$ 63,797.02
	Ventra LXP 2.67 2GB 500 GB	75	$ 45,074.25
	UltraTouch USB Keyboard	120	$ 4,797.60
	DigiPad Mousepad	339	$ 3,010.32
	Computer Speakers	115	$ 2,643.85
	LightTouch Optical Mouse	95	$ 1,519.05
August 2007		**6,145** $	**729,641.87**
	17" LCD Monitor	1,650	$ 387,733.50
	Ventra LXP 2.67 2GB 500 GB	390	$ 234,386.10
	Computer Speakers	1,300	$ 29,887.00
	LightTouch Optical Mouse	1,475	$ 23,585.25
	UltraTouch USB Keyboard	530	$ 21,189.40
	Ventra Ultra 3.00 2GB 750 GB	30	$ 19,529.70
	DigiPad Mousepad	758	$ 6,731.04
	Ventra LX 2.33 1GB 300 GB	12	$ 6,599.88
September 2007		**6,810** $	**734,299.45**
	17" LCD Monitor	1,260	$ 296,087.40
	Ventra Ultra 3.00 2GB 750 GB	225	$ 146,472.75
	Ventra LXP 2.67 2GB 500 GB	205	$ 123,202.95
	Ventra LX 2.33 1GB 300 GB	100	$ 54,999.00
	UltraTouch USB Keyboard	1,370	$ 54,772.60
	Computer Speakers	1,200	$ 27,588.00
	LightTouch Optical Mouse	1,325	$ 21,186.75
	DigiPad Mousepad	1,125	$ 9,990.00
		13,962 $	**1,675,531.76**

Figure 6.42   Report Before Adding Product Category Group

Now we need to add our new custom group. The question is, How? In this case we won't be changing the existing group, because we still need to see sales by calendar month. We need to add the group as a second group beneath the existing Calendar Month group. It's been a while since we actually added a group, so as a reminder, you need to click the Group Expert button (Figure 6.43).

Figure 6.43   Group Expert Button

In the Group Expert dialog box you need to select the Product Category formula we just created. It will be added as the second group.

Once you've added the Product Category group, your report should now look like Figure 6.44.

Hedijetijak Electronics Corporation

National Sales Report

Month/Year	Product	Qty	Revenue
July 2007		**1,007**	**$ 211,590.44**
Legacy Products			
	Ventra LXP 2.67 2GB 500 GB	75	$ 45,074.25
	Computer Speakers	115	$ 2,643.85
New Products			
	Ventra Ultra 3.00 2GB 750 GB	98	$ 63,797.02
	DigiPad Mousepad	339	$ 3,010.32
	LightTouch Optical Mouse	95	$ 1,519.05
Strategic Products			
	Ventra LX 2.33 1GB 300 GB	165	$ 90,748.35
	UltraTouch USB Keyboard	120	$ 4,797.60
August 2007		**6,145**	**$ 729,641.87**
Legacy Products			
	17" LCD Monitor	1,650	$ 387,733.50
	Ventra LXP 2.67 2GB 500 GB	390	$ 234,386.10
	Computer Speakers	1,300	$ 29,887.00
New Products			
	LightTouch Optical Mouse	1,475	$ 23,585.25
	Ventra Ultra 3.00 2GB 750 GB	30	$ 19,529.70
	DigiPad Mousepad	758	$ 6,731.04

Figure 6.44 Adding Product Category Custom Group

Now we need to make a couple of minor changes. First, we'll indent the new Product Category group header to the right. Next, we'll add subtotals for our new group (this is a basic part of the requirement — to see total sales by product category within a given month).

Question: What is the fastest way to create these new subtotals?

Answer: Clone the existing Calendar Month subtotals and place them in the Product Category group header.

In case you've forgotten how to clone objects in Crystal Reports, all you need to do is hold down the `Ctrl` key on your keyboard and then drag the object to the desired location. In our case we'll simply `Ctrl` + drag the Calendar Month subtotals down to the Product Category group header below. Unless you're very steady with the mouse, you may need to realign the new subtotal with the other objects in that column.

Reminder

When performing formatting tasks in the Design tab, consider zooming the layout up from 100%. You do this by sliding or clicking the zoom control at the bottom left.

Now our report looks like Figure 6.45.

Hedijetijak Electronics Corporation

National Sales Report

Month/Year	Product	Qty	Revenue
July 2007		**1,007**	**$ 211,590.44**
Legacy Products		**190**	**$ 47,718.10**
	Ventra LXP 2.67 2GB 500 GB	75	$ 45,074.25
	Computer Speakers	115	$ 2,643.85
New Products		**532**	**$ 68,326.39**
	Ventra Ultra 3.00 2GB 750 GB	98	$ 63,797.02
	DigiPad Mousepad	339	$ 3,010.32
	LightTouch Optical Mouse	95	$ 1,519.05
Strategic Products		**285**	**$ 95,545.95**
	Ventra LX 2.33 1GB 300 GB	165	$ 90,748.35
	UltraTouch USB Keyboard	120	$ 4,797.60
August 2007		**6,145**	**$ 729,641.87**
Legacy Products		**3,340**	**$ 652,006.60**
	17" LCD Monitor	1,650	$ 387,733.50
	Ventra LXP 2.67 2GB 500 GB	390	$ 234,386.10
	Computer Speakers	1,300	$ 29,887.00

Figure 6.45 Product Category Group with Subtotals

In just a few minutes you've successfully transformed an existing sales report into an updated version that will meet the new needs of the sales department. And you'll make the VP of sales very happy.

But of course, as the saying goes, the reward for a job well done is that you get another job to do well, which is the case here. After having expressed her complete satisfaction with your report, the VP of sales immediately asks if it might be possible to see a slightly different version of the report. All she wants is a version that's grouped first by product category and then by calendar month.

Fortunately for you, this isn't at all difficult to do in Crystal Reports. Before we make our change, however, let's save the work we've done so far on our Chapter 6 – Custom Group Using a Formula 3 report. Now do another Save As and save the report this time as Chapter 6 – Custom Group Using a Formula 4.

Changing the order of groups in Crystal Reports is quite simple. There are two ways of doing it: the fun way and the not-so-fun way. We'll show you the not-so-fun way first. You can change the order of your groups by simply opening the Group Expert and then selecting a group and clicking the up or down arrows on the top right on the screen (Figure 6.46).

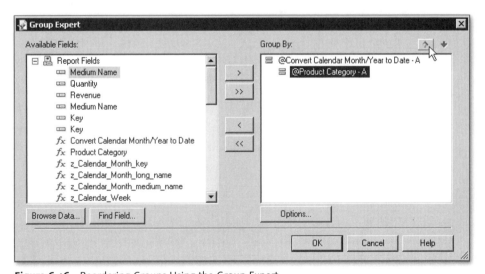

Figure 6.46 Reordering Groups Using the Group Expert

This method works just fine. It's just not as gratifying as the second method. The other way to reorder groups is by dragging the group header section up or down in the Design tab. In our case, we can drag the Product Category group header up until it's switched with the Calendar Month group header.

The trick to doing this is to grab the group header in the left margin of the Design tab using your mouse (Figure 6.47).

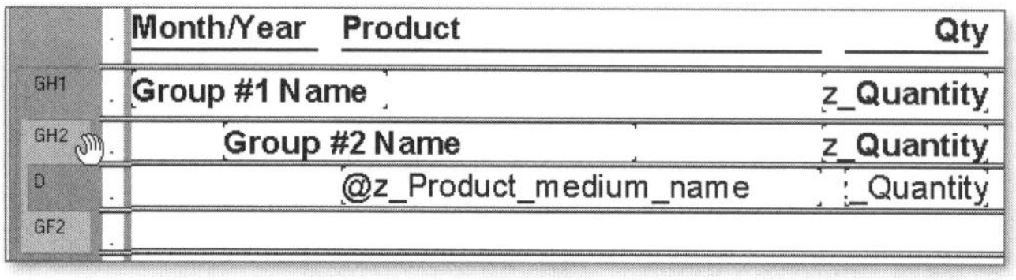

Figure 6.47 Grabbing the Group Header

Notice that when you do this your cursor turns into a little hand. But the best part is next: you can now drag the group header section up until you see a dark blue line appear around Group 1 (Figure 6.48).

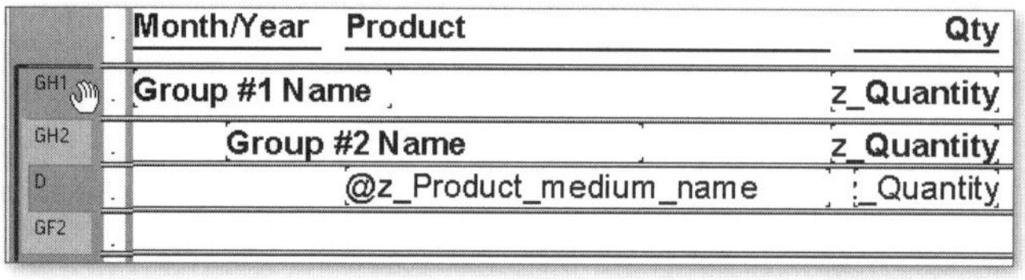

Figure 6.48 Swapping Groups in the Design Tab

The only visual change you might notice in the Design tab is the group names: they'll switch both names and position, as you can see in Figure 6.49.

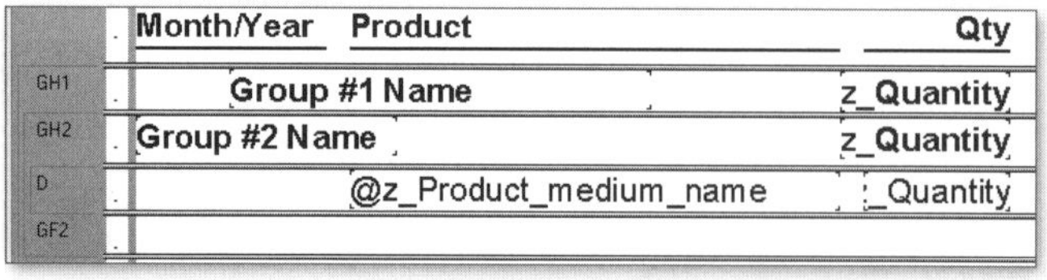

Figure 6.49 Groups Swapped in Design Tab

Notice that in the Design tab you cannot immediately tell what you're grouping by for each group, especially when showing short section names, as we are here. All you see is GH1 and GH2. A quick way to see what you're grouping by for any one group is to "hover" your mouse over the left margin of the group header (Figure 6.50).

Figure 6.50 Displaying the Group Name in the Design Tab

Now all we need to do is swap the horizontal positions of the two headers by moving Group #1 Name back to the left and Group #2 Name over to the right and change the first column header to "Product Category" (Figure 6.51).

Product Category	Product	Qty
Group #1 Name		z_Quantity
Group #2 Name		z_Quantity
@z_Product_medium_name		Quantity

Figure 6.51 Changing Position of Group Headers

The final change we'll make is to change the display of the Revenue column from two decimal places to zero decimal places (this is the most common display setting for summary reports).

Pop Quiz

Question: What's the fastest way to change the decimal place settings for these four objects (detail, grand total, and two subtotals)?

Answer: Select all four in the Design tab and then click the Decrease Decimals button two times.

When finished, your new report should now look like Figure 6.52.

Hedijetijak Electronics Corporation

National Sales Report

Product Category	Product	Qty		Revenue
Legacy Products		**6,195**	**$**	**1,146,603**
July 2007		**190**	**$**	**47,718**
	Ventra LXP 2.67 2GB 500 GB	75	$	45,074
	Computer Speakers	115	$	2,644
August 2007		**3,340**	**$**	**652,007**
	17" LCD Monitor	1,650	$	387,734
	Ventra LXP 2.67 2GB 500 GB	390	$	234,386
	Computer Speakers	1,300	$	29,887
September 2007		**2,665**	**$**	**446,878**
	17" LCD Monitor	1,260	$	296,087
	Ventra LXP 2.67 2GB 500 GB	205	$	123,203
	Computer Speakers	1,200	$	27,588

Figure 6.52   Completed Report with Product Category and Calendar Month Groups

Let's make on final "tweak" on this report before we move on. You may notice that there's a space between the Calendar Month groups. We'd like to tighten up this space to reduce the length of our report.

Pop Quiz

Question: What's causing this extra space?

Answer: The group footer for Group #2 (Calendar Month).

You should remember from our first lesson how to change the size of a section. In case you don't, all you need to do is grab the bottom border of the section and drag up or down. Reduce the size of group footer 2. This is how you adjust spacing in Crystal Reports — by changing the size of individual sections.

Let's take a second to review what we just did (and the implications of how we did it). Having created a perfectly useful report, we were rewarded by being asked to create another version. So far, nothing unusual. However, we've just run headlong into the Achilles' heel of Crystal Reports: they tend to reproduce like rabbits.

This has always been the single biggest "push back" from IT concerning Crystal Reports — the fact that they have traditionally been very static in nature. In other words, if I wanted a slightly different version of an existing report, that meant having to create a completely new report. True, I could begin with the existing report as a starting point, but when I was finished I still ended up with two separate reports (as we have in our exercise). You can guess why this might be a problem: maintenance. This is the biggest reason there are so many "orphaned" reports out there. It simply becomes too difficult to maintain all of the different versions that tend to get created over time.

This is why one of the new features available in Crystal Reports 2008 is so exciting (and powerful). This feature is called *non-data parameters*. As you might imagine, we'll be covering this in detail in a later lesson. For now, all you need to know is that these non-data parameters (or prompts) allow report consumers to select various options that can then be used to dynamically change the layout of the report. In Crystal Reports terminology, this is called *dynamic formatting*.

This new development is huge because it provides a mechanism to "stretch" your Crystal Reports to accommodate more than a single report requirement. And depending on how good you get at using this new feature, you can potentially create a single report that can meet the demands of many different report requirements.

That's about it for grouping for now — at least as a separate topic. We'll be using groups from time to time throughout the remainder of this book. Now we need to move on to our final topic of this chapter: summaries.

6.1.4 Leveraging Built-In Summary Functions in Crystal Reports

We've already introduced you to one of the built-in summary functions in Crystal Reports: the Sum function. This is by far the most popular summary function in Crystal Reports (or in any other reporting application).

The Sum function is both useful and simple to understand. However, there are many other built-in summaries that you can leverage in Crystal Reports. Let's take a look at a few of these in more detail.

First, if you want to see a list of all of the numeric summary functions in Crystal Reports, you can right-click on any numeric field (key figure) in the Detail section and select INSERT • SUMMARY. This will take you to the list in Figure 6.53.

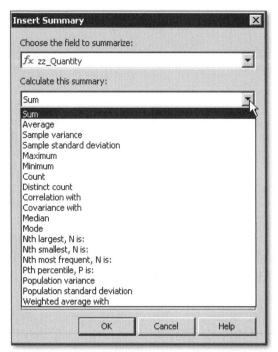

Figure 6.53 Built-in Numeric Summaries in Crystal Reports

The second most common numeric function is Average. Again, this is a fairly simple summary to understand. The one thing you may want to know is that you cannot use average to calculate the average of a percentage. If you need to calculate the average of a percentage, you must use the Weighted Average With function.

The next two functions on the list are, like some of the other summary functions, probably not used very much in the real world, except perhaps by those brave few who understand statistics. These are Sample Variance and Sample Standard Deviation. The easiest to understand of the other statistical functions are Median and Mode, with Median being the exact middle value of a series of numbers and the Mode being the most frequent value. Because this isn't a statistics class, we'll skip over the remaining statistical functions.

Before moving on, we'll mention two more commonly used summaries: Count and Distinct Count. Even though these summaries show up in the list of numeric summaries, they really aren't numeric summaries at all. They're simply used to count rows (in the case of Count) or distinct values of a field in the current set of data (Distinct Count).

When you use the Count function, it doesn't matter which field you select when creating the summary. All this function does is count the number of rows in a set of records. If you put this summary in the footer of a report, it will always return the same number as the record counter at the bottom of the Crystal Reports window.

Distinct Count is a little trickier because it discriminates when it's counting. It evaluates the value of a field when it performs a count and only counts a particular value once. When it's finished it returns the number of distinct values for that field.

Lest you think that these 19 summary functions are all you get with Crystal Reports, we should mention that several hundred more are available for your use in the Formula Editor. These 19 are the only ones you can quickly enter in the Design tab by right-clicking a field and selecting INSERT • SUMMARY. The several hundred additional formulas require just a bit more work. You must include them in a formula before you can put them in your report. Also, these functions include not only summary functions but a host of other specialized functions that perform a wide array of services for you whenever you're creating formulas in Crystal Reports. Figure 6.54 lists all of the types of functions that are available.

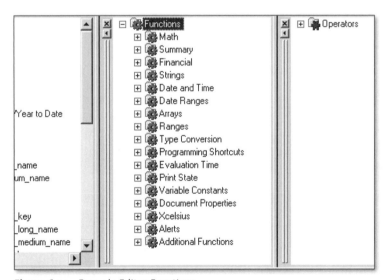

Figure 6.54 Formula Editor Functions

We'll get a chance to use a few more of the built-in summaries and some more of the other Formula Editor functions throughout the remainder of this book. Now, we're going to wrap up this chapter with a look at another very handy feature of Crystal Reports: Conditional Summaries.

6.2 Conditional Summaries Using Running Totals

Our final two topics in this chapter will cover conditional, or selective, summaries. This means we'll no longer be summarizing every numeric (or text) value indiscriminately, but we'll be telling Crystal Reports when (or under what condition) to summarize a particular value.

Much like the concept of custom groups, conditional summaries provide you as the report developer with a far greater degree of flexibility to deal with special report requirements — in this case, the need to summarize data only when it meets certain criteria.

As usual, there are many reasons why you might want to perform a conditional summary when creating a report using Crystal Reports. We'll cover a few examples to give you a feel for why this is a valuable feature and how best to use it.

Let's use our last report as a starting point. First, make sure you've saved it, and then let's do another Save As, and this time call it "Chapter 6 – Running Totals."

To start, let's take a look at our current report (Figure 6.55).

As you can see, our report is organized (grouped) by product category and then by calendar month. One advantage of doing this is that it allows us to quickly generate subtotals for our two key figures, one at each group level. So in our case we can quickly see the totals for each product category and for each month within that particular product category. All in all, it's a very useful report.

As it turns out it, could be a bit more useful. Our VP of sales appreciates the information provided by this report, but she's finding it difficult to see totals for each of the three computer products that Hedijetijak Electronics produces. Because these products are the mainstay of the company, it's always a good idea to get an idea of how they are selling in virtually every sales report.

Hedijetijak Electronics Corporation

National Sales Report

Product Category	Product	Qty	Revenue
Legacy Products		6,195	$ 1,146,603
July 2007		190	$ 47,718
	Ventra LXP 2.67 2GB 500 GB	75	$ 45,074
	Computer Speakers	115	$ 2,644
August 2007		3,340	$ 652,007
	17" LCD Monitor	1,650	$ 387,734
	Ventra LXP 2.67 2GB 500 GB	390	$ 234,386
	Computer Speakers	1,300	$ 29,887
September 2007		2,665	$ 446,878
	17" LCD Monitor	1,260	$ 296,087
	Ventra LXP 2.67 2GB 500 GB	205	$ 123,203
	Computer Speakers	1,200	$ 27,588

Figure 6.55 National Sales Report by Product Category and Month

There are two alternatives for handling this requirement. The first is to create another report that's organized (grouped) by product first instead of product category. That way you'd always get a total for each product. However, this would mean both creating and running a whole new report. Also, the VP of sales likes the idea of being able to see both sets of totals in one report. It's just more convenient. Besides, she heard that this is not a problem with Crystal Reports.

The second option is to create a series of conditional summaries in the existing report that calculate these totals for us. In Crystal Reports there are a couple of ways to accomplish this. The first is to use a built-in feature called a running total. The second is to use a formula to create a conditional total. Let's look at the running total first.

First, the Running Total formula could have perhaps been given a better name. A more accurate name would have been Conditional Total because, although a Running Total formula can be used as an actual running total, it almost never is. (A running total is a total that increments for each row of data so that you see the total increasing as you progress through your report.) In almost every case you're using a Running Total formula for its ability to attach a condition to the summary function you're performing.

Let's use a running total to create a summary that totals up the sales for the first of our computer products — the Ventra LX. The way you create a running total is very similar to how you insert a built-in summary; you right-click a detail field and select INSERT • RUNNING TOTAL.

But before we do that, we need to take care of a preliminary step. Earlier, when we created our custom group formula called Product Category, we stated that it's always best to reference a key (or code) when using any characteristic in a formula. At that time we assumed you already knew the codes associated with each product.

But what if you don't know them? How can you look them up? Well, there's no need to look them up because we have access to the code already. We just need to add it to our report. Simply take the z_Product_key formula and add it to the Detail section to the right of the Revenue field (Figure 6.56).

Product Category	Product	Qty	Revenue	
Legacy Products		**6,195**	**$ 1,146,603**	
July 2007		**190**	**$ 47,718**	
	Ventra LXP 2.67 2GB 500 GB	75	$ 45,074	PDS03
	Computer Speakers	115	$ 2,644	PDS08
August 2007		**3,340**	**$ 652,007**	
	17" LCD Monitor	1,650	$ 387,734	PDS05
	Ventra LXP 2.67 2GB 500 GB	390	$ 234,386	PDS03
	Computer Speakers	1,300	$ 29,887	PDS08

Figure 6.56 Product Key and Detail Section

Now we know the correct code for each product. At this point it's a good idea to note the code for each computer product:

▶ Ventra LX: PDS01

▶ Ventra LXP: PDS03

▶ Ventra Ultra: PDS02

Now that we have the correct code for our three computer products, we can create a running total that calculates total revenue by product.

The key figure we'll apply our Running Total to is Revenue. Right-click the Revenue key figure in the Detail section and then select INSERT • RUNNING TOTAL. You should then see the dialog box shown in Figure 6.57.

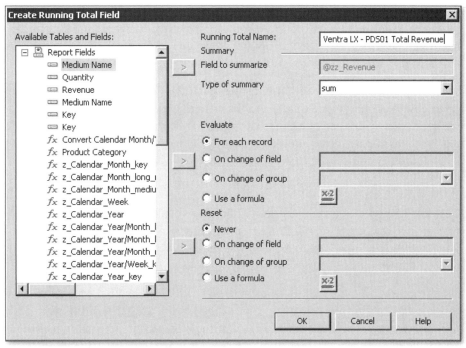

Figure 6.57 Create Running Total Field Dialog Box

First, you need to give your running total a descriptive name. We'll name it "Ventra LS – PDS01 Total Revenue" because we'll be generating a total for the Ventra LX (code PDS01).

The next option is grayed out because we began this running total by right-clicking the z_Revenue key figure. If we hadn't (and had started in the Field Explorer), we'd choose the key figure to summarize here.

The next option is Type of Summary. You almost always use the Sum summary when creating a running total, as is the case here.

The trick behind the Running Total formula is the next section, Evaluate. Here is where you tell the running total when to sum (or add) the Revenue key figure. You'd never use the first option (For Each Record). Doing so would turn the running total into an ordinary summary (just as if you had selected INSERT • SUMMARY and selected the Sum summary).

The next two options (On Change of Field and On Change of Group) are used only in very specific situations, with On Change of Group being the most commonly used. The option we're going to use is the final option (Use a Formula), which is by far the most commonly used option. You use this virtually every time you create a running total. This is because this option allows you to supply your own condition that tells the running total when to sum the key figure you've selected.

Select the Use a Formula option and then click the Formula button to the right (which is no longer grayed out). This take us to the Formula Editor. Here is where we need to provide the condition that triggers the running total. We want to add the Revenue key figure whenever the product key (or code) is equal to "PDS01," so our formula will simply be:

```
{@z_Product_key} = 'PDS01'
```

That's it. This type of formula is called a Boolean formula, and it reads like a comparison (we're comparing the Product key to the text "PDS01"). The result is that whenever this comparison is true, the Revenue key figure will be added to our total. If the comparison isn't true, the Revenue key figure is skipped.

We can now click Save and Close to save our formula. The final option we need to set is the Reset option at the bottom of the screen. This determines when our Running Total will be reset back to zero. In the case of a grand total (which sums across every record in the report), you'd leave this at the default, which is Never. Of the remaining options, the most commonly used, is On Change of Group. You use this option if you're creating a running total at the group level rather than the report level, like we are here.

Because our report requirement is to calculate a grand total for each computer product, we'll keep the default setting of Never. Click OK, and you'll see something like Figure 6.58.

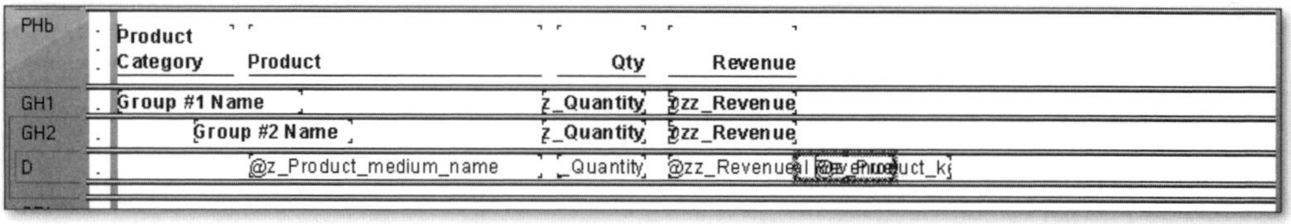

Figure 6.58 Running total in the Detail Section

As you can see, our Running Total formula was automatically inserted into the Detail section right next to the key figure we had selected (Revenue). By doing so it placed itself right on top of the z_Product_key formula.

Hot Tip

You need to always be careful not to allow objects in Crystal Reports to overlap. You almost never want this to happen. If it does, you should immediately separate them before moving on. If you don't, things can begin to get cluttered.

Move the z_Product_key formula to the right and then format the Running Total formula to display zero decimal places. Now your report should look something like Figure 6.59):

September 2007	**2,675**	**$**	**177,650**		
Ventra Ultra 3.00 2GB 750 GB	225	$	146,473		PDS02
LightTouch Optical Mouse	1,325	$	21,187		PDS07
DigiPad Mousepad	1,125	$	9,990		PDS04
Strategic Products	**2,297**	**$**	**233,107**		
July 2007	**285**	**$**	**95,546**		
Ventra LX 2.33 1GB 300 GB	165	$	90,748	90,748	PDS01
UltraTouch USB Keyboard	120	$	4,798	90,748	PDS06
August 2007	**542**	**$**	**27,789**		
UltraTouch USB Keyboard	530	$	21,189	90,748	PDS06
Ventra LX 2.33 1GB 300 GB	12	$	6,600	97,348	PDS01
September 2007	**1,470**	**$**	**109,772**		
Ventra LX 2.33 1GB 300 GB	100	$	54,999	152,347	PDS01
UltraTouch USB Keyboard	1,370	$	54,773	152,347	PDS06
	13,962	**$**	**1,675,532**		

Figure 6.59 Running Total in the Preview Tab

Now we can see the running total in action. It starts off as zero (displayed as a blank field) and then begins incrementing by adding the Revenue key figure for the Ventra LX. As you can see, the total increments three times, once for each time the Ventra LX is listed in the report. We end up with a grand total for this product of $152,347.

Now we need to do some formatting to make things a bit more presentable. First, we need to see the grand total for each product in the report footer, not in the Detail section as it is now. The report footer is where you put grand total summaries. To do this, we just need to move the running total into the report footer. However, before we do that we need to make more room in the report footer so we can insert our three running totals.

When you need to add room in a header or footer to accommodate additional objects, it can be advantageous to split the section rather than to expand it. Splitting sections provides you with greater flexibility and increases your layout options as you continue to expand your report. In our example we'd like to keep the existing grand total summaries separate from the running total formulas we're adding. Later when we look at conditional formatting of sections, we'll get a chance to see this additional flexibility in action.

Earlier when we created our master template, we split our page header into two sections and put the header objects in one section (company name, report title) and the column headers in the other. Now we're going to split the report footer so we can put our three running totals in their own section apart from the existing grand totals.

To split any section, you right-click in the left margin of the section and select Insert Section Below (Figure 6.60).

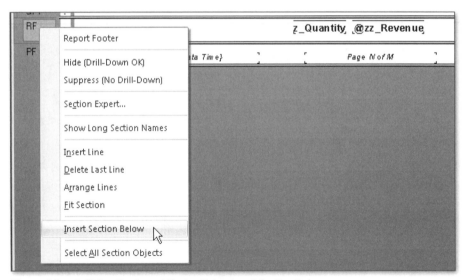

Figure 6.60 Splitting the Report Footer Using Insert Section Below

You should now have Report Footer a (RFa) and Report Footer b (RFb). To give us room for our running total formulas, make the new Report Footer b bigger by dragging the bottom border of the section down.

Hot Tip

When you know you're about to add several (or many) objects to any section, it's best to give yourself plenty of room by generously resizing the section. You can never have too much room while you're in the process of placing all of your objects, and you can always tighten up the section when you're finished.

Our newly expanded report footers should now look like Figure 6.61.

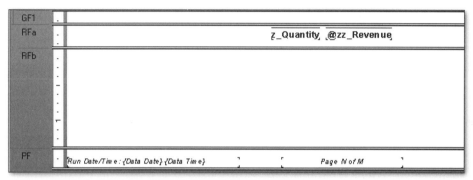

Figure 6.61 Spilt Report Footer – RFa and RFb

Now it's time for a mid-term formatting exam. We'll help you get started, but it will be up to you to finish. This is a good chance to see how well your formatting skills are doing so far.

First, we'll insert a text object to create a label for our three running totals. The labels should read "Revenue Totals for Computer Products." Place this text object near the top left of Report Footer b. Make it bold, italic, and 11-point size. Now create another text object below that reads "Ventra LX" and make it bold. Drag the Running Total formula we created in the Detail section to the right of the Ventra LX label (running totals don't need to be in the Detail section to create a grand total). Align these objects so that Report Footer b looks something like Figure 6.62.

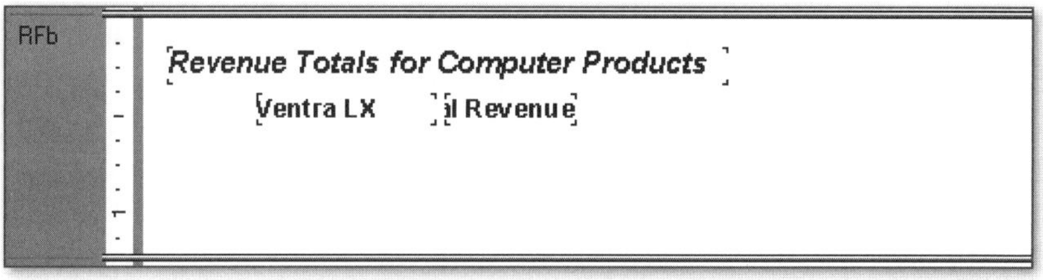

Figure 6.62 Report Footer b with First Running Total

Now create two more running totals for the other two computer products (Ventra LXP – PDS03 and Ventra Ultra – PDS02). Add these two new running totals with their corresponding text labels to Report Footer b. When finished, your Report Footer b in the Preview tab should look like Figure 6.63.

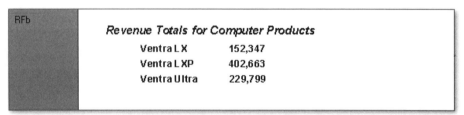

Figure 6.63   Report Footer b with Running Totals

Now it's time for a couple of finishing touches. First, add a dollar sign (fixed) to the beginning of the revenue totals. To format all three at the same time you can select them all, right-click one of them, and select Format Objects. Finally, we'll add a box around our header label and the three running totals. You create a box by clicking the Insert Box button (Figure 6.64).

Figure 6.64   Insert Box Button

After you click the Insert Box button, simply drag a box around the header and three running totals in Report Footer b. You can click and drag any edge of the box to move it and any handle to resize it. Now your completed report footer should look something like Figure 6.65.

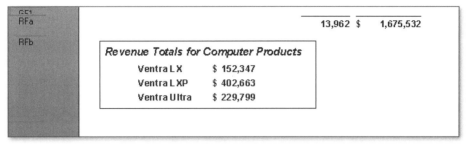

Figure 6.65 Completed Report Footers a and b

Although the Running Total formula is quite handy in these situations because it's relatively quick and easy to create, it does come with two limitations:

▸ You cannot create a chart from a running total.

▸ Running total formulas work only when place in a footer (group footer or report footer). They won't work when placed in a header.

Earlier when we began looking at summaries, we mentioned that it's not uncommon to place summaries in group headers (or even in the report header). If running total formulas (which are really conditional total formulas) don't function in the report header or a group header, is there some other way to display a conditional total in a header? Fortunately the answer is "yes." Let's wrap up this chapter by showing you how.

6.3   Conditional Summaries Using a Formula

First, we need to save our previous report. Let's do a Save As and save our report as "Chapter 6 – Conditional Summaries Using a Formula."

We're going to fulfill the same requirement we handled previously with the Running Total formula with the combination of three standard Crystal Reports formulas and the built-in Sum function. The first step is to create our three formulas.

Our first formula will total up the revenue for the Ventra LX. Create a new formula (not a running total but a regular formula) and call it "Ventra LX Revenue." The contents of the formula should be:

```
If {@z_Product_key} = 'PDS01'
 then {@zz_Revenue}
else
 0
```

If the Product Key of the current record is "PDS01," then the result of this formula will be the value of the current zz_Revenue alias (which is just the Revenue amount). Otherwise, the result will be zero. Now we just need to do the same for the other two computer products.

We can simply place these three formulas in the Detail section. We'll first move the z_Product_key formula to the left. After we make them bold with zero decimal places, the report looks like Figure 6.66 in the Preview tab.

Legacy Products	6,195	$	1,146,603			
July 2007	190	$	47,718			
Ventra LXP 2.67 2GB 500 GB	75	$	45,074 PDS03	0	45,074	0
Computer Speakers	115	$	2,644 PDS08	0	0	0
August 2007	3,340	$	652,007			
17" LCD Monitor	1,650	$	387,734 PDS05	0	0	0
Ventra LXP 2.67 2GB 500 GB	390	$	234,386 PDS03	0	234,386	0
Computer Speakers	1,300	$	29,887 PDS08	0	0	0
September 2007	2,665	$	446,878			
17" LCD Monitor	1,260	$	296,087 PDS05	0	0	0
Ventra LXP 2.67 2GB 500 GB	205	$	123,203 PDS03	0	123,203	0
Computer Speakers	1,200	$	27,588 PDS08	0	0	0
New Products	5,470	$	295,822			
July 2007	532	$	68,326			
Ventra Ultra 3.00 2GB 750 GB	98	$	63,797 PDS02	0	0	63,797
DigiPad Mousepad	339	$	3,010 PDS04	0	0	0
LightTouch Optical Mouse	95	$	1,519 PDS07	0	0	0
August 2007	2,263	$	49,846			
LightTouch Optical Mouse	1,475	$	23,585 PDS07	0	0	0
Ventra Ultra 3.00 2GB 750 GB	30	$	19,530 PDS02	0	0	19,530
DigiPad Mousepad	758	$	6,731 PDS04	0	0	0
September 2007	2,675	$	177,650			
Ventra Ultra 3.00 2GB 750 GB	225	$	146,473 PDS02	0	0	146,473
LightTouch Optical Mouse	1,325	$	21,187 PDS07	0	0	0
DigiPad Mousepad	1,125	$	9,990 PDS04	0	0	0
Strategic Products	2,297	$	233,107			
July 2007	285	$	95,546			
Ventra LX 2.33 1GB 300 GB	165	$	90,748 PDS01	90,748	0	0
UltraTouch USB Keyboard	120	$	4,798 PDS06	0	0	0
August 2007	542	$	27,789			
UltraTouch USB Keyboard	530	$	21,189 PDS06	0	0	0
Ventra LX 2.33 1GB 300 GB	12	$	6,600 PDS01	6,600	0	0
September 2007	1,470	$	109,772			
Ventra LX 2.33 1GB 300 GB	100	$	54,999 PDS01	54,999	0	0
UltraTouch USB Keyboard	1,370	$	54,773 PDS06	0	0	0

Figure 6.66 Conditional Total Formulas in the Detail Section

As you can see, each formula returns either the Revenue amount for a particular computer product or a zero. Now to create our summaries, we simply treat these formulas as we would any other numeric field (or key figure). We can right-click them one at a time and select INSERT • SUMMARY. We can then move them from the report footer to the report header (or into one of the group headers if you want to see a subtotal as well).

We'll move them into the report header. We can then unsuppress the report header to see the result (you can right-click in the left margin of the report header and select Don't Suppress) (Figure 6.67).

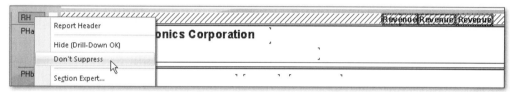

Figure 6.67   Selecting Don't Suppress in the Report Header

Now the top of our report should look like Figure 6.68.

Figure 6.68   Conditional Totals in Report Header

If you look back a few pages to the three running total formulas we put in the report footer, you'll see that these totals are exactly the same. All we need to do to finish these up is add the same type of formatting that we did for our running totals. Feel free to do so if you'd like some practice.

Because these report header totals don't need to be displayed in our final layout, we can suppress the report header again to make them go away.

Before we wrap up this chapter on grouping and summarizing, we'll show you something that will help you in your development efforts. Notice that we now have some extra stuff in our Detail section. We're still displaying the z_Product_key formula along with our three conditional formulas that we used for our product summaries (Figure 6.69).

Product Category	Product	Qty	Revenue				
Legacy Products		**6,195**	**$**	**1,146,603**			
July 2007		**190**	**$**	**47,718**			
	Ventra LXP 2.67 2GB 500 GB	75	$	45,074	PDS03	0	45,074	0
	Computer Speakers	115	$	2,644	PDS08	0	0	0
August 2007		**3,340**	**$**	**652,007**			
	17" LCD Monitor	1,650	$	387,734	PDS05	0	0	0
	Ventra LXP 2.67 2GB 500 GB	390	$	234,386	PDS03	0	234,386	0
	Computer Speakers	1,300	$	29,887	PDS08	0	0	0

Figure 6.69 Extra Formulas in the Detail Section

These are considered extra because we don't need (or want) to see them in the final report layout. We have three ways to make them go away:

▶ We can delete them. Now that we have created the grand total summaries using these formulas, we can remove them from the report canvas, and the summaries will continue to work correctly.

▶ We can suppress them.

▶ We can move them to another detail section and suppress the section.

Although we don't technically need these formulas any more (because the summaries will work fine without them), it can be quite useful to keep them around. The reason for this is that they can provide feedback to you as a developer if you need to troubleshoot a report or if you simply want to get a better idea of what is taking place "behind the scenes." Therefore, we recommend keeping any such background formulas in your report.

Our two choices then become to either suppress them directly or move them to another section and suppress the entire section. To suppress them directly you select all of the objects at once and click the Suppress button (Figure 6.70).

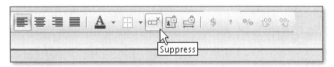

Figure 6.70 Suppress Button

Although this works fine, the potential problem with this method is that the formulas are still taking up space in our Detail section. This isn't a problem now, but it can become a problem if we decide to add additional objects to the Detail section of our report. Then they can get in the way.

Therefore, we recommend that you always create a second Detail section (by splitting the section) and then place any extra formulas that you don't want to have displayed in your final report in the second Detail section. By now you should know how to split a section. Create a second Detail section now (Detail b or Db). Next, select all four of the extra formula fields, and then just press the Down Arrow on your keyboard to move them into the second Detail section.

Finally, to make these fields disappear you simply suppress the second Detail section (Detail b) by right-clicking in the left margin and selecting Suppress.

> **Hot Tip**
>
> It's a good idea to change the color of anything you leave in your report (whatever color you like). That way, if you forget to suppress the section, it will stand out when you view your report.

When finished, your Detail sections should look like the following in the Design tab (assuming you have selected the Show Hidden Sections option on the Layout tab in the FILE • OPTIONS dialog box) (Figure 6.71).

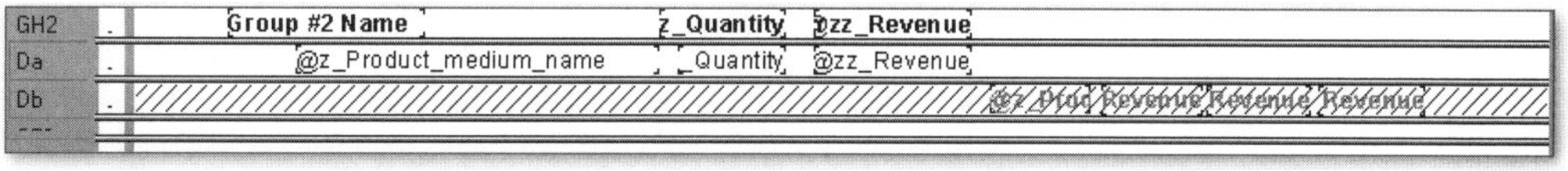

Figure 6.71 Suppressed Detail b Section

When you switch to the Preview tab you won't see the suppressed section, as shown in Figure 6.72.

Product Category	Product	Qty	Revenue
Legacy Products		6,195	$ 1,146,603
July 2007		190	$ 47,718
	Ventra LXP 2.67 2GB 500 GB	75	$ 45,074
	Computer Speakers	115	$ 2,644
August 2007		3,340	$ 652,007
	17" LCD Monitor	1,650	$ 387,734
	Ventra LXP 2.67 2GB 500 GB	390	$ 234,386
	Computer Speakers	1,300	$ 29,887
September 2007		2,665	$ 446,878
	17" LCD Monitor	1,260	$ 296,087
	Ventra LXP 2.67 2GB 500 GB	205	$ 123,203
	Computer Speakers	1,200	$ 27,588

Figure 6.72 Report in Preview Tab after Suppressing Detail b

> **Important Note**
>
> Although it's nice to be able to hide formulas in a suppressed Detail section as we've just done, when working with a BW query as your data source, you need to be careful not to put anything in a suppressed section that would result in the generation of more summary detail rows than required by the report. When you add a new characteristic to a report against a BW query, it can (but not always) result in the creation of additional aggregates by SAP NetWeaver BW that then get sent to your report (in the form of additional rows).

Because this behavior is specific to reports developed against a BW query can be a bit difficult to conceptualize (or explain, for that matter), it will be worthwhile to include a quick example before we wrap up this chapter. This is such an important concept to grasp when working with Crystal Reports in an SAP NetWeaver BW environment that it's worth the time to emphasize the point a bit further.

Let's say you've just received a new requirement to create a simple list report that returns the total revenue for each sales channel. You remember that you recently created a very similar report that lists revenue by channel product name, so you decide it would be best to modify that report to save time. You open the original report, which currently returns 19 rows of data — one for every combination of sales channel and product currently in the data (Figure 6.73).

Channel	Product Name	Revenue
Internet	Ventra LX 2.33 1GB 300 GB	122,098
Internet	Ventra Ultra 3.00 2GB 750 GB	86,582
Internet	Ventra LXP 2.67 2GB 500 GB	342,564
Internet	DigiPad Mousepad	9,395
Internet	17" LCD Monitor	448,831
Internet	UltraTouch USB Keyboard	64,768
Internet	LightTouch Optical Mouse	37,976
Internet	Computer Speakers	57,475
Fax	Ventra Ultra 3.00 2GB 750 GB	65,099
Fax	DigiPad Mousepad	622
Phone	Ventra Ultra 3.00 2GB 750 GB	78,119
Phone	Ventra LXP 2.67 2GB 500 GB	60,099
Phone	DigiPad Mousepad	9,226
Phone	17" LCD Monitor	234,990
Phone	UltraTouch USB Keyboard	15,992
Phone	LightTouch Optical Mouse	8,315
Phone	Computer Speakers	2,644
Other	Ventra LX 2.33 1GB 300 GB	30,249
Other	DigiPad Mousepad	488

Figure 6.73 Simple Revenue List Report

Because the new report requirement is to display only revenue by sales channel, all we need to do now is remove Product from our report. But rather than simply deleting it from the report, you decide to create a second Detail section, move the Product Name characteristic to the new section, and then suppress the section. After doing this your Design tab now looks like Figure 6.74.

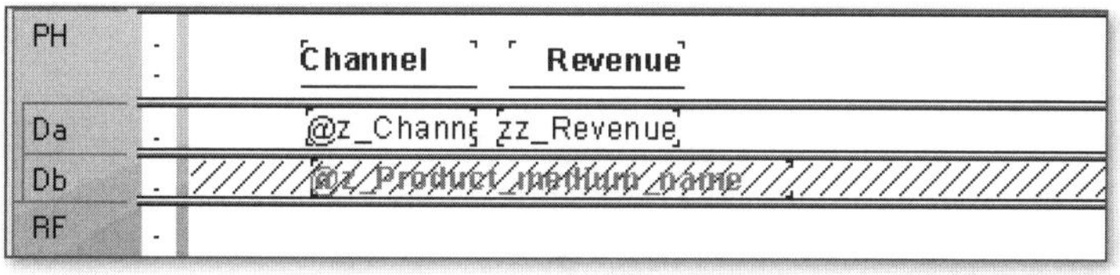

Figure 6.74 Product Name in Suppressed Detail Section

Pop Quiz

Question: What will our report look like now in the Preview tab? How many records do you expect to see?

Answer: We'll see the same number of records that we saw before. The only difference will be that you'll no longer see the Product Name.

When you click the Preview tab, you'll see the report shown in Figure 6.75.

Channel	Revenue
Internet	122,098
Internet	86,582
Internet	342,564
Internet	9,395
Internet	448,831
Internet	64,768
Internet	37,976
Internet	57,475
Fax	65,099
Fax	622
Phone	78,119
Phone	60,099
Phone	9,226
Phone	234,990
Phone	15,992
Phone	8,315
Phone	2,644
Other	30,249
Other	488

Figure 6.75 Report with Product Name Suppressed

267

So what's happening here? Why are we getting the same number of rows as we did before? The reason is because the Product Name characteristic is still being used in your report and is therefore being used by SAP BW to generate the aggregated key figures (revenue) for your report. SAP BW doesn't know (or care, for that matter) that you're not actually showing the Product Name in your report any longer. As long as you're using any characteristic anywhere in your report, SAP BW will factor it in when generating the key figure summaries for your report.

> **Important Tip**
>
> If a characteristic (or key figure) is being used somewhere in your report, there will always be a green checkmark next to it in the Field Explorer. If for some reason you find your report returning more rows than you expected, you can scan down through the Field Explorer and find all active characteristics by looking for the green checkmark.

There are times when you'll want to keep both of these in the same report. This would make sense when you want to see revenue by sales channel and by both sales channel and product name in the same report. We'll show you examples of this later.

Let's assume for the sake of our example that you have no intention of ever including Product in your report. In this case, the simplest way to get to the correct number of aggregates (rows) is to completely remove Product Name from the report. We'll right-click in the left margin of Detail b and select Delete Section (Figure 6.76).

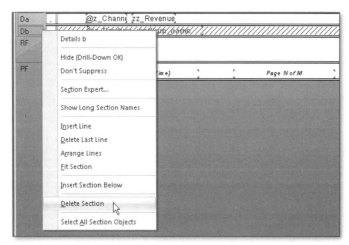

Figure 6.76 Delete Section

Now when we switch to the Preview tab we see the same thing as before. Why is that?

It's because whenever you remove any characteristic from your report, Crystal Reports doesn't automatically refresh the report. It only does this when you add a characteristic. To see the what the new record set will look like, you have to click the Refresh button. After doing this, you should now see something like Figure 6.77.

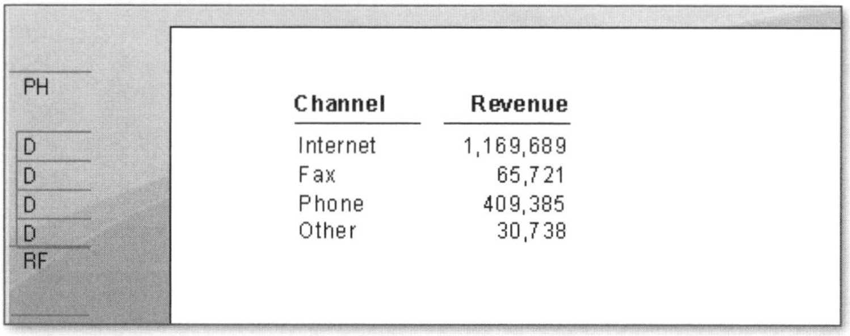

Channel	Revenue
Internet	1,169,689
Fax	65,721
Phone	409,385
Other	30,738

Figure 6.77   Revenue by Sales Channel with Four Rows

Now our report is down to only the four records (aggregates) that are necessary to display revenue by sales channel.

Again, we want to emphasize that there are definitely times when it's perfectly fine to have extra characteristics in your report that aren't displayed in the Preview tab — at least not initially displayed. One of the most useful features in Crystal Reports is the ability to create drill-down reports, which we'll show you how to create in a later lesson. The main thing we want you to understand for now is that there will be times when you accidentally place (or leave) a characteristic in your report and that you can figure out how to fix it.

One last thing: there's no Where Used command in Crystal Reports like there is in the Query Designer to help you find where a particular characteristic is being used in a Crystal Report. You can go to VIEW • REPORT EXPLORER, which can help you find objects that are actually on the report canvas. However, this behavior occurs whenever a characteristic is used (or referenced) anywhere in your report, including formulas (regular formulas, running totals, formatting formulas, record selection, etc.), and used for creating groups or performing sorts.

6.4 Summary

▸ Creating groups in Crystal Reports is very common and is used primarily for creating additional summaries of your key figures.

▸ The simplest and most common type of group uses an existing characteristic.

▸ You can use specified order grouping to order a group in any order you determine. You can also use it to create simple custom groups.

▸ The ability to create custom groups using a formula is a very powerful feature of Crystal Reports. This feature enables you to quickly respond to the changing needs of business end users who need to look at their data in new ways that aren't directly supported by the data.

▸ Although it's always preferable to group by data from the original source system, this isn't always possible or practical.

▸ A number of built-in summary functions are available in Crystal Reports for summarizing both numeric and text fields.

▸ The Running Total formula provides a way to apply a condition to a summary function. Such functions only work when placed in a footer section (a group footer or report footer). They don't work when placed in a header section.

▸ You can create your own conditional summaries by using a Crystal Reports formula along with a standard built-in summary function. The advantage of doing this is that you can place your conditional summary in the report or group header and you can also create a chart using the summary.

Please Read Carefully Before Proceeding!

The knowledge and skills you've obtained up to this point in the book are the baseline core skills required for any Crystal Reports developer to be successful in creating reports against SAP NetWeaver BW. If you didn't learn anything else, you could still most likely meet most reporting requirements in a typical SAP NetWeaver BW environment.

One reason for this is the nature of the data that's stored in SAP BW. Because it has already been organized into a more reportable form, for the most part you end up simply organizing and summarizing data to meet many report requirements. Another reason is that in most organizations the core reports required to run any business are typically not very exotic or complex in nature.

Certainly there are more skills you can (and will) learn as you continue to develop your ability to create reports using Crystal Reports. But before moving on to any new skills, it is critical that you immediately apply the ones you've just learned.

Although we've made every effort to make our hands-on exercises as real world as possible, there's no substitute for learning on your own system, using your own data. It's then, and only then, that you truly begin to see lasting and permanent change.

So here's your mid-term homework assignment. You must complete this assignment before moving on to the remainder of this book. Failing to do so could significantly reduce your overall chances of success:

▶ First, you need to make sure you're completely set up to create reports against SAP NetWeaver BW. You'll need to ensure that:

  ▶ You've installed Crystal Reports 2008 correctly.

  ▶ You've installed the Integration for SAP client software.

  ▶ Your BASIS security team has added you to the Crystal Developer role.

  ▶ You have access to the InfoProviders in your functional area, at a minimum.

▶ Second, you need to locate at least one SAP BW data source you can use to begin creating practice reports. If you need help locating an appropriate data source (InfoCube or MultiProvider), you should find someone in your IT department who can help you. If you can't locate someone quickly in IT, then you might try asking someone who's an SAP BEx power user (typically an analyst or business process expert).

▶ Take the time to create a master query for at least one InfoProvider for use with Crystal Reports. Don't be too concerned at this point about getting it exactly right. The important thing is that you have something you can practice with. If you cannot create BW queries yourself, you need to request that one be created for you, typically by someone in your IT department.

▶ Once the master query is finished, use it to create a Crystal Reports template. Remember to create all your alias formulas for each characteristic and key figure in the query. Also take the time to create a standard header and footer.

▶ Now, time to practice. You should go back through the exercises we covered in the first half of this book and try them out using your own data. Do your best to "translate" the exercise so that it makes sense using the data from your own SAP BW system.

▶ Practice as much as you can. Be creative. Try different things out to see how they affect your report. Remember to make good use of Undo. Because you'll be working in a nonproduction environment, you really can't hurt anything, no matter what you try.

▶ Pay attention to the little things. The more efficient you become at basic layout skills, the faster you'll be in producing your final results. If you develop good habits early on, it will save you many hours of wasted effort going forward.

▶ Most likely any query you use for Crystal Reports will have one or more BW variables. These are used to create user prompts when the query is run, which are used to filter the data coming from the query. For now just answer the prompts appropriately when you run your report. We'll learn much more about variables and parameters in the following lesson.

Very rarely do you want all the data returned from a BW query, or from any other data source, for that matter. A common practice when developing reports is to provide a way for the end user to select a subset of the data each time the report is run. In this chapter, we look at various methods for allowing the user to have control over the final data set returned to the report.

7 Picking and Choosing

In this and the following lesson we look at different ways to ask the report consumer (end user) a question and then use the answer to accomplish a variety of useful tasks. This is a very important topic for a lot of reasons, the main one being that it provides a way to provide the report consumer with the ability to gain some degree of control over the final report.

The specific mechanisms that allow us to provide this higher level of control are *BW variables* and *Crystal Reports parameters*. As you'll soon see, in the case of a BW variable the two are one in the same: The report consumer sees a BW variable as just another Crystal Reports parameter.

The primary benefit of both of these is the greater degree of flexibility they provide you as a report developer, especially in the case of Crystal Reports parameters. In this chapter we'll focus on the *record filtering* capabilities of the BW variable and the Crystal Reports parameter. In the following chapter we'll look specifically at how to leverage a Crystal Reports parameter to "extend" the functionality and look of your report.

7.1 Filtering Data with a BW Variable

You use a BW variable in Crystal Reports for one thing: to filter (or select) the data coming from the BW query. The key advantage of a BW query when used for filtering data is that the filtering is done on the backend, or at the database, where you typically (but not necessarily always) want this to occur.

The first thing we need to do is show you how you can add an existing BW variable to a BW query. Almost all BW queries have at least one variable to provide basic filtering functionality. This is especially true as the size of the InfoCube (or Multi-Provider) increases. The more data you have on the backend, the more important it becomes to provide a way to filter it.

The BW query we used in our earlier lessons didn't contain any variables. We'll now go back and add one. Because time period filters are by far the most common type of data filter you see in any BW query, we'll add one to the Calendar Year/Month characteristic. As a reminder, the purpose of this book isn't to teach you how to create BW queries, so we'll cover only the basics here.

After we open our existing query, we right-click the Calendar Month/Year characteristic and select Restrict (Figure 7.1).

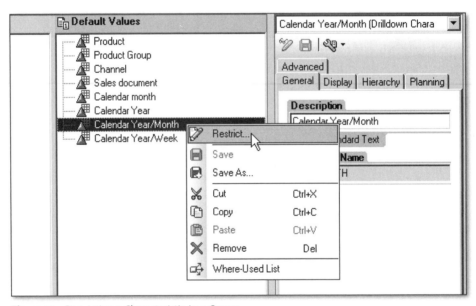

Figure 7.1 Restricting a Characteristic in a Query

Next we'll see the Select Values for Calendar Year/Month dialog box. We need to change the Show pull-down menu to Variables (Figure 7.2).

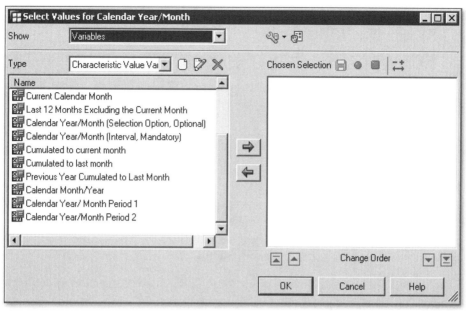

Figure 7.2 Select Values Dialog Box Showing Variables

We can now select the appropriate variable for our query. When selecting variables for use with Crystal Reports, there are two different factors to consider: the type of variable and whether it's mandatory or optional. The four types of variables that are used with Crystal Reports are:

▶ Single value

▶ Multiple single values

▶ Interval

▶ Selection option

The single value variable is the simplest to use and to handle in Crystal Reports. However, it's the most limited of the four in that the user is limited to a single input value. Multiple single values, as it sounds, allows the user to enter multiple single values. The interval variable allows the user to select a single range of values, and the selection option provides the greatest range of options of all: The user can input single values, ranges, or multiple single values and ranges.

Whenever you use a query with one or more variables as a data source in Crystal Reports, a parameter is created for each of the BW variables in the query. You don't have any control over this as a Crystal Reports developer. The only thing you can control is the number and type of variables you have in your query.

> **Note**
>
> The fact that Crystal Reports can also filter data by itself adds a considerable degree of flexibility when it comes to filtering data coming from a BW query. Although it's true that most of time the filtering will still be done at the backend using a BW variable, there are definitely situations where it's advantageous or even preferred to filter at least some of the data within Crystal Reports.

Regarding variable types, although the selection option variable type is definitely the most flexible and powerful in terms of providing input options for the end user, it's also the most difficult to handle within Crystal Reports in terms of the task of displaying the user's response(s) in the report header. As you'll see shortly, this is the most challenging aspect of working with BW variables in Crystal Reports.

The bottom line on variable types is that you should only use selection option variables when the user requires the greater degree of flexibility they provide. If that's not a requirement, you should consider using one of the other variable types.

In our example query we'll select the variable called Calendar Year/Month (Interval, Mandatory). We can tell by the name of this variable that the type of variable is Interval and that it's a mandatory variable (the user must provide a valid value). Although you're not required to add this information to any variable name, it's helpful to do so. If this information isn't provided as part of the name, you have to edit the variable to determine this information.

After adding the variable we then save the BW query.

> **Note**
>
> Whenever you save any changes to a BW query, depending on how your SAP NetWeaver BW system is configured, you might see a dialog box that will ask you to attach your changes to either a new transport or an existing transport. If you have no idea what a transport is, find someone in your IT department to help you.

Now that we've updated our query, let's create a new report against the query so you can see how the variable looks in Crystal Reports. From within Crystal Reports we need to click the Create New Report from a Query button on the SAP toolbar. When we open the Field Explorer and expand the Parameter node, we should see something like Figure 7.3.

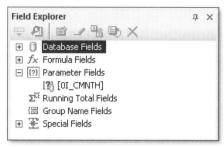

Figure 7.3 Field Explorer Showing Parameter Created by BW Variable

The name given to the parameter created by the BW variable is the technical name of the variable.

As a reminder, the one thing all parameter fields have in common is that they provide a way for report consumers to provide input that you, the report developer, can use. You'd always use a BW variable for record selection.

When we right-click our new parameter that's tied to a BW variable, we'll see the list shown in Figure 7.4 displayed in the middle of the dialog.

Value	Description
[0CALMONTH].[200707]	July 2007
[0CALMONTH].[200708]	August 2007
[0CALMONTH].[200709]	September 2007
[0CALMONTH].[000000]	Not assigned
Click here to add item	

Figure 7.4 Pick List for a BW Variable Parameter

This is the pick list portion of the parameter dialog box. The reason these values are here is because Crystal Reports automatically populates the pick lists of parameters created by BW variables from master data tables in SAP NetWeaver BW. The list is very short and therefore quite unusual. Most pick lists created by BW variable parameters are much longer. However, by default Crystal Reports limits the number of entries to a few hundred.

Depending on how many variables are in your BW query and how much master data is attached to the characteristics they are associated with, this process of creating pick lists for each parameter can take some time – sometimes a lot of time. It's not uncommon for it to take several minutes or more for the Design tab to appear after selecting a query when first creating a report in Crystal Reports.

This is another reason why it's is important that you make every effort to ensure that your master BW queries are completely finished before you create your Crystal Reports templates. This is especially true for BW variables. Once you have all your variables in place, you can create your Crystal Reports template and then you can create your pick lists just one time for all of your future Crystal Reports reports. This is potentially a big time saver.

> **Important Note**
>
> This pick list is a *static list* that's created as a one-time courtesy by Crystal Reports to help you as the report developer (and only you) whenever you run this report in Crystal Reports. This list isn't used whenever your report gets published into SAP BusinessObjects Enterprise and then viewed online by report consumers. Report consumers will always be presented a *dynamic pick list* when viewing reports created using BW queries (assuming the report was published correctly). We'll discuss publishing your reports later in Chapter 11.

There's typically so much confusion on this point that it bears repeating: The list that's created the first time you access a BW query as a data source when creating a new report in Crystal Reports isn't intended to be used by the report consumer when running and viewing reports in SAP BusinessObjects Enterprise. It's created for one purpose only: to help you as the report developer when running the report in Crystal Reports.

Below the pick list are a series of options (which we'll cover in more detail shortly), several of which are grayed out and cannot be modified. That's because these are determined by the type of BW variable that created this parameter and cannot be changed (Figure 7.5).

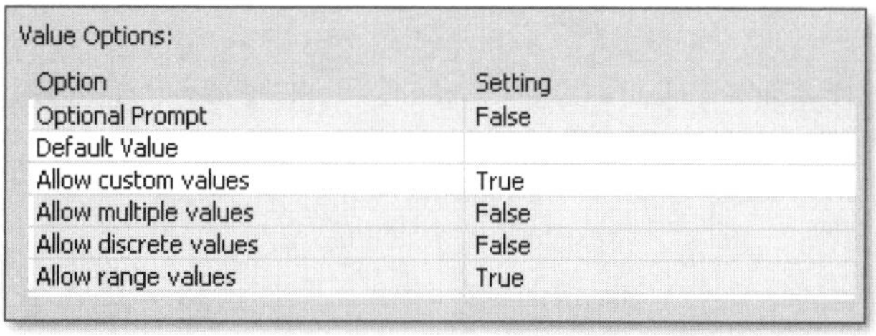

Figure 7.5 Value Options Grayed Out for a BW Variable

Although we've made the point that it's always best to ensure that all of your BW variables are in place before beginning any new report development (or creating a master template) against a particular BW query, we recognize that this isn't always the case. There will be times when you must add a variable to an existing query that's already been used to create one or more reports in Crystal Reports. In this case you must tell the report about the new variables.

You do this with the Verify Database command under the Database menu. Let's demonstrate how this works. We'll open an existing report that uses the query we just added a variable to a moment ago (Chapter 7 – Sales Report by Month). When we open the report and look at the Field Explorer, we notice that there are no parameter fields. That's because when we first created this report, the underlying BW query didn't include any variables. But now we've added a variable, and we want to use it in this report.

Go to DATABASE • VERIFY DATABASE. After a short while, you should see something like Figure 7.6.

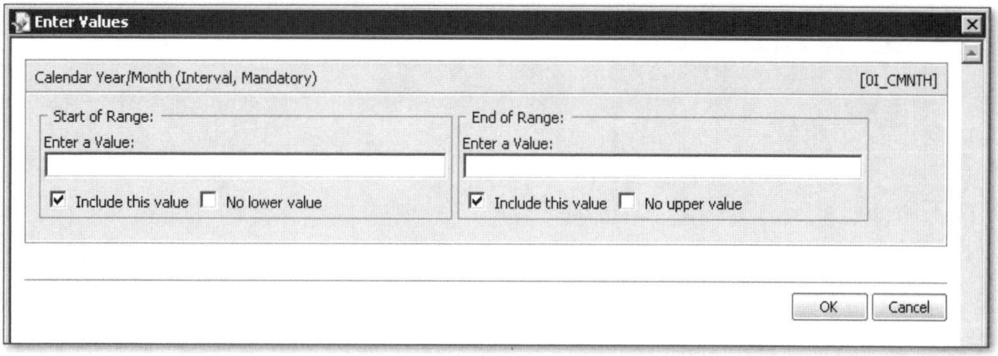

Figure 7.6 BW Variable Input Screen

What just happened (and the reason it took a little while) is that Crystal Reports just went back and checked to see the current structure of its source BW query. After checking, it found a new BW variable and presented its input dialog box on the screen.

At this point you don't have to answer this prompt. Crystal Reports is simply showing you the new BW variable it found. It will show you any BW variable it finds at this point, regardless of whether it's new or not. We can simply click Cancel to go on. Next we'll see the message shown in Figure 7.7.

Figure 7.7 Verify Database File Changed Message

Even though the message says "database file," we know it's actually a BW query. After we click OK, we'll get a message confirming that everything is back in order (Figure 7.8).

Figure 7.8 The Database Is Up to Date

When we edit our newly created parameter, we see that the pick list is empty (Figure 7.9).

Value	Description
Click here to add item	

Figure 7.9 Empty Pick List for Newly Created BW Variable Parameter

We have any pick list values this time because Crystal Reports only generates a pick list for a parameter linked to a BW variable the first time you access the query to create the new report. It doesn't generate a pick list every time you add a variable after that point and perform a Verify Database.

To get a pick list for our new parameter, fortunately we don't have to manually enter one for ourselves. The best way to populate this new pick list is to create another report against the query and then export and import the newly created pick list.

We already have a new report open (from when we earlier accessed our query after adding the BW variable). We'll go to that report and right-click the parameter in the Field Explorer and select Edit. Next we'll click the Actions button toward the middle of the dialog box and select Export (Figure 7.10).

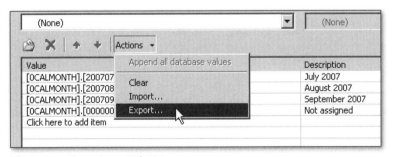

Figure 7.10 Exporting a Pick List

Next, save the pick list as "Calendar Year Month pick list." It's a good idea to create a folder called "Pick Lists" to keep all of your exported pick lists because this can be a fairly common occurrence, especially in a rapidly changing environment.'

Now we go back to our other report and edit the same parameter there, only this time we select Import instead of Export. After selecting the pick list we just saved, we now see the newly updated list in our dialog box. When we save our changes and click the Refresh button, we'll see the dialog box shown in Figure 7.11.

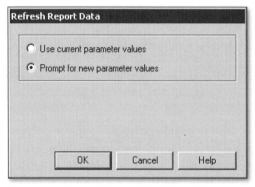

Figure 7.11 Refresh Report Data Dialog Box

If we select Prompt for New Parameter Values. we'll see our new parameter input dialog where we can select our data range (Figure 7.12).

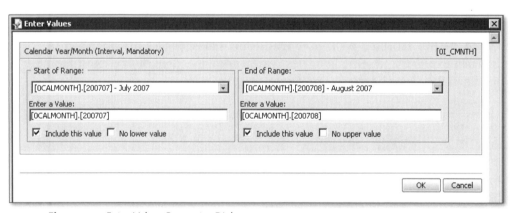

Figure 7.12 Enter Values Parameter Dialog

The data in this InfoProvider is quite limited (just three months). For the sake of demonstration, we'll select July 2007 to August 2007 as our range. After we click OK, our report will look like Figure 7.13.

Hedijetijak Electronics Corporation

National Sales Report

Month/Year	Product	Qty	Revenue
July 2007		1,007 $	211,590.44
	Ventra LX 2.33 1GB 300 GB	165	$ 90,748.35
	Ventra Ultra 3.00 2GB 750 GB	98	$ 63,797.02
	Ventra LXP 2.67 2GB 500 GB	75	$ 45,074.25
	UltraTouch USB Keyboard	120	$ 4,797.60
	DigiPad Mousepad	339	$ 3,010.32
	Computer Speakers	115	$ 2,643.85
	LightTouch Optical Mouse	95	$ 1,519.05
August 2007		6,145 $	729,641.87
	17" LCD Monitor	1,650	$ 387,733.50
	Ventra LXP 2.67 2GB 500 GB	390	$ 234,386.10
	Computer Speakers	1,300	$ 29,887.00
	LightTouch Optical Mouse	1,475	$ 23,585.25
	UltraTouch USB Keyboard	530	$ 21,189.40
	Ventra Ultra 3.00 2GB 750 GB	30	$ 19,529.70
	DigiPad Mousepad	758	$ 6,731.04
	Ventra LX 2.33 1GB 300 GB	12	$ 6,599.88
		7,152 $	941,232.31

Figure 7.13 Report Filtered by July and August 2007

As you can see, filtering your data in Crystal Reports using a BW variable is fairly straightforward. The only real trick you've learned so far is how to generate a pick list whenever you add a BW variable after the report has already been started. You'll find out that using BW variables for record filtering in Crystal Reports isn't very difficult to figure out. However, displaying the report consumer's variable selections in your report is another matter altogether.

> **Warning**
>
> What we're about to cover is perhaps the trickiest and most difficult element to understand when you're developing reports in Crystal Reports against an SAP BW query.

It's quite common to want to display the report consumer's responses to the BW variables in your Crystal Reports report. This process is handled automatically for you when you run a BW query with the Excel analyzer tool in SAP BEx. However, it isn't handled automatically when you run a report from within Crystal Reports. Through the current version of Crystal Reports (2008) the process is still a manual process that's handled via formulas.

The good news is that other developers have run into this issue before you and have created a series of prebuilt formulas to display BW variable responses in Crystal Reports. You can access and download these formulas at (INSERT DOWN-LOAD INFORMATION HERE). These formulas are free, and you can use them in any of your reports. There's a separate formula for each of the four variable types we mentioned earlier (single value, multiple single value, interval, and selection option). You must match up the correct formula to the type of variable you're using for the formula to work.

For now we won't go into a detailed explanation. We'll simply show you how to use one of these formulas as an example. In our current example, we've added a BW variable to select a range of calendar months. If you recall, the type of variable we used was an interval variable. An interval variable in Crystal Reports is referred to as a *range* parameter.

If you have a hard time figuring out what type of variable you're working with, you can go back and look up the variable type in the Query Designer. Another way to do this is to edit the parameter and look at the value options, as in Figure 7.14.

Value Options:	
Option	Setting
Optional Prompt	False
Default Value	
Allow custom values	True
Allow multiple values	False
Allow discrete values	False
Allow range values	True

Figure 7.14   Value Options for a BW Interval Variable

You can figure out the type of variable by examining the settings for the following three options:

▸ Allow multiple values

▸ Allow discrete values

▸ Allow range values

The settings for each of the four BW variable types are:

▸ Single value: False, True, False

▸ Multiple single values: True, True, False

▶ Interval: False, False, True

▶ Selection option: True, True, True

As you can see, in our case the type of BW variable we're using for filtering on calendar month is interval. When selecting time periods like this, it's is common to use an interval type variable to capture a range of periods.

To make things as clear as possible, let's first create a couple of formulas that will extract the two input values from the variable response and display those on the report as-is. Then we'll show you how to format the values into a month and year.

Create a formula and call it "Display Beginning Value." The contents of the formula will be:

```
minimum({?[0I_CMNTH]})
```

We're using a function here called the *minimum* function. Its purpose is to extract the first value out of range. Because the [0I_CMTNH] parameter is defined to be a range parameter, it's a valid argument for the minimum function.

Now let's create a similar formula and call it "Display Ending Value." It will be almost identical to our first formula but will use the *maximum* function:

```
maximum({?[0I_CMNTH]})
```

We can now save and close the formula. When we get back to the Design tab, we'll need to unsuppress the report header and then place these two formulas side by side in the report header. When we view our report in the Preview tab, we should see something like Figure 7.15.

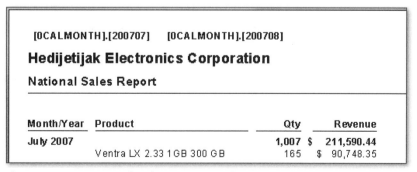

Figure 7.15 Beginning and Ending Parameter Values

As you can see, we're now able to see the variable responses we entered when we last ran this report. The next logical question would be, Why is each entry prefaced with [0CALMONTH]? This behavior is unique to parameters created for a BW variable. When you simply display the response as-is, you'll initially see the technical name of the associated characteristic from the BW query appended to the user's response. Each of these will be enclosed by square brackets and separated by a period.

If you're wondering why, the quick answer would be, "This is just the way it works." The challenge (as you might imagine) is to get from these two pieces of "raw material" to something end users are going to want to see in their reports. Accomplishing this will require some creative formatting formulas, which is where our special free variable formatting formulas come in. We recommend using ours unless you like a challenge.

For a time period range, like we have here, it's best to format each value separately and then join them together in a text object. The main reason for this is that our formatting formula is going to take the year and month text ("YYYYMM") and convert it into a date. This will make it easier to format into our final output of "Month Year."

All we'll do is go back to our original Display Beginning Value formula and replace the contents with the following:

```
local stringVar Value:= Minimum({?[0I_CMNTH]});
local numberVar start:= instr(Value, '.') + 2;
local stringVar Yr_Month:= mid(Value, start, 6);
local numberVar nYear:= ToNumber(Yr_Month[1 to 4]);
local numberVar nMonth:= ToNumber(Yr_Month[5 to 6]);
Date(nYear, nMonth, 1)
```

Because the focus of our lesson isn't formulas, we won't take any time to explain how this formula works. If you're new to Crystal Reports and have little or no experience with formulas, the best way to approach this is to simply copy and paste and then substitute your parameter into the formula (in this example it goes in once in the first line). Then just look at your report to ensure that it worked.

Let's copy what we've just done, save it, and then edit the Display Ending Value formula. Paste the formula and simply change the minimum function in the first line to maximum. Close and save the formula.

Now when we preview our report, we should see Figure 7.16.

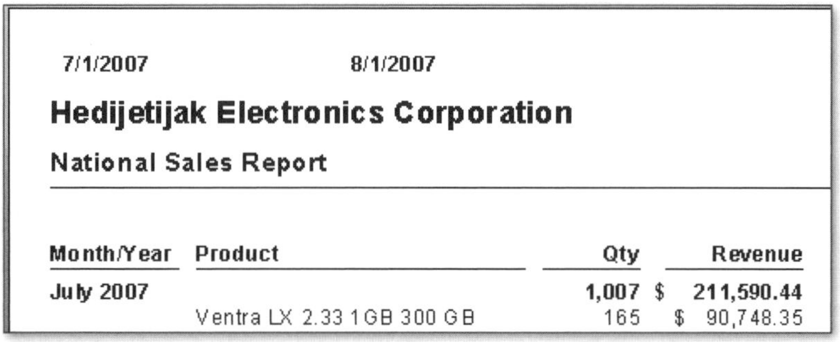

7/1/2007		8/1/2007		
Hedijetijak Electronics Corporation				
National Sales Report				
Month/Year	**Product**		**Qty**	**Revenue**
July 2007			1,007 $	211,590.44
	Ventra LX 2.33 1GB 300 GB		165	$ 90,748.35

Figure 7.16 Beginning and Ending Parameter Values Converted to Dates

Now that we've separated the beginning and ending values in each parameter and converted them to dates, we can format them as "Month/Year" and combine them into a text object.

To do this, select both objects, right-click, and then select Format Objects. Click the Date tab and then select the March 1999 option. When we return to our report, it will look like Figure 7.17.

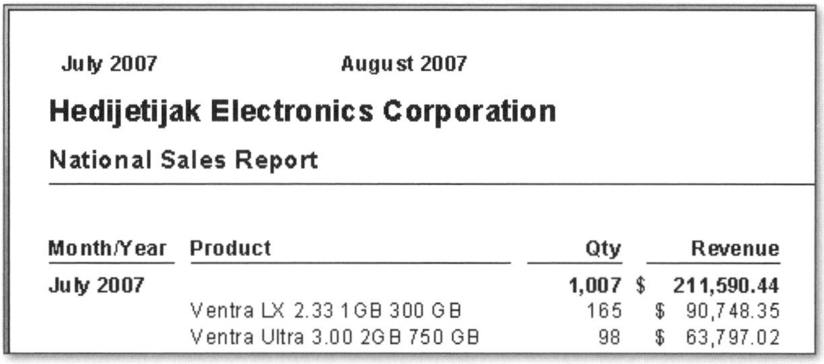

July 2007		August 2007		
Hedijetijak Electronics Corporation				
National Sales Report				
Month/Year	**Product**		**Qty**	**Revenue**
July 2007			1,007 $	211,590.44
	Ventra LX 2.33 1GB 300 GB		165	$ 90,748.35
	Ventra Ultra 3.00 2GB 750 GB		98	$ 63,797.02

Figure 7.17 Beginning and Ending Parameter Values Formatted as Month/Year

The last step is the easiest. We first need to create some space in our page header so we can put our new parameter display formulas in the page header below the report title (National Sales Report). We can then move the horizontal line down and insert a blank text box between the report title and the line (Figure 7.18).

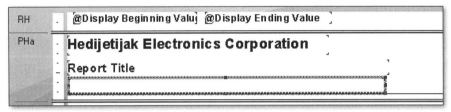

Figure 7.18 Empty Text Object in Page Header a

Formatting Tip

When you're about to insert objects (text, fields, formulas) into a text object, it's a good idea to expand the text object so that it's big enough to accommodate all of the objects. Otherwise, the text object will expand vertically (up and down) when you insert the objects.

Now we need to drag the Display Beginning Value formula into the text object. Then double-click the text object to select the contents and click after the formula field you just inserted. Enter a space, the word "to," and another space. Now drag the Display Ending Value formula after the word "to." When you look at the report in the Preview tab, it should look like Figure 7.19.

Hedijetijak Electronics Corporation

National Sales Report

July 2007 to August 2007

Month/Year	Product	Qty	Revenue
July 2007		**1,007** $	**211,590.44**
	Ventra LX 2.33 1GB 300 GB	165	$ 90,748.35
	Ventra Ultra 3.00 2GB 750 GB	98	$ 63,797.02

Figure 7.19 Final Variable Display

Because this variable is a mandatory variable, there's is no need to deal with the possibility of there being no value entered by the end user (this results in a NULL value). When handling optional parameters, you have to take into account the possibility of the input value being NULL, which adds to the complexity of the logic.

One final note: When displaying the user response to a BW variable in Crystal Reports, you only have direct access to the key (or code) associated with the characteristic, not the descriptive text. In our example we were able to leverage the Date function to convert the time period key (in the form of YYYYMM) to create our final display (in the form of Month/Year). However, with any other characteristic, you'll only be able to display the key.

Before we move on, do a Save As and save your report as "Chapter 7 – BW Variables."

7.2   Filtering Data with a Crystal Reports Parameter

Like a BW variable, a Crystal Reports parameter can also be used to filter the data coming from SAP NetWeaver BW. However, when used in a report that uses a BW query as its data source, a standard Crystal Reports parameter cannot be used to filter data at the database. That always requires a BW variable. However, it can be used to filter data at the frontend, which as it turns out, can be quite useful.

If you're an IT person, you may be having a hard time with that statement, because conventional wisdom states that it's always preferable to filter data at the database (or at the source) rather than at the client (or frontend). That's true — when it's both possible and practical.

There are situations where it simply isn't possible to filter the data at the database level using a BW variable. This would be any time you need to filter by something that's not directly available in the source data. (If this sounds familiar, it should. It's essentially the same issue we discussed when we covered custom groups — only this time we aren't grouping but filtering.)

One example is filtering by a *key figure* (a numeric field). You simply can't do this with a BW variable. However, you can do this with a Crystal Reports parameter. Another example would be when you want to filter on some sort of concatenated field, where two or more fields are being combined to form a compound field.

A more practical use of a Crystal Reports parameter is when filtering by a BW variable may be possible but isn't very practical. You can get into a situation with variables where you begin to over-filter your query. A query can become overloaded with too many variables and become unwieldy and cumbersome to execute. And filtering with a BW variable requires that you execute the query each time you filter in a different way, which can end up taking a lot of time.

Up until Crystal Reports 2008 you also had to rerun the report every time you wanted to filter your report a different way using a Crystal Reports parameter. Not anymore. This latest version of Crystal Reports introduces a new type of report filter: the *saved data filter*. This takes record filtering to a whole new level.

With the introduction of the saved data filter in Crystal Reports, you now have the option of performing a two-stage filter of your data: the first using one or more BW variables (your "heavy hitters") and the second using one or more Crystal Reports parameters that perform a secondary saved data filter.

Perhaps we should take a second to explain exactly what we mean by saved data filter. When you run a Crystal Reports report (either directly from within Crystal Reports or from SAP BusinessObjects Enterprise), all of the data that's retrieved from your data source is stored temporarily within the Crystal Reports file (known in tech circles as an RPT file).

Important Note

Under the File menu is an option called Save Data with Report. The default setting for this option is on. This is a very handy feature of Crystal Reports that can save you a lot of development time.

With this setting turned on, whenever you save a report, any data that was retrieved from your data source is saved with the report. There are two ways you can tell that a report has saved data. First, when you open the report, start off in the Preview tab looking at the report with data instead of the Design tab. Second, depending on the number of records being saved, the RPT file can get quite large. This is the only real disadvantage of saving data with your report — file size.

The good thing about saving data with your report is that it can save you a lot of time over the long run. That's because once you have your data saved locally, you can continue to develop your report without having to continually retrieve data from your data source.

Let's say you're working on a report, and you just ran it for the first time to test it out. Because it's running against a very large InfoCube, it takes about 10 minutes to retrieve all of the data. It's time for lunch, so you decide to save your report and close Crystal Reports. If you don't save your report with data, when you get back from lunch what's the first thing you're going to need to do? Refresh your report again and wait 10 more minutes.

Multiply this over and over for every Crystal Reports report you may be working on at any given moment, and you can see why it would be more efficient in the long run to save data with all of your reports. Another benefit is that you no longer need to have a live connection to your original data source when you save data with your reports. The only time you'd have to go back to the data source is if you either add an object (characteristic or key figure) or when you want to run the report with a different set of filter values.

> **Important Note**
>
> When publishing your reports to SAP BusinessObjects Enterprise, don't save data with the report. We'll look at publishing in detail in a later lesson.

Whenever an end user either runs your report live or schedules it for later viewing in SAP BusinessObjects Enterprise, the same thing happens. All of the data that's retrieved is stored in a saved data object (but in this case the object is not on your local machine but on a central server).

One of the key benefits of Crystal Reports when teamed up with SAP BusinessObjects Enterprise is the ability to schedule "long runners" to run at off-hours and then view them later. In this scenario even though the report may have taken quite some time to run when scheduled (let's say 15 minutes or so), the response time when viewed later is very good, perhaps near real time. This is because all of the data that was in SAP NetWeaver BW is now stored in a local saved data object that is typically much more responsive than the live database.

As usual, the best way to see this is to see it in action. The first step is to create a new Crystal Reports parameter for our saved data filter. As a reminder, when using a BW variable to filter at the source database, you don't have to create a Crystal Reports parameter to prompt the user. Crystal Reports created one for you. Now we'll have to create one ourselves.

We'll begin with the report we were just working on when we added the BW variable for filtering by calendar month: Chapter 7 – BW Variables. Immediately do a Save As and rename it "Chapter 7 – Crystal Parameters."

In this example we'll show you how you can filter on a key figure, something you can't do with a BW variable.

The first step in this process is to create a new Crystal Reports parameter that we can use to prompt the user for a response. All we need to do is go to the Field Explorer, right-click Parameters, and select New. Next you'll see the Create New Parameter dialog box (Figure 7.20).

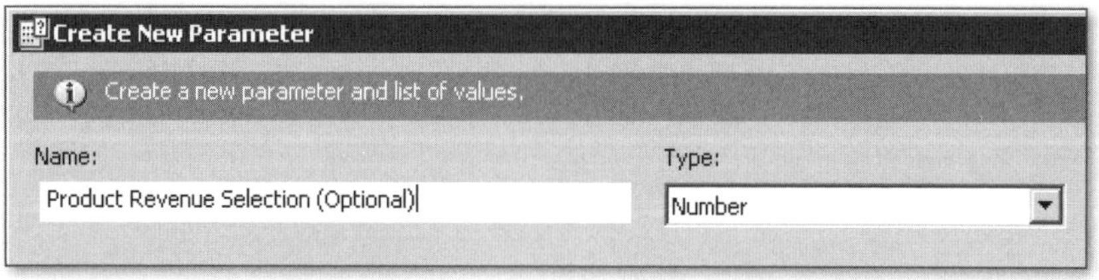

Figure 7.20 Create New Parameter

First, let's name our parameter "Product Revenue Selection (Optional)." You should always make the parameter name as descriptive and easy to understand as possible (not technical). This is how end users will identify your parameter when running your report. You should also indicate whether the parameter is mandatory or optional (as it is in our case).

Next, we need to give our parameter a type. This is important because the type you select needs to match the input the user will be entering and the way you'll be using the input in your report. In our example we'll be prompting the user for a range of numbers to filter the Revenue key figure, so we need to set the type to Number.

Next, we need to set some Value Options at the bottom of the dialog box (Figure 7.21).

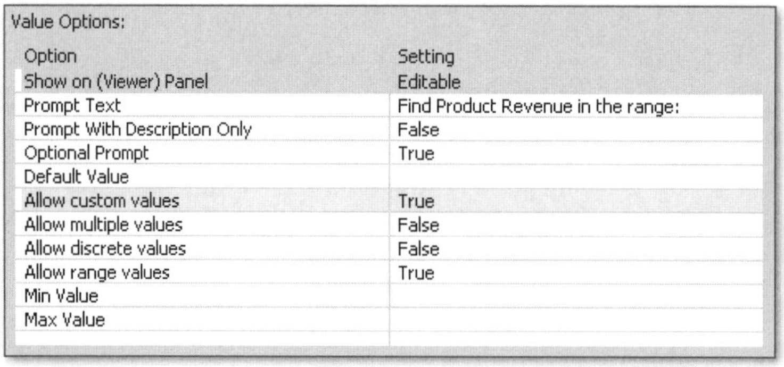

Figure 7.21 Value Options for Crystal Reports Record Filter Parameter

The first option is Show on (Viewer) Panel. This is a new option available in Crystal Reports 2008. It allows us to prompt the user from within the Crystal Viewer (in SAP BusinessObjects Enterprise) after the report has been executed. When users make their selection from within the Viewer, the report will be filtered locally, not on the SAP NetWeaver BW server. We'll leave this at the default setting (Editable).

The next option we want to set is Optional Prompt. We'll set this to True. This is very important because it allows us now to use this prompt to create a "post" or secondary filter that the user can execute after the first record filter has completed (assuming there was an initial filter, which is normally the case).

The Allow Custom Values option is grayed out because there are no entries in the pick list above. As soon as you enter at least one item in the pick list (or import a list), this option becomes active. Typically when you're filtering on a numeric value, it doesn't make sense to create a pick list, which is the case here.

Because we're setting up a single range parameter the next three options should be configured as follows:

▶ Allow Multiple Values: False

▶ Allow Discrete Values: False

▶ Allow Range Values: True

Now that we've set all of the appropriate options, we can now click OK to save our parameter.

Once we've created a parameter, the next step is to use it somewhere in our report. Simply creating a parameter won't create a prompt on the screen when you run the report. In order to be prompted the parameter has to first be put to use in some capacity. We'll use this parameter to perform a client-side record selection, also known as a saved data filter.

The quickest and easiest way to accomplish this is to right-click the detail field or formula you want to filter your report by (in our case the zz_Revenue formula) and select Select Expert Saved Data from the menu (Figure 7.22).

Figure 7.22 Select Expert Saved Data

Next we'll see the Select Expert Saved Data dialog box. We can pull down the menu on the left and change the selection from Is Any Value to Is Equal To. Then we need to pull down the menu on the right and select our newly created parameter from the list, as shown in Figure 7.23.

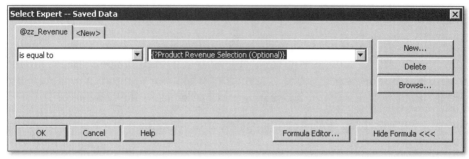

Figure 7.23 Select Expert Dialog Box

The Select Expert is a quick and easy way to create simple record selection formulas without having to write any code. It's a great way for beginners to create filters for their reports, and even seasoned report developers use it for basic record selection in Crystal Reports. However, there will be times when the record selection requirement is too complex to handle with the Select Expert alone. If that's the case, you'll need to create your own record selection formula.

To view the saved data selection formula we just created using the Select Expert, you can follow the menu path REPORT • SELECTION FORMULAS • SAVED DATA (Figure 7.24).

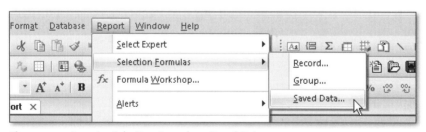

Figure 7.24 Report – Selection Formulas – Saved Data

Next we see the Saved Data formula that we created using the Select Expert Saved Data (Figure 7.25).

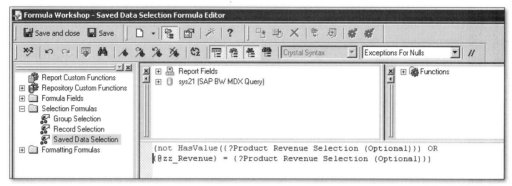

Figure 7.25 Saved Data Selection Formula

Here's another formula, this time one to use to select records for our report from saved data. The good thing about this formula is that the Select Expert created it for us. If you're curious about how this formula works, we'll take a second to explain it.

```
(not HasValue({?Product Revenue Selection (Optional)}) OR
{@zz_Revenue} = {?Product Revenue Selection (Optional)})
```

The first part of the formula uses two operators: `not` and `HasValue`. The following part is a reference to the parameter we just created (all parameters in formulas begin with a "?").In plain English this would mean, "The parameter doesn't not have a value." But in a formula like this the subject comes last and not first.

The second half of the formula (after the `OR`) is a simple comparison. It compares the zz_Revenue key figure to the parameter we created.

The entire formula from beginning to end reads something like this: The parameter has no value OR revenue is equal to the parameter." If the first part is true (the parameter has no value), then the equation is satisfied, and it goes no further (in other words, nothing happens and no filtering takes place). However, if the first part is false (the parameter does have a value), then the second part of the formula is evaluated. At that point we're looking only for revenue amounts that are equal to the parameter value.

We hope you're beginning to get this, at least a little. Learning how to create efficient and effective record selections in Crystal Reports (whether by using the Select Expert or by entering them manually) is a very useful skill and can significantly increase the record filtering options you can provide your end users.

Important Note

If you were paying close attention, you noticed that the last half of our record selection uses the "=" comparison (equal sign) to compare the revenue amount to our parameter. If you recall, the parameter we created is a range parameter. You might expect that we would have used a comparison such as "in" or perhaps "between." To keep things simple, however, whenever you compare anything in Crystal Reports to a parameter, you always use the "=" operator, no matter what kind of parameter you're using.

Now we're ready to put our parameter and record selection to the test. Click Save and Close (or the Close button at the top right) to go back to the Design tab. Then click the Preview tab. You'll see the screen shown in Figure 7.26.

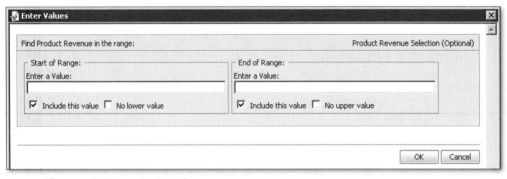

Figure 7.26 Parameter Entry Screen

Now that we've used our parameter in the Saved Data Selection Formula, we're being prompted to enter a response. Because we made it an optional parameter, we don't have to enter anything at this time. To see how this works, simply click OK without entering any values.

You now see the report as it's currently filtered using the BW variable we added as part of our first lesson in this chapter. To see the full effect of this pairing of a BW variable filter with a Crystal Reports saved data filter, click the Refresh button and run the report again. We're given the choice to either Use the Current Parameter Values or Prompt for New Parameter Values. We'll select the second option so we can run the report using a different set of values (Figure 7.27).

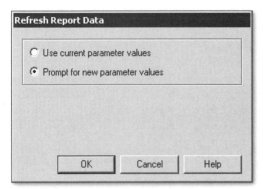

Figure 7.27 Refresh Report Data Dialog Box

When we click OK, we see the next screen (Figure 7.28).

| Enter Values | [x] |

Calendar Year/Month (Interval, Mandatory)   [OI_CMNTH]

Start of Range:
[0CALMONTH].[200707] - July 2007

Enter a Value:
[0CALMONTH].[200707]

☑ Include this value ☐ No lower value

End of Range:
[0CALMONTH].[200708] - August 2007

Enter a Value:
[0CALMONTH].[200708]

☑ Include this value ☐ No upper value

Find Product Revenue in the range: Product Revenue Selection (Optional)

Start of Range:
Enter a Value:

☑ Include this value ☐ No lower value

End of Range:
Enter a Value:

☑ Include this value ☐ No upper value

OK Cancel

Figure 7.28 Parameter Input Screen with Two Parameters

Now we see both our BW variable parameter at the top and our standard Crystal Reports parameter at the bottom. Just to get a different record set back from SAP NetWeaver BW, let's change the Calendar Month range to August 2007 to September 2007. Because the second parameter is optional, we'll leave it blank for now. After setting the first parameter, we'll click OK and see the report in the Preview tab (Figure 7.29).

297

Hedijetijak Electronics Corporation

National Sales Report

August 2007 to September 2007

Month/Year	Product	Qty	Revenue
August 2007		6,145 $	729,641.87
	17" LCD Monitor	1,650	$ 387,733.50
	Ventra LXP 2.67 2GB 500 GB	390	$ 234,386.10
	Computer Speakers	1,300	$ 29,887.00
	LightTouch Optical Mouse	1,475	$ 23,585.25
	UltraTouch USB Keyboard	530	$ 21,189.40
	Ventra Ultra 3.00 2GB 750 GB	30	$ 19,529.70
	DigiPad Mousepad	758	$ 6,731.04
	Ventra LX 2.33 1GB 300 GB	12	$ 6,599.88
September 2007		6,810 $	734,299.45
	17" LCD Monitor	1,260	$ 296,087.40
	Ventra Ultra 3.00 2GB 750 GB	225	$ 146,472.75
	Ventra LXP 2.67 2GB 500 GB	205	$ 123,202.95
	Ventra LX 2.33 1GB 300 GB	100	$ 54,999.00
	UltraTouch USB Keyboard	1,370	$ 54,772.60
	Computer Speakers	1,200	$ 27,588.00
	LightTouch Optical Mouse	1,325	$ 21,186.75
	DigiPad Mousepad	1,125	$ 9,990.00
		12,955	**$ 1,463,941.32**

Figure 7.29   Report Filtered by AUG and SEP 2007

When you click the Parameters button in the Preview Panel on the left side of the screen, you'll see the parameter we created at the top of the Preview Panel. You may have to resize the Preview Panel to see all of the prompting text, as shown in Figure 7.30.

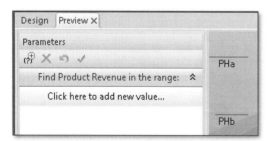

Figure 7.30   Parameter in the Preview Panel

Now we can click where it says Click Here to Add New Value... to add a range of values for the revenue key figure. When the Enter Values dialog box appears, we'll enter "20000" for the Start of Range and "30000" for End of Range. Now click OK.

The report doesn't get filtered until you click the Apply Changes button at the top of the Preview Panel (Figure 7.31).

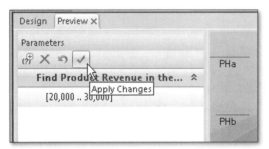

Figure 7.31 Apply Changes Button in the Preview Panel

Now when we look at the report in the Preview tab, we only see revenue amounts that range between $20,000 and $30,000 (Figure 7.32).

Hedijetijak Electronics Corporation
National Sales Report

August 2007 to September 2007

Month/Year	Product	Qty	Revenue
August 2007		**3,305** $	**74,661.65**
	Computer Speakers	1,300	$ 29,887.00
	LightTouch Optical Mouse	1,475	$ 23,585.25
	UltraTouch USB Keyboard	530	$ 21,189.40
September 2007		**2,525** $	**48,774.75**
	Computer Speakers	1,200	$ 27,588.00
	LightTouch Optical Mouse	1,325	$ 21,186.75
		5,830 $	**123,436.40**

Figure 7.32 Report Filtered by 20,000 to 30,000 Range

If you're unfamiliar with SAP BEx reporting, this may not seem like much of a feature — to be able to filter by a key figure — but with the standard Excel analyzer in SAP BEx this isn't possible. You'd have to bring all of the data into Excel and figure out how to filter it out afterward.

> **Important Reminder**
>
> Keep in mind that our saved data filter works without having to rerun the query, which is another key advantage of performing this type of post filter in Crystal Reports. We can continue selecting various ranges for revenue amount, and the report will never be refreshed. You could actually disconnect from SAP NetWeaver BW, and the filter would work just fine.

This point is so important it's worth repeating: When you filter data in Crystal Reports with a saved data filter the BW query isn't executed again. This combination of BW variable filters up front (the primary filter) and Crystal Reports parameters afterward (the secondary filter) is a great way to divide the task of record selection to make it as efficient and user friendly as possible.

Let's look at one more example of using a Crystal Reports parameter to perform a secondary (saved data) filter. The example we just looked at was one that wasn't possible to perform using the standard Excel analyzer tool because we were filtering our data on a key figure. We'll now look at an example of how you can filter data in Crystal Reports using a formula that has been used to create a custom group. Before we move on, however, be sure to save the current report as "Chapter 7 – Crystal Parameters."

For our next example let's start with a report we created in Chapter 7 called Chapter 6 – Custom Group Using a Formula 4. This is the report where we created a custom group called Product Category. We now want to not only be able to group by Product Category but to filter by it as well.

The first step, as before, is to create the parameter. We'll name it "Product Category (Optional)" and give it a type of String (the default setting). This time we'll create a pick list of values for users to select from. The values we want are shown in Figure 7.33.

Value	Description
Legacy Products	
New Products	
Strategic Products	
Click here to add item	

Figure 7.33 Pick List for Product Category Parameter

Next, we want to set the Value Options as shown in Figure 7.34.

Value Options:	
Option	Setting
Show on (Viewer) Panel	Editable
Prompt Text	Select one or more Product Categories:
Prompt With Description Only	False
Optional Prompt	True
Default Value	
Allow custom values	False
Allow multiple values	True
Allow discrete values	True
Allow range values	False
Min length	
Max length	
Edit mask	

Figure 7.34 Value Options for Product Category Parameter

Notice that we set the Allow Custom Values option to False this time because we want to force our users to select a value from our pick list. In this case we don't want them entering a value themselves.

We can now click OK to save our parameter settings. The next step, just like before, is to use this parameter in our saved data selection formula. The last time we did this we right-clicked a field in the Design tab (the revenue key figure) and selected Select Expert Saved Data. This worked because the revenue key figure was on the Design tab and it was a detail field (not a summary).

In this report the Product Category formula isn't in the Detail section of the Design tab, but is being used to group our report (as Group 1). Therefore, we cannot right-click the formula anywhere in the report, so in this case we'll go to REPORT • SELECT EXPERT • SAVED DATA (Figure 7.35).

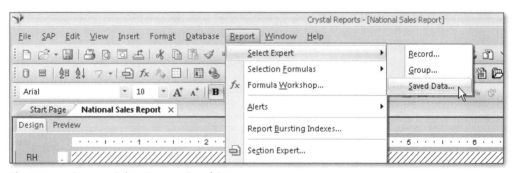

Figure 7.35 Report – Select Expert – Saved Data

We now see the Choose Field dialog box, where we can select the Product Category formula (Figure 7.36).

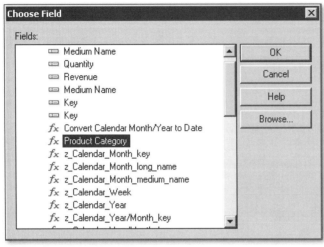

Figure 7.36   Choose Field for Select Expert

After clicking OK, we can see the Select Expert Saved Data dialog box. We can now change Is Any Value to Is Equal To and select our parameter in the second pull-down menu on the right (Figure 7.37).

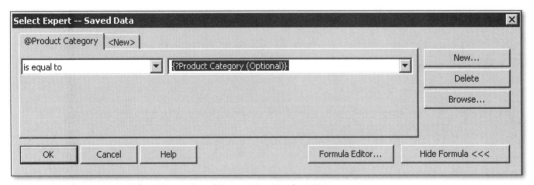

Figure 7.37   Select Expert Saved Data Using Product Category

We can now click OK and return to the Design tab.

Pop Quiz

Question: What will happen when we click the Preview tab?

Answer: We'll be presented with our new parameter now that we've referenced it in the Select Expert Saved Data dialog box. However, because it's optional, we can simply close the window without responding.

After we click the Preview tab and cancel the parameter dialog box that appears, we'll see our current report with all three product categories listed (Figure 7.38).

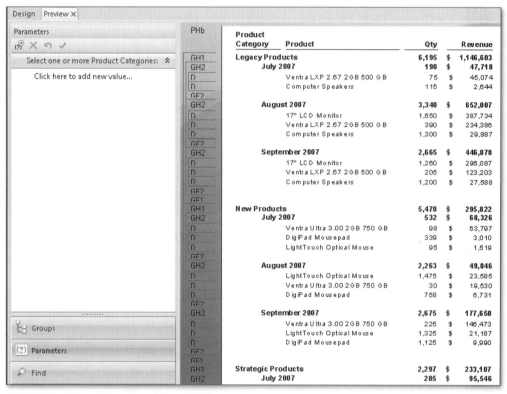

Figure 7.38 Report Showing All Three Product Categories

Notice our newly created parameter at the top of the Preview Panel on the left. As a reminder, the reason it's displayed in the Preview Panel and we can enter a response is because we selected Editable for the Show on (Viewer) Panel option when we created the parameter.

By clicking the Click Here To Add New Value... button and then using the pull-down menu, we can select Legacy Products from our pick list (this is the list we created when creating the parameter). Repeat this process to select Strategic Products (Figure 7.39).

Figure 7.39   Selecting Legacy and Strategic Products

Now click the Apply Changes button to apply our filter. You should now see something like Figure 7.40.

Product Category	Product	Qty	Revenue
Legacy Products		**6,195**	**$ 1,146,603**
July 2007		**190**	**$ 47,718**
	Ventra LXP 2.67 2GB 500 GB	75	$ 45,074
	Computer Speakers	115	$ 2,644
August 2007		**3,340**	**$ 652,007**
	17" LCD Monitor	1,650	$ 387,734
	Ventra LXP 2.67 2GB 500 GB	390	$ 234,386
	Computer Speakers	1,300	$ 29,887
September 2007		**2,665**	**$ 446,878**
	17" LCD Monitor	1,260	$ 296,087
	Ventra LXP 2.67 2GB 500 GB	205	$ 123,203
	Computer Speakers	1,200	$ 27,588
Strategic Products		**2,297**	**$ 233,107**
July 2007		**285**	**$ 95,546**
	Ventra LX 2.33 1GB 300 GB	165	$ 90,748
	UltraTouch USB Keyboard	120	$ 4,798
August 2007		**542**	**$ 27,789**
	UltraTouch USB Keyboard	530	$ 21,189
	Ventra LX 2.33 1GB 300 GB	12	$ 6,600
September 2007		**1,470**	**$ 109,772**
	Ventra LX 2.33 1GB 300 GB	100	$ 54,999
	UltraTouch USB Keyboard	1,370	$ 54,773
		8,492	**$ 1,379,710**

Figure 7.40   Report Showing Two Selected Product Categories

Save this report as "Chapter 7 – Crystal Parameters 2."

In this example, we demonstrated two key benefits of using a Crystal Reports parameter to perform a saved data filter:

▶ We can filter our report by something that doesn't exist in the data (at the source level). We accomplish this by filtering not on a field but on a formula.

▶ We can perform a sequence of filters quickly and efficiently because the saved data filter occurs locally and doesn't require a reexecution of the BW query.

A couple of final thoughts: Although, as we've mentioned, you'd normally want to perform the bulk of your record selection using one or more BW variables, there may be times when you want to do more filtering after the fact using one or more saved data filters. This becomes a viable option especially when a report is being scheduled to run off-hours rather than live (on demand).

Lastly, we should point out that BW variables have one distinct advantage over a standard Crystal Reports parameter: They can be restricted using SAP NetWeaver BW roles. This prevents end users from selecting values that they're not allowed to see, which of course, is essential for any kind of sensitive or unauthorized data.

7.3 Summary

▶ There are two mechanisms you can use to allow your users to filter the data in your SAP NetWeaver BW reports: the BW variable and the Crystal Reports parameter.

▶ A BW variable in a BW query used in Crystal Reports automatically creates a Crystal parameter to capture the end user response.

▶ The pick list that Crystal Reports creates for you for a BW variable is a static pick list intended for use by you as the report developer. When end users run the report in SAP BusinessObjects Enterprise, they're presented with a dynamic pick list.

▶ If you add a variable to a query after having started your Crystal Reports report against that query, you have to do a Verify Database to be able to see the new variable.

▶ If your new variable still doesn't appear in Crystal Reports, close Crystal Reports, relaunch, and try again.

- If you need to populate a pick list for a BW variable parameter, you can create a new report against the query, export the pick list, and import it into your original report.

- You can use Crystal Reports parameters to create data filters that are not possible or practical to perform using a BW variable. Two examples of this are filtering on a key figure and filtering on a custom field (formula).

- You can use a saved data filter to perform a secondary filter to supplement your primary filters that are being performed by one or more BW variables. This "tag team" approach to record selection can provide your end users with a more efficient and more user-friendly way to get exactly the data they're looking for.

Up to now, perhaps the single biggest push back on the idea of creating reports using Crystal Reports has been the sheer number of reports you typically end up creating to handle all the various "looks" that are necessary to meet differing report requirements. With Crystal Reports 2008 you can now create a single report that can be re-formatted dynamically by the end user. Now, finally, a single report can function as many.

8 Flexible Formatting

When we positioned the four BI frontend tools available from SAP and SAP Business Objects in Chapter 2 (Understanding the New SAP BI Toolset), we made the point that Crystal Reports has always been known to be a great choice for creating static, operational reports. Although that's true, it's also true that over the years Crystal Reports has picked up a fair amount of dynamic formatting capabilities, particularly with the release of Crystal Reports 2008.

End users like more options, not less. Typically if they're given the choice of seeing their data one way or in several different ways, they'll choose the latter. This is just common sense. It's one of the inherent strengths of the more dynamic and open interfaces of products like SAP BusinessObjects Web Intelligence and Voyager/"Pioneer." They give the end user an almost limitless number of choices when it comes to how they want to see their data.

But as we discussed in Chapter 2, with added flexibility comes added complexity, in this case in the form of a more complex user interface. Although it's true that many end users are capable of navigating these more flexible and powerful interfaces, there are also many who either can't or, more commonly, won't.

This has always been the biggest issue with the SAP BEx Excel analyzer tool (which, in technical terms, is a true OLAP user interface). It does provide the end user with a high degree of flexibility and functionality. The problem has always been that, for the majority of end users, the interface has proven to be too cumbersome and complicated for them to handle effectively. So many of them end up looking at just one or perhaps two or three different views of their data, which defeats the purpose of having a highly flexible OLAP interface in the first place.

Although Crystal Reports will never be able to match the high degree of flexibility you can get with an OLAP interface or with an ad hoc interface such as SAP BusinessObjects Web Intelligence, it's capable of providing both dynamic formatting and basic interactive functionality. The strength of Crystal Reports is that it provides this functionality in a very simple, easy to navigate interface. Crystal Reports is designed to limit the number of layout and formatting options presented to the end user. You, as the report designer, determine how much flexibility you want the end user to have by designing it into your report.

In this chapter, we'll cover some of the ways you can add greater flexibility and additional functionality to your reports. The general technique you'll be learning to accomplish this is called conditional formatting. This is when you format an object or section in Crystal Reports based upon some condition, which can be activated (or triggered) in one of two ways: by the data or by the end user.

We'll first show you how to conditionally format your report using values from the data, and then we'll show you ways to create dynamic report layouts that the end user can select using a parameter.

8.1   Using the Highlighting Expert

First, we'll look at a common formatting request: flagging (or highlighting) certain data values. There are a variety of ways to flag data in a report, but perhaps the most common is to use is color.

> **Important Note**
>
> Keep in mind that using color in a report to highlight data is only effective when the report is either viewed on the screen or printed using a color printer.

Crystal Reports has a Highlighting Expert that's designed for this very purpose. Let's look at a couple of examples of how you can use it. To start off, we'll open a report we created earlier: Chapter 7 – Sales Report by Month. Right away do a Save As and call it "Chapter 8 – Highlighting Expert."

The classic way to highlight data is to use a technique called *traffic lighting*. This is when you use three colors (green, yellow, and red) to represent data values that are good, marginal, or bad (or improving, flat, or decreasing). The simplest way to implement traffic lighting in Crystal Reports is to use the Highlighting Expert to apply color to the key figure itself.

Here's what the report should look like before we get started (Figure 8.1).

Month/Year	Product	Qty	Revenue
July 2007		**1,007**	**$ 211,590.44**
	Ventra LX 2.33 1GB 300 GB	165	$ 90,748.35
	Ventra Ultra 3.00 2GB 750 GB	98	$ 63,797.02
	Ventra LXP 2.67 2GB 500 GB	75	$ 45,074.25
	UltraTouch USB Keyboard	120	$ 4,797.60
	DigiPad Mousepad	339	$ 3,010.32
	Computer Speakers	115	$ 2,643.85
	LightTouch Optical Mouse	95	$ 1,519.05
August 2007		**6,145**	**$ 729,641.87**
	17" LCD Monitor	1,650	$ 387,733.50
	Ventra LXP 2.67 2GB 500 GB	390	$ 234,386.10
	Computer Speakers	1,300	$ 29,887.00
	LightTouch Optical Mouse	1,475	$ 23,585.25
	UltraTouch USB Keyboard	530	$ 21,189.40
	Ventra Ultra 3.00 2GB 750 GB	30	$ 19,529.70
	DigiPad Mousepad	758	$ 6,731.04
	Ventra LX 2.33 1GB 300 GB	12	$ 6,599.88
September 2007		**6,810**	**$ 734,299.45**
	17" LCD Monitor	1,260	$ 296,087.40
	Ventra Ultra 3.00 2GB 750 GB	225	$ 146,472.75
	Ventra LXP 2.67 2GB 500 GB	205	$ 123,202.95
	Ventra LX 2.33 1GB 300 GB	100	$ 54,999.00
	UltraTouch USB Keyboard	1,370	$ 54,772.60
	Computer Speakers	1,200	$ 27,588.00
	LightTouch Optical Mouse	1,325	$ 21,186.75
	DigiPad Mousepad	1,125	$ 9,990.00
		13,962	**$ 1,675,531.76**

Figure 8.1 Initial Sales Report

The data in our report isn't necessarily the best for illustrating this type of high-lighting, but it will do for learning the basics of this technique. Let's assume that the VP of sales wants to highlight monthly sales figures based on the following criteria:

▸ Green – revenue over $100,000

▸ Yellow – revenue from $50,000 to $100,000

▸ Red – revenue below $50,000

Once we know our parameters, we're ready to apply our highlighting. Just right-click the zz_Revenue key figure in the Detail section and select Highlighting Expert (Figure 8.2).

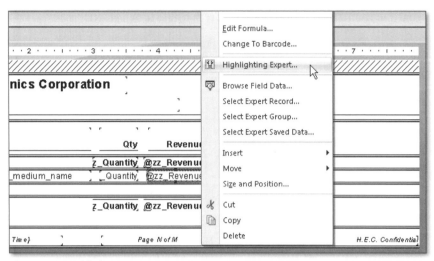

Figure 8.2 Highlighting Expert Menu Option

Next you'll see the Highlighting Expert dialog box. Click the New button at the bottom right to add a new condition. Our first condition will highlight all sales below $50,000 in red (Figure 8.3).

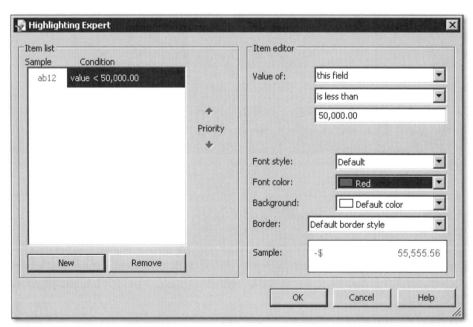

Figure 8.3 Adding a Condition in the Highlighting Expert

Notice that we left the first pull-down menu as the default value of This Field. In most cases the condition will be based on the value of the field you're applying the highlighting to (in our case Revenue). However, the Highlighting Expert is capable of testing the value of any other field available in the data source of the report.

The next condition is a bit trickier to pull off because we're using color to highlight our revenue key figure. The middle color of a traffic light is yellow, which works well on a real traffic light but not so well on a piece of paper, where it washes out and becomes difficult to see. Therefore, if you're going to highlight data in your report using yellow, you have to change the background color of the field to provide some contrast. It's is also helpful to change the font style to bold to help make it more legible on the screen. Therefore, our settings for the yellow band of numbers should look like Figure 8.4).

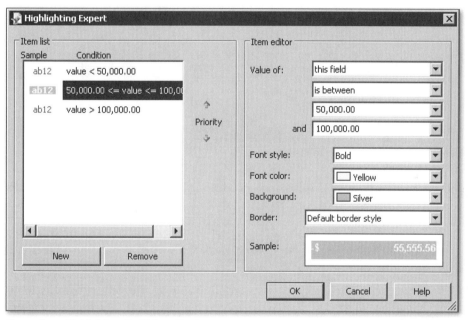

Figure 8.4   Highlighting the Yellow Band

The last band of numbers to highlight is the high end numbers, or those that are greater than $100,000. These, of course, will be our green numbers. Once we've completed our three conditional bands, we can click OK and then preview our report. It should look like Figure 8.5).

Month/Year	Product	Qty	Revenue
July 2007		**1,007**	**$ 211,590.44**
	Ventra LX 2.33 1GB 300 GB	165	$ 90,748.35
	Ventra Ultra 3.00 2GB 750 GB	98	$ 63,797.02
	Ventra LXP 2.67 2GB 500 GB	75	$ 45,074.25
	UltraTouch USB Keyboard	120	$ 4,797.60
	DigiPad Mousepad	339	$ 3,010.32
	Computer Speakers	115	$ 2,643.85
	LightTouch Optical Mouse	95	$ 1,519.05
August 2007		**6,145**	**$ 729,641.87**
	17" LCD Monitor	1,650	$ 387,733.50
	Ventra LXP 2.67 2GB 500 GB	390	$ 234,386.10
	Computer Speakers	1,300	$ 29,887.00
	LightTouch Optical Mouse	1,475	$ 23,585.25
	UltraTouch USB Keyboard	530	$ 21,189.40
	Ventra Ultra 3.00 2GB 750 GB	30	$ 19,529.70
	DigiPad Mousepad	758	$ 6,731.04
	Ventra LX 2.33 1GB 300 GB	12	$ 6,599.88
September 2007		**6,810**	**$ 734,299.45**
	17" LCD Monitor	1,260	$ 296,087.40
	Ventra Ultra 3.00 2GB 750 GB	225	$ 146,472.75
	Ventra LXP 2.67 2GB 500 GB	205	$ 123,202.95
	Ventra LX 2.33 1GB 300 GB	100	$ 54,999.00
	UltraTouch USB Keyboard	1,370	$ 54,772.60
	Computer Speakers	1,200	$ 27,588.00
	LightTouch Optical Mouse	1,325	$ 21,186.75
	DigiPad Mousepad	1,125	$ 9,990.00
		13,962	**$ 1,675,531.76**

Figure 8.5 Revenue Key Figure Highlighted

Although this technique is fairly simple and straightforward, as you can see, it does come with some limitations:

▸ This works fine when viewing the report on a computer screen or when it's printed on a color printer, but doesn't work at all when printed on a black and white printer (as in this book).

▸ It's is not particularly attractive, especially the way the yellow band is highlighted. There's just not any elegant way to highlight text in yellow on a white piece of paper.

▸ The Highlighting Expert is only capable of evaluating the value of a single field (which can be any field in your data source). Sometimes your condition will require the evaluation of more than one field.

Before we move on from the Highlighting Expert, we should point out that you can also apply a variety of border styles to your highlighted field to help draw distinctions between your various bands of numbers. Also, if you do decide to highlight any numbers in a report using only color, you should always supply a legend (usually in the page footer) that explains the meaning of the various colors.

8.2   Applying Conditional Formatting Using a Formula

Once you get beyond the most basic highlighting needs, you'll find yourself needing to bypass the Highlighting Expert and create your own custom formatting formulas that you attach to objects in your report. There are a many more options available to you as a developer when you learn how to apply your own formatting using formulas. Once you understand the basic technique, the possibilities are only limited by your imagination and creativity.

Although you can use a formatting formula to change the color of a field, you normally wouldn't do this, for the simple reason that you can do this much more easily using the Highlighting Expert (as we've just seen). Once you get beyond the highlighting of text, the most common technique involves the *conditional suppression* of a variety of objects to draw attention to various value points in your data.

Hot Tip

As you'll see as we move on through the rest of this book, conditional suppression is a key skill to master if you want to get the most out of Crystal Reports. Beyond basic formatting and grouping skills this may be the most valuable skill for you to learn.

If you haven't yet, save the previous example report. Now go back and open the Chapter 7 – Sales Report by Month report and immediately do a Save As. Call the new report "Chapter 8 – Conditional Formatting Using a Formula."

We're going to highlight two advantages of this technique in the following example. First, we'll use objects (instead of colored text) to highlight our data values. Second, we'll use two conditions to determine the appropriate highlighting rather than just one. Our VP of sales has just refined the conditions for highlighting the revenue figures in our report. She's decided that she's only interested in tracking the big-ticket items that Hedijetijak Electronics sells — items priced at $500 or more.

When we look back at our report, we notice we have a bit of a problem. The two key figures available from our BW query are Quantity (quantity sold) and Revenue. The item price isn't available as a key figure.

Important Note

It's not at all unusual for individual item characteristics (such as price) to not be available as key figures when working with data coming from SAP NetWeaver BW. If you recall, the whole idea of a data warehouse is to provide summary, not detail-level, data. Unless something like price is deliberately included as part of the design of the source InfoCube, you cannot count on it being available for use (at least not directly) in your report.

Fortunately we can easily reverse-engineer the price for each item by simply dividing the revenue key figure by quantity (this assumes, of course, that the price of a individual item is always the same, as it is in our case). This requires that we create a formula. It's been a little while since our last formula, but you should be able to start a new formula by now. Let's name it "Unit Price."

This formula is going to be quite simple. The formula is:

```
{@zz_Revenue} / {@zz_Quantity}
```

That's it. After saving and closing our new formula, we need to move our Revenue column (detail field, summaries, and column header) to the right to make room for our new item price formula. After this, we need to insert our new formula into the Detail section between the Quantity field and Revenue. After formatting it with a $ and adding a column header, our report should now look like Figure 8.6.

Month/Year	Product	Qty	Unit Price	Revenue
July 2007		**1,007**		**$ 211,590.44**
	Ventra LX 2.33 1GB 300 GB	165	$ 549.99	$ 90,748.35
	Ventra Ultra 3.00 2GB 750 GB	98	$ 650.99	$ 63,797.02
	Ventra LXP 2.67 2GB 500 GB	75	$ 600.99	$ 45,074.25
	UltraTouch USB Keyboard	120	$ 39.98	$ 4,797.60
	DigiPad Mousepad	339	$ 8.88	$ 3,010.32
	Computer Speakers	115	$ 22.99	$ 2,643.85
	LightTouch Optical Mouse	95	$ 15.99	$ 1,519.05

Figure 8.6 Adding the Unit Price Formula

Pop Quiz

Question: What's the fastest way to create the new Unit Price column header?

Answer: Clone the Qty header by holding down the `Ctrl` key and dragging it to the right. Then double-click the cloned copy and change the text.

We know which of our products are our big hitters (over $500 per unit price). Now all we need to do is figure out a good way to highlight our revenue figures based on the new criteria we just received from the VP of sales. This is where we get to be a little more creative.

Once we move past using colored text using the Highlighting Expert, it's now up to us to choose a method to highlight values in our data. One common method is to use a combination of graphic objects and conditional suppression. The trick to making this work is that you need to either create or find your own graphic because the only graphic shape available to you within Crystal Reports is a square. (There's also a line, but although you're not likely to use a square to highlight data, you're even less likely to use a line.)

We suggest that if you want to do any serious highlighting using the technique we're about to show you, you should invest in some simple clip art to make your life easier. The types of shapes you need are very limited, so you'll find that a very limited number of graphic shapes is all you'll need. For now, if you don't want to take the time to find some clip art to complete the following exercise, you can use the Paint program that comes with Windows (or your favorite graphics program) to create your own.

In our example we'll be using three objects to highlight the revenue key figure: a green circle, a yellow triangle, and a red X. Our first step is to copy and paste these three graphics into our Detail section, as in Figure 8.7.

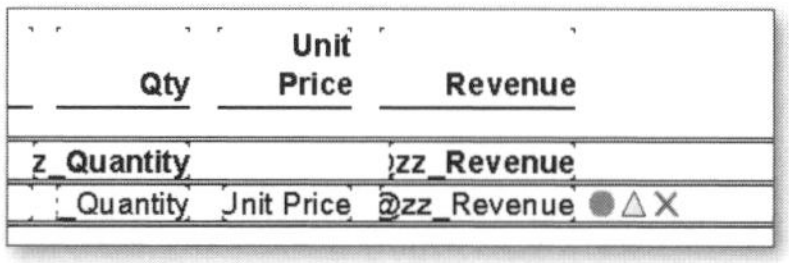

Figure 8.7   Copy and Paste Graphic Objects

Now when we preview our report, we see Figure 8.8.

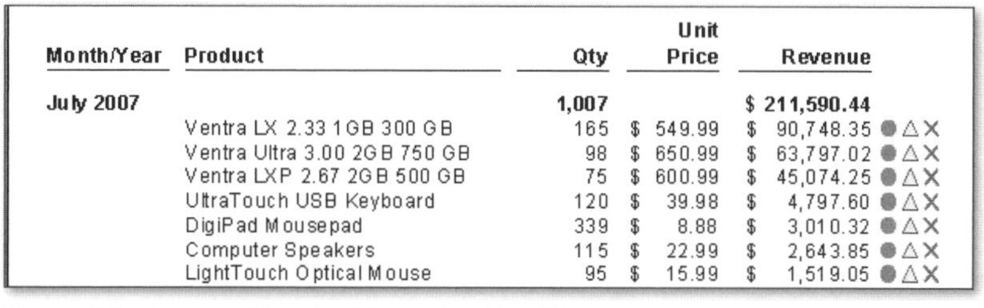

Figure 8.8   Preview Showing Three Graphic Objects

315

The trick now is to show only the one graphic that applies to the particular revenue figure (or no graphic at all). Again, this is all handled using conditional suppression. Let's start with our green circle. Right-click the green circle (or whatever other graphic you're using to represent the good band) and select Format Graphic (Figure 8.9).

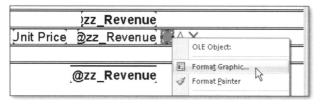

Figure 8.9   Format Graphic Menu Item

You'll see the Format Editor dialog box. Next we need to click the formula icon next to the Suppress option (Figure 8.10).

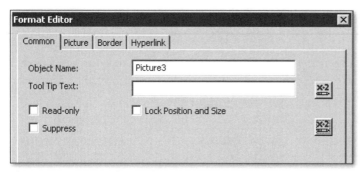

Figure 8.10   Format Editor Dialog Box

Now we need to create a formula that will suppress our green circle (which indicates the good revenue numbers).

Hot Tip
The key to understanding conditional suppression is to make yourself stop for a second and think backward. What we're doing here is creating a formula that will determine when we don't want to see the green circle, not when we do. You're initial gut reaction (especially when you're just getting started) will be to create a formula that will determine when you want to display the object, not suppress it. If when you finish your formula, you end up with the exact opposite result of what you had expected, just go back and reverse your logic.

With that in mind, the formula we want to create to suppress our green circle is the following:

```
If {@Unit Price} > 500
  then
  if {@zz_Revenue} < 100000
  then True
  else
  False
else
  True
```

Because this type of conditional suppression logic is quite common, we'll take the time to fully explain the logic of this formula.

The first condition we want to consider is the new condition just introduced by our VP of sales, namely, that she's only interested in highlighting products whose unit price is greater than $500. Because of this, right away we want to delineate between products whose unit price is $0 to $500 and those that are above $500.

Our first test is to determine if the unit price is greater than $500. If so, we proceed with our test of the Revenue key figure to determine whether or not we need to suppress the graphic (in this case, a green circle). If the unit price is not greater than $500 the formula drops down to the final Else statement, which is `else True`.

> **Important Note**
>
> A result of True in a suppression formula means the object will be suppressed. A result of False means it will not be suppressed.

So far this means the green circle will be suppressed for all items with a unit price of under $500. (This will be true for all three of our graphic objects because we aren't concerned about flagging or highlighting any of the products that sell for less than $500.)

What do we do with the items whose unit price is above $500? That's when we drop down into our second If statement (this type of formula is called a *nested If* formula because there's a second If statement nested inside of the first If statement). For these items we now need to evaluate a second value, the Revenue key figure. Our logic says that if the revenue key figure is less than $100,000 we'll suppress the green circle.

Again, this will at first seem backward to you. As we said before, take the time to think backward, and it will all make sense. Remember, because we're answering the question, "When do you want the green circle to *not* appear?" not "When do you want to see the green circle?" it makes sense that our condition would say "less than $100,000" not "more than $100,000."

The acid test of this logic is to take a peek at your report in the Preview tab to see what happens to the green circle. Let's take a look (Figure 8.11).

Month/Year	Product	Qty	Unit Price	Revenue		
July 2007		1,007		$ 211,590.44		
	Ventra LX 2.33 1GB 300 GB	165	$ 549.99	$ 90,748.35	△	X
	Ventra Ultra 3.00 2GB 750 GB	98	$ 650.99	$ 63,797.02	△	X
	Ventra LXP 2.67 2GB 500 GB	75	$ 600.99	$ 45,074.25	△	X
	UltraTouch USB Keyboard	120	$ 39.98	$ 4,797.60	△	X
	DigiPad Mousepad	339	$ 8.88	$ 3,010.32	△	X
	Computer Speakers	115	$ 22.99	$ 2,643.85	△	X
	LightTouch Optical Mouse	95	$ 15.99	$ 1,519.05	△	X
August 2007		6,145		$ 729,641.87		
	17" LCD Monitor	1,650	$ 234.99	$ 387,733.50	△	X
	Ventra LXP 2.67 2GB 500 GB	390	$ 600.99	$ 234,386.10 ●	△	X
	Computer Speakers	1,300	$ 22.99	$ 29,887.00	△	X
	LightTouch Optical Mouse	1,475	$ 15.99	$ 23,585.25	△	X
	UltraTouch USB Keyboard	530	$ 39.98	$ 21,189.40	△	X
	Ventra Ultra 3.00 2GB 750 GB	30	$ 650.99	$ 19,529.70	△	X
	DigiPad Mousepad	758	$ 8.88	$ 6,731.04	△	X
	Ventra LX 2.33 1GB 300 GB	12	$ 549.99	$ 6,599.88	△	X
September 2007		6,810		$ 734,299.45		
	17" LCD Monitor	1,260	$ 234.99	$ 296,087.40	△	X
	Ventra Ultra 3.00 2GB 750 GB	225	$ 650.99	$ 146,472.75 ●	△	X
	Ventra LXP 2.67 2GB 500 GB	205	$ 600.99	$ 123,202.95 ●	△	X
	Ventra LX 2.33 1GB 300 GB	100	$ 549.99	$ 54,999.00	△	X
	UltraTouch USB Keyboard	1,370	$ 39.98	$ 54,772.60	△	X
	Computer Speakers	1,200	$ 22.99	$ 27,588.00	△	X
	LightTouch Optical Mouse	1,325	$ 15.99	$ 21,186.75	△	X
	DigiPad Mousepad	1,125	$ 8.88	$ 9,990.00	△	X
		13,962		$ 1,675,531.76		

Figure 8.11   Green Circle Suppressed

Let's see how we did. Looking at the July revenue figures, there are no products that sold more than $100,000 in that month, so none of them deserve a green circle. So far, so good.

When we drop down to the August numbers, we have our first green circle. Does it pass the test? First, we need to ensure that the unit price is over $500, and that's the case here. Next, the revenue key figure needs to be over $100,000. Ditto on that. The same is true for the following item that has a green circle.

So far we're doing fine. We've successfully highlighted the high end of our product revenue numbers. Now let's move to the yellow triangle to take care of the middle numbers (between $50,000 and $100,000).

Pop Quiz

Question: What would be a good shortcut for creating our next formula?

Answer: Copy and paste the first suppression formula we created and then modify it.

After copying and pasting our first formula into the suppression formula for the yellow triangle graphic, we'll change it to look like the following:

```
If {@Unit Price} > 500
 then
 if {@zz_Revenue} < 50000 or {@zz_Revenue} >= 100000
 then True
 else
 False
else
 True
```

The initial condition remains unchanged, as it will for the next object (the red X). All three share the condition that we're only interested in highlighting items whose unit price is over $500.

What changes is the second condition. For the yellow triangle, we again need to ask ourselves the question, "When do we want the yellow triangle to go away?" The answer is whenever the revenue key figure is *either* less than $50K (these will soon get a red X) *or* greater than $100,000 (which we just handled with the green circle).

Again, the proof is in the pudding, as they say. Once you save and close this formula, you should see the results shown in Figure 8.12 in the Preview tab.

Month/Year	Product	Qty	Unit Price	Revenue	
July 2007		**1,007**		**$ 211,590.44**	
	Ventra LX 2.33 1GB 300 GB	165	$ 549.99	$ 90,748.35	△X
	Ventra Ultra 3.00 2GB 750 GB	98	$ 650.99	$ 63,797.02	△X
	Ventra LXP 2.67 2GB 500 GB	75	$ 600.99	$ 45,074.25	X
	UltraTouch USB Keyboard	120	$ 39.98	$ 4,797.60	X
	DigiPad Mousepad	339	$ 8.88	$ 3,010.32	X
	Computer Speakers	115	$ 22.99	$ 2,643.85	X
	LightTouch Optical Mouse	95	$ 15.99	$ 1,519.05	X
August 2007		**6,145**		**$ 729,641.87**	
	17" LCD Monitor	1,650	$ 234.99	$ 387,733.50	X
	Ventra LXP 2.67 2GB 500 GB	390	$ 600.99	$ 234,386.10 ●	X
	Computer Speakers	1,300	$ 22.99	$ 29,887.00	X
	LightTouch Optical Mouse	1,475	$ 15.99	$ 23,585.25	X
	UltraTouch USB Keyboard	530	$ 39.98	$ 21,189.40	X
	Ventra Ultra 3.00 2GB 750 GB	30	$ 650.99	$ 19,529.70	X
	DigiPad Mousepad	758	$ 8.88	$ 6,731.04	X
	Ventra LX 2.33 1GB 300 GB	12	$ 549.99	$ 6,599.88	X
September 2007		**6,810**		**$ 734,299.45**	
	17" LCD Monitor	1,260	$ 234.99	$ 296,087.40	X
	Ventra Ultra 3.00 2GB 750 GB	225	$ 650.99	$ 146,472.75 ●	X
	Ventra LXP 2.67 2GB 500 GB	205	$ 600.99	$ 123,202.95 ●	X
	Ventra LX 2.33 1GB 300 GB	100	$ 549.99	$ 54,999.00	△X
	UltraTouch USB Keyboard	1,370	$ 39.98	$ 54,772.60	X
	Computer Speakers	1,200	$ 22.99	$ 27,588.00	X
	LightTouch Optical Mouse	1,325	$ 15.99	$ 21,186.75	X
	DigiPad Mousepad	1,125	$ 8.88	$ 9,990.00	X
		13,962		**$ 1,675,531.76**	

Figure 8.12　Yellow Triangle Suppressed

We've passed the test. We now see only three yellow triangles, with each next to an item that sells for more than $500 per unit and whose revenue amount for that month was between $50,000 and $100,000.

The last item is the red X. Again, you might want to copy and paste the original suppression formula and make the appropriate changes. The final suppression formula should look like the following:

```
If {@Unit Price} > 500
  then
  if {@zz_Revenue} >= 50000
  then True
  else
  False
else
  True
```

By now this should be looking a little more familiar. As before, the only thing that changes is the revenue condition. This time we'll suppress the red X whenever the revenue key figure is less than or equal to $50,000.

Important Note

You have to be careful that you handle the "border" points between your different bands correctly. If one band is taking the exact border value (in our case $50,000 and $100,000), you need to be careful that the neighboring band doesn't take it as well. If you do, and you get a value that's exactly that amount, you'll have two graphics showing up in your report.

Let's take a look at our report (Figure 8.13).

Month/Year	Product	Qty	Unit Price	Revenue	
July 2007		**1,007**		**$ 211,590.44**	
	Ventra LX 2.33 1GB 300 GB	165	$ 549.99	$ 90,748.35	△
	Ventra Ultra 3.00 2GB 750 GB	98	$ 650.99	$ 63,797.02	△
	Ventra LXP 2.67 2GB 500 GB	75	$ 600.99	$ 45,074.25	X
	UltraTouch USB Keyboard	120	$ 39.98	$ 4,797.60	
	DigiPad Mousepad	339	$ 8.88	$ 3,010.32	
	Computer Speakers	115	$ 22.99	$ 2,643.85	
	LightTouch Optical Mouse	95	$ 15.99	$ 1,519.05	
August 2007		**6,145**		**$ 729,641.87**	
	17" LCD Monitor	1,650	$ 234.99	$ 387,733.50	
	Ventra LXP 2.67 2GB 500 GB	390	$ 600.99	$ 234,386.10	●
	Computer Speakers	1,300	$ 22.99	$ 29,887.00	
	LightTouch Optical Mouse	1,475	$ 15.99	$ 23,585.25	
	UltraTouch USB Keyboard	530	$ 39.98	$ 21,189.40	
	Ventra Ultra 3.00 2GB 750 GB	30	$ 650.99	$ 19,529.70	X
	DigiPad Mousepad	758	$ 8.88	$ 6,731.04	
	Ventra LX 2.33 1GB 300 GB	12	$ 549.99	$ 6,599.88	X
September 2007		**6,810**		**$ 734,299.45**	
	17" LCD Monitor	1,260	$ 234.99	$ 296,087.40	
	Ventra Ultra 3.00 2GB 750 GB	225	$ 650.99	$ 146,472.75	●
	Ventra LXP 2.67 2GB 500 GB	205	$ 600.99	$ 123,202.95	●
	Ventra LX 2.33 1GB 300 GB	100	$ 549.99	$ 54,999.00	△
	UltraTouch USB Keyboard	1,370	$ 39.98	$ 54,772.60	
	Computer Speakers	1,200	$ 22.99	$ 27,588.00	
	LightTouch Optical Mouse	1,325	$ 15.99	$ 21,186.75	
	DigiPad Mousepad	1,125	$ 8.88	$ 9,990.00	
		13,962		**$ 1,675,531.76**	

Figure 8.13 Red X Suppressed

We're almost finished. So far our suppression formulas have passed their individual tests. A final test is to check that no one item has more than one graphic displayed, which is the case with our report. If for some reason a particular item had more than one graphic showing, we'd need to go back and review our suppression logic.

The final step is fairly simple: We need to align the three graphics so they're sitting on top of each other (stacked). The easiest way to do this is to select all three, right-click, and select Align and then Centers. Our final highlighted report now looks like Figure 8.14.

Month/Year	Product	Qty	Unit Price	Revenue	
July 2007		**1,007**		**$ 211,590.44**	
	Ventra LX 2.33 1GB 300 GB	165	$ 549.99	$ 90,748.35	△
	Ventra Ultra 3.00 2GB 750 GB	98	$ 650.99	$ 63,797.02	△
	Ventra LXP 2.67 2GB 500 GB	75	$ 600.99	$ 45,074.25	X
	UltraTouch USB Keyboard	120	$ 39.98	$ 4,797.60	
	DigiPad Mousepad	339	$ 8.88	$ 3,010.32	
	Computer Speakers	115	$ 22.99	$ 2,643.85	
	LightTouch Optical Mouse	95	$ 15.99	$ 1,519.05	
August 2007		**6,145**		**$ 729,641.87**	
	17" LCD Monitor	1,650	$ 234.99	$ 387,733.50	
	Ventra LXP 2.67 2GB 500 GB	390	$ 600.99	$ 234,386.10	●
	Computer Speakers	1,300	$ 22.99	$ 29,887.00	
	LightTouch Optical Mouse	1,475	$ 15.99	$ 23,585.25	
	UltraTouch USB Keyboard	530	$ 39.98	$ 21,189.40	
	Ventra Ultra 3.00 2GB 750 GB	30	$ 650.99	$ 19,529.70	X
	DigiPad Mousepad	758	$ 8.88	$ 6,731.04	
	Ventra LX 2.33 1GB 300 GB	12	$ 549.99	$ 6,599.88	X
September 2007		**6,810**		**$ 734,299.45**	
	17" LCD Monitor	1,260	$ 234.99	$ 296,087.40	
	Ventra Ultra 3.00 2GB 750 GB	225	$ 650.99	$ 146,472.75	●
	Ventra LXP 2.67 2GB 500 GB	205	$ 600.99	$ 123,202.95	●
	Ventra LX 2.33 1GB 300 GB	100	$ 549.99	$ 54,999.00	△
	UltraTouch USB Keyboard	1,370	$ 39.98	$ 54,772.60	
	Computer Speakers	1,200	$ 22.99	$ 27,588.00	
	LightTouch Optical Mouse	1,325	$ 15.99	$ 21,186.75	
	DigiPad Mousepad	1,125	$ 8.88	$ 9,990.00	
		13,962		**$ 1,675,531.76**	

Figure 8.14   Final Highlighted Report

As a reminder, any time you use either color or a graphic (or both) to highlight values in a report, you should include a legend to help the user understand what it all means, like in the example shown in Figure 8.15.

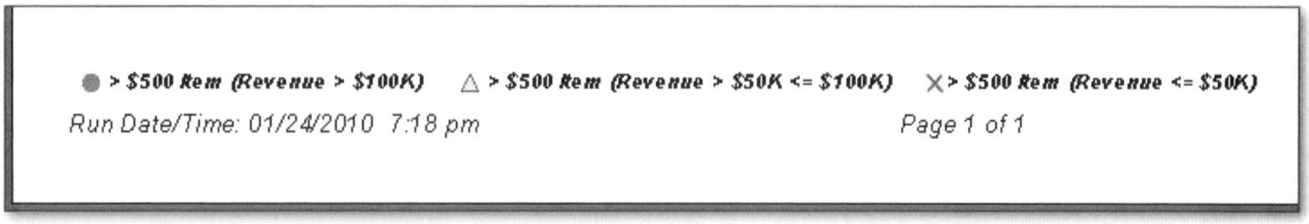

● > *$500 Rem (Revenue > $100K)*   △ > *$500 Rem (Revenue > $50K <= $100K)*   ✕ > *$500 Rem (Revenue <= $50K)*

Run Date/Time: 01/24/2010 7:18 pm   *Page 1 of 1*

Figure 8.15   Highlighting Legend in Page Footer

Pop Quiz:

Question: If you don't see your graphics after placing them in the page footer to make your legend, why aren't they showing up?

Answer: You copied and pasted them from your Detail section and forgot to delete the suppression formula.

One benefit of using different shapes when highlighting values in a report is that it translates nicely to a black and white printout of the report. That way you're not dependent on a color printer for your highlighting to make sense to the end user.

Before we leave this topic of highlighting data, we should do a little reality check to get our bearings:

▶ First, you may be getting the impression that once you get beyond the world of the Highlighting Expert and using colored text highlighting data in Crystal Reports gets a bit tricky. This is absolutely correct. Because Crystal Reports is a general-purpose report writer that can be used to handle a wide range of reporting requirements, it tends to be somewhat limited in certain specialized applications (such as traffic lighting or exception reporting).

▶ If you require sophisticated (and more automated) highlighting capabilities, you may want to look into SAP BusinessObjects Xcelsius Enterprise or Voyager/"Pioneer." These tools are specifically designed to provide a rich, graphical data analysis environment. Although you can create some "dashboard-like" interfaces with Crystal Reports (if you're creative and good with formulas), no one should ever expect Crystal Reports to produce the kind of dashboard or cockpit interfaces that SAP BusinessObjects Xcelsius Enterprise is capable of producing. And remember, SAP BusinessObjects Xcelsius Enterprise dashboards can be inserted directly into Crystal Reports 2008, giving you the best of both worlds.

▶ In terms of level of complexity, the suppression formulas we just showed you are somewhere around a 2 or 3 on a scale of 1 to 10, with 10 being the highest level of complexity. If these formulas have your head spinning, this might be a good point to give your future as a report writer some serious thought. This is not meant to scare you. You rarely get above a 4 or 5 level of complexity when dealing with SAP NetWeaver BW. However, you must be able to handle the level of formulas we just covered to succeed as a report developer in this environment. There's no getting around it.

▶ We cannot emphasize enough how important it is for you to get as comfortable as possible as soon as possible with this concept of conditional suppression. This is a critical key that unlocks a whole new level of possibilities in your report development endeavors. And whereas it's handy in suppressing individual objects in your report (as we've just seen), it really gets exciting when you start applying it to entire sections of your report, as we're are about to see next.

8.3   Stretching Your Reports with Conditional Suppression

Right about now is when things really start to get interesting. First, if you've made it this far, you're to be congratulated. You're already most of the way to becoming fully equipped to be successful in developing Crystal Reports reports in an SAP NetWeaver BW environment.

This section, in many ways, is the pivotal section in this book. To understand why, we need to take a minute to review where we've come from and where we're going.

We've already established in a variety of ways that different users require different ways of looking at their data. This should be obvious by now. It's also just as true that the needs of any individual user will change over time and from situation to situation. One day a certain approach may work fine, whereas the next day a new approach (or technique) is required.

That said, certain general observations can be made regarding any group of business end users and their ability to consume information through any BI interface:

▶ The average business end user is busy — very busy. Therefore, they typically don't have the time (or patience) to learn the latest new way of looking at their data, no matter how intuitive it may be. That's just reality. This is the biggest determiner of how sophisticated you can get in your approach to delivering information to business end users.

▶ Although most end users appreciate flexibility in any BI interface, there's is a limit to the amount of flexibility they can realistically handle. And they usually reach this limit faster than the people in IT think they will. This is the biggest reason why many well-intentioned ad hoc initiatives don't ever catch on with many users.

▶ As you might imagine, this has always somewhat perplexed the developers of BI (reporting) interfaces, and many have made efforts to study this issue in hopes of figuring out ways to help end users become capable of dealing with some of the more complex BI interfaces (such as OLAP).

▶ What they're finding out is that, for the most part, *it is what it is*. There really isn't a problem at all — only a very simple, basic fact: Most business end users will never be able to handle any kind of BI interface beyond a basic reporting interface (such as Crystal Reports). This has very little to do with the capabilities of the end user and almost everything to do with the inherent complexity of working with data. For the most part this will never change, and all the hand-wringing on the part of BI vendors isn't going to change this fact.

▶ Does this mean there's no place for the more advanced BI tools (ad hoc, OLAP, data analysis, predictive analytics, etc.)? Absolutely not. In any organization there will be a subset of end users who possess either the skills or the motivation (or perhaps both) necessary to take full advantage of these more advanced BI interfaces. But it would be a highly unusual organization where that subset becomes the majority.

▶ The bottom line: It can be safely stated that the majority of business end users require a BI interface that's designed to be a "package and deliver" system where information is assembled and preformatted for them. All they need to do, for the most part, is select from a (intentionally) limited set of options to produce the results they need to get their questions answered. It's quick, it's easy, and it doesn't take days of training to figure out how to get it done.

This brings us to our current topic: how to stretch what was at first a static Crystal Reports report into a more dynamic reporting interface, in other words, how to take a single-purpose snapshot of your data and turn it into a multipurpose collection of looks so you can meet the requirements of what would have been several reports in a single Crystal Reports report.

8.3.1 The Classic Crystal Drill-Down

To get started, we'll briefly show you how this was done before Crystal Reports 2008, because, although we'll encourage you to handle this primarily using the new method, there's still some value in doing it the old way for certain reporting requirements.

To begin, let's start with a report we created Chapter 6 that we called Chapter 6 – Custom Group Using a Formula 4. We're starting with this report because it contains two groups that will work well for our example. Immediately do a Save As and call the new report "Chapter 8 – Classic Drill-Down."

The report should currently look something like Figure 8.16.

Hedijetijak Electronics Corporation

National Sales Report

Product Category	Product	Qty	Revenue
Legacy Products		6,195	$ 1,146,603
July 2007		190	$ 47,718
	Ventra LXP 2.67 2GB 500 GB	75	$ 45,074
	Computer Speakers	115	$ 2,644
August 2007		3,340	$ 652,007
	17" LCD Monitor	1,650	$ 387,734
	Ventra LXP 2.67 2GB 500 GB	390	$ 234,386
	Computer Speakers	1,300	$ 29,887
September 2007		2,665	$ 446,878
	17" LCD Monitor	1,260	$ 296,087
	Ventra LXP 2.67 2GB 500 GB	205	$ 123,203
	Computer Speakers	1,200	$ 27,588
New Products		5,470	$ 295,822
July 2007		532	$ 68,326
	Ventra Ultra 3.00 2GB 750 GB	98	$ 63,797
	DigiPad Mousepad	339	$ 3,010
	LightTouch Optical Mouse	95	$ 1,519
August 2007		2,263	$ 49,846
	LightTouch Optical Mouse	1,475	$ 23,585
	Ventra Ultra 3.00 2GB 750 GB	30	$ 19,530
	DigiPad Mousepad	758	$ 6,731

Figure 8.16 Sales Report with Two Groups in the Preview Tab

When we look at the report in the Design tab, it looks like Figure 8.17.

PHa	**Hedijetijak Electronics Corporation**		
	Report Title		
PHb	Product		
	Category Product	Qty	Revenue
GH1	Group #1 Name	z_Quantity	@zz_Revenue
GH2	Group #2 Name	z_Quantity	@zz_Revenue
D	@z_Product_medium_name	Quantity	@zz_Revenue
GF2			
GF1			
RF		z_Quantity	@zz_Revenue

Figure 8.17 Sales Report with Two Groups in the Design Tab

As you can see here in the Design tab, the report has two groups and a Detail section. The first group is our custom group, Product Category, the second group is Calendar Month, and the detail displays Product. This is known as a *grouped detail report*. A drill-down report in Crystal Reports is when the initial report layout is only at a group level, and the user has the ability to "drill down" into the details of the report.

We'll begin by creating a single-level drill-down report. After that we'll create a two-level drill-down report. In general, the three primary steps to creating a drill-down report in Crystal Reports are:

▶ Move any group summaries to the group header (if not already there).

▶ Suppress the group footer(s).

▶ Hide the Detail section (and any group headers that you want to make "drill-able" starting with the bottommost group).

In our example we can skip the first step because our summaries are already in the group headers. The next step is to suppress the appropriate group footers. For our initial single-level drill-down report we'll need to suppress only the footer for group 2. You suppress any section by right-clicking in the left margin of the section and selecting Suppress (No Drill-Down) (Figure 8.18).

Lastly, we need to hide the Detail section. The difference between suppress and hide is that when you suppress a section, the user will never see it (at least with absolute suppression as opposed to conditional suppression), but when you hide a section, the user will have the option of drilling down to see the section if needed.

By right-clicking and selecting Suppress (No Drill-Down), we apply absolute suppression. As we'll see shortly, you apply conditional suppression by applying the suppression using a formula.

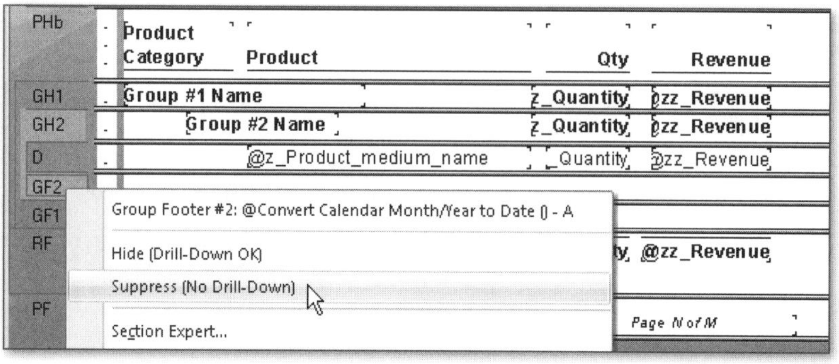

Figure 8.18 Suppress (No Drill-Down) Menu Item

After right-clicking in the left margin of the Detail section and selecting Hide (Drill-Down OK), our report should now look like Figure 8.19.

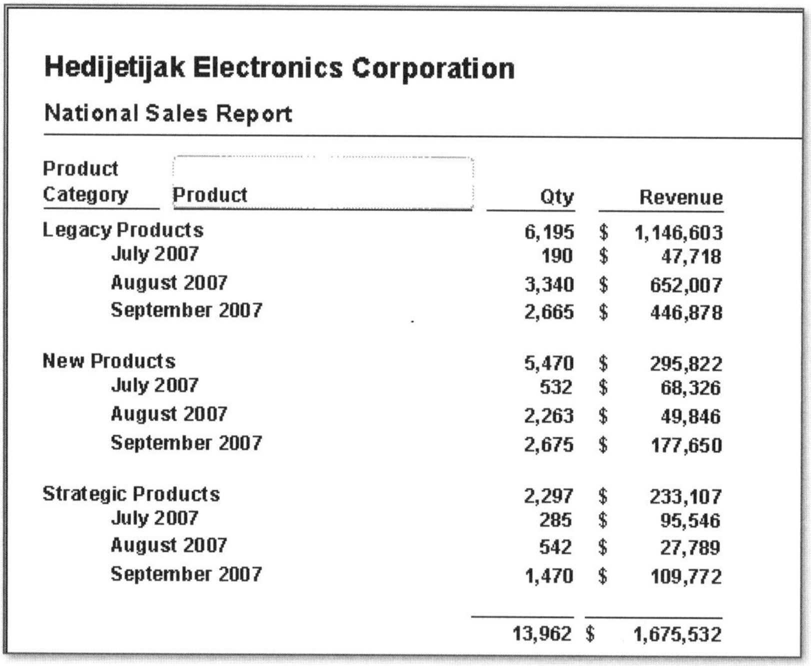

Figure 8.19 Initial Single-Level Drill-Down in the Preview Tab

That's all we need to do to create a fully functioning single-level drill-down report. You'll notice right away that something is missing — for now. The product detail data has disappeared. This is because it's now hidden in our initial view. If we now want to see the product detail for any month, we simply double-click either the name of the month on the left or one of the two summaries on the right. After double-clicking the September 2007 summary under Legacy Products, we see Figure 8.20.

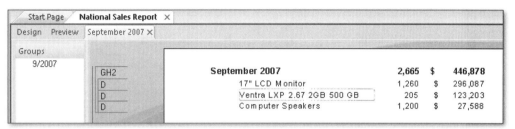

Figure 8.20 September 2009 Drill-Down

Notice that when we double-clicked the September 2007 summary, we generated a third tab at the top of our report called September 2007. Essentially, we've "peeled off" the detail data beneath the summary and set it aside as its own mini-report.

If you're at all observant, you may notice something a bit fishy going on here. If you look closely, you'll notice that we've lost our context. We can see the product detail now for September 2007, but for which product category? This isn't the total sales across all product categories but for one product category. If you recall, we double-clicked the September 2007 entry within the Legacy Products group. Of course, your end users may not remember that when they perform a drill-down on the Web. Besides, if you wanted to print this mini-report and take it to a meeting, you'd have to scribble Legacy Products at the top — not a good option.

Fortunately there's a quick fix for this. Let's close our drill-down tab first (just click the x on the tab). Now go to FILE • REPORT OPTIONS. We'll now select the option Show All Headers on Drill Down (Figure 8.21).

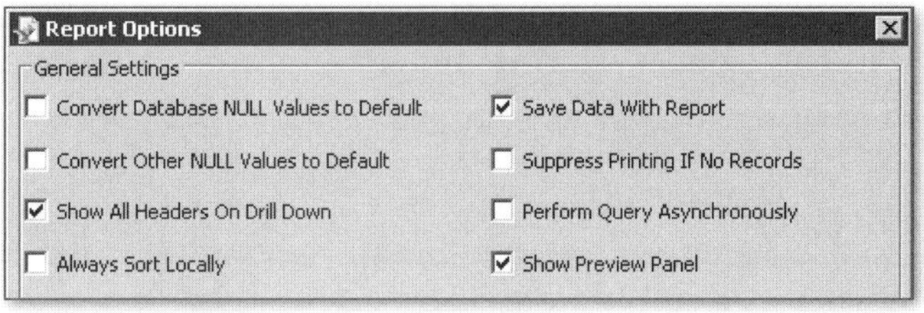

Report Options

General Settings

☐ Convert Database NULL Values to Default   ☑ Save Data With Report

☐ Convert Other NULL Values to Default   ☐ Suppress Printing If No Records

☑ Show All Headers On Drill Down   ☐ Perform Query Asynchronously

☐ Always Sort Locally   ☑ Show Preview Panel

Figure 8.21 Show All Headers on Drill Down

Now let's double-click the same September 2007 summary within the Legacy Products group. We now see the report shown in Figure 8.22.

Hedijetijak Electronics Corporation

National Sales Report

Product Category	Product	Qty	Revenue
Legacy Products		6,195	$ 1,146,603
	September 2007	2,665	$ 446,878
	17" LCD Monitor	1,260	$ 296,087
	Ventra LXP 2.67 2GB 500 GB	205	$ 123,203
	Computer Speakers	1,200	$ 27,588
		13,962	$ 1,675,532

Figure 8.22 September 2009 Drill-Down with Headers

Now things are looking better. We've have retained our context by "carrying forward" the group 1 header. Notice we've have also retained our page header. But, once again, if you're observant, you'll notice that we've introduced a new issue. We've also carried forward our report footer, which is still displaying the grand total for the entire report, not just the September totals for the Legacy Products. The option we just selected should have read Show All Headers *and Footers* on Drill Down because, as you can see, that's exactly what it does.

As you might imagine, there's a fix for this: conditional suppression. What we need to do is suppress the report footer whenever we (or our end user) perform a drill-down into detail. Fortunately for us, this is a lot easier than it used to be because we can now figure out where we are in our report (which level) by referencing a fairly recent addition to Crystal Reports, the DrillDownGroupLevel function.

Time for another formula. This one is going to be very short and to the point. Create a new formula and call it "DrillDownGroupLevel." You might want to copy the name before you click OK because the contents of the formula will be just the name of the formula, DrillDownGroupLevel. After entering this (or pasting it), close and save the formula.

A Reminder About Functions

We've utilized several functions up to this point in the book (ToNumber, Date, Minimum, Maximum). Functions are used within formulas to perform a specific task that would otherwise be either very difficult or impossible to perform with a formula.

The DrillDownGroupLevel formula has one purpose: to tell you what level you're at in your report as you're drilling-down into the report. The levels begin at 0 in the initial Preview tab and proceed to 1 when you drill into Group 1, 2 for Group 2, 3 for Group 3, and so on. Whenever you create any sort of drill-down group, it's a good idea to create a DrillDownGroupLevel formula and place it in the Detail section of your report and every group header section.

Let's do that. Once we've placed this formula in the Detail section and the two group headers (and applied some formatting), the report will look like Figure 8.23 when we go to the Preview tab.

Product Category	Product	Qty	Revenue	
Legacy Products		6,195	$ 1,146,603	0
	July 2007	190	$ 47,718	0
	August 2007	3,340	$ 652,007	0
	September 2007	2,665	$ 446,878	0

Figure 8.23   DrillDownGroupLevel Formula in the Preview Tab

As you can see, DrillDownGroupLevel returns a value of 0 when we're are looking at the report in the Preview tab. Notice that it returns the same value regardless of which section it's sitting in. In this case, the value is 0 in both the Group 1 header and the Group 2 header. This is because, even though this function does have the word *group* in its name, DrillDownGroupLevel returns the drill-down level only, not the group number. So, no matter where this function sits in your report, in the Preview tab it will always return 0.

Now let's see what happens when we double-click the September 2007 summary again to perform a drill-down. The Drill-Down tab now looks like Figure 8.24.

Now we can clearly see we're at DrillDownGroupLevel 2. So what happened to level 1? Did we bypass it somehow? Not exactly. If you recall, we hid only the Detail section of our report, not Group 2 (which we'll do next). Because we drilled down into Group 2, we went straight to drill-down level 2.

Hedijetijak Electronics Corporation

National Sales Report

Product Category	Product	Qty	Revenue	
Legacy Products		6,195	$ 1,146,603	2
	September 2007	2,665	$ 446,878	2
	17" LCD Monitor	1,260	$ 296,087	2
	Ventra LXP 2.67 2GB 500 GB	205	$ 123,203	2
	Computer Speakers	1,200	$ 27,588	2
		13,962	$ 1,675,532	

Figure 8.24 DrillDownGroupLevel Formula in the Drill-Down Tab

If you're a bit confused, this is quite normal. This idea of drill-down levels is a little hard to get your mind around at first. This is why we had you create the Drill-DownGroupLevel formula and place it in the Detail section and in every group header in your report. Now there's no room for confusion. You always know which level you're looking at.

Pop Quiz

Question: Now that we know the Preview tab is at level 0, how can we ensure that the report footer displays on this level only?

Answer: Apply a conditional suppression formula that says to suppress the report footer whenever the DrillDownGroupLevel is not 0.

To accomplish this, close the Drill-Down tab and then right-click in the left margin of the Report Footer. Select Section Expert. You'll see the window shown in Figure 8.25.

Figure 8.25 Section Expert – Suppress Formula Button

On the right is a Suppress (No Drill-Down) option, and next to it is a formula button. Click the formula button. Now enter the following short formula:

```
DrillDownGroupLevel <> 0
```

That's it. Save and close the formula.

> **Hot Tip**
>
> Be sure to click the OK button now in the Section Expert. If you click the Close button at the top right, it's the same as clicking Cancel, and you'll lose all your changes.

Perform another drill down as before. This time you'll see that the report footer with the grand total has disappeared (Figure 8.26).

Hedijetijak Electronics Corporation

National Sales Report

Product Category	Product	Qty		Revenue	
Legacy Products		6,195	$	1,146,603	2
September 2007		2,665	$	446,878	2
	17" LCD Monitor	1,260	$	296,087	2
	Ventra LXP 2.67 2GB 500 GB	205	$	123,203	2
	Computer Speakers	1,200	$	27,588	2

Figure 8.26   Drill-Down with Report Footer Suppressed

Now we have a usable drill-down layout that could be printed as a fully functional report. In this example the drill-down "slice" is quite small (only three detail lines). However, it's not unusual at all for a drill-down to be many pages by itself.

> **Important Note**
>
> The real power of a drill-down report in Crystal Reports is that you can not only provide your end user with a simple, point-and-click method to extract detail information, but you can deliver it as a fully formatted report suitable for printing.

Before we move on, let's take one more look at the "top" level of our report (the Preview tab) (Figure 8.27).

Product Category	Product	Qty	Revenue	
Legacy Products		**6,195**	$ **1,146,603**	0
	July 2007	**190**	$ **47,718**	0
	August 2007	**3,340**	$ **652,007**	0
	September 2007	**2,665**	$ **446,878**	0

Figure 8.27   Preview Tab with Incorrect Header

You may notice that we still have one more formatting issue to deal with in our initial report view. Because we've hidden the product detail in our initial view, the Product column heading is no longer necessary, at least not until we perform our drill-down. Knowing what you now know, what would be one way to make this column header disappear in the initial Preview tab but re-appear when we perform our drill-down?

Conditionally suppress it, of course. All we need to do is right-click the header in the Design tab and select Format Text. On the Common tab you should see the Suppress option. Click the Formula button across from it and enter the following formula:

```
DrillDownGroupLevel <> 0
```

Notice that this suppression formula is exactly the opposite of the one we entered for the report footer, which should make sense. We wanted the report footer to appear in the Preview tab and disappear when we drill down. We want the column header to disappear in the Preview tab and appear when we drill down.

As you might imagine, the acid test for determining if you got your conditional suppression formula logic correct is to look at your report in the Preview tab. When we do, we'll see the Figure 8.28.

Product Category	Qty	Revenue	
Legacy Products	**6,195**	$ **1,146,603**	0
July 2007	**190**	$ **47,718**	0
August 2007	**3,340**	$ **652,007**	0
September 2007	**2,665**	$ **446,878**	0

Figure 8.28   Preview Tab with Correct Header

Now our column headers match the data being displayed in the initial Preview tab. The only potential issue we might have to deal with is spacing. As you can see, now that we've eliminated the product description in the middle of the report, we now have a gap between the group headers on the left side of the report and the summaries on the left. We'll show you how you can take care of these types of situations shortly.

For now let's take things to the next level. We now want to "roll up" our report again so that it initially displays only the top-level totals for the three product categories. Then we want to be able to drill down into the calendar month group totals and then finally to the product detail. This will then become a two-level drill-down report.

Pop Quiz

Question: How will we "collapse" our single-level drill-down into a two-level drill-down report?

Answer: Suppress Group Footer 1 and hide Group Header 2.

Once we've have done this, our Preview tab should look like Figure 8.29.

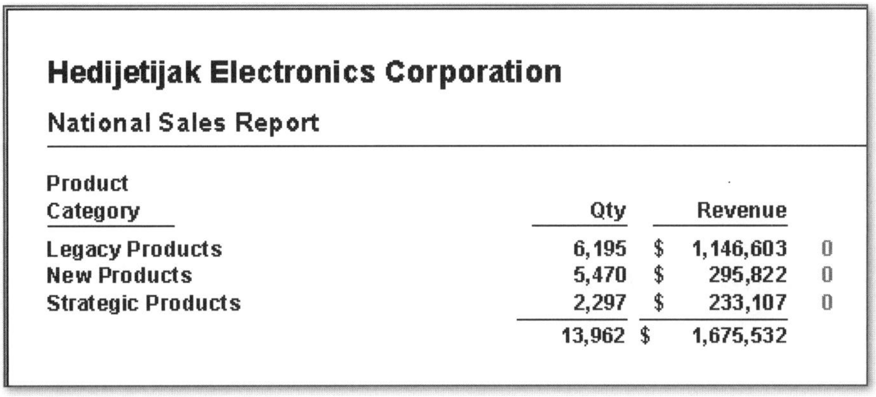

Hedijetijak Electronics Corporation

National Sales Report

Product Category	Qty	Revenue	
Legacy Products	6,195	$ 1,146,603	0
New Products	5,470	$ 295,822	0
Strategic Products	2,297	$ 233,107	0
	13,962	$ 1,675,532	

Figure 8.29   Two-Level Drill-Down in the Preview Tab

Now let's drill down into our report to the first drill-down level (Figure 8.30).

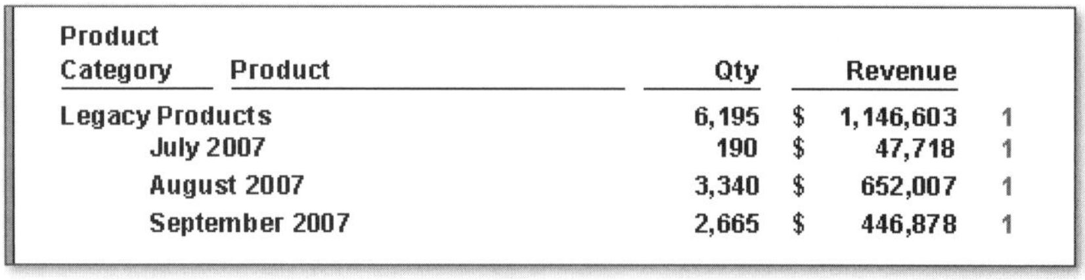

Product Category	Product	Qty		Revenue	
Legacy Products		6,195	$	1,146,603	1
	July 2007	190	$	47,718	1
	August 2007	3,340	$	652,007	1
	September 2007	2,665	$	446,878	1

Figure 8.30 Two-Level Drill-Down with Incorrect Level 1 Header

What happened? The Product column header has returned too soon. We need it to appear when we drill down to the next level (level 2), not at this level.

We did this intentionally to make the point that, as you make changes to any drill-down report, from time to time you may have to adjust your conditional suppression formulas. Before, when we had just a one-level drill-down, the conditional suppression formula we used for the Product column header worked just fine (DrillDownGroupLevel = 0). But now that we've inserted another level between the top level and the Product detail level, this no longer works. We now need to suppress this column header for both levels 0 and 1 (or when the DrillDownGroupLevel is not equal to 2).

After adjusting the conditional suppression formula so that it now reads "DrillDownGroupLevel <> 2," the first level of our drill-down report looks correct, as shown in Figure 8.31.

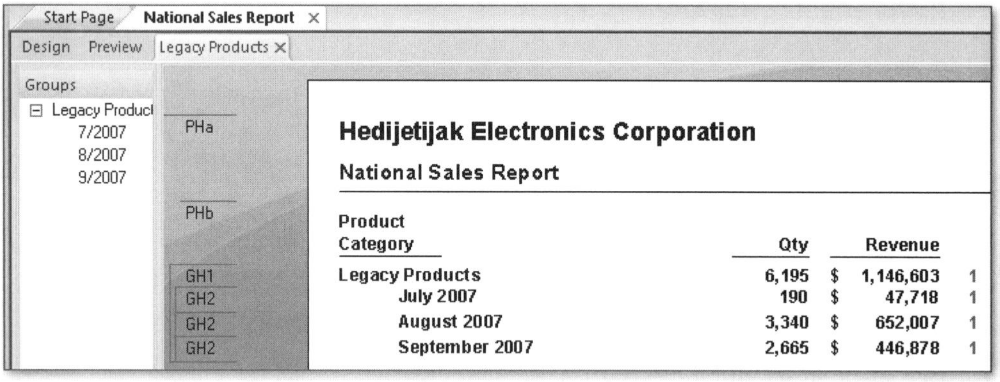

Figure 8.31 Two-Level Drill-Down with Correct Level 1 Header

Because we've added a second drill-down level, we can drill down one more time to the detail level from here by double-clicking one of the group 2 names or either of the summaries on the right. After drilling down one more time, the next Drill-Down tab should look something like Figure 8.32.

Figure 8.32 Two-Level Drill-Down Showing Level 2

Now it's almost perfect. We only have two adjustments we need to make. The first one should be fairly obvious. We're still showing the formula we created to show us which level we're currently on (DrillDownGroupLevel). Now that we no longer need it (at least for now), we can simply suppress it to make it disappear. The quickest and easiest way to do that is to select the formula and then click the Suppress button (Figure 8.33).

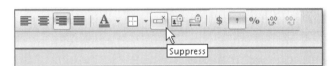

Figure 8.33 Suppress Button

That was easy enough to catch and fix. However, if you look back at the second level of our drill-down you should be able to catch one last issue (hint: it has to do with math, specifically, sums). The issue is that when we now drill down to the second level, the Product Category summaries won't be accurate. This is because they still sum the total for all calendar months, even though we've drilled into a single calendar month.

So it looks like we need to include just one more conditional suppression. What condition will we use to cause the Product Category subtotals to go away when we drill all the way down to the Product detail? The condition should read "Drill-

DownGroupLevel = 2." Now when we drill down to the second level, it should look like Figure 8.34.

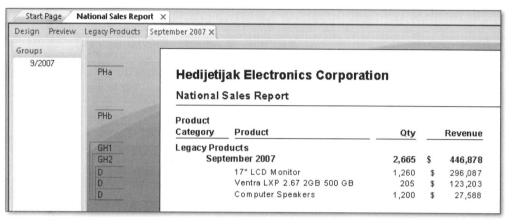

Figure 8.34 Completed Two-Level Drill-Down Showing Level 2

We've now successfully designed a classic two-level drill-down that's formatted correctly at each level.

Although this method has always been an effective way to enable the end user to navigate from summary-level data down to details, it's always suffered from one significant shortcoming: You're limited to drilling into one summary value at a time. Once you drill into a particular value, you have to go back to the preview to drill into another. This also means that there's no way to see all summary nodes expanded at one time in the main report (just as you'd perform an "expand" in a pivot table in Microsoft Excel).

Therefore, we recommend that you use the following method for almost all your drill-down requirements. However, the previous method is not completely without merit. There are certain specific report requirements where it remains the best option.

8.3.2 Drill-Down Report Using a Parameter and Conditional Suppression

The following method is possible because of new functionality available in Crystal Reports 2008 that allows end users to respond to parameters without having to rerun the report. We mentioned these in the preceding chapter when we introduced parameters. Now we'll get the chance to combine a view-time parameter with conditional suppression to create an "expand all, collapse all" drill-down report.

To begin, we'll go back to the report we started with when we created our classic drill-down report: "Chapter 7 – Custom Group Using a Formula 4." Do a Save As and call it "Chapter 8 – Expand All Collapse All Drill-Down Report."

Essentially our report requirement and objective remain the same as our previous example. We'd like to provide the end user with a summary report that initially shows totals by product category only, but then give the user the option to see revenue by calendar month and then finally by product. However, the user has requested that they be able to see all members of each level at the same time in one report.

Let's get started.

Pop Quiz

Question: To be able to allow the end user to determine the level to be displayed in the report, what's the first thing we need to do?

Answer: Create a parameter for capturing the user's request.

First, we'll create a parameter that will present our end user with three report detail level choices. The top part of the parameter dialog box should look like Figure 8.35.

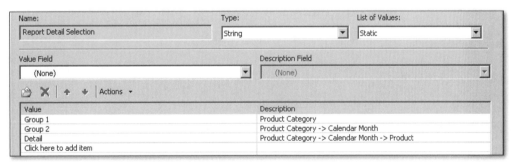

Figure 8.35 Report Detail Selection Parameter

You might notice we're doing something a little different from the parameters we created earlier. With this parameter we're creating a pick list with both a Value and a Description. This is because we want to present the end use with only the descriptions but reference the *value* when we create our conditional suppression formulas. We can do this by setting the Prompt with Description Only option to True. We should also set a default value of Group 1 from the pull-down menu.

Once we're finished, we can use this parameter and the pick list values we created to conditionally suppress sections in our report based upon the user's selection. Let's handle the first selection first: when the user selects Product Category (Group 1) from the pick list.

Let's look at the report the way it currently looks without any conditional suppression applied (fully expanded) (Figure 8.36).

Hedijetijak Electronics Corporation

National Sales Report

Product Category	Product	Qty	Revenue
Legacy Products		6,195	$ 1,146,603
July 2007		190	$ 47,718
	Ventra LXP 2.67 2GB 500 GB	75	$ 45,074
	Computer Speakers	115	$ 2,644
August 2007		3,340	$ 652,007
	17" LCD Monitor	1,650	$ 387,734
	Ventra LXP 2.67 2GB 500 GB	390	$ 234,386
	Computer Speakers	1,300	$ 29,887
September 2007		2,665	$ 446,878
	17" LCD Monitor	1,260	$ 296,087
	Ventra LXP 2.67 2GB 500 GB	205	$ 123,203
	Computer Speakers	1,200	$ 27,588
New Products		5,470	$ 295,822
July 2007		532	$ 68,326
	Ventra Ultra 3.00 2GB 750 GB	98	$ 63,797
	DigiPad Mousepad	339	$ 3,010
	LightTouch Optical Mouse	95	$ 1,519
August 2007		2,263	$ 49,846
	LightTouch Optical Mouse	1,475	$ 23,585
	Ventra Ultra 3.00 2GB 750 GB	30	$ 19,530
	DigiPad Mousepad	758	$ 6,731

Figure 8.36 Sales Report Fully Expanded in the Preview Tab

Now let's look at the report in the Design tab (Figure 8.37).

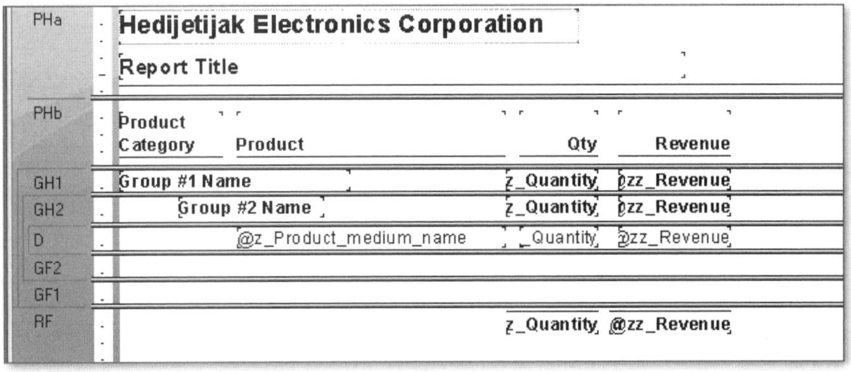

PHa	Hedijetijak Electronics Corporation

Report Title

PHb	Product				
	Category	Product		Qty	Revenue
GH1	Group #1 Name			z_Quantity	@zz_Revenue
GH2		Group #2 Name		z_Quantity	@zz_Revenue
D			@z_Product_medium_name	Quantity	@zz_Revenue
GF2					
GF1					
RF				z_Quantity	@zz_Revenue

Figure 8.37   Sales Report Fully Expanded in the Design Tab

Looking at our report in the Design tab, we need to decide which section (or sections) need to be suppressed whenever the end user selects Product Category from our pick list. In this case we'll want to suppress (starting from the top) Group Header 2, Detail, Group Footer 2, and Group Footer 1. If you recall from our first drill-down exercise, we'll also want to suppress the Product column header because the products and product totals will be suppressed.

Now we should right-click in the left margin of Group Header 2 (GH2) and select Section Expert. Click the Formula button next to the Suppress option. The formula we want to enter is:

```
{?Report Detail Selection} = 'Group 1'
```

Formula Tip

Never type in the name of a field, formula, or parameter into a formula. You should always select these from the Report Fields pane of the Formula Editor.

Notice that we're referencing the value from our parameter pick list and not the description. Even though we've configured our parameter to display the description to the end user, Crystal Reports always references (or uses) the value.

Before we save this formula we should copy the entire contents because we'll be using this exact same formula three more times. Now click Save and Close. When you get back to the Section Expert dialog box, don't click OK. We can stay in the Section Expert to apply this same suppression logic to the other three sections.

Click Details on the left side of the dialog box. Now click the Formula button next to Suppress again. Paste the formula and then click Save and Close. Do the same thing again for Group Footer 2 and Group Footer 1. When finished, we can now click OK at the bottom of the Section Expert.

The last item we need to suppress is the Product column header. Right-click the text box and select Format Text. Click the Formula button next the Suppress option and paste the formula text. Save and close and then click OK.

When we click the Preview tab, we'll now be presented with a parameter value entry screen (Figure 8.38).

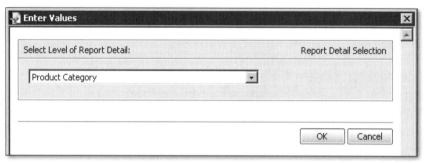

Figure 8.38   Enter Values for Report Detail Selection

We'll leave the default value for now (Product Category). When we see the report in the Preview tab it now looks like Figure 8.39.

Product Category	Qty	Revenue
Legacy Products	6,195	$ 1,146,603
New Products	5,470	$ 295,822
Strategic Products	2,297	$ 233,107
	13,962	$ 1,675,532

Figure 8.39   Sales Report Displaying Group 1

So far, so good. We've successfully created the top-level summary look for our report. Now we need to move on to the next level. To proceed, we need to ask ourselves, "Which sections do I need to suppress when the user selects the option for Product Category → Calendar Month?"

The correct answer is, "The same as last time except for Group Header 2." The next question then becomes, "How?" Currently the conditional suppression formula for Group Header 2 is:

```
{?Report Detail Selection} = 'Group 1'
```

Pop Quiz

Question: Do we need to change the suppression formula for Group Header 2 so that it will be displayed when the end user selects the option Product Category → Calendar Month?

Answer: No.

When the end user selects the second option (Product Category → Calendar Month), the value they're selecting for the Report Detail Selection parameter is Group 2. According to our current suppression formula for Group Header 2, what will happen to this section when the user selects Group 2?

Nothing (the section won't be suppressed).

This is because a value of Group 1 must be selected to trigger a suppression of Group Header 2. So for this section, no further action is required.

Let's move on to the next section, which is the Detail section. Currently the suppression formula for the Detail section is the same suppression formula we used for Group Header 2, which is:

```
{?Report Detail Selection} = 'Group 1'
```

If we leave the Detail suppression formula as-is, what will happen when the end user selects the second option (value = Group 2)? Just as before with Group Header 2, the formula won't trigger a suppression of the section. However, when the user selects the second option, we want the Detail section to be suppressed. In other words, we want the Detail section to be suppressed whenever the user selects either the first option (Group 1) or the second option (Group 2).

We therefore need to change our suppression formula for the Detail section so that it looks like the following:

```
{?Report Detail Selection} in ['Group 1', 'Group 2']
```

What about the next section down (Group Footer 2)? Because we want it to remain suppressed when the user selects the second option, we need to change its suppression formula to the same as the Detail section above (just copy and paste).

Are we finished? How about the final section (Group Footer 1)? As it turns out, our report will look a little cleaner if we allow this section to display when the user selects the second option, so we can leave its suppression formula as-is.

There's one more item we need to modify, and that's the Product column header. Its suppression formula needs to mirror that of the Detail section because it's tied to the Detail section (again, copy and paste the above suppression formula).

Once we're done, we need to test our new suppression logic. To do so, we need to select the second option in the pick list of our parameter. Because we defined this parameter as a view-time parameter (Show on (Viewer) Panel = "Editable") we can now make a new selection for this parameter directly from within the Preview tab without having to rerun the report.

In the Preview tab we need to click the Parameters button at the bottom of the viewer panel on the left. Now we can see the prompting text of our parameter at the top of the panel. Just click the existing selection (Product Category) once and then click the pull-down menu on the right. You'll now see the options shown in Figure 8.40.

Figure 8.40 Selecting a Parameter Option in the Viewer Panel

Once we've selected the second option in the list, we can then click the Apply Changes icon (green check mark) above (Figure 8.41).

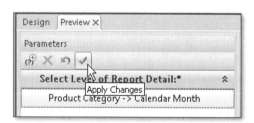

Figure 8.41 Apply Changes Icon

Our report now looks like Figure 8.42.

Product Category	Qty	Revenue
Legacy Products	6,195	$ 1,146,603
July 2007	190	$ 47,718
August 2007	3,340	$ 652,007
September 2007	2,665	$ 446,878
New Products	5,470	$ 295,822
July 2007	532	$ 68,326
August 2007	2,263	$ 49,846
September 2007	2,675	$ 177,650
Strategic Products	2,297	$ 233,107
July 2007	285	$ 95,546
August 2007	542	$ 27,789
September 2007	1,470	$ 109,772
	13,962	$ 1,675,532

Figure 8.42 Sales Report Displaying Groups 1 and 2

You may see now why we didn't choose to suppress Group Footer 1 when the user selects this option. This is what is giving us our space between the Product Category groups.

The final situation we need to handle is when the user selects the third option, which is to show everything all the way down to the detail section (Product).

Pop Quiz

Question: What do we need to do to handle this situation?

Answer: Nothing.

This last scenario is the easiest of the three, because it requires us to do nothing. When the user selects the option to see all three levels of the report (Group 1, Group 2, and Detail) we don't need to apply any suppression at all. So that means we are done. To test and see if this is really true, let's select the third option and click the Apply Changes button. We should now see a fully expanded report (which is really just our original report with no suppression) (Figure 8.43).

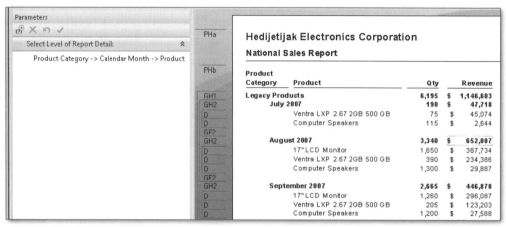

Figure 8.43 Sales Report Displaying Groups 1, 2, and Detail

That's the basic process of expanding and collapsing sections using a view-time parameter. As you practice this technique of applying conditional suppression based upon a user's parameter selection, you'll find yourself becoming more and more proficient, and as you do, you'll find it to be invaluable in helping you provide the kind of flexibility your end users are looking for.

8.3.3   Adding Versatility with Dynamic Groups

We'll leave you with just one more practical example of how you can add extended functionality to your reports in Crystal Reports so you can potentially meet the demands of several report requirements in a single report. With this technique you can create a limited, but effective, "slice and dice" interface through the use of dynamic groups.

In Chapter 7 we showed you how to create both standard and custom groups in Crystal Reports. At that time, the custom group was created by first creating a formula that essentially created a new characteristic that didn't exist in the source data. In the following example, we'll create a different kind of custom group. We'll allow the end user to select the characteristic he wants to group by for each of our two groups.

Before we move on, if you haven't done so already, let's save the work from our previous exercise. Do a Save As and save a copy as "Chapter 8 – User Selectable Groups."

As before, any time we allow the user to select anything in Crystal Reports the first thing we need is a parameter, so create a new parameter. This parameter will be used to allow the end user to select how the report is to be grouped. Here are the settings we need for this parameter (if a value is not specified, just keep the default value):

- Name: Report Groups
- Type: String
- Pick List Values:
  - Product Category then Channel
  - Channel then Product Category
- Show on (Viewer) Panel: Editable
- Prompt Text: Group Report By . . .
- Default Value: Product Category then Channel
- Allow Custom Values: False

Now that we have our parameter, the next step is to create two custom group formulas. Let's create our first formula and call it "Group 1." Now enter the following into the Formula Editor:

```
If {?Report Groups} = 'Product Category then Channel'
 then {@Channel_name}
else
 {@z_Calendar_Month_medium_name}
```

> **Reminder**
>
> You can double-click the {?Report Groups} parameter in the top-left pane of the Formula Editor under the Report Fields node. The same is true for the two formulas (starting with "@"). You should always do this rather than attempt to type them in yourself.

We hope you can decipher this formula yourself by now. This is a simple If statement that checks the value of the {?Report Groups} parameter and then sets the value of the formula to either the {@Product Category} or the {@z_Channel_name} alias.

Now we need to create a second formula and call it "Group 2." You can do this directly from within the Formula Editor simply by clicking the New button at the top. The contents of this formula will be very similar to the previous formula, only backward:

```
If {?Report Groups} = 'Channel then Product Category'
 then {@Product Category}
else
 {@z_Channel_name}
```

The last step is to change our existing two groups so that they group by these two group formulas. We just need to right-click in the left margin and select Change Group. Then change the formula we're grouping by from @Product Category to @Group 1 and then click OK (Figure 8.44).

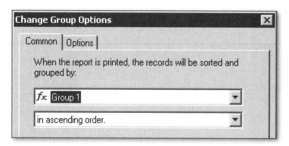

Figure 8.44 Change Group to Group 1 Formula

Now we need to do the same thing for Group 2, except this time, of course, we'll set the formula we're grouping by to the @Group 2 formula.

You may notice that we changed to Channel from Calendar Month in this example for one of our group selections. This is because you cannot group by two different data types using the same formula. Channel is a text (string) field, whereas Calendar Month is a date field. If you recall from our lesson on custom groups in Chapter 7, we converted the original Calendar Month characteristic to a date field so that we could sort it in chronological order. If we kept it as a string, it would have sorted in alphabetical order. Now that it's a date, we cannot select from Calendar Month and a text field when selecting a particular field to group by.

> **Hot Tip**
>
> A formula in Crystal Reports always results in a particular data type (string, numeric, date). Therefore, you cannot create a custom group formula that allows a user to select from fields that are different data types.

Now when we switch to the Preview tab, we'll see the parameter screen shown in Figure 8.45.

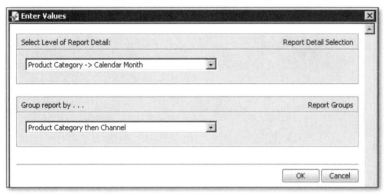

Figure 8.45   Parameter Entry Screen with "Group Report By" Parameter

For the level of detail we'll select the second option (Product Category → Calendar Month).

> **Note**
>
> You may notice that our level of detail parameter selections no longer make sense now that our groups are no longer static as they were before but dynamic (user selectable). Don't worry. We'll fix this in a minute.

After we make our selections and click OK the report looks like Figure 8.46.

Now that we've made our report groups dynamic, our Select Level of Report Detail prompt no longer makes sense. First, Calendar Month is not currently an option for either group. Second, we cannot hard-code any particular order (Product Category → Channel or Channel → Product Category) because the report can now be in either order.

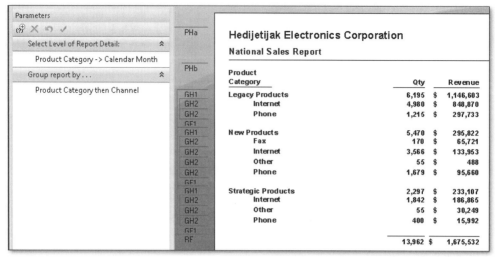

Figure 8.46 Report Grouped by Product Category then Channel

To fix this, we need to make our report level parameter pick list choices generic rather than specific. Right-click the Report Detail Selection parameter in the Field Explorer and select Edit. Now let's change the descriptions of our pick list value items to those shown in Figure 8.47.

Value	Description
Group 1	Level 1
Group 2	Level 1 -> Level 2
Detail	Level 1 -> Level 2 -> Level 3
Click here to add item	

Figure 8.47 Changing the Pick List Descriptions

For this parameter we've selected the option to display only the description to the user and not the value. The value (on the left) has not changed, so we don't need to make any changes to our conditional suppression formulas that we created to display or hide our group and detail sections. This is the primary benefit of showing the user the description rather than the value when configuring a parameter. We can make any changes we want to the description without having to change any of the formulas on our report that reference this parameter.

Let's click OK to save our changes. Now when we preview our report the Report Detail Selection parameter looks like Figure 8.48.

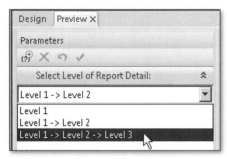

Figure 8.48 New Report Detail Selection Parameter Pick List

Whenever you combine the added functionality of both user-selectable level of detail and user-selectable groups, you must make the level of detail selection generic, as we've just done. This is because you have no way of knowing what the user has selected for each of the groups in the report.

Let's change the Group Report By... parameter to Channel then Product Category and then click the Apply Changes button. Our report now looks like Figure 8.49.

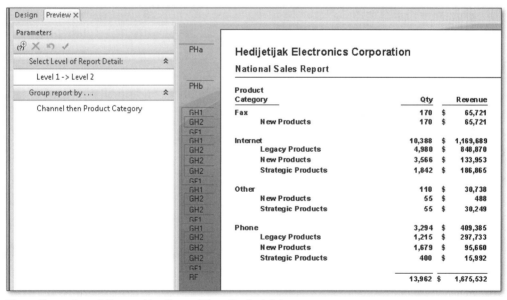

Figure 8.49 Report Grouped by Channel then Product Category

Do you notice anything that needs to be fixed now? If you look closely, you'll see that the column header for Group 1 is incorrect now that we've selected Channel for our first group.

> **Important Note**
>
> You may be noticing that as we make certain changes to our report, it sometimes necessitates another change somewhere else in the report. This happens for two reasons: First, we started our report from an existing report and, second, we're intentionally "stretching" a report to cover multiple report requirements. This is a normal part of the process when your goal is to get the most use possible from a single Crystal Reports report. Remember, the alternative is much worse. That would be to create a separate report for each new requirement. So far, we could have up to six separate reports.

Now for our final test on conditional formatting. How should we handle this situation? We need two different column headings for Group 1: one for when we select Product Category for our first group and one for when we select Channel.

There are two ways to handle this: One requires the use of a formula as our column heading (which produces a dynamic header based on our parameter selection), and the other is to create a second header and use conditional suppression to suppress one or the other. For the sake of consistency we'll go with the second option.

First, we need to create our second header. All we need to do is clone the first header (Ctrl + drag) and then change the text to Channel (be sure the text is at the bottom of the text box). Next, we need to apply a conditional suppression formula to each of our two headers.

The formula for the Product Category header should be as follows:

```
{?Report Groups} = "Channel then Product Category"
```

The formula for the Channel header should be as follows:

```
{?Report Groups} = "Product Category then Channel"
```

> **Reminder**
>
> To apply conditional suppression to a text box in Crystal Reports, right-click the text, select Edit Text, and then click the Formula button next to the Suppress option.

The final step is to align the two column headers so they're directly on top of each other. The quickest way to do this is to select both headers, right-click on the Product Category header on the left, and then select ALIGN • MIDDLES followed by ALIGN • CENTERS.

Now when we preview our report, it should look like Figure 8.50.

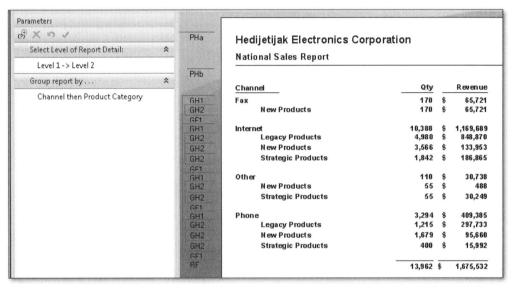

Figure 8.50 Completed Report Grouped by Channel then Product Category

Now, as a final test, we can switch our group selection back to Product Category then Channel. Now the report looks like Figure 8.51.

Bonus Exercise

As an additional exercise, you can create a second column header for Group 2. This will require that you move the header for Group 2 to the right a bit and that you insert two more headers — one for Product Category and the other for Channel.

Bonus Exercise Pop Quiz

Question: What would be the fastest way to create the column headers for Group 2?

Answer: Clone (or copy) the Group 1 column headers then adjust the conditional suppression formulas (basically switch them).

353

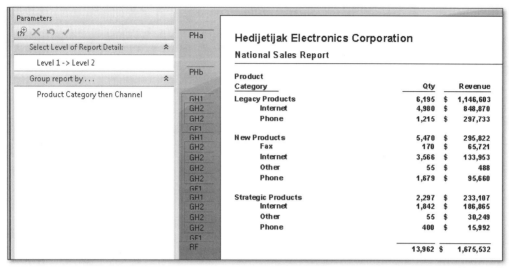

Figure 8.51 Completed Report Grouped by Product Category then Channel

That concludes our chapter on flexible formatting. The examples we've given here represent a small fraction of the many different ways you can leverage this one simple feature of Crystal Reports to stretch a single report to allow it to function as many.

As a final reminder, it's not at all uncommon to have a difficult time at first with conditional suppression, because it's easy to get things backward. Even the most seasoned Crystal Reports developer will create a conditional suppression formula that results in the exact opposite result from what was intended. If this happens to you, just get used to going back and reversing your logic, and everything will turn out just fine.

If you stick to it and become proficient at this one skill, you'll find that it will open up a whole new world of possibilities as you develop your reports in Crystal Reports. Now when your end users ask you if you can create another version of a report that looks or functions a certain way, you just might be able to take your existing report and make it work.

This one skill will help you deal with what's perhaps the biggest complaint that end users tend to have when it comes to reporting in general: the sometimes overwhelming number of reports they have to deal with to find what they need. The fewer reports that end users have to deal with the more likely they are to actually use them.

8.4   Summary

▸ Although Crystal Reports is known more as an operational, static reporting tool, it's possible to design more flexible reports that provide both feedback to the end user (in the form of flags or highlighting) and the ability to select from a variety of possible report layouts.

▸ You can use the Highlighting Expert to quickly and easily flag data values using font color and style. The Highlighting Expert works well when the condition is driven by the value of a single field. If more than one field must be tested you must use a custom formula to control your highlighting.

▸ If you require either a different method for highlighting (something besides font color or style) or if your condition is based on the value of more than one field, you must use a custom formatting formula.

▸ The most common type of custom highlighting involves the use of conditional suppression. You can use various graphic objects to draw attention to certain data values in your report.

▸ Conditional suppression of sections provides a way for the report developer to stretch a single Crystal Reports report to meet additional formatting requirements. This is almost always preferred to creating another report to meet the additional requirement.

▸ Another method for extending the functionality of a report created in Crystal Report is the use of dynamic groups. These are groups that are created based upon the response by the end user to a custom group parameter.

▸ Conditional formatting is one of the most powerful and useful features of Crystal Reports. It provides you as the developer with a way to avoid having to create a new report every time an end user requests a slightly different look from an existing report. The better you get at this skill, the fewer report objects you'll have to create — and the fewer reports your users will have to deal with.

A commonly used feature of SAP NetWeaver BW and SAP ECC is the hierarchy. With Crystal Reports 2008 you are able to leverage your existing hierarchies to organize your data without having to create an additional front end data structure.

9 Handling Hierarchies

If you've been around SAP systems for any length of time, you've at least heard of *hierarchies*. Hierarchies are especially prevalent when you're working with financial data, but they're not limited to the area of finance. They can, and are, used in all of the functional areas of SAP systems to organize data into a custom hierarchy.

Perhaps the most commonly recognized hierarchy in the world of business is the *organizational* hierarchy, probably because most people like to have a sense of where they fit in and where everyone else sits in the organization. The power of a hierarchy is both its flexibility and its ability to simply and clearly communicate relationships.

Hierarchies are flexible in that they provide a way to organize data in any way that makes sense. This is similar in concept to the custom groups we created in Chapter 7, only now we can organize the data values into *levels*, which makes hierarchies even more flexible that custom groups.

However, as we've said several times now in this book, with added flexibility comes added complexity, in this case in the form of additional maintenance requirements. Because hierarchies are created (or rather, assembled) manually, whenever a change in structure is required, it must be made manually as well.

Hierarchies are created and maintained in SAP NetWeaver BW (and SAP ERP Central Component) by either someone in IT or someone on the business side, usually a business process expert (BPX) or analyst. In this chapter we'll show you how to properly handle these hierarchies so that you can leverage them in Crystal Reports.

At this point we're going to abandon any pretense of you trying to "follow along" with us as we go through the exercises in this chapter. These exercises will be more "show and tell" than the previous exercises because, although it may have been a challenge for you to have the same sort of InfoProvider available to you in the exercises up to now, it's virtually impossible for you to have the same hierarchies available.

However, this isn't going to be a problem. In this chapter we'll carefully lay out the process of incorporating a hierarchy into your Crystal Reports report step by step so that you'll be able to transfer this knowledge to any hierarchy in SAP NetWeaver BW and be successful.

9.1 Building a Hierarchy Using Hierarchical Grouping

The example we'll use in this lesson will cover what is perhaps the most common use of a hierarchy in SAP NetWeaver BW: to provide the correct structure to build a financial statement.

To correctly utilize a hierarchy in Crystal Reports you must first know that it exists and second know where it's been applied. At first this may seem obvious, but it's not unheard of for someone to use a query that has an active hierarchy in a report created in Crystal Report and not even know that the hierarchy exists. And you won't know it exists if the person who created the query hasn't told you or you haven't looked at the query yourself (using the Query Designer) and discovered it on your own. The point is that it's not obvious in Crystal Reports that any given characteristic has an active hierarchy attached to it.

Normally once you're told (or discover) that a hierarchy exists in a BW query, you'll know the characteristic that it's been applied to. A hierarchy is *always* attached to a particular characteristic. For financial accounting this characteristic is going to be G/L Account.

Once you know which characteristic the hierarchy has been assigned to, you need to create (typically) four alias formulas. In our example the characteristic is G/L Account, so our four aliases will be:

▶ G/L Account Node ID

▶ G/L Account Key

▶ G/L Account Name

▶ G/L Account Long Name

In most situations you'll have access to both the Name and Long Name attributes for the characteristic you're working with. However, sometimes you'll only have access to one. If you have both, then alias both of them so you can use either one in your report.

As usual, you'll want to alias any key figures that you'll be using in your report. In our example we've aliased two key figures:

- zz_Previous_Year
- zz_Current_Year

The final formula you'll want to create is critical for making sense of your hierarchy, in particular if you decide to use conditional suppression to selectively hide or display individual levels within the hierarchy (as we'll show you how to do). The purpose of this function is to return the current level of the hierarchy (level 1 is the top level, 2 is next, and so on). The formula looks like the following:

```
Hierarchylevel(Groupinglevel({@z_GL_Account_Node_ID}))
```

This formula uses two functions in Crystal Reports (Hierarchylevel and Groupinglevel). The argument for Groupinglevel is the alias for the characteristic Node ID, which in our case is @z_GL_Account_Node_ID. This in turn is used as the argument for Hierarchylevel.

> **Important Note**
>
> If this step seems a bit odd, we suggest that you just accept it and go on. It will make more sense in a moment when we use this in our report. This is just something that you need to remember to do each time you work with a hierarchy in Crystal Reports. After your first two or three hierarchies it will become routine.

Now we have the basic building blocks in place that we need to re-create our G/L account hierarchy (financial statement) in Crystal Reports.

The next step is to create a group, and group by the Characteristic Node ID alias formula that you just created (in our example, G/L Account Node ID). When you create the group, you should select Original Order for the sort order. If you keep the default setting (Ascending), depending on how your hierarchy was created, you can sometimes end up with your hierarchy in the wrong order.

The Common tab of the Insert Group dialog box should look like Figure 9.1.

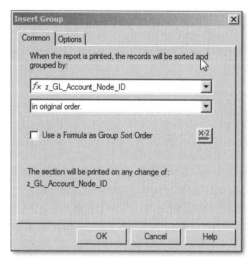

Figure 9.1 Insert Group Using Node ID

Now we need to select the Options tab of the Insert Group dialog box to change the name of our group. You never keep the name of the group as the default (which would be the Node ID) because you'd almost never want to display the node ID in your report as your group name by itself. However, there are times when you might combine it with one of the descriptive fields, as we will shortly. On the Options tab select the Customize Group Name Field checkbox and then click the radio button next to Use a Formula as Group Name, as shown in Figure 9.2.

Figure 9.2 Options Tab of the Insert Group Dialog

Now click the Formula button next to Use a Formula as Group Name. Our formula will simply be the alias for either one of our characteristic names (Name or Long Name). Usually when working with G/L Accounts, you'll want to use the long name, but this will depend on your specific report requirement. We'll use the alias @z_GL_Account_Long_Name.

Now we will add our two key figures to the report.

Hot Tip

When adding key figures to a report that uses a hierarchy, you place the key figures in the group header of the hierarchy group you just created, not the Detail section. You then suppress the Detail section and the group footer.

After placing the two key figures in the group header and suppressing both the Detail section and the group header, our Design tab looks like Figure 9.3.

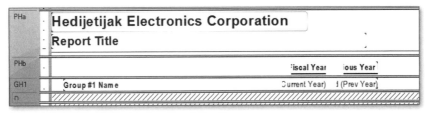

Figure 9.3   Design Tab with Group and Key Figures

We can now and run the report to see what it looks like so far. Our initial Preview tab now looks like Figure 9.4.

Important Note

Because we selected Original Order when we grouped on the G/L Account Node ID, the order of the hierarchy nodes from top to bottom is currently correct. However, the hierarchy levels have not yet been re-created. That step comes next.

Our next step is to re-create (or reassemble) the levels of the hierarchy by using a feature in Crystal Reports called Hierarchical Grouping. Go to the Report menu and select Hierarchical Grouping Options ... Now select the checkbox next to Sort Data Hierarchically. Next we need to select the characteristic parent node ID from the pull-down menu for the Parent ID field option.

Hedijetijak Electronics Corporation
Financial Statement

	2008	2007
Financial Statement (USA)		
ASSETS	1,560,397	1,409,178
Cash & Pooled Cash	1,372,165	1,136,881
CASH ON HAND		
CHANGE FUNDS		
PETTY CASH FUNDS	13	15
CASH IN TRANSIT TO TREASURY		
IMPREST CHECKING - OTHER	1	1
OPERATING CASH	1,383,602	1,162,698
CASH INTERFUND CLEARING	775	(5,480)
CASH INTER-COMPANY CODE CLEARING	3,841	5
WARRANTS PAYABLE FOR CONVERSION ONLY	(17)	(26)
WARRANTS PAYABLE RECONCILIATION ACCOUNT FOR WARRAN	(16,051)	(20,331)
Other Receivables, net	53,290	168,805
INTEREST RECEIVABLE -INVESTMNT		

Figure 9.4   Preview Tab with Group and Key Figures

In our example the Hierarchical Group Options dialog box looks like Figure 9.5.

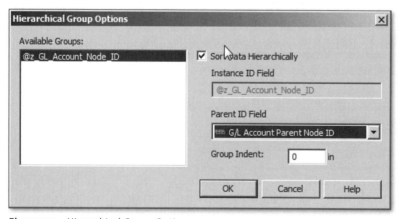

Figure 9.5   Hierarchical Group Options

Important Note

Don't enter anything in the Group Indent field. This was put here so that each level of the hierarchy can be indented by a certain width (in inches). It works fine except for one issue: It indents not only the hierarchy node name (label) but the key figures as well. You normally don't want the key figures to be indented along with the node names. We'll show you a way to indent only the node names.

When we look at our report again, we won't notice anything different, although something did happen "behind the scenes" (for now). Although not immediately apparent, the structure of the hierarchy (each level and all its nodes) has been reconstructed. We now just need to create an indent to be able to actually see the structure.

But before we do, we need to add our Hierarchy Level formula that we created earlier to our group header. We'll place it at the beginning of the section to the left of the hierarchy node name. When we preview the report, we now see something like Figure 9.6.

Hedijetijak Electronics Corporation
Financial Statement

	2008	2007
1 Financial Statement (USA)		
2 ASSETS	1,560,397	1,409,178
3 Cash & Pooled Cash	1,372,165	1,136,881
4 CASH ON HAND		
4 CHANGE FUNDS		
4 PETTY CASH FUNDS	13	15
4 CASH IN TRANSIT TO TREASURY		
4 IMPREST CHECKING - OTHER	1	1
4 OPERATING CASH	1,383,602	1,162,698
4 CASH INTERFUND CLEARING	775	(5,480)
4 CASH INTER-COMPANY CODE CLEARING	3,841	5
4 WARRANTS PAYABLE FOR CONVERSION ONLY	(17)	(26)
4 WARRANTS PAYABLE RECONCILIATION ACCOUNT FOR WARRAN	(16,051)	(20,331)
3 Other Receivables, net	53,290	168,805
4 INTEREST RECEIVABLE -INVESTMNT		

Figure 9.6 Hierarchy Level Formula in the Preview Tab

In our example we can now see that there's one top-level node (level 1) called Financial Statement (USA). This is the highest level of the hierarchy and always consists of just one node. Below that is a level 2 node called ASSETS. Below that is a level 3 node called Cash & Pooled Cash. Below that is a series of level 4 nodes.

Now that we've have re-created the levels of our hierarchy, we can create the indention of each level. To do this, we need to right-click on the node label (the group name) and select Size and Position. Next you'll see the dialog box shown in Figure 9.7.

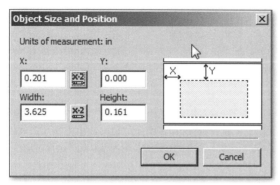

Figure 9.7   Object Size and Position

The next step is to click the Formula button for the X coordinate setting. This setting determines the horizontal positioning of an object using a formula. The formula we need to enter is the following:

```
{@Hierarchy Level} * 150
```

The contents of the formula is the @Hierarchy Level formula times 150. The 150 represents the number of "twips" (pixels) to move the object to the right. As you move down throughout the hierarchy and the level increases, the object (the group name) moves further to the right. If you want less of an indent, reduce the number below 150. If you want a larger indent, increase it.

> **Important Note**
>
> This is another one of those steps when dealing with hierarchies in Crystal Reports that may seem a bit odd at first. Again, it's best just to accept it and move on. This is simply the way you create an indent.

Now our report should look something like Figure 9.8.

Those are the basic steps for re-creating a hierarchy structure in Crystal Reports and indenting the hierarchy levels. Let's now look at some additional fine-tuning you can do when working with hierarchies.

> **Important Note**
>
> The following hierarchy formatting tips are presented as examples of how you can apply custom formatting to an SAP NetWeaver BW hierarchy in Crystal Reports. Because every hierarchy is configured differently, it's impossible to create an example that will apply in every situation. We'll make every effort to make our examples as generic as possible so they can be applied to the widest range of possibilities.

Hedijetijak Electronics Corporation

Financial Statement

		2008	2007
1	Financial Statement (USA)		
2	ASSETS	1,560,397	1,409,178
3	Cash & Pooled Cash	1,372,165	1,136,881
4	CASH ON HAND		
4	CHANGE FUNDS		
4	PETTY CASH FUNDS	13	15
4	CASH IN TRANSIT TO TREASURY		
4	IMPREST CHECKING - OTHER	1	1
4	OPERATING CASH	1,383,602	1,162,698
4	CASH INTERFUND CLEARING	775	(5,480)
4	CASH INTER-COMPANY CODE CLEARING	3,841	5
4	WARRANTS PAYABLE FOR CONVERSION ONLY	(17)	(26)
4	WARRANTS PAYABLE RECONCILIATION ACCOUNT FOR WARRAN	(16,051)	(20,331)
3	Other Receivables, net	53,290	168,805
4	INTEREST RECEIVABLE -INVESTMNT		

Figure 9.8 Report with Levels Indented

9.2 Custom Formatting for Hierarchies

There will be times when you'll leave your hierarchy as-is after applying the previous basic steps. Once you've completed these steps you'll have completely replicated the structure of the SAP NetWeaver BW hierarchy in Crystal Reports. However, sometimes you maywant to tweak the look and feel of a hierarchy to fulfill particular reporting requirements.

The first change we're going to make is a very common one. In our example we're currently displaying only the G/L account description, not the actual account number. Because it's almost always a requirement to display both the account and the description, we'll show you how.

The account number (or for another characteristic, the code) is returned as the characteristic *key*. If you recall, one of our beginning steps was to create a series of aliases of our hierarchy characteristic, so we already have one for the G/L account key.

The simplest way to append the key to the description is to change the group name. We'll right-click in the left margin of our group and select Change Group.

Next, we'll select the Options tab and click the Formula button next to the Use a Formula as Group Name option. Our new group name formula will be:

```
{@z_GL_Account_Key} + ' - ' + {@z_GL_Acct_Long_Name}
```

This will concatenate the G/L account key with a " – " and then the G/L account long name. When we look at our report in the Preview tab, we now see something like Figure 9.9.

Hedijetijak Electronics Corporation
Financial Statement

		2008	2007
1	BAUS - Financial Statement (USA)		
2	BAUS6 - ASSETS	1,560,397	1,409,178
3	BAUS14 - Cash & Pooled Cash	1,372,165	1,136,881
4	1101000000 - CASH ON HAND		
4	1101100000 - CHANGE FUNDS		
4	1101200000 - PETTY CASH FUNDS	13	15
4	1101300000 - CASH IN TRANSIT TO TREASURY		
4	1103200000 - IMPREST CHECKING - OTHER	1	1
4	1110000000 - OPERATING CASH	1,383,602	1,162,698
4	1110000010 - CASH INTERFUND CLEARING	775	(5,480)
4	1110000015 - CASH INTER-COMPANY CODE CLEARING	3,841	5
4	2200000000 - WARRANTS PAYABLE FOR CONVERSION ONLY	(17)	(26)
4	2200000003 - WARRANTS PAYABLE RECONCILIATION ACCOUNT FOR WARRAN	(16,051)	(20,331)
3	BAUS16 - Other Receivables, net	53,290	168,805
4	1130000000 - INTEREST RECEIVABLE -INVESTMNT		
4	1133400000 - A/R RECON ACCOUNT FOR DAMAGE CLAIMS	3,110	3,033

Figure 9.9 Hierarchy with G/L Account Key Added

As you can see, we solved one problem but created another. This is because not only do the G/L accounts have a value for the key (the account number), but all the summary nodes do as well. Their key is not a G/L account number but a unique identifier for that particular summary node (the ASSETS summary node is BAUS6). This is a standard feature of every SAP NetWeaver BW hierarchy.

So our challenge now becomes how to display the key (account number) for the actual G/L accounts only and not for the hierarchy summary nodes. We've just stumbled upon a very common issue when it comes to applying custom formatting to an SAP NetWeaver BW hierarchy in Crystal Reports — the need to correctly distinguish between the *summary* nodes and the *postable* nodes of an SAP NetWeaver BW hierarchy.

Every SAP NetWeaver BW hierarchy is made up of two types of nodes: summary nodes and postable nodes. The postable nodes are always at the bottom of the hierarchy. In other words, as you work your way down from the top level of the hierarchy, you'll eventually reach the last (or bottom) level. That's the postable node. In our example it's the total for a particular G/L account. You cannot go any further down than this level in this hierarchy.

All of the nodes above the postable nodes in a hierarchy are summary nodes. These nodes are put there by whoever creates the hierarchy. A summary node provides a way to summarize all of the postable nodes below that particular point in the hierarchy.

One of the keys to handling hierarchies successfully in Crystal Reports is to become skilled at finding ways to distinguish between the summary nodes and postable nodes in any given hierarchy. There's no flag or any other kind of identifier to tell one from the other. One hint: This almost always will be done by identifying some difference in the characteristic key.

There are times, however, when you can simply use the level of the hierarchy node to determine which nodes are summary nodes and which are postable nodes. This would be in the case of a *balanced* hierarchy. A balanced hierarchy is one where all of the postable nodes are at the same level. The most common type of hierarchy where you'd see this is where you have one level of summary nodes followed by a single level of postable nodes (a two-level hierarchy).

However, in our case we're working with the more common type of hierarchy, an *unbalanced* hierarchy. In an unbalanced hierarchy the postable nodes can be at any level (below the top level). In Figure 9.10 we can see a portion of our hierarchy that clearly shows that we're working with an unbalanced hierarchy.

As you can see, the 3 series G/L accounts are all at level 5 in the hierarchy, and the 7 series are all at level 8 (except for the first one, which is at level 9). The point of all this is that when you're working with an unbalanced hierarchy (the most common situation), you cannot use the hierarchy level to determine which nodes are the postable nodes.

Fortunately for us there's a way to distinguish between the G/L account nodes and the summary nodes in our hierarchy — the key. The key for the G/L accounts is always a number (numeric text), and the key for the summary nodes always starts with BAUS. We can use either one of these to determine when to append our key to the description in our group name.

4	BAUS58 - Unreserved Undesignated	(1,239,801)	(1,029,786)
5	3340000000 - FB-UNRESERVED/UNDESIGNATED	(1,217,230)	43,023
5	3340000100 - FUND BALANCE INDIRECT COSTS N	(3,280)	
5	3340000101 - FUND BALANCE INDIRECT COSTS P	(4,749)	
5	3340000120 - FUND BALANCE CONSTRUCTION ENG N	(3,187)	
5	3340000121 - FUND BALANCE CONSTRUCTION ENG P	(11,356)	
5	3380000001 - IGFA ROAD EQUIPMENT DEPRECIATION		
5	3380000002 - IGFA OTHER DEPRECIATION		
5	3380000010 - IGFA BUILDING DEPRECIATION		
5	3380000060 - IGFA ITS/TOC DEPRECIATION		
5	3385000190 - FB SEC COST ELEMENT CLR PROJECTS N		(3,466,403)
5	3999999999 - BATCH INPUT CLEARING		2,393,593
4	BAUS77 - YTD Increase (Decrease)	(152,818)	(228,563)
5	BAUS59 - REVENUES, EXPENDITURES AND CHANGES IN FB	(152,818)	(228,563)
6	BAUS60 - REVENUES	(572,438)	(512,769)
7	BAUS61 - Taxes		
8	BAUS63 - Sales and Use		
9	7100000001 - AVIATION SALES TAX		
7	BAUS62 - Licenses, Permits, and Fines	(5,305)	(7,723)
8	7420000050 - ACCESS PERMIT FEES	(69)	(71)
8	7421000052 - OVERSIZE PERMIT		
8	7421000054 - OVERWEIGHT PERMIT	(4,202)	(6,627)
8	7421000062 - OUTDOOR ADVERT CONTROL PERMITS	(180)	(135)
8	7430800038 - MOTORCYCLE OPER LICENSES		
8	7550100032 - LEAF		
8	7570000082 - MISCELLANEOUS FINES	(5)	(108)
8	7587000021 - DMG CLAIM RECOV INDIV N	(413)	(266)
8	7587000023 - DMG CLAIM RECOV INDIV P		(20)
8	7587000024 - DAMAGE CLAIM RECOVERY MATERIAL	(348)	(407)
8	7587000025 - DAMAGE CLAIM RECOVERY EQUIPMENT	(87)	(90)

Figure 9.10 Unbalanced Hierarchy

We'll choose to identify the summary nodes as those nodes whose key begins with BAUS. Now all we need to do is go back to our group name formula and change it to the following:

```
If {@z_GL_Account_Key} startswith "BAUS"
 then {@z_GL_Acct_Long_Name}
else
 {@z_GL_Account_Key} + ' - ' + {@z_GL_Acct_Long_Name}
```

This formula should be self-explanatory. It simply states that any node whose key begins with BAUS (the summary nodes) will display only the descriptive text, and the G/L accounts (the postable nodes) will display both the account number and the descriptive text.

When we now look at our report it looks like Figure 9.11.

Hedijetijak Electronics Corporation
Financial Statement

		2008	2007
1	Financial Statement (USA)		
2	ASSETS	1,560,397	1,409,178
3	Cash & Pooled Cash	1,372,165	1,136,881
4	1101000000 - CASH ON HAND		
4	1101100000 - CHANGE FUNDS		
4	1101200000 - PETTY CASH FUNDS	13	15
4	1101300000 - CASH IN TRANSIT TO TREASURY		
4	1103200000 - IMPREST CHECKING - OTHER	1	1
4	1110000000 - OPERATING CASH	1,383,602	1,162,698
4	1110000010 - CASH INTERFUND CLEARING	775	(5,480)
4	1110000015 - CASH INTER-COMPANY CODE CLEARING	3,841	5
4	2200000000 - WARRANTS PAYABLE FOR CONVERSION ONLY	(17)	(26)
4	2200000003 - WARRANTS PAYABLE RECONCILIATION ACCOUNT FOR WARRAN	(16,051)	(20,331)
3	Other Receivables, net	53,290	168,805
4	1130000000 - INTEREST RECEIVABLE -INVESTMNT		
4	1133400000 - A/R RECON ACCOUNT FOR DAMAGE CLAIMS	3,110	3,033

Figure 9.11 Key Added for G/L Accounts Only

There are times when you'll want to suppress the display of a particular node, type of node, or entire levels in your hierarchy. First we'll show you how to suppress a particular level. In our case, the topmost level of our hierarchy (level 1) is the Financial Statement (USA) node. This node is functioning only as a label for the hierarchy and is not of any real use to us, so we want to suppress it.

Because this is the only node at level 1 of our hierarchy, the simplest thing to do is to suppress the group header section when the hierarchy level is 1. We need to right-click in the margin of our group header and select Section Expert. Then click the Formula button next to the Suppress option. Our conditional suppression formula will be quite simple:

```
{@Hierarchy Level} = 1
```

Once we save this and go back to the Preview tab, our report will look like Figure 9.12.

Hedijetijak Electronics Corporation

Financial Statement

		2008	2007
2	ASSETS	1,560,397	1,409,178
3	Cash & Pooled Cash	1,372,165	1,136,881
4	1101000000 - CASH ON HAND		
4	1101100000 - CHANGE FUNDS		
4	1101200000 - PETTY CASH FUNDS	13	15
4	1101300000 - CASH IN TRANSIT TO TREASURY		
4	1103200000 - IMPREST CHECKING - OTHER	1	1
4	1110000000 - OPERATING CASH	1,383,602	1,162,698
4	1110000010 - CASH INTERFUND CLEARING	775	(5,480)
4	1110000015 - CASH INTER-COMPANY CODE CLEARING	3,841	5
4	2200000000 - WARRANTS PAYABLE FOR CONVERSION ONLY	(17)	(26)
4	2200000003 - WARRANTS PAYABLE RECONCILIATION ACCOUNT FOR WARRAN	(16,051)	(20,331)
3	Other Receivables, net	53,290	168,805
4	1130000000 - INTEREST RECEIVABLE -INVEST MNT		
4	1133400000 - A/R RECON ACCOUNT FOR DAMAGE CLAIMS	3,110	3,033

Figure 9.12 Hierarchy with Level 1 Suppressed

As you can see, our level 1 node has disappeared, and now our hierarchy begins with our first level 2 node (ASSETS).

Another common requirement is to be able to expand or collapse the hierarchy, which means we'll need to selectively display or hide the G/L account nodes. This will require that we first create a parameter to allow our end user to select the appropriate level of detail. Because we already covered how to create parameters in an earlier lesson, we'll simply show you the finished parameter entry (Figure 9.13).

Hedijetijak Electronics Corporation

Financial Statement

		2008	2007
2	ASSETS	1,560,397	1,409,178
3	Cash & Pooled Cash	1,372,165	1,136,881
3	Other Receivables, net	53,290	168,805
3	Intrafund Receivables	52,704	49,027
3	Due from Other Governments	55,878	18,848
3	Due from Other Funds	14,330	5,290
3	Inventories	588	227
3	Prepaids, Advances and Deferred Charges	57	611
3	Restricted Cash and Pooled Cash	11,386	29,488
3	Investments		
2	LIABILITIES/FUND BALANCE	(1,560,397)	(1,409,178)
3	LIABILITIES	(156,392)	(121,340)
4	Tax Refunds Payable		
4	Accounts Payable and Accrued Liabilities	(115,444)	(105,057)

Parameters
Show account level detail?
No

PHa
PHb
GH1
GH1
GH1
GH1
GH1
GH1
GH1
GH1
GH1
GH1
GH1
GH1
GH1

Figure 9.13 Report with G/L Account Level Suppressed

Now we need to make an adjustment to our conditional suppression formula for our group header.

Our new conditional suppression formula will now look like the following:

```
If {@Hierarchy Level} = 1
 then True
else
if {?Show Account Level} = 'No'
 then if not({@z_GL_Account_Key} startswith "BAUS")
 then True
 else
 False
```

This formula first tests if the hierarchy level is 1. If so, the section is suppressed. If it is not level 1, we then check the user's response to the Show Account Level parameter. If the response is "No" (they don't want to see the account-level detail), then any hierarchy node that doesn't start with BAUS (the G/L account nodes) will be suppressed.

To test this, we can go to the Preview tab and select "No" for the Show Account Level parameter. Our report now looks like Figure 9.14.

Our next formatting tip will show you how to format the summary nodes and key figures in bold and the G/L Account nodes in normal style. First we need to select both the Group Name (the node description) and the two key figures. Next, right-click one of the objects and select Format Objects. Then select the Font tab and finally the Formula icon next to the Style option.

Our conditional formatting formula will look like the following:

```
If {@z_GL_Account_Key} startswith "BAUS"
 then crBold
else
 DefaultAttribute
```

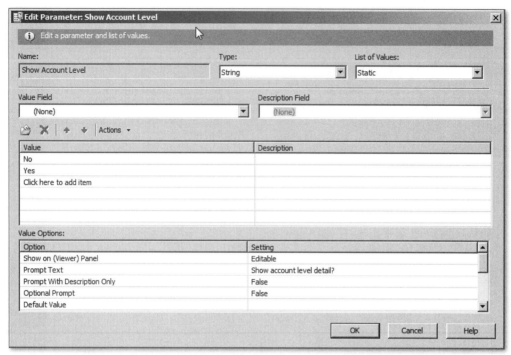

Figure 9.14 Show Account Level Parameter

This will result in the summary nodes (the key begins with BAUS) being bold and the G/L account nodes having the Default Attribute (the current setting). For this to work, however, we must reset the default setting of the group name, which is currently set to bold. We can set this by just selecting the group name and clicking the Bold button in the Formatting toolbar.

Now when we look at our report in the Expanded view, it should look like Figure 9.15.

Let's show you one more handy formatting trick that can help you improve the overall appearance of your report. This technique will provide a way to apply varying levels of gray to the background of our group header based on the current level of the hierarchy.

To set the background color of our group header we need to right-click in the left margin of the section and select Section Expert. Then select the Color tab and finally the Formula button for the Background color option.

Hedijetijak Electronics Corporation
Financial Statement

		2008	2007
2	ASSETS	1,560,397	1,409,178
3	Cash & Pooled Cash	1,372,165	1,136,881
4	1101000000 - CASH ON HAND		
4	1101100000 - CHANGE FUNDS		
4	1101200000 - PETTY CASH FUNDS	13	15
4	1101300000 - CASH IN TRANSIT TO TREASURY		
4	1103200000 - IMPREST CHECKING - OTHER	1	1
4	1110000000 - OPERATING CASH	1,383,602	1,162,698
4	1110000010 - CASH INTERFUND CLEARING	775	(5,480)
4	1110000015 - CASH INTER-COMPANY CODE CLEARING	3,841	5
4	2200000000 - WARRANTS PAYABLE FOR CONVERSION ONLY	(17)	(26)
4	2200000003 - WARRANTS PAYABLE RECONCILIATION ACCOUNT FOR WARRAN	(16,051)	(20,331)
3	Other Receivables, net	53,290	168,805
4	1130000000 - INTEREST RECEIVABLE -INVESTMNT		
4	1133400000 - A/R RECON ACCOUNT FOR DAMAGE CLAIMS	3,110	3,033
4	1133400010 - A/R RECONCILIATION ACCOUNT FOR REAL ESTATE	6	52

Figure 9.15 Report with Conditional Bold Formatting

The conditional formatting formula for our background color will be as follows:

```
If {?Show Account Level} = 'Yes'
 then
 if not({@z_GL_Account_Key} startswith "BAUS")
 then
 if remainder(groupnumber, 2) <> 0
 then Color (245,245,245)
 else
 NoColor
 else
 Color(235,235,235)
 else
 if {@z_GL_Account_Key} in ['BAUS6', 'BAUS5', 'BAUS59']
 then Color(225,225,225)
 else
 if {@z_GL_Account_Key} in ['BAUS7', 'BAUS9', 'BAUS60', 'BAUS67',
 'BAUS68']
 then Color(235,235,235)
 else
 NoColor
```

The preceding conditional formatting formula is not meant to impress or scare you, only to give you an idea of the extent to which you can customize the look and feel of a report when necessary. As you might imagine, you can go quite a bit further, depending on how complex your formatting requirements are.

Before we explain the preceding formula, it would be a good idea to explain first the Color function that's used in the formula. The Color function accepts three arguments that represent the level of Red, Green, and Blue (RGB values) that will be used to create the final color. When you use the same value for all three arguments, you end up with a shade of gray. The higher the number, the lighter the shade. The highest number possible is 255.

A high-level explanation of the preceding formula would look something like the following:

▶ If the end user wants to see the G/L Account level detail (an answer of Yes to the Show Account Level parameter), then format every other G/L account node with a light gray color and format each summary node with a slightly darker shade of gray.

▶ If the end user wants to see only the summary nodes (an answer of No' to the Show Account Level parameter), then format three of the higher-level summary nodes in a shade of gray and format five nodes at a lower level in a slightly lighter shade of gray.

Figure 9.16 shows what the report looks like when the user chooses to see the G/L Account level detail.

Figure 9.17 shows what it looks like when the user chooses the summary-only version of the report.

Note

We've left the Hierarchy Level formula visible at the left of each hierarchy node in our examples so we can see the hierarchy level of each node. A finished report would have this formula suppressed.

Figure 9.16 Report Showing G/L Accounts with Custom Formatting

Figure 9.17 Report Showing Summary Nodes with Custom Formatting

It's important that you not get caught up in the particulars of this one conditional formatting formula at this point. If you do, then you're missing the point of this lesson. Our primary objective is to expose you to some of the ways you can control the final look and feel of a report that uses an SAP NetWeaver BW hierarchy. As we mentioned earlier, there are many different reasons why you might want to change the appearance of this type of report. So far we've covered only a few.

And, as we've been saying at various places throughout this book, because Crystal Reports is a versatile, multipurpose report development tool, it's designed to provide you as the report developer with an almost unlimited degree of control over the final output of your report. Because of this, there are no automatic ways to handle special nuances and tweaks like the ones we just covered. Other more specialized tools may offer more of a point-and-click way to set these types of options, but typically they're limited to a relatively small set of options. If your needs extend past these built-in, options you may be out of luck.

So, once again, we're back to the fundamental principle of increased flexibility bringing increased complexity. If you want the opportunity to do more with a single product, you have to be willing to handle more complexity. This again is the primary reason why Crystal Reports is definitely not an end user BI tool.

> **Reality Check**
>
> If this last formula is, for whatever reason, simply too complex for you to get your mind around, you need to consider again whether or not you should move forward in your plans to become a Crystal Reports developer. To be truly proficient in handling the kinds of report requirements you typically see in an SAP NetWeaver BW environment you simply must be able to handle this level of complexity.

9.3   Taking Hierarchies to the Next Level

The last topic we want to cover regarding hierarchies deals with situations where you want to add an additional level of detail to a report that uses an SAP NetWeaver BW hierarchy. Although it's true that the majority of reports that use an SAP NetWeaver BW hierarchy will never go beyond the structure of the hierarchy in terms of detail, one of the advantages of Crystal Reports when dealing with SAP NetWeaver BW hierarchies is that you have the option of adding an additional layer (or layers) of detail.

For this exercise, we'll switch to a different report and hierarchy. This report is a training attendance report that uses a hierarchy to organize the various training courses that Hedijetijak Electronics offers its employees. Figure 9.18 shows what the report looks like with only the hierarchy characteristic (Course) active.

Hedijetijak Electronics Corporation
Course Attendance

Microsoft Project 2007 Professional	22
50050984 - Microsoft Project 2007 Professional	11
50051791 - Microsoft Project 2007 Professional	11
Microsoft Word 2003 Level 1	25
50038508 - Microsoft Word 2003 Level 1	10
50038509 - Microsoft Word 2003 Level 1	5
50046844 - Microsoft Word 2003 Level 1	1
50050974 - Microsoft Word 2003 Level 1	9
Microsoft Word 2003 Level 2	23
50038514 - Microsoft Word 2003 Level 2	10
50038515 - Microsoft Word 2003 Level 2	4
50046845 - Microsoft Word 2003 Level 2	1
50050980 - Microsoft Word 2003 Level 2	8
Microsoft Word 2003 Level 3	19
50041831 - Microsoft Word 2003 Level 3	2
50042662 - Microsoft Word 2003 Level 3	10
50046843 - Microsoft Word 2003 Level 3	7

Figure 9.18 Course Attendance Report with Hierarchy Only

This report has worked fine for the director of training at Hedijetijak Electronics until recently. Now the needs to be able to quickly see a list of employee numbers for each of the employees who attended a particular training course. To handle this requirement you decide to simply add the employee ID characteristic to the Detail section of this report.

After doing this, you run the report again and it looks like Figure 9.19.

As you can see, our totals are no longer correct for any of our summary nodes. In fact, the summary node totals are all the same (1). What happened?

What you have seen here is the effect of adding anything to the Detail section beneath a hierarchy that results in the creation of additional aggregates. The original report aggregated at the course level because the lowest level of detail that was included in the report was Course. This is the characteristic that's associated with the hierarchy used in this report. Therefore, the totals we were seeing in the original report were the totals for each course as returned in the key figure from the BW query.

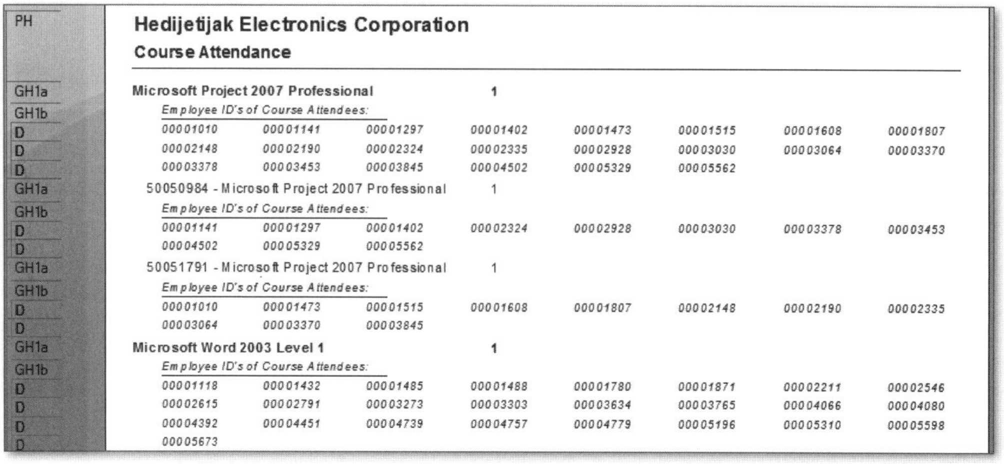

Figure 9.19 Course Attendance Report with Employee Detail

Hot Tip

When you're including only the characteristic associated directly with the hierarchy in your report, you can put the key figures in the group header, and they'll return the correct summary for that hierarchy node. However, if you add any lower-level characteristic to the report (either in the Detail section or in a lower-level group), then the key figures no longer work as summary node totals.

To fix this problem we need to add summaries to our group headers to total up the number of employees who attended each course, just like you would in any normal Crystal Reports report (with no hierarchy). All we need to do is right-click the Employee ID field in the Detail section, select INSERT • SUMMARY, and then select the Count summary function. After placing this in the group header (and applying our conditional formatting), the report now looks like Figure 9.20.

If you compare our totals here with the totals we had originally when we were using only the hierarchy characteristic, you'll see that they're the same. However, we now have access to additional detail information that we didn't have before.

Also, based on what you now know about conditionally suppressing sections in a hierarchy, you could provide the user with the option (using a parameter) to display or hide the employee detail in the report.

That's all we'll cover concerning hierarchies for now. As you've seen, Crystal Reports does a good job of allowing you to leverage the existing hierarchies that your organization has developed for use with your BW queries. Once you learn the few steps it takes to re-assemble them in Crystal Reports, from then on it's up to you how far you want to take them in making your reports more presentable, and useful, to your end users.

```
PH        Hedijetijak Electronics Corporation
          Course Attendance

GH1a      Microsoft Project 2007 Professional        22
GH1b      Employee ID's of Course Attendees:
D           00001010    00001141    00001297    00001402    00001473    00001515    00001608    00001807
D           00002148    00002190    00002324    00002335    00002928    00003030    00003064    00003370
D           00003378    00003453    00003845    00004502    00005329    00005562
GH1a      50050984 - Microsoft Project 2007 Professional    11
GH1b      Employee ID's of Course Attendees:
D           00001141    00001297    00001402    00002324    00002928    00003030    00003378    00003453
D           00004502    00005329    00005562
GH1a      50051791 - Microsoft Project 2007 Professional    11
GH1b      Employee ID's of Course Attendees:
D           00001010    00001473    00001515    00001608    00001807    00002148    00002190    00002335
D           00003064    00003370    00003845
GH1a      Microsoft Word 2003 Level 1                  25
GH1b      Employee ID's of Course Attendees:
D           00001118    00001432    00001485    00001488    00001780    00001871    00002211    00002546
D           00002615    00002791    00003273    00003303    00003634    00003765    00004066    00004080
D           00004392    00004451    00004739    00004757    00004779    00005196    00005310    00005598
D           00005673
```

Figure 9.20 Course Attendance Report with Corrected Totals

9.4   Summary

▶ Crystal Reports provides full support for your existing SAP NetWeaver BW hierarchies through the Hierarchical Grouping feature.

▶ It's important that you make use of the HierarchyLevel function in Crystal Reports when working with hierarchies to ensure that you always know the hierarchy level of each node.

▶ Assembling the basic structure of a hierarchy in Crystal Reports is a fairly straightforward process. The challenge then becomes formatting the hierarchy to meet particular reporting requirements.

▶ An essential part of applying any conditional formatting to a hierarchy is being able differentiate between the hierarchy summary nodes and postable nodes.

▶ There's a wide variety of techniques you can learn to help you refine the appearance and functionality of your hierarchies in Crystal Reports.

▶ You can add additional details to a report that uses a hierarchy. However, when you do, you'll need to create your own summary functions to aggregate your key figures for your hierarchy summary nodes.

Sometimes you just can't put everything in one report, but you would still like to keep it all together in one place. Subreports provide you with a way to combine data from different data sources into a single report.

10   Extending Reports Using Subreports

In this final report development chapter we'll cover one of the features in Crystal Reports that allows you to extend your report beyond the reach of its data source — the subreport. A subreport is the mechanism within Crystal Reports that provides a way to retrieve data from a completely separate data source from the main report. It's a report within a report.

One of the inherent challenges in any reporting environment is *scope*. Every data source on the planet is limited to some degree in its scope, or the range of information that can be accessed within the confines of that one data source. It's simply impossible to see everything in one place.

The most limited data source is the single table within a transactional system (such as SAP ERP Central Component). You can't get any more limited than this. As a data source, a single transactional table will provide you with a very limited range of information, normally only information pertaining to a single entity (customer, vendor, etc.) and often only a limited amount of information about that one entity.

Because of this limitation, it's very common to combine multiple tables into a single data source when working with a transactional system. The most common method of doing this is joining the tables within the reporting application. Crystal Reports does this quite well, and it's routinely done when creating reports in a standard SQL-based environment (such as SQL Server or Oracle). Because Crystal Reports also integrates directly with SAP ERP Central Component (SAP R/3), you can also join tables within SAP ERP Central Component as easily as you can in an SQL environment.

There are also several backend options for combining data in a transactional environment, the most common ones being *views, queries,* and *stored procedures*. In the

SAP ERP Central Component world, InfoSets and ABAP (or SAP) queries are two of the most commonly used mechanisms for bringing more information together.

Of course, as we've discussed on several occasions in this book, the basic premise of the data warehouse (such as SAP NetWeaver BW) is to bring disparate transactional data together in one place so that end users can see more of their business data at one time through a single interface. It some ways this is simply taking the idea of the view, stored procedure, or query and extending it further by bringing even more data together and "time synchronizing" it so that historical information can be analyzed accurately. Of all possible reporting data sources, the data warehouse has the greatest potential for bringing the widest spectrum of data into a single place.

But even a data warehouse has its limitations. There's only so much that can be brought together into an InfoProvider in SAP NetWeaver BW. One method for getting around this limitation is something called the *MultiProvider.* A MultiProvider is a combination of InfoProviders (InfoCubes, DSOs) that essentially functions as a view. But, as you might expect, there are even limitations with Multiproviders, the most common of which is performance. They can also be difficult to create and maintain.

One of the newer approaches that's gained popularity over the past several years is something called data federation. The idea behind data federation is to provide a meta-layer that virtually combines data from a wide array of disparate data sources (relational databases, flat files, XML files, Web services, etc.) into a cohesive, unified data source. The concept is really more of a response to how difficult (and time-consuming) it can be to combine multiple sources of data into one physical data source than anything else.

Because of the inherent challenges of trying to combine a wide range of data into a single data source on the backend it's been necessary to come up with new ways to combine disparate data sources on the frontend. The SAP BEx Report to Report Interface (RRI) is one example of this. The Crystal Reports subreport, which has been around for quite some time, is very similar in concept to the Report to Report Interface in SAP BEx.

One last practical observation before we move on: As you can tell by now, this issue has been around for quite some time, ever since the first relational database. And although technically speaking, it will always make the most sense to combine and integrate disparate data either on the backend or virtually through some sort of meta-layer technology, these approaches share one common enemy that, practically speaking, makes them sometimes impractical: time.

As we mentioned earlier in this book, changes made to the backend always take longer than changes made to the frontend of any data system. That's just the way things work. What frontend solutions lack in terms of permanence and maintainability they, in some ways, make up for with increased responsiveness and flexibility.

So for situations where you're being told that the long-term solution is going to be a long time coming, we present to you the "just do it now" solution: the subreport.

10.1 The Query to Query Subreport

For our first example we'll look at a situation where you want to combine data from one BW query with another BW query through a subreport.

> **Important Note**
>
> Just as with the previous lesson on hierarchies, don't try to follow along exactly with each exercise. It's highly unlikely that you have the same data sources configured on your SAP NetWeaver BW system. Just as before, we'll make every effort to make this lesson as general as possible to make it transferable to almost any environment and reporting requirement.

Our first example will cover a scenario that's quite common in the world of SAP NetWeaver BW: getting to the detail. You may recall from our earlier discussions of the benefits and challenges of the data warehouse that perhaps the biggest challenge facing anyone developing reports in a data warehouse environment is reporting at the detail, or document, level.

Data warehouses aren't designed to provide end users with ready access to document-level data, especially when dealing with large volumes of data. This is the highest level of detail possible in any data warehouse as it gets down to the individual transaction level. As you might imagine, once you get to millions of rows of data, it begins to become impractical to retrieve this amount of data in one shot.

The SAP BEx Excel analyzer tool uses *drill-down* and *drill-across* to allow users to go from one level of detail down into the next. This is a common way to get specific pieces of detail data without having to bring all of the detail across for the entire set of summary data. The technique you're about to learn is the Crystal Reports way to perform the same sort of drill-down into detail. The advantage of this approach is that it gives users access to detail information without having to retrieve all of the detail data in the original data set (or report).

Before we go on, however, some initial definitions may help us get started on the right footing. A subreport is essentially a report within a report. You're placing a Crystal Reports report within a section of another Crystal Reports report, which now becomes the main report. Up to now we've been working with just a single Crystal Reports report at a time.

A subreport can be placed into any section within a Crystal Reports report except for the page header or page footer. The placement of a subreport is driven by its purpose (or why you need the subreport). There are two basic types of subreports: *unlinked* and *linked.* Linked subreports are the more common and will be the type used in our exercises. A linked subreport is synchronized (or related) to a particular characteristic value.

The purpose of a linked subreport is to retrieve additional information related to a particular characteristic value in the main report. Because of this, it's always placed in the same section as the characteristic it's related to. So if the purpose of a subreport is to retrieve detail information about customers, and my main report is grouped by customer (Group 1), the linked subreport will be placed in either the header or footer for Group 1. However, if the main report lists individual customers in the Detail section the linked subreport will be placed there instead.

Linked subreports are almost never placed in the report header or footer. This makes sense because this would mean the related characteristic would have to have the exact same value across the entire data set in the main report (for instance, every row has the same customer value).

Unlinked subreports aren't nearly as common as linked subreports. The data in an unlinked subreport is not related to (or synchronized with) the data in the main report in any way. The data in an unlinked subreport can be completely unrelated to the data in the main report. Unlike linked subreports, unlinked subreports are almost always placed in the report header or footer.

A subreport can either be a *standard* subreport or an *on-demand* subreport. A standard subreport runs every time the section it appears in displays in the report. So if the subreport is placed in the header for Group 1 and there are 20 unique members in group 1, the subreport will run 20 times when the main report is run.

> **Warning**
>
> Be careful when placing a standard subreport in the Detail section of any report. In a report based on a BW query it actually isn't uncommon to have a subreport placed in the Detail section because the data being retrieved is summarized data (even though it's presented in the Detail section). In other words, the number of rows returned is normally restricted. However, keep in mind that the subreport will execute once for every time the Detail section is displayed in the Preview tab. For reports that return a large number of rows this quickly becomes impractical due to performance constraints.

Often when using a linked subreport, you'll want to make it an on-demand subreport. Like the name suggests, this type of subreport only executes when the end user activates it (by double-clicking it). The advantage of this is increased performance and efficiency because the detail data is retrieved only when needed. The primary disadvantage (or rather, limitation) is that, because this is an interactive feature, it only works when the report is viewed online.

Because we'll be performing a drill-down detail using a subreport, we'll make it a linked on-demand subreport. In an SAP NetWeaver BW environment this is perhaps the most common type of subreport used.

For the sake of context, let's take a quick look at the query being used for our main report (the Sales Overview – Crystal Master query) (Figure 10.1).

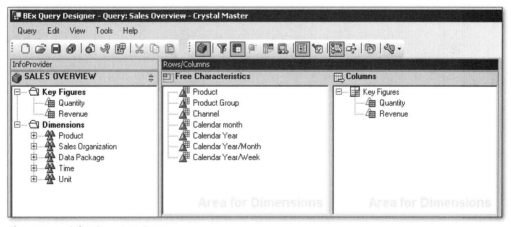

Figure 10.1 Sales Overview Query

Besides the four time period characteristics, this query contains the following three characteristics:

▶ Product

▶ Product Group

▶ Channel

We've already created several reports that use this query as its data source. Let's open one now to use as our starting point — the Chapter 7 – Sales Report by Month report. Now let's do a Save As and call it "Chapter 10 – On Demand Subreport."

Our report currently looks like Figure 10.2.

Hedijetijak Electronics Corporation

National Sales Report

Month/Year	Product	Qty	Revenue
July 2007		1,007 $	211,590.44
	Ventra LX 2.33 1GB 300 GB	165	$ 90,748.35
	Ventra Ultra 3.00 2GB 750 GB	98	$ 63,797.02
	Ventra LXP 2.67 2GB 500 GB	75	$ 45,074.25
	UltraTouch USB Keyboard	120	$ 4,797.60
	DigiPad Mousepad	339	$ 3,010.32
	Computer Speakers	115	$ 2,643.85
	LightTouch Optical Mouse	95	$ 1,519.05

Figure 10.2 National Sales Report by Month

Our report currently displays the lowest level of detail possible given the characteristics that are available in our BW query, which is the product level. Note that the Sales Overview query doesn't contain any document-level characteristics (in this case, Sales Document). If we were to include Sales Document in our query and include it in our current report (by grouping on Product and then putting Sales Document data in the Detail section), we'd be retrieving all of the sales document data for all products in the report every time we run the report.

This might be fine if (a) we want to see all of the detail every time we run the report and (b) the report will run in a reasonable amount of time (and not time out). As we've said before, this isn't always the case. It's quite common for a report that includes document-level characteristics to either run for a very long time or not run at all. In these cases you have to break up your report into two pieces: a main report with the top-level summary characteristics and an on-demand subreport that retrieves the document-level detail information.

A key part of this process is the structure of the BW query for the subreport. For the on-demand subreport to work correctly, the query must include the following:

▶ The document level characteristic (in our case, Sales Document) and any other detail-level characteristics or attributes the end user wants.

▶ Any other characteristic required to filter the data to match the data in the main report. These characteristics should be filtered using a variable. The need for this additional characteristic filter is determined by the filters and groupings in the main report.

▶ The appropriate key figure(s).

▶ A "link" characteristic with a variable. This characteristic will be the "common" characteristic used to synchronize the summary data from the main report with the detail data in the subreport. In our example this will be Product.

In Figure 10.3 we can see the how the BW query we'll use for our subreport is structured.

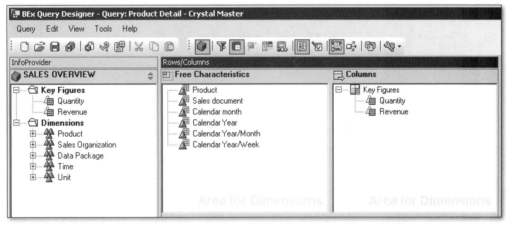

Figure 10.3 Product Detail Query

You can see that this query differs from the query for our main report in that it doesn't include Channel or Product Group but does include Sales Document. The one characteristic they share in common (other than the time period characteristics) is Product. This common characteristic will be used (along with Calendar Month) to link the main report with the subreport.

> **Important Note**
>
> To successfully link a main report with a subreport when both use BW queries as their data source, the two queries must share at least one common characteristic, and the query for the subreport must have a variable attached to the common characteristic.

The next step is to create the subreport. There are two ways to create a subreport in Crystal Reports. One doesn't work with BW queries, so we'll use the other, and that is to create the subreport in advance (just like any other report) and then select it when we create the subreport within the main report. (The option that doesn't work is to create the subreport on-the-fly when you go to insert a subreport into your main report.)

Because you already know how to create a new report, we won't bother showing you the steps we took to create our simple detail subreport.

> **Pop Quiz**
>
> **Question:** What's the preferred method for creating a new Crystal Reports report from a BW query?
>
> **Answer:** Start with a Crystal Reports template.

Although this is true, you can cut yourself a bit of slack in these types of situations where you're creating a "one-off" subreport for a particular purpose. For these types of reports you may decide it's not worth the extra effort to create a full template and just start directly from the BW query. This is perfectly acceptable. As a rule, however, you still want to create master templates for your heavy-hitter queries that you use regularly to meet ongoing report requirements. Our simple list report looks like Figure 10.4.

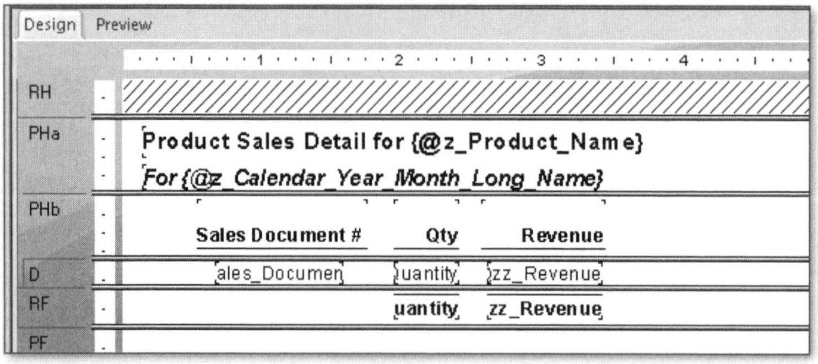

Figure 10.4 Product Sales Detail Subreport

You might notice that we've inserted both the Product Name and the Calendar Month in the Page Header of our report (soon to become a subreport). We point this out because this would be unusual to do in a standard report because it would only make sense to do if the values for both Product Name and Calendar Month were constant for the entire report. This would be quite unusual for a normal report.

However, this is definitely not unusual for a subreport. In fact, we've limiting our subreport to a single Product and Calendar Month by design. This is because our goal is to allow the end user to double-click a particular Product Name in the main report and retrieve detailed sales data for only that product for a particular month. If you look back at our main report in Figure 10.1, you'll see that when you select a particular product in the report, you're at the same time selecting a particular month because the data is first grouped by Calendar Month before you get to Product. In this way Calendar Month is acting as a contextual filter.

Now let's take another look at our original monthly sales report in the Design tab (Figure 10.5).

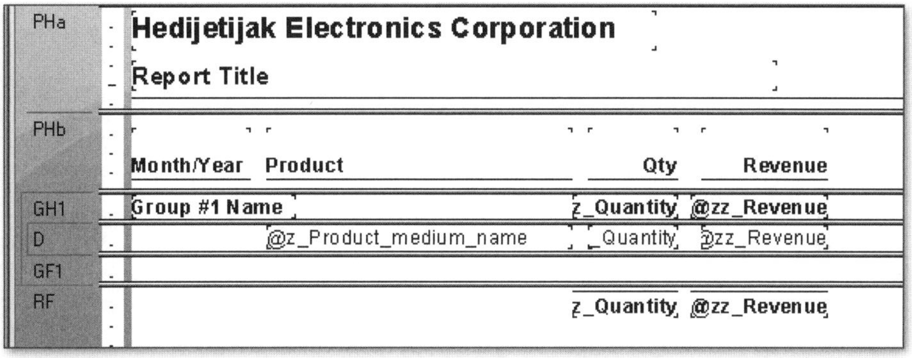

Figure 10.5 Monthly Sales Report Before Subreport

Remember, our goal is to allow the end user to double-click a particular product and retrieve detailed sales information about that product. What that means in practical terms is that we're going to replace the existing Product Name alias formula in the Detail section with an on-demand subreport.

To begin, we'll delete the existing alias formula from the Detail section. Now we have a place to put our on-demand subreport, as you can see in Figure 10.6.

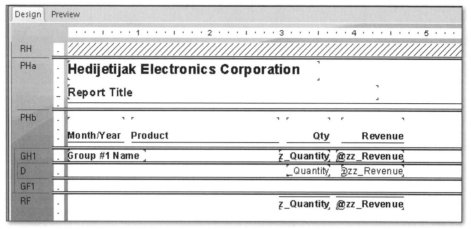

Figure 10.6 Deleting the Product Name from the Detail Section

The next step is to insert our subreport. We need to click the Insert Subreport button in the Insert toolbar (Figure 10.7).

Figure 10.7 Insert Subreport Button

After clicking this button we should see the Insert Subreport dialog box, as shown in Figure 10.8.

The first thing we need to do is select our existing subreport. This is where we *don't* choose the second option (Create a Subreport with the Report Wizard). We need to choose the first option (Choose an Existing Report) and select the Product Sales Detail subreport.

Next we need to select the On-demand Subreport option at the bottom on the dialog box. Just as it sounds, this option turns our otherwise normal subreport into an on-demand subreport. As a reminder, if we don't do this, the subreport would run every time the section it sits in appears in the Preview tab.

Next we need to establish our link from the main report to the subreport. This is a critical step in the process, and you must take care to perform it correctly. We do this by first selecting the Link tab at the top of the dialog box (Figure 10.9).

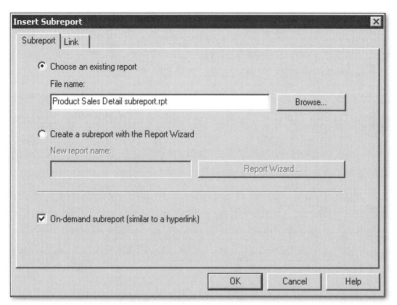

Figure 10.8 Insert Subreport Dialog Box

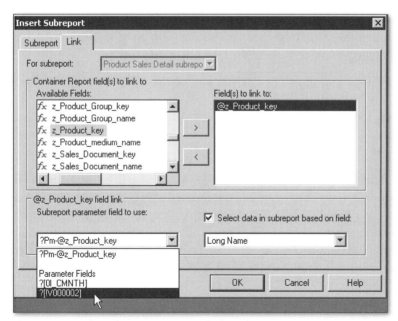

Figure 10.9 Linking the Main Report with the Subreport

The next step is to select the characteristic (or characteristics) in the main report that will be used to create the link to the subreport. This is the part that can get a little tricky. To get this right you need to understand exactly how these two reports need to be linked to keep the data between the two synchronized.

It should be fairly obvious that at least one of our links needs to be Product, because the goal of this subreport is to retrieve detailed sales information about a particular product. When we click a product in the main report, information about that product will be passed to the subreport and used to restrict the data set of the subreport.

We hope that by now it makes sense that the information that needs to be passed to the subreport should always be the characteristic key, not a descriptive name. A key is always going to be a unique value and will not change over time. The descriptive text for any characteristic (short name, medium name, and/or long name) can change at any time.

In our example, then, we'll choose the z_Product_key alias formula to begin forming our link. Once we click it and move it to the right, the two options at the bottom of the dialog box become active. The option on the left (Subreport Parameter Field To Use) initially appears with the value "?Pm-@link_field." You don't want to use this parameter field to establish your link to the subreport. This option is used for linking subreports that don't use a BW query as a data source.

You'll find the correct choice by clicking the pull-down menu on the left. When you do, you'll see any BW variables that are part of the subreport's source BW query (refer back to Figure 10.8). Your link to any subreport that uses a BW query as a data source is always created by selecting the appropriate BW variable from the subreport's BW query.

This example should give you a good idea of the kinds of things you sometimes have to deal with when working with BW queries and things like variables. In our list we have two variables (0I_CMNTH and !V000002). If you have no idea which of these two is the correct variable to use with Product, you might be able to select it by a process of elimination (0I_CMNTH most likely belongs to Calendar Month). Sometimes, however, you won't be able to recognize any of the variables listed by their technical names.

If you have no idea what variable belongs to what characteristic, you can either find someone in your organization who does (perhaps the person who created the query), or you can figure it out yourself by going to the subreport and editing the variable parameter. When we open our Product Sales Detail subreport and edit the *!V000002* parameter, we'll see something like Figure 10.10.

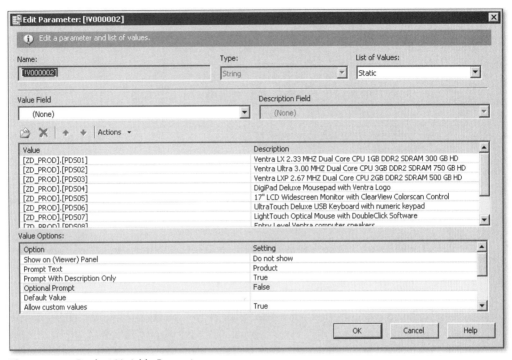

Figure 10.10   Product Variable Parameter

Now we see that this variable is being used to filter the Product characteristic. We can tell both by the list of values and the prompt text at the bottom (Product). The prompt text of a variable parameter will always be the descriptive text of the BW variable.

Now that we've selected the Product key as our subreport link, we can click OK to insert our subreport. After you click OK, you'll find a rather large blue rectangle attached to your cursor. This is your subreport waiting to be placed in the main report.

> **Hot Tip**
>
> Don't try to place the subreport yet in the Detail section (its final resting place). Because it's rather large, it will make a mess of your Detail section. The best thing to do at this point is to place it temporarily someplace where it will comfortably fit until you can resize and format it.

A good place to put our subreport for now is in the Report Footer. After we place it in the Report Footer, our report will look like Figure 10.11.

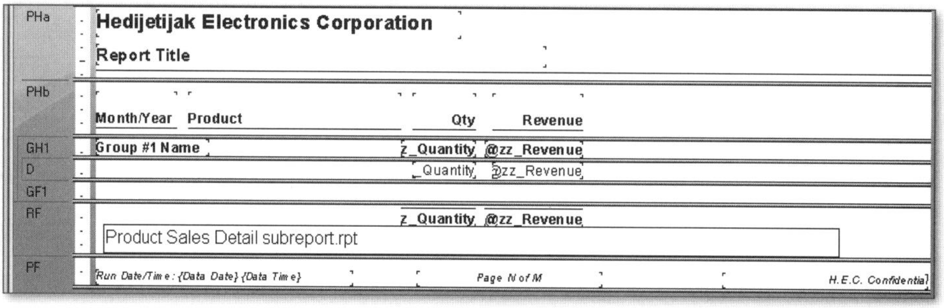

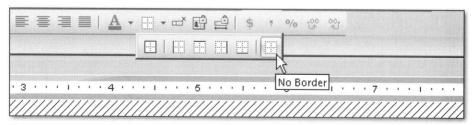

Figure 10.11 Placing the Subreport Temporarily in the Report Footer

Now we have some work to do to seamlessly integrate our newly created subreport into the Detail section of our report. The first step is to reduce it down to a size that will fit neatly into the Detail section in the spot where the Product name used to be.

Right away we'll need to get rid of the box around the subreport. You almost never want to have a box around your subreports, which is unfortunate, because the default setting (as you can see) is to put a box around the subreport. We can now select the subreport and click the No Border button in the Formatting toolbar (Figure 10.12).

Figure 10.12 No Border Button

Next we need to apply some formatting to our subreport to allow it to blend seamlessly into the Detail section. Right-click the subreport and select Format Subreport from the menu (Figure 10.13).

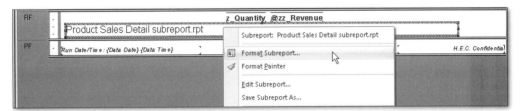

Figure 10.13 Format Subreport Menu Item

Now we can select the Font tab of the Format Editor and set the font size to 10 and change the color of the font to Blue (Figure 10.14). We're using blue because this will indicate to the end user that this is a hyperlink.

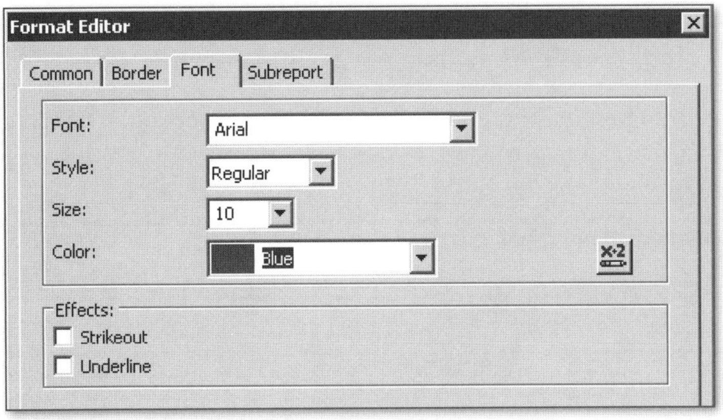

Figure 10.14 Changing the Font for the Subreport

Next, select the Subreport tab in the Formula Editor (Figure 10.15).

Here we should double-check to ensure that the On-demand Subreport option is selected, which it is. Now we'll change the name of the subreport so that it displays the current product name for the section where it sits (in our case, the Detail section). We do this by clicking the Formula button next to the On-demand Subreport Caption option. The formula contents will be:

```
{@z_Product_medium_name}
```

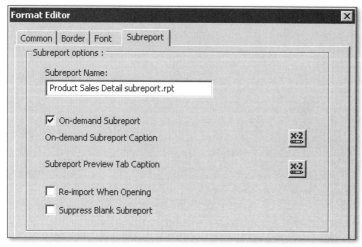

Figure 10.15   Subreport Tab

This means the Product medium name will now be displayed as the title of the subreport in the main report. And because we changed the font size to 10, it will blend in perfectly with the rest of the items in the Detail section.

The final step is to resize the subreport and place it in the Detail section, where the Product name was before (Figure 10.16).

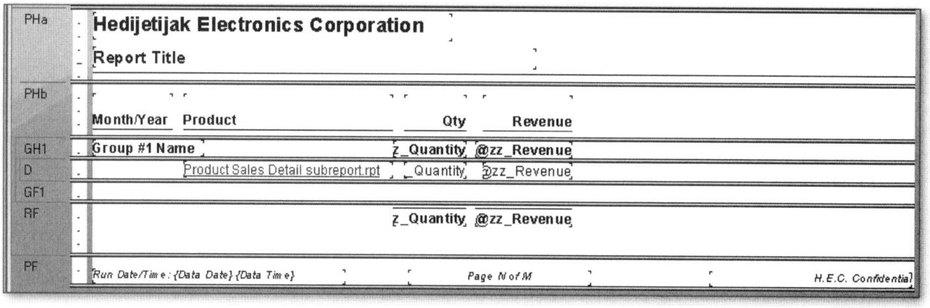

Figure 10.16   Subreport Formatted and Placed in Detail Section

Now we're ready to run our main report and test our on-demand subreport. When we click the Refresh button, we get see the Enter Values dialog box (Figure 10.17).

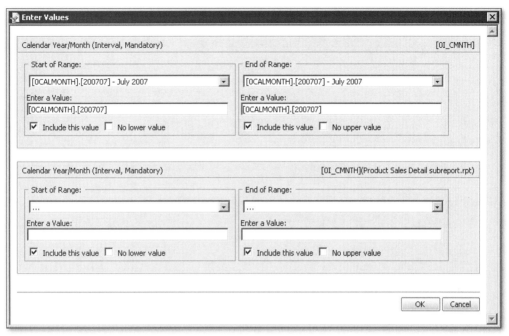

Figure 10.17 Enter Values Dialog Box with Extra Parameter

Something doesn't look quite right here. For some reason we're seeing double. The Calendar Month parameter is showing up twice now, whereas before it was only showing up once. What happened?

We've done this intentionally to show you something that can easily happen when you link a subreport that has a BW query as its data source into a main report. We left a BW variable in the subreport "unlinked" with the main report. If will recall, we only selected z_Product_key as a link from the main report to the subreport (linked to the variable for Product in the subreport). However, there are two variables in the BW query behind the subreport, not just one.

What we're seeing in the Enter Values dialog box of the main report is what you'll see whenever this happens. We see the Calendar Month variable from the main report at the top and the one from the subreport at the bottom. We can tell it's coming from the subreport because the subreport name is appended to the end of the parameter name (Product Sales Detail subreport.rpt).

> **Hot Tip**
>
> You never want to leave a variable parameter in a subreport unattached from the main report. You need to always provide a link from the main report to the variable parameter in the subreport. If for some reason the variable is simply an "extra" that's unnecessary for establishing the link, you should remove it from the subreport query.

To fix this situation we need to click Cancel, right-click the subreport, and select Change Subreport Links. We can then select the Calendar Year/Month key and link it to the 0I_CMNTH variable at the bottom left (Figure 10.18).

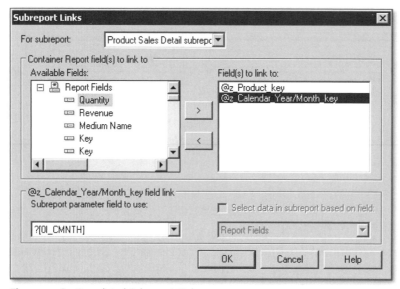

Figure 10.18   Completed Subreport Links

When you're creating links between the main report and the subreport when both reports use a BW query as a data source, there are two different methods for forming the link:

▶ Main report characteristic linked to subreport variable parameter

▶ Main report variable parameter linked to subreport variable parameter

In this example we linked two characteristics from the main report to two variable parameters in the subreport. We did this for two reasons:

- First, the main report doesn't have a variable for Product. Therefore, we have to use the Product key characteristic to establish the link to the Product variable parameter in the subreport.

- Second, to keep the Calendar Month synchronized between the main report and the subreport it's necessary to link a contextual value for Calendar Month rather than the value entered for the BW variable parameter.

In our example, if we had linked the Calendar Month variable parameter in the main report to the corresponding variable parameter in the subreport, it would result in the subreport returning summaries for the same calendar months that were selected for the main report. This would work whenever the user selected a single calendar month.

But what would happen if the user selected more than one month? Now the two reports will be out of sync. When the user double-clicks a particular product in the main report, that product is displayed in the context of a particular month. To keep the data in the two reports in sync, you'll need to link that particular month's value to the subreport, not the overall selection used to generate the entire main report.

Perhaps the best way to explain how this works is to show you. First, we'll run our report and activate the on-demand subreport while it's linked correctly. Then we'll link it the wrong way to show the difference.

We'll refresh the report again. When we do, we see just a single variable parameter for Calendar Year/Month. This is because we linked the Calendar Year/Month characteristic to the variable parameter in the subreport (Figure 10.19).

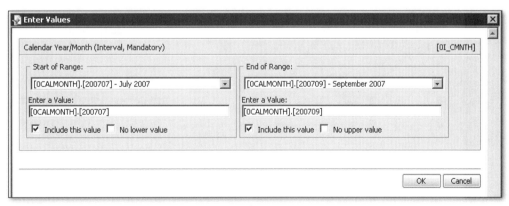

Figure 10.19 Enter Values with Variable Parameter from Main Report

We'll select the range of July 2007 to September 2007 and click OK. We now see the main report in the Preview tab (Figure 10.20).

Hedijetijak Electronics Corporation

National Sales Report

Month/Year	Product	Qty	Revenue
July 2007		**1,007 $**	**211,590.44**
	Ventra LX 2.33 1GB 300 GB	165	$ 90,748.35
	Ventra Ultra 3.00 2GB 750 GB	98	$ 63,797.02
	Ventra LXP 2.67 2GB 500 GB	75	$ 45,074.25
	UltraTouch USB Keyboard	120	$ 4,797.60
	DigiPad Mousepad	339	$ 3,010.32
	Computer Speakers	115	$ 2,643.85
	LightTouch Optical Mouse	95	$ 1,519.05

Figure 10.20 Main Report Showing On-Demand Subreport Links

Now we can see our on-demand subreport links that we formatted to display the product name in the form of a hyperlink. To test our on-demand subreport, let's click the Ventra Ultra 3.00 value for July 2007. We'll see the subreport shown in Figure 10.21.

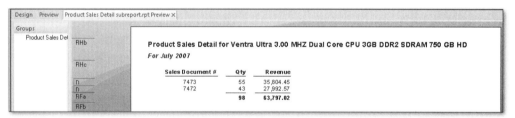

Figure 10.21 Detail Subreport for Ventra Ultra 3.00 July 2007

If you compare the totals for this subreport to the summary totals for the Ventra Ultra 3.00 in July 2007 from the main report, you'll notice that they're the same.

Now let's link these reports the wrong way. In the Design tab we'll right-click the subreport and select Change Subreport Links. Now we'll remove the z_Calendar_Year/Month_key entry on the right and replace it with the variable parameter from the main report, as shown in Figure 10.22.

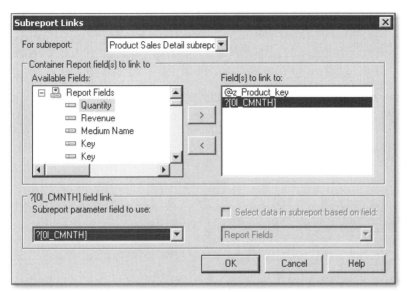

Figure 10.22 Incorrect Link Between Variable Parameters

Now when we click the Ventra Ultra 3.00 value for July 2007, we see the subreport shown in Figure 10.23.

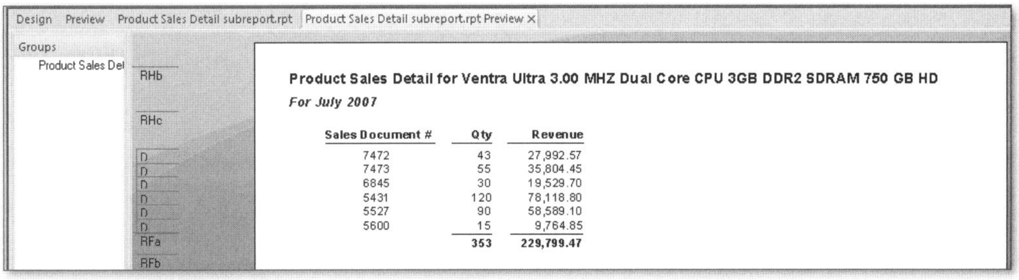

Figure 10.23 Detail Subreport with Summaries for all Months

Now that we've linked the variable parameter from the main report to the corresponding variable parameter in the subreport, we're getting the summaries for the Ventra Ultra 3.00 for all three months, not just for July. This is because the link is doing exactly what we told it to do: return the same calendar months that were selected by the end user for the main report. Because our selection for the main report was for three months of data and we linked this selection to the subreport variable parameter, we're now getting three months of data in the subreport.

Before we go back and return this link to its original setting, let's make one more formatting change. You may have noticed that when we activate our on-demand subreport it appears in a separate tab with the label Product Sales Detail subreport. rpt Preview. This isn't very user friendly.

Fortunately we can change this by right-clicking the subreport and selecting Format Subreport again. Now we can click the Subreport tab and then the Formula button next to Subreport Preview Tab Caption. We should now enter the following formula:

```
"Detail for " + {@z_Product_medium_name}
```

Now we can close and save this and click OK. When we click the same entry again, we'll see the subreport preview tab shown in Figure 10.24.

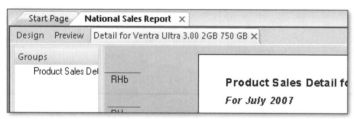

Figure 10.24   Subreport Preview Tab Formatted with Product Name

We'll now go back and fix the Calendar Month subreport link so that it once again uses z_Calendar_Year/Month_Key for the link to the subreport variable parameter. Let's test our link one more time to make sure it's working correctly. This time we'll click on the 17" LCD Monitor entry for September 2007. Our subreport preview now looks like Figure 10.25.

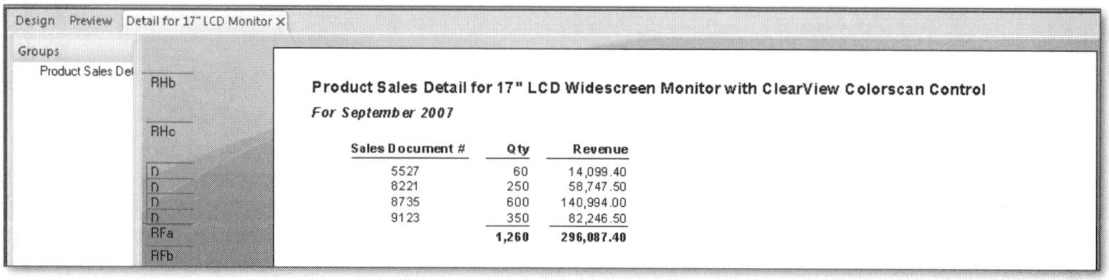

Figure 10.25   Detail Subreport for 17" Monitor Sept 2007

The main benefit of this solution is that it provides you as a developer with a seamless way to deliver to your end users not only a high-level summarized look at their data but a way to quickly and easily drill down into additional detail. However, this solution depends on the detail information your users are looking for having been brought over into SAP NetWeaver BW from the original transaction system. There will be times when this is not the case. In our next example we'll look at how you can bridge the gap between SAP NetWeaver BW and your transactional data using a subreport.

10.2 The Query to SAP ERP Central Component (SAP R/3) Subreport

In this exercise we'll show you how to link a summary report that uses a BW query as its data source to detail information stored in SAP ERP Central Component (or SAP R/3). Although it's normally preferable to first move the required detail information into SAP NetWeaver BW (normally into a DSO), there are times when this is either not practical or just hasn't been done due to lack of time or resources (a common occurrence).

> **Important Disclaimer**
>
> We won't be considering any special security requirements as we move on to accessing data directly from SAP ERP Central Component. We'll only say at this time that any time you begin to provide access into SAP ERP Central Component transactional data, you must ensure that any confidential or secure information is protected from any one in your organization who has Crystal Reports and the Integration for SAP Solutions kit installed. The Security Definition Editor is provided as part of the Integration for SAP Solutions as one way to help ensure that your SAP ERP Central Component data remains secure.

This will be our final report development exercise and, given the nature of the data sources we'll be using, will function as more of an example than a hands-on exercise. The important thing here is to pick up on the basic techniques being presented so that you'll be able to apply them to your own report requirements.

Our new report requirement follows a familiar theme: the plant maintenance department has been using an equipment inventory report for some time and wants to add some additional functionality. Whenever someone looks up a particular piece of equipment (especially when it's a vehicle), it would be very useful if certain aspects of the maintenance history for that piece of equipment could be retrieved quickly and easily. This has become a common need for the maintenance department, and currently they have to look this up using several transactions in SAP ERP Central Component, which can take a long time.

Figure 10.26 shows the current equipment inventory report.

Equipment Inventory

Equipment Type	Count
TR TANDEM DUMP	467

Equip #	Equipment Name	Plant	Manufacturer	Model#
70000849	TR TANDEM DUMP	2001	FORD	L 9000
70000092	TR TANDEM DUMP	2001	IHC	2574
70003268	TR TANDEM DUMP	2001	IHC	2574
70000811	TR TANDEM DUMP	2001	MACK	RD688S
70000429	TR TANDEM DUMP	2001	IHC	2574
70000342	TR TANDEM DUMP	2001	IHC	2574
70001036	TR TANDEM DUMP	2001	IHC	5600I
70003516	TR TANDEM DUMP	2001	INTERNATIONAL	5600I 6X4
70000489	TR TANDEM DUMP	2001	FORD	L 9000
70000114	TR TANDEM DUMP	2001	IHC	2574
70000613	TR TANDEM DUMP	2001	IHC	F 2574
70002044	TR TANDEM DUMP	2001	IHC	F 9370
70000798	TR TANDEM DUMP	2001	MACK	RD688S

Figure 10.26 Equipment Inventory Report

The existing equipment inventory report is run out of SAP NetWeaver BW using a BW query as the data source. It has already been proposed that the requested maintenance data be moved into SAP NetWeaver BW as well, but for now there are no plans (or the required resources) to get this done anytime in the near future. A recent rash of lapses in vehicle maintenance has created a sense of urgency to find a better way to track the maintenance history to help determine exactly what kind of work has been performed and when.

The director of plant maintenance has contacted you and asked if you could look into modifying the existing report somehow to include equipment maintenance records. You think there may be a way and ask for a plant maintenance business process expert (BPX) to help determine exactly which SAP ERP Central Component tables are required to pull the necessary information together. Given the requirements, you're able to determine that the following SAP ERP Central Component tables must be accessed to get the required information:

- AFIH – Maintenance Order Header
- AUFM – Movement Goods for Order

▸ MAKT – Material Descriptions

▸ T001L – Storage Locations

▸ T156T – Movement Type Text

▸ T353IT – Maintenance Activity Type Description

▸ SKAT – G/L Account Master Record (Chart of Accounts: Description)

> **Important Note**
>
> The above SAP ERP Central Component tables are presented here simply as examples. The specific tables required to produce any particular SAP ERP Central Component report (such as a maintenance history report) will depend on the specific requirements of the report.

Based on the specifications developed by the plant maintenance BPX, you create a report using the Open SQL driver in Crystal Reports that accesses the required tables in SAP ERP Central Component, which when run looks like Figure 10.27.

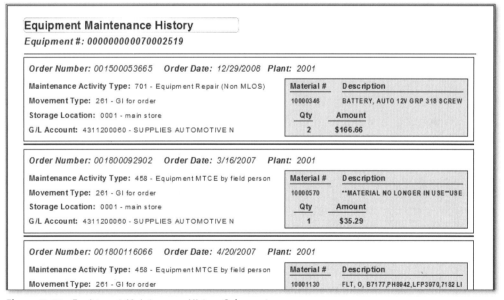

Figure 10.27 Equipment Maintenance History Subreport

One of the keys to making this work is that there must a way to connect (or link) the equipment inventory report with the equipment maintenance report. For this to happen there must be a common field, which in this case is Equipment Number.

Your goal is to replace the existing Equipment Number column in the equipment inventory report (the first column) with an on-demand subreport that will take us to the maintenance records for that particular piece of equipment.

Although both reports contain a field called Equipment Number, upon further investigation we discover a bit of an issue. If you look carefully at the two report samples above you'll notice that the Equipment Number in the equipment inventory report is an eight-digit number. This is how Equipment Number is being stored in SAP NetWeaver BW. However, in SAP ERP Central Component the Equipment Number is padded with 10 zeros, making it impossible to match the two numbers as-is. For your link to work, there must be an exact match between the two numbers, just as when you're joining two tables in a standard SQL environment.

So your challenge is to figure out a way to make an equipment number in your main report (such as 70003489) match up with the same equipment number in the subreport (which looks like 000000000070003489). Fortunately, Crystal Reports provides a way to link these two "unlinkable" fields. We need to transform one of the fields so that it matches the other. The question now becomes, "Which one do we change so that it fits the other?"

Although at first glance it may seem to make sense to change the number in the SAP ERP Central Component subreport (by removing the extra zeros), in reality you *never* want to do this. The reason for this is that it will "break" the record selection you want in the subreport. It's not important that you understand why for now, only that you know that you never change the subreport field to match the main report field. It's always the other way around.

So in our case, we'll need to create a link formula in the main report that will transform the SAP NetWeaver BW equipment number into a form that will match up with the SAP ERP Central Component equipment number. Our formula will look like the following:

```
'0000000000' + {@z_Equipment_Key}
```

Now we have a field (or formula) in our main report that we can use to establish our link to the SAP ERP Central Component subreport. We can insert our subreport to begin the process. We should click the Insert Subreport button in the Insert toolbar (Figure 10.28).

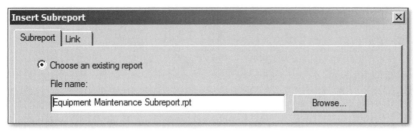

Figure 10.28 Insert Subreport Dialog Box

We should now select the report called Equipment Maintenance Subreport and select the checkbox to make this subreport an on-demand subreport.

Important Reminder

Although it's true that any report selected as a subreport is really just another ordinary Crystal Reports report, it must be designed beforehand specifically with the thought of it being used as a subreport within this specific main report. It would be dumb luck if you picked some other report just because it contained Equipment Number and you somehow made it work.

Subreport Design Hint

Our example subreport works correctly with our main report because the contents of the subreport display information related to a single piece of equipment. This means that the subreport should always be designed around the link field (in our case, Equipment Number).

Now we need to establish our all-important link between the main report and the subreport. First, we select the Link tab in the Insert Subreport dialog box (Figure 10.29).

The field we need to select from the main report is not a field at all, but a formula (@Equipment Link). This is the formula we just created that pads the equipment number in the main report with 10 zeros so that it will match exactly the equipment number in our subreport. Once we select this formula for our link, we'll see ?Pm-@Equipment Link appear in the Subreport Parameter Field To Use field at the bottom left.

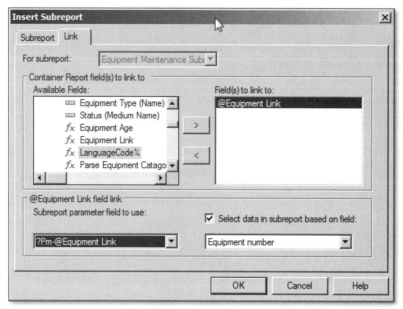

Figure 10.29 Setting up the Subreport Link

Important Note

Earlier, when we established a link between a main report built on a BW query and a subreport that also used a BW query as its data source, we had you override this entry with a BW variable entry from the pick list. If you click the pull-down menu now, you'll find nothing there. This is because you only override this default selection when linking to a subreport built off of a BW query.

Now we need to select the field in the subreport that will match our @Equipment Link formula in the main report and that will be Equipment Number. It's critical that you make the correct connection here, or your subreport won't work.

After we click OK we'll temporarily place the subreport in the Report Footer so we can begin changing its appearance, as shown in Figure 10.30.

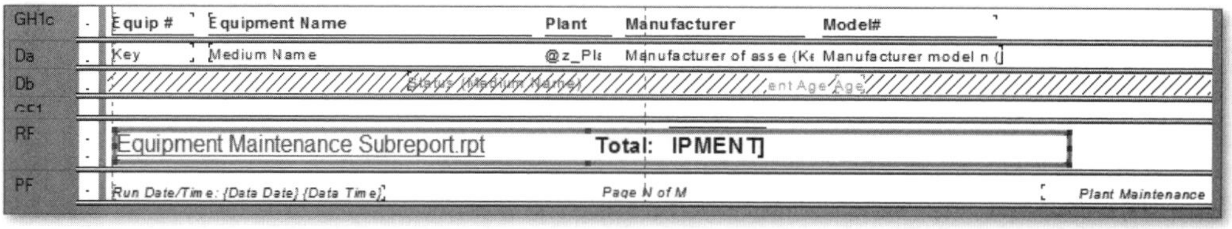

Figure 10.30 Temporary Placement of the Subreport

We now right-click the subreport and select Format Subreport. First, we'll select the Font tab and set the font size to 9 to match the rest of the objects in the Detail section. Next we'll select the Subreport tab to set the On-demand Subreport Caption to the following:

```
{@z_Equipment_Key}
```

After we click OK, we'll need to resize the subreport so that it's the same size as the Equipment Number field in the report.

Pop Quiz

Question: What's the fastest way to make the subreport the same size as the Equipment Number field in the first column?

Answer: Select both the subreport and the Equipment Number field, right-click the Equipment Number field and select Size and then Same Size.

Now that our subreport is the same size as the field, all we need to do is remove the original field and replace it with our subreport. Our report now looks like Figure 10.31.

Equipment Inventory

Equipment Type	Count			
TR TANDEM DUMP	467			

Equip #	Equipment Name	Plant	Manufacturer	Model#
70000849	TR TANDEM DUMP	2001	FORD	L 9000
70000092	TR TANDEM DUMP	2001	IHC	2574
70003268	TR TANDEM DUMP	2001	IHC	2574
70000811	TR TANDEM DUMP	2001	MACK	RD688S
70000429	TR TANDEM DUMP	2001	IHC	2574
70000342	TR TANDEM DUMP	2001	IHC	2574
70001036	TR TANDEM DUMP	2001	IHC	56001
70003516	TR TANDEM DUMP	2001	INTERNATIONAL	5600i6X4
70000489	TR TANDEM DUMP	2001	FORD	L 9000
70000114	TR TANDEM DUMP	2001	IHC	2574
70000613	TR TANDEM DUMP	2001	IHC	F 2574
70002044	TR TANDEM DUMP	2001	IHC	F 9370
70000798	TR TANDEM DUMP	2001	MACK	RD688S
70000485	TR TANDEM DUMP	2001	FORD	L 9000

Figure 10.31 On-Demand Subreport Placed in the Detail Section

Now we're ready to test our subreport. To activate the subreport we simply click the on-demand subreport for a particular piece of equipment. Let's click 70000432. After a few seconds the next thing we see is Figure 10.32.

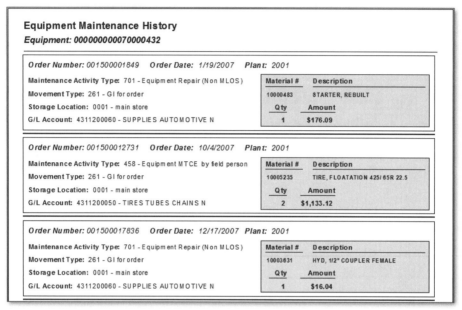

Figure 10.32 Equipment Maintenance History for 70000432

Before we wrap up, we need to take care of a couple of formatting issues. First, let's remove the zeros from in front of the equipment number in the heading of the subreport.

> **Hot Tip**
>
> When you need to make a change to a subreport, just right-click the subreport (in Design or Preview) and select Edit Subreport.

Whenever you edit a subreport, a new tab is created next to the Preview tab that's essentially a new Design tab for the subreport (Figure 10.33).

Start Page	**Equipment Inventory** ×
Design Preview	Equipment Maintenance Subreport.rpt ×

Figure 10.33 Subreport Design Tab

Now that we're editing the subreport, we can change the Equipment Number formula so that it looks like the following:

```
{AFIH.EQUNR}[11 to 20]
```

This will eliminate the 10 extra zeros at the front of the equipment number. Next let's change the subreport preview tab caption so that it's more user friendly. We need to right-click the subreport, select Format Subreport, and then click the Subreport tab. Now click the Formula button text to the Subreport Preview Tab Caption option. The formula will look like the following:

```
{@z_Equipment_Key} + ' - ' + {@z_Equipment_Name}
```

With these two changes, our subreport and subreport preview tab now look like the following:

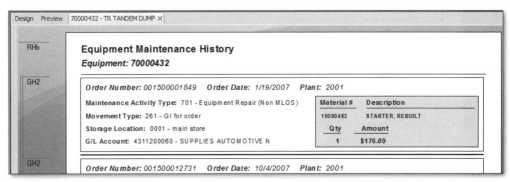

Figure 10.34 Subreport with New Title and Preview Tab

Now our report is almost finished. The last thing we need to do is add is the equipment name to the subreport header and we'll be done. The problem is that right now the equipment name isn't included in any of the SAP ERP Central Component tables being used in our subreport. The preferred way of handling this is always to add it to the data source of the subreport if possible. We could do this because there's an equipment name lookup table available in SAP ERP Central Component called EQKT. However, we're going to pretend for a moment that is doesn't exist so we can leave you with a final Crystal Reports tip.

As we've said, this book isn't necessarily a "deep dive" onto all of the features of Crystal Reports. Our primary objective has been to focus on those specific skills necessary to get up and running as quickly as possible with developing Crystal

Reports in an SAP NetWeaver BW environment. We haven't deviated very far from that path throughout all of our exercises.

However, here at the end of our journey we want to take things one level deeper to highlight just one example of how Crystal Reports provides the skilled developer with the tools necessary to meet even the most difficult and demanding reporting requirements. This next tip is a more advanced skill in Crystal Reports and involves the use of a subreport along with a pair of formulas that use something Crystal Reports calls a *shared variable*.

A shared variable in Crystal Reports is used to pass information from the main report to a subreport or from subreport back to the main report. As you begin using subreports there will be times when you don't want (or need) to see another report, but you only want specific information from a different data source to use in your main report. You use shared variables to pass this information "behind the scenes."

As usual, the best way to understand this is to see it. Let's show you how.

The first thing we're going to do is create a formula in our main report to capture the equipment name using a shared variable. We could create a new formula for this purpose, but we already have an alias formula for Equipment Name in the Detail section called z_Equipment_Name. We can modify this formula for our purposes by simply changing it to the following:

```
shared stringVar Equipment_Name:={0EQUIPMENT_Z0EQUIPMENT_Q001_
CR.[0EQUIPMENT]-[50EQUIPMENT]}
```

As a reminder, the `{0EQUIPMENT_Z0EQUIPMENT_Q001_CR.[0EQUIPMENT]-[50EQUIPMENT]}` in the above formula is the technical name for the equipment name (actually medium name). If you go back to our lesson on aliases in Chapter 5, you'll recall why we created these aliases to begin with: to shield ourselves from these not-so-intuitive BW technical names.

What we've just done is modify our alias to turn it into a shared variable that can be now be passed to our subreport. As you'll see in a moment, it will still work as an ordinary field in our main report. The only difference now is that the value can be shared with our subreport.

Before you save the formula and close it, it's a good idea to copy the first part of the formula as follows:

```
shared stringVar Equipment_Name
```

The reason for this is that this will become the formula in our subreport to receive the value from the main report. To create this formula we need to right-click the subreport and select Edit Subreport. Now we need to create another formula in the subreport and call it Equipment Name. Now simply paste the portion of the previous formula that you just copied into that formula:

```
shared stringVar Equipment_Name
```

After we save and close this formula, we need to insert it into the report title (separated with a dash):

Figure 10.35 Inserting Equipment Name Formula in Subreport Title

That's it. Now we're ready to see if our shared variable is working correctly. When we click on the 70000432 equipment number in the main report, our subreport now looks like Figure 10.36.

Equipment Maintenance History
Equipment: 70000432 - TR TANDEM DUMP

Order Number: 001500001849	Order Date: 1/19/2007	Plant: 2001		

	Material #	Description
Maintenance Activity Type: 701 - Equipment Repair (Non MLOS)	10000483	STARTER, REBUILT
Movement Type: 261 - GI for order		
Storage Location: 0001 - main store	Qty	Amount
G/L Account: 4311200060 - SUPPLIES AUTOMOTIVE N	1	$176.09

Figure 10.36 Completed Equipment Maintenance History Subreport

Now our report and subreport are complete. We have a solution that will provide the plant maintenance department with the additional real-time detail information they need. And we created it in about an hour.

It's fitting that we conclude the hands-on lessons with an example of the versatility and depth that makes Crystal Reports the "Swiss Army knife" of BI tools. Many other handy features and techniques are ready and waiting for you to take advantage of once you become proficient in the basics. The key for you now is to practice the fundamentals that you've learned so far so that you can build a solid foundation to grow on.

We have one more practical chapter to go before we reach our parting conclusions. This chapter, however, has nothing to do with the creation of reports, but rather the distribution of the reports you've already created. That, in the words of Paul Harvey, is "the *rest* of the story."

10.3 Summary

▸ A subreport is a report within a report. Whenever you have a subreport, the original report is called the main report.

▸ There are two types of subreports — unlinked and linked. They can be used either as a standard subreport or as an on-demand subreport. When you're working with SAP NetWeaver BW, the most common type used is a linked on-demand subreport.

▸ A query to query subreport is a great way to split a report into a high-level summary view and a low-level detail view. The query used for the subreport must have a variable that links back to the main report to ensure that the subreport is filtered correctly by SAP NetWeaver BW.

▸ If you want access to real-time detail data from SAP ERP Central Component, it's possible to create a subreport using ECC data and link it back to the main report using a common (or key) field.

▸ There are times when it may be necessary to create a custom link field if there's is no direct match between the main report and subreport data sources. This is a common occurrence when combining SAP NetWeaver BW with SAP ERP Central Component data in one report.

▸ You can use a shared variable to pass information from the main report to the subreport or from the subreport back to the main report. This is especially useful when you don't need an entirely different report but just some specific data from another data source to include in your main report.

Creating a report is only half the story. The other half is getting noticed. How your reports get delivered to and consumed by your end users is as important as the creation of the report itself.

11 Getting Published

Now that we've completed the report development lessons, you might be tempted to think that we're done. Not so fast. Creating reports is only part of the story. The next step is getting noticed.

A well-designed, accurate, and timely report without an efficient and effective way to distribute it is like being all dressed up with no place to go. It can be argued that, from a pure cost-effectiveness perspective, the way you distribute reports is at least as important to your organization's bottom line as the way you design them. In many organizations this is the weak link in the process of getting information out the hands of the few and into the hands of the many.

In all of the previous lessons we learned the basics of how to effectively create business content (reports) from SAP NetWeaver BW using Crystal Reports. Here at the end, in this brief chapter, we're going to cover the basics of how to deliver that content to the end user community in your organization. The term for this process is, appropriately enough, called *publishing*.

11.1 How Not to Get Noticed

Before we look at how to best distribute your reports, we thought we'd take a few minutes to review some of the ways not to do it. In virtually every organization the most common method for distributing reports is the *spreadmart*.

You may be familiar with the spreadmart. If you're part of the target audience for this book, you may be running one at your desk right now. And as much as industry pundits like to poke fun at (and deride) the thousands upon thousands of spreadmarts sprinkled throughout the world's organizations, the fact of the matter is without them commerce would immediately (and spectacularly) come to a grinding halt.

Because they perform such a vital function in an organization, the answer of course isn't to get rid of them, but instead to *upgrade* them. There's nothing fundamentally wrong with the function of a spreadmart. The function they serve is vital to the health of any organization. Rather, the problem is how they perform that function.

Essentially there are at least two major flaws with this approach to distributing information:

▸ **It's a terribly inefficient (and sometimes painful) process.**
A spreadmart is the consummate bottleneck. If you currently operate a spreadmart in your organization, you know exactly what we're talking about. Downloading, reassembling, and formatting information using a spreadsheet is a labor-intensive process that can consume many hours of time for an individual report.

▸ **It is very difficult (or impossible) to control.**
This is pain felt not on an individual level, but at a corporate or organizational level. Nothing can keep a comptroller up at night in this new age of Sarbanes-Oxley more than the thought of dozens of little isolated spreadmarts pumping out unregulated, unsupervised, and unapproved information throughout the organization. In a privately held company this issue it not so much lack of compliance but a simple lack of control. In a publicly traded company, however, the potential ramifications of the free flow of unregulated information throughout the organization can be quite serious indeed.

However, even with these (and other) rather serious problems, it's not reasonable or practical to simply rid an organization of spreadmarts. It's our contention that these will always perform a vital function in any organization simply because they are an organization's "last stand" in the battle for timely, accurate, and relevant information. The combination of someone who both understands the business and is skilled at creating powerful, complex spreadsheets is invaluable.

So how can an organization upgrade their existing spreadmarts to help mitigate the inherent risks involved in the process? By implementing an efficient, easily accessible information distribution platform that serves as the organization's "gold standard" for information dissemination. And by doing so you address the two biggest problems with the spreadmart: inefficiency and lack of control.

For Crystal Reports this system is called SAP BusinessObjects Enterprise. The combination of SAP BusinessObjects Enterprise and Crystal Reports is what gives an organization the efficiency and control that it needs to make the distribution of information both cost effective and reliable.

Implementing SAP BusinessObjects Enterprise in an organization brings some very practical benefits, perhaps the greatest of these being an increase in the baseline flow of useful information throughout the organization. We use the word *useful* here quite deliberately. People deal with a lot of "noise" in organizations today, most of it coming from their inbox. However, although the volume may be quite high, the quality is often very low. One of the benefits of SAP BusinessObjects Enterprise is that it creates a separate "quiet place" where only business-relevant information is disseminated and discussed. Think of it as an internal social network for business.

A second significant benefit of SAP BusinessObjects Enterprise is that it provides an organization with a set of standardized, tested, and IT-approved reports that serve as a gold standard for every other type of report (including those produced by spreadmarts) in the organization. These reports have been put through a rigorous testing process and have been approved by the appropriate authorities before being made available to the organization at large. And, most importantly, by design, they cannot be modified by anyone in the organization who doesn't have the proper authorization to do so.

So part of any organization's overall BI strategy should be to carefully lay out a foundation of consistent, nonmodifiable business content (such as Crystal Reports) made easily accessible by anyone in the organization using a standard Web interface (such as SAP BusinessObjects Enterprise).

11.2 Publishing Reports to SAP BusinessObjects Enterprise

Now let's turn our attention to the right way to get noticed: by publishing your reports to SAP BusinessObjects Enterprise.

> **Important Note**
>
> If by chance your organization implemented SAP BusinessObjects Enterprise before they implemented SAP NetWeaver BW and/or SAP BusinessObjects Enterprise is currently being used to publish non–SAP NetWeaver BW reports, be aware that the process for publishing reports in an SAP NetWeaver BW environment is completely different from the "standard" publishing process used in other environments (such as SQL Server or Oracle).

Before we proceed, we need to make a few assumptions about your particular environment. First (and this is a pretty safe assumption), we'll assume that your organization has implemented the standard dev-test-production three-tiered landscape for SAP NetWeaver BW. This is where you have three separate SAP NetWeaver BW instances: one for development, the next for testing (quality), and the final one for production (the system that the organization actually uses to run the business).

Second, we're assuming that the BW Publisher has been installed and configured on your SAP BusinessObjects Enterprise server(s). As a report developer you don't need to know much about the BW Publisher — only that it must be installed properly before you can begin publishing reports into SAP BusinessObjects Enterprise from Crystal Reports. If you're unsure if this is the case, you should contact someone within your IT department to find out. The best person to ask would be whoever has been designated to administer your SAP BusinessObjects Enterprise servers.

In a typical three-tiered landscape, the basic publishing process is as shown in Figure 11.1.

At the far left of the process (and at the beginning) is you and Crystal Reports. The first step in the process is to save your Crystal Reports report into a role in SAP NetWeaver BW (just as you would with a standard BW query). There will be special roles that have been previously set up by your BASIS team for the express purpose of saving Crystal Reports reports that are to be published into SAP BusinessObjects Enterprise.

When saving a Crystal Reports report into SAP NetWeaver BW you can simultaneously publish (save) a copy into the corresponding SAP BusinessObjects Enterprise system. In a three-tiered SAP NetWeaver BW landscape there will typically be three matched SAP BusinessObjects Enterprise systems (although this isn't required). However, as a report developer, it's not important that you know how SAP BusinessObjects Enterprise has been matched up with your SAP NetWeaver

BW landscape. All you have to do is click a button, and everything else happens automatically from then on.

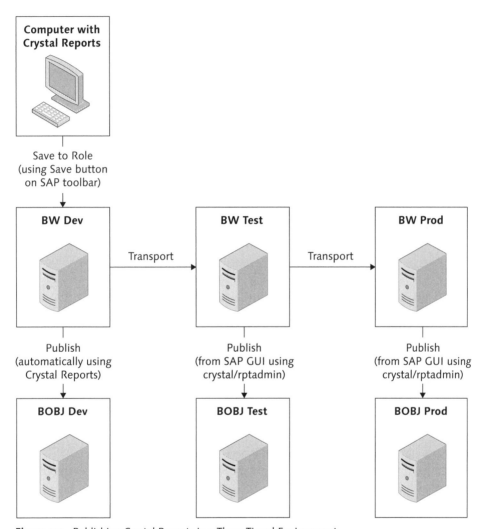

Figure 11.1 Publishing Crystal Reports in a Three-Tiered Environment

To begin the process, you simply click the Save button on the SAP toolbar. After authenticating to SAP NetWeaver BW, you'll see a selection of roles where you can save your Crystal Reports report.

> **Important Note**
>
> The roles you see in this list depend on the authorizations assigned to your SAP NetWeaver BW login ID. A subset of these roles (or perhaps all of them) should be the roles set up by your BASIS team and/or your SAP BusinessObjects Enterprise administrator for the express purpose of publishing Crystal Reports reports into SAP BusinessObjects Enterprise. If you're unsure which roles are the Crystal Reports roles, you should contact your BASIS team or your SAP BusinessObjects Enterprise administrator.

Once you've selected the appropriate role and clicked Save, you'll be presented with a dialog box with the option "Automatically Publish to Enterprise." Make sure this option is selected. This will ensure that the report is also published (saved) to the corresponding SAP BusinessObjects Enterprise system.

Once you've saved your report into SAP NetWeaver BW and published it into the corresponding SAP BusinessObjects Enterprise system, your job as report developer is done. It's the responsibility of the SAP BusinessObjects Enterprise system administrator to ensure that the report is promoted up the landscape. As shown in Figure 11.1, the report object (.rpt) is transported from the development environment into the test (or quality) SAP NetWeaver BW environment, and the SAP BusinessObjects Enterprise administrator will then publish it from there to the corresponding SAP BusinessObjects Enterprise system. Once the report has been approved in the test environment, it's transported into the production SAP NetWeaver BW environment, where it's finally published to the SAP BusinessObjects Enterprise production system — that is, if you do things the standard way.

11.3 Fast-Track Publishing

What we have just described would normally be considered best practice for publishing from Crystal Reports. But, as we've discussed on several occasions in this book, real life is seldom "normal."

The biggest problem with starting this process by publishing reports into a development environment is that SAP NetWeaver BW development environments rarely approximate the real-world production system. Usually they're not even close. If your SAP NetWeaver BW development environment holds anything close to the amount of data stored in your production environment, you would be the exception to the rule. Most organizations don't have either the capacity or the bandwidth to keep the development system in sync with the production system.

So what's the problem? As we mentioned early on inthis book, perhaps the biggest factor to consider when creating any kind of BI content is performance (especially as data volumes and the necessary level of detail increases). Content created and delivered using Crystal Reports tends to lean toward the higher level of detail and, when working with SAP NetWeaver BW as a data source, this often means including more characteristics than you might see in an OLAP report or perhaps a dashboard interface.

The practical fallout from this is that it's extremely important (vital, in fact) that your Crystal Reports reports be developed in as close a data environment as possible to the final production environment. In an ideal world these environments would be identical in every way (hardware, configuration, and data load). However, as we've just said, it's rare to find a development environment that closely approximates the production environment.

So what should your Crystal Report development strategy be if you find yourself in same situation as the majority SAP NetWeaver BW installations, where your development environment is a mere shadow of production? First, don't develop your Crystal Reports reports in a dev environment. This is an easy decision for a lot of reasons, including the following:

▶ First, doing your Crystal Reports development in a "light" development environment will lure your developers into a false sense of security and cause them to make unwise design decisions that must later be either revised or, in a worst-case scenario, scrapped entirely. Often a report will run just fine in development but then fall apart when run under a full data load in test or production.

▶ This problem is often exacerbated by the fact that development data is notorious for being riddled with "junk" data. So, not only is the amount of data not realistic, but the data itself isn't realistic. Besides the amount of data, there's perhaps nothing more important when developing any kind of BI content that having real-world data available from the very start.

▶ SAP NetWeaver BW isn't an operational or transaction system. It's a reporting system. Having a three-tiered environment makes perfect sense when creating function modules or custom ABAP code for your SAP ERP Central Component transactional system. However, SAP NetWeaver BW is an offline reporting environment. And you don't run or change anything using a report. You use reports to look at data.

All this is to say, you would be hard pressed to find any reason to develop Crystal Reports in an SAP NetWeaver BW development environment when the development data is either significantly less than or of significantly inferior quality to that in production — or both.

"Not a problem here," you say. "We're careful to ensure that our SAP NetWeaver BW development environment is kept in sync with our production environment on a regular basis." In this situation it seems quite reasonable to proceed with your initial Crystal Reports development in the SAP NetWeaver BW development environment. After all, your report developers will be getting a realistic look at what they can expect to see in the final production environment and design their reports accordingly.

In this scenario it would be perfectly fine to create your reports in Crystal Reports and publish them initially to the SAP NetWeaver BW development environment — if you have the time and don't mind doing things twice. Let's explain.

Your developers would create the report in development and publish it into the SAP BusinessObjects Enterprise development environment. Let's assume the end users (or perhaps the developer) give it their stamp of approval to go to the next step in the process. The next step would be to transport the report into the SAP NetWeaver BW test environment and then publish it into the SAP BusinessObjects Enterprise test system. Now the same users will again test the report (or perhaps for the first time) using test data, which is going to be virtually the same — or exactly the same — data that was used in development.

So what's going to happen? If the data is virtually the same, and the end users had previously approved the version that was in development, this becomes a rubber stamp step in the process because the only thing that has changed is the location of the report. And, amazingly enough, it still works the same as before. So we just interrupted our end users' busy schedule to have them tell us what they told us before.

What if this is the first time the users have seen the report? This isn't unusual, because it's normal for developers to move content to test without the end users having seen it. If the user immediately approves it, you're on to production. However, this never happens. The users will find some things that need to be changed with the report and, you guessed it, now the developer must go back to the copy in development to make the requested changes. The changes are then made, and the new version is saved to SAP NetWeaver BW development and then published into the SAP BusinessObjects Enterprise development system.

The next step is to retransport the revised report object (.rpt) back up into the SAP NetWeaver BW test environment and then republish it into the SAP BusinessObjects Enterprise test system. And usually transports only occur at predetermined times during the day (normally once or twice). So if you miss a transport, you have to wait for the next opportunity to transport. Of course, you can always request an emergency transport (with the commensurate forms and approvals), which, because this can become such a common occurrence when developing reports in Crystal Reports, begins to erode the whole purpose of the emergency transport request.

After all of this, the users can finally test the report again. And guess what happens next?

Rewind and do it all over again. You almost never get the report right on the first revision. In fact, it's rare to get it right on even the second or third try. It's not uncommon to cycle through this test and revise process many times before the report passes inspection.

And this is precisely why the "dev to test to production" path ends up being a path of "slow and painful death" for both the developer and the end user. If you'll recall from our discussion of the report specification and development process in Chapter 2, one of the things that the typical business end user doesn't have is a lot of extra time. And we're not talking about the time it takes to provide feedback on revising the report. That's a given and can't be avoided. It's the length of the revision cycle required to go back to dev and back to test that begins to drive them (and the developer) a bit crazy.

> **Bottom Line**
>
> No matter how you look at it, it simply doesn't make sense to force your Crystal Reports developers to create and modify their reports in the SAP NetWeaver BW development environment. Absolutely no one wins in this scenario.

Now let's look at the test and revise cycle, where the report is both created and modified in the SAP NetWeaver BW test (or quality) environment. In this scenario when the end user requests a change to the report, the Crystal Reports developer immediately changes the report in the SAP NetWeaver BW test environment, saves it back to SAP NetWeaver BW, and the report is automatically published into the SAP BusinessObjects Enterprise test system, where it's immediately available for the user to test again — no transports, no additional publishing, and no requests to BASIS and/or the SAP BusinessObjects Enterprise administrator to get involved. Just quick, immediate turnaround. In this scenario a request can be made, the change be made to the report, and the results made available to the end user in a matter of minutes, rather than hours (or sometimes days).

Hottest Tip of All

If you don't take anything else away from this book, if you help your organization implement this one simple procedural change in your development cycle, you can potentially save your organization hundreds (if not thousands) of hours of wasted time over the life of a typical Crystal Reports SAP NetWeaver BW implementation.

One more thought: if it's so much more efficient to begin your Crystal Reports development in a test (quality) environment, wouldn't it be even more efficient to develop reports directly in production?

Strictly and technically speaking, the answer would be, "Yes." Of course this would be best in terms of pure efficiency. After all, there's literally no wasted effort going on here. There's no doubt this would decrease the overall development cycle even more — but how much? As it turns out, not very much. At least not nearly as much as moving the report design and modification process from development to test. The reason for this is that the real time savings is in reducing the length of the test and revise cycle. Once that is finished (the report is signed off and ready to go) the last step of moving it to production is usually a very small part of the overall process, so you're not adding much by taking that final step.

So although you may make some gains in terms of overall efficiency, you achieve this at the expense of increased risk. It's rarely a good idea to develop anything (even something like a report in a data warehouse environment) in the production system. This is of course because this is the system that end users in the organization are actually using for their reporting and analysis. And although it's true that, relatively speaking, report development isn't as risky as other forms of development, it's still quite possible to adversely affect the overall performance of the production system with the additional overhead of development work.

Because of this, you'd be hard-pressed to find situations where it makes sense to create reports in a production SAP NetWeaver BW environment. However, in smaller, more focused warehouse environments with very tight development cycles (translated: get it done now), it certainly can make sense to create your reports directly in production. This is a judgment call that needs to be made by the business end users and IT to determine whether or not it makes sense.

As we wrap up this chapter, here are a few more clarifying points on creating and publishing reports in Crystal Reports for SAP NetWeaver BW:

▶ Usually it still makes sense to continue developing your BW queries in a development environment. Very little (or nothing) is gained by moving your development of queries into the test or quality environment. Because characteristics and key figures in a query aren't active until they're actually used in a Crystal Reports report, there's is no real need for testing the performance of a query designed for use with Crystal Reports. Performance testing should be done within Crystal Reports, ideally in a fully loaded test environment.

▶ It's critical that all Crystal Reports reports using a BW query as their data source be published to SAP BusinessObjects Enterprise using the the BW Publisher. From within Crystal Reports this is accomplished by selecting the Automatically Publish to Enterprise option as described earlier in this chapter. When transported to the next SAP NetWeaver BW environment, the BW Publisher is invoked via special transaction on the SAP NetWeaver BW server (/crystal/rptadmin). If this isn't done and the report is published in the standard way (as in a SQL environment or when publishing reports created in SAP ERP Central Component or SAP R/3), then the end user won't be presented with a dynamic pick list when running the report in SAP BusinessObjects Enterprise and won't be able to utilize personal variants.

▶ Also, by using the BW Publisher to publish modified Crystal Reports SAP NetWeaver BW report into SAP BusinessObjects Enterprise, you ensure that any existing report instances are retained in history. Because Crystal Reports can be scheduled in SAP BusinessObjects Enterprise for later viewing, any report can have any number of historical instances associated with it. If you publish a modified version of the report back into SAP BusinessObjects Enterprise without using the the BW Publisher, you'll lose any existing instances.

11.4   Summary

▶ The creation of a report in Crystal Reports is only part of the overall solution. Once a report has been developed it must be distributed quickly and efficiently to the appropriate audience of end users.

▶ SAP BusinessObjects Enterprise is a Web-based report (BI content) distribution and management system that allows end users to access reports themselves using a standard web browser.

▶ Two benefits of combining Crystal Reports content with SAP BusinessObjects Enterprise is that it increases the baseline amount if BI content available to your end user community and provides a gold standard of BI content by which other more ad hoc and custom reports can be compared.

▶ The process of transferring a Crystal Reports report into SAP BusinessObjects Enterprise is called publishing. The BW Publisher is used to publish Crystal Reports reports that use a BW query as their data source into SAP BusinessObjects Enterprise.

▶ The standard starting point for both developing and publishing from Crystal Reports is an SAP NetWeaver BW development environment. However, it makes more sense to begin your Crystal Reports development (and publishing) process in a test or quality environment. There are two primary reasons for this: The data in most development environments is usually sparse and often unrealistic and, more importantly, the process of going back in development to make changes and then publishing revised versions into quality will greatly increase the length of your test and revise cycle.

▶ Perhaps nothing else will produce greater returns in terms of pure efficiency of effort than adopting a two-tiered development and publishing approach with Crystal Reports, especially in a high-volume development environment.

From a pure return of investment perspective, Crystal Reports is much more about volume and ease of access than making reports look pretty. The most pressing need in most organizations today is not how to make information look better, but how to make information available — information available to the many and not just to the few.

12 Moving On

As we said at the beginning of our journey, our goal has been to provide you with the knowledge and skills necessary to begin developing Crystal Reports in an SAP BI environment as quickly and a efficiently as possible. We've endeavored to share with you those skills most necessary to be successful when working within the often unique and specialized world of SAP NetWeaver BW.

We hope you've gotten the impression that, whereas Crystal Reports is certainly the premier BI interface for developing "print ready" BI content, it also provides you with a wide variety of functionality that goes beyond simply putting a "pretty face" on your data. Crystal Reports is a full-featured BI content development environment that has developed a well-deserved reputation for being able to handle almost any type of tricky BI reporting requirement you can throw at it.

And, as we explained at the beginning, the goal of this book has not been to cover every aspect and feature available within Crystal Reports. If that were the case, this book would be easily twice the length (and weight) that it is. We have intentionally reduced the scope and content of this book for one simple reason: Right now it isn't necessary. In fact, it would most likely just get in the way.

Your most pressing need is to put into practice the skills we've taught you throughout the many hands-on lessons in this book. It's much more important that you master what you have learned up to now than that you learn about any additional features or functionality in Crystal Reports.

With this in mind, please allow us to leave you with a short, concise game plan for moving forward in your efforts to master Crystal Reports development in the world of SAP BW. First, we begin with some personal notes for you as a report developer. We'll end with a suggested strategy for helping your organization maximize its investment in the integration of Crystal Reports and SAP BW.

12.1 A Personal Report Development Game Plan

▶ **Be realistic**
It's important that you begin with simple report requirements, especially if you're a beginner to Crystal Reports and/or reporting in general. Even if you're familiar with creating BI content using other BI tools (perhaps SAP BEx), you still need to make sure you don't overreach your capabilities at the onset. It's important that you gain some quick wins to help boost your confidence and keep yourself motivated.

▶ **Enlist the help of others**
If for some reason you're unable to get connected successfully to SAP NetWeaver BW from within Crystal Reports, you'll need the help of your BASIS security team, your SAP BusinessObjects Enterprise administrator, or both. If you're not familiar with creating BW queries, you'll need to find someone in your organization who can help you, whether to create them for you or to help you learn how to create them for yourself.

▶ **Keep it simple**
Avoid the temptation to overreach when specifying and designing reports, especially early on in your development efforts. It's better to quickly create a simple, elegant report that works than spin your wheels trying to do something new and different.

▶ **Take time to master the basics**
The better you get at making your reports look polished and professional, the more valuable you'll become to your organization. The almost limitless capability of Crystal Reports to format the layout of reports is what it's known for. If you don't take the time to learn how to make your reports look good, you'll miss out on one of the fundamental advantages of using Crystal Reports.

▶ **Take advantage of online help**
The online help feature of Crystal Reports is quite good and very thorough. It's especially good for learning more about formulas and functions. You can learn about any feature or function in Crystal Reports easily and quickly using the online help.

▶ **Be patient while learning formulas**

In many ways, your ability to utilize and master the formula functionality of Crystal Reports is what will set you apart and enable you to accomplish things that might be difficult or impossible to do with other BI tools. More than any other function in Crystal Reports, it takes time and persistent effort to get really good at creating formulas. In the end, everyone learns formulas by finding a need for them. Once you find a need, then you'll learn.

▶ **Know where to find outside help**

Some of the best places to find help outside your organization are the various SAP Community Network Forums (*http://forums.sdn.sap.com*). The two forums you might find most useful are:

  ▶ The Crystal Reports Design Forum

  ▶ The Integration Kits – SAP Forum

▶ **Conduct an on-site custom lab session**

If there are others in your organization who are also developing Crystal Reports against SAP BW, perhaps the best way to take your skills (and theirs) to the next level is to bring in a qualified resource who can conduct a hands-on lab session (or series of sessions) where you and your co-workers work together designing and creating reports on your own system. Because this type of training uses your organization's data and the examples being used are actual reports, this type of training provides the greatest return possible to the organization. And, because the reports created during the lab session are meant to be "production ready" when completed, the return on investment in the training session is almost immediate.

12.2 Putting it All Together – The ReportMart

Finally, we leave you with an overall strategy, or blueprint, for how you can help your organization maximize its investment in Crystal Reports and SAP NetWeaver BW. The goal of these final points is to summarize everything we've learned thus far into a single, concise battle plan that clearly defines for you and your organization the "sweet spot" of this integration between Crystal Reports and SAP NetWeaver BW.

As we've seen time and time again throughout our exercises, Crystal Reports is a versatile, well-rounded BI tool that's capable of handling a wide array of BI reporting requirements. And whereas it makes sense to position Crystal Reports as the highly formatted reporting solution for SAP BW, it would be a great mistake to stop there. Used properly and in conjunction with SAP BusinessObjects Enterprise, Crystal Reports can be much more than just a way to create "pretty reports."

By now you should be quite familiar with the concept of the data warehouse. In essence, a data warehouse is a place where transactional data from across your organization can be gathered, standardized, and summarized to provide an offline reporting environment to support the ongoing operations of the organization.

An offshoot of the data warehouse is the data mart. There are differences in opinion about what exactly differentiates a data mart from a data warehouse, but we can safely state the following as key differentiators:

▶ A data mart is smaller in scope than a data warehouse. Whereas the data in a data warehouse may come from virtually every functional area in an organization, a data mart is normally confined to a single functional area (such as sales or accounting).

▶ Normally data is stored in a data warehouse at a lower level of granularity than a data mart. This means that most data warehouses are designed to provide better access to more detailed information than the typical data mart.

Part of the appeal of a data mart is its size. It's smaller. And smaller means easier (and therefore less costly) to build and maintain.

One type of data mart, known as the dependent data mart, is a subset of a data warehouse. In other words, a portion of the data from the data warehouse is fed into the data mart on a regular basis. In many ways this is simply a way to off-load the processing of the reporting requests to a different server or environment. You can think of this as a way of "stepping down" a large volume of data and dividing it up into more manageable portions.

Crystal Reports 2008, when combined with the scheduling capabilities of SAP BusinessObjects Enterprise, provides a similar way to step down the data within SAP NetWeaver BW into more "bit-size" chunks, but on a much smaller scale. We call this the *ReportMart*. Here's how it works:

▶ First, make it a practice to avoid creating "single-look" Crystal Reports reports and instead make it your goal to always provide multiple looks and layers (groupings) within a single report.

- Always strive to make your reports as flexible as possible by allowing users to select their own groups and group order. You should also always provide the option to drill down through your groupings into the detail.

- Whenever possible, leverage the saved data filter functionality in Crystal Reports so your users can "post-filter" your report at view time without having to rerun the report.

- Once you've created your flexible, drillable, and post-filterable report, you can publish the report and schedule it to run on a regular basis in SAP BusinessObjects Enterprise. Each time it's run data is retrieved from SAP NetWeaver BW and saved on the SAP BusinessObjects Enterprise server as a *saved data object*, or instance.

- Your end users are now free to view the report instance any time they want (as long as it remains on the SAP BusinessObjects Enterprise server). And because you've been careful to provide them with their top two or three options in terms of report layout and structure, they're able to get the data they need in the look and level of detail they require quickly and easily.

- Done correctly, this solution allows you to create a self-service BI environment where end users can not only find the exact information they need, but can retrieve it in a print-ready format.

The key to maximizing your investment in Crystal Reports is to get past this notion that Crystal Reports is the best solution for highly formatted reports. Yes, this is certainly true. Of all of the BI tools available from SAP, Crystal Reports is the one that provides the skilled report developer with the greatest degree of control over the final look and feel of a report. But it would be a big mistake to stop there.

From a pure return of investment perspective, Crystal Reports is much more about volume and ease of access than making reports look pretty. The most pressing need in most organizations today is not how to make information look better, but how to make information available — information available to the many and not just to the few.

The Author

 **Mike Garrett** is an independent consultant and has been working with the Crystal Reports and its SAP Integration Kit for over 8 years. He helped with the fist installation of Crystal Reports solution for SAP BW 3.x in 2002. Since then he has worked one-on-one and in group situations with more developers and business analysts in implementing this solution than probably anyone else in the field. He has delivered custom end-user training to hundreds of business users and has been able to experience first-hand what it takes for the average end user to learn and master this solution. He was previously with Apple Computers for 6 years.

Index

D

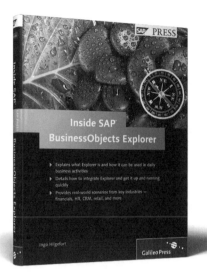

Explains what Explorer is and how it can be used in daily business activities

Details how to integrate and get Explorer up and running quickly

Uses real-world scenarios to show how it works in financials, HR, CRM, and retail

Ingo Hilgefort

Inside SAP BusinessObjects Explorer

With this book you'll learn what SAP BusinessObjects Explorer is, and find out how to install, deploy, and use it. Written for people who are interested in bringing Business Intelligence to business users, this book will teach you how to use it in your SAP environment and address specific questions about how it works with your existing SAP tools and data. After reading this book, you'll understand why and how to leverage Explorer to bring quick and easy access to data analysis to users throughout your company.

307 pp., 2010, 69,95 Euro / US$ 69.95
ISBN 978-1-59229-340-7

>> www.sap-press.com

Provides a complete end-to-end overview of the BusinessObjects integration

Teaches you how to set up your NetWeaver 7.0 system for using Crystal Reports, Xcelsius, Web Intelligence, and more BO tools

Includes best practices for portal integration, security, and troubleshooting

Ingo Hilgefort

Integrating SAP BusinessObjects XI 3.1 Tools with SAP NetWeaver

This book is about the integration of BusinessObjects BI tools (release XI 3.1) with SAP NetWeaver 7.0 and SAP ERP 6.0 landscapes. Whether you are a BW administrator, technical consultant, or implementation project lead, you will learn about the actual installation and configuration of the software in combination with the SAP system. You will get started with the BusinessObjects software but will also understand how the SAP NetWeaver BW concepts are being mapped to BusinessObjects software.

258 pp., 2009, 68,– Euro / US$ 85.00
ISBN 978-1-59229-274-5

>> www.sap-press.com